PARTNERS FOR POSSIBILITY

Praise for the book

Stories of Impact is just that, a brilliant reflection of the impact that partnerships have had in raising the quality of education in many of South Africa's schools. The testimonies are vivid in reflecting the chilling reality that is South Africa's mainly township education today – but they also serve to punctuate how disadvantage can turn to advantage through collaboration and on-site partnership support. This book is a must-read for anyone who is committed to redressing the imbalances in our society. It will frustrate, it will inspire, but it will activate too. These stories are a template for 'stronger together'. *Stories of Impact* is a manifestation of the Champion South Africa mantra 'Champion People Build Champion People, Champion People Build Champion Nations'...

Ashraf Garda
Chief Driver - Champion South Africa, Host of the Ashraf Garda Show and Champion South Africa podcasts, Moderator, MC, Speaker and Media Trainer

This new book by Partners for Possibility (PfP) demonstrates why the programme was chosen in 2018 as one of six winners of the prestigious WISE Award which recognises innovative projects that are successfully addressing education challenges. These moving accounts show how the programme is empowering school leaders in South Africa to lead change under extraordinarily challenging circumstances with the powerful support of their peers in education and in business. Their stories also illustrate how PfP is creating opportunities for school and business leaders to build on their shared expertise and develop collective capacity for school improvement across local ecosystems through being part of a leadership community of practice. I am delighted that details about the PfP programme are being shared and promoted through WISE.

Dr Asmaa Al-Fadala
Director of Research, WISE (World Innovation Summit for Education)

When reading this book one is struck by the passion for doing something that would appear impossible. Not only that it had a whole heap of theoretical 'underpins' and a coherence that was not perhaps immediately apparent to the participants (unless you have read the first book). And if that was not enough, it enabled a thousand weird and unique partnerships to form and change the world. If you want to change the world through people, then this is a great practical example of awesome stuff done by apparently ordinary people with the hidden hand of Louise and her team making it all happen.

Bob Head
Director of companies and Catalyst for the Dinokeng Scenarios

The relevance, uniqueness and impact of the Partners for Possibility programme are undisputable. It's relevance stems primarily from two fundamental concerns in South Africa – the first is the lack of inspirational, effective leadership in organisations at virtually all levels. The second reality is the disappointingly poor quality of education in our country. PfP offers a solution to both these challenges and needs. It is a powerful and practical leadership development programme for both business leaders and school principals. From a leadership perspective, it opens eyes, broadens outlooks, brings about mind shifts, deepens insight and, in many cases, it transforms both the business leader as well as the school principal. Thanks to the improvement in leadership effectiveness in the participating schools, a much stronger platform is created for the financial sustainability of the institution. Another positive outcome is a much higher level of involvement by parents and more motivated teachers. All of this, ultimately, culminates in better education. More than a thousand case studies provide convincing evidence of the positive impact of this amazing initiative. The PfP programme is uniquely South African. It is an extraordinary story of courage, commitment, caring and hope. PfP is about things that move the human spirit – of giving, learning, sharing and discovering – for the good of all!

Brand Pretorius
Former MD of Toyota SA Marketing and retired CEO of McCarthy Limited
Author, speaker, leadership coach and director of companies

Post 1994 South Africa adopted a great constitution that provided for equal rights for every citizen and implemented policies that enhanced human rights. However, what we failed to do is to help our more privileged citizens to fully comprehend what the impact of apartheid was on the vast majority of South African communities. We acted as if passing laws and introducing policies would change people's behaviour, attitudes and practices towards each other.

Even today, many people have great difficulty accepting that they have benefitted from our historical past and they do little to understand the past or help to make the future better.

This book provides fascinating reports and stories about partnerships, journeys and the South African spirit of Ubuntu. It tells of the tremendous assistance provided to school leaders in disadvantaged communities to improve their school environment so that teaching and learning are significantly enhanced. The multiplier effect of this intervention is enormous since it impacts the learners, the teachers, the parents and the extended community. It gives hope, self-respect and restores dignity to all those who participate.

However, the less recognised and lauded aspect of the programme is the opportunity it provides many advantaged South Africans to find out first-hand what the daily struggles are that disadvantaged communities have to navigate as a result of South Africa's history. This experience makes individuals realise their historic advantage and gives them a non-threatening avenue toward small, but tangible, acts of reparation.

And finally, it equips these individuals to speak about the real South African inequalities within their social circles and in this way create a better understanding among South Africans of the need for us to work together to build a better society.

The Partners for Possibility programme is therefore much more than just a leadership and school improvement intervention, it is also about changing attitudes amongst South Africans in a way that helps us build a better society for all the people of South Africa.

'We delight in the beauty of the butterfly, but rarely admit the changes it has gone through to achieve that beauty.' (Maya Angelou)

Brian Figaji
Education Leader and Director of Companies

South Africa confronts an urgent and massive task of improving the learning outcomes achieved by its schools. The challenge is widely recognized; many dedicated education sector professionals, at all levels, are working hard to address it. There is an intensified focus on the goal of ensuring that every child can read for meaning by age 10. Curriculums are being improved; new systems are being put in place; investments are being made in teacher training. This is all to the good – but is it enough?

For all of the determined efforts of educationalists, there is a striking lack of attention to the 'softer' side of what it takes to achieve results: motivating teachers and learners; engaging parents and communities. Inspiration matters – inspired people are the ones who make the effort and add the extra perspiration needed to achieve great things.

For the past decade, Partners for Possibility has been working to support the evocation of agency within schools and between schools and communities. It has helped to catalyze new partnerships, new relationships, new possibilities for learning and mutual learning –possibilities which connect principals, teachers, business executives, and community leaders. As described in this book, much has been learned from this effort – lessons about what works and also lessons in humility. The journey sometimes has been a lonely one – technical professionals (educationalists are no exception) aren't always eager to embrace those from outside their specialty who want to engage. But for all organisations, schools included, the task of evoking agency is key for performance. Partners for Possibility has much valuable experience to share as to how this can be achieved. I applaud their efforts – and welcome this book, which communicates vividly what has been learned.

Brian Levy
Academic Director (2012-2019), Nelson Mandela School of Public Governance, University of Cape Town; Professor of the Practice of International Development, School of Advanced International Studies, Johns Hopkins University

Partners for Possibility is changing the way we view the role of civil society and business in education. The programme has the potential to break the 'silo syndrome effect' between schools and the business fraternity and dispel the notion that business can inject only monetary value into our schools. Some of the well-constructed stories in this book lend themselves to becoming very useful real-life case studies for training intervention purposes.

Brian White
Northern Cape Department of Education

Business leaders are ideally suited to bring a different perspective to running a school. They operate in an ever-changing environment. 'Disruptive Thinking' is the norm for them, but not so in schools, and their support in getting schools principals to think differently about education is invaluable.

One of the great strengths of PfP is that the relationship between Business Leader and Principal is reciprocal. The business leader gets to understand the deep problems in running a school and the principals gets to be exposed to Business principles.

Prof Brian O'Connell has said that being a school principal in a school that serves a disadvantaged community is one of the most challenging jobs in our country. I would add that it is also, without doubt, the most important job in our country.

If one considers that PfP has interacted with more than 1,200 schools, each with about 1,000 pupils, it gives one an idea of their reach and influence. They are certainly doing their bit to address the challenges facing education. Well done Louise and your team, for capturing the experiences, stories, and the massive changes that have occurred as a result of your programme.

Bruce Probyn
Coach: Principals Academy Trust

Partners for Possibilty not only brings hope to schools in distress and their leaders, but brings real inspiration to the executives who benefit considerably through their involvement in education. This book gives deep insight through first person accounts of the shared experiences of head teachers and the execs who give freely of their time to help create a future for children let down by a dysfunctional system which betrays the dreams and aspirations of tens of thousands of children every year. None of this is possible without the dogged determination of Louise van Rhyn whose purpose is ensuring others find theirs. Her story is one of extraordinary courage and determination.

Bruce Whitfield
Author, Speaker and Radio Host

The great Irish author, philosopher and educator Charles Handy once wrote that in society there were three occupations for which no qualification and no training existed: politician, parent and manager. 'Unfortunately,' Handy commented, 'these occupations are three of the most important'. Since Handy made this observation, there has been some progress in the preparation and development for the latter two occupations, but there is still a long road to travel. This book provides a compelling account of a driving vision and a set of practical approaches to support the development of the third of Handy's groups, school 'managers' – principals and leaders – and the corresponding positive impact on the business leaders who partner with them. It documents the incredible power of partnerships, communities, dialogue and joint experiences, often across wide cultural chasms. It is also a testament to the power of storytelling. The book demonstrates the huge potential of learning from working and learning through sharing – the '70' and '20' in the 70:20:10 approach – and ways these can be turned into reality. This is a book every educator and every business leader looking to make a difference should read.

Charles Jennings
Co-founder, 70:20:10 Institute

In South Africa we really need to tell our good news stories. Here is one such story, the record of people whose lives have been touched for the better through being involved in the Partners for Possibility programme. Being a principal in our country can be a lonely and thankless job. PfP has provided partners for our school leaders, and this book captures both the stories of the principals and their business partners as they have found each other and, together, made a difference in schools across our country. If you want to find out how our schools are doing better, and who are the main players in this improvement, then read this book.

David de Korte
South African Principals Association President

The authenticity of this book is that it does not try and ingratiate itself with funders who want numbers to show that it works. Certainly, one measure of progress is improved school marks, and it's encouraging to see some evidence of better grades in partnership schools. But the main message from this book is that relationships that affirm, unite and enable form the lasting fabric with which to raise the state of education in South Africa. If principals and teachers feel inspired and supported, they will inspire and support children to find their own place in society. If our main goal is to build a better nation, the best measure of achievement is whether a child who struggles at school still feels like a 'somebody' and leaves with a strong sense of hope and possibility, even if they do not complete Grade 12. Children motivated in this way do better at school anyway. It's always great to see the fruits of our labour, but the real visionaries are content to till the soil and sow the seeds for a harvest that others may reap. I suspect that's how Partners for Possibility will ultimately be recognised.

David Harrison
Chief Executive Officer, DG Murray Trust

From its humble beginnings 10 years ago, to where it is now, the journey of the PfP movement that Louise van Rhyn started has been truly remarkable. To the point where the quantitative data that many people look for to measure the programme's success is emerging. Regrettably though, some people still ignore the qualitative data – the stories that show how lives have been impacted by the work done by PfP. The inspiring stories in this book are testament to the difference that PfP has and continues to make. As you read these stories you can feel the impact that PfP has had on principals, business leaders, teachers, students and communities You can feel how people have been moved and motivated by this initiative and how their hope has been restored. Despite doubt and tough times Louise has shown immense resilience and, through PfP, has continued to make a difference in our country and communities.

Deon Myburgh
Manager ICT Operations, Mediclinic Southern Africa

Partners for Possibility is a role model for how to start a movement. This collection of stories proves, with concrete examples, what an impact they've had already. Please follow their lead.

Derek Sivers
Author: 'How to Start a Movement'

This collection of inspiring stories shows that when different groups come together in long-term partnerships, rather than in aid, real change can take place. Business leaders who have worked with school principals recount moments where their courage and perseverance was tested and where their worldviews were fundamentally altered. What these leaders found was not a community project where they were giving and others were receiving but a space where they could also grow, learn and find support.

Diane Radley
Trustee DG Murray Trust and Director of Companies

In terms of education, South Africa is doubly challenged. Not only are we dealing with a broken education system – the lingering effects of Apartheid era segregation and ripple effect of embedded inequality – but also a generic problem of a traditional education template (spawned in the 19th century), which is proving wholly out of place for the 21st century. Add to that the rise of Gen Z, the world's first generation of true digital natives, and the question of whether or not we are preparing our youth for the future of work, becomes more complex, and pressing. The Partners for Possibility programme has married business leadership with education leadership with remarkable results. But we still have a very long way to go. I hope that anyone who reads this book will realise that interventions can be made, as long as we think about problem solving differently. In a disruptive era, businesses themselves are learning that unusual collaborations are proving to increase the innovation process. Partners for Possibility has blazed new trails in education. Let's turn those trails into well-worn pathways.

Dion Chang
Founder, Flux Trends

Reading the stories of impact in the second book by Partners for Possibility, I am filled with hope and am truly inspired. The powerful quote by Andy Andrews, 'you have been created in order that you might make a difference. You have within you the power to change the world,' truly applies to each member of this incredible team.

It is my heartfelt wish that more leaders across the country embrace the opportunities that Partners for Possibility offers for making a meaningful difference in arguably the most important sector of our country, namely educating our youth.

Dot Field
Founder Dot Field Consulting

I defy anyone who reads this moving collection of real-life stories not to be inspired by them and their heroes and heroines. This is how communities in South Africa could and should team up, and work together, for the benefit of all. I salute all contributors to this brilliant and life-changing educational initiative.

Erica Platter
International award-winning author, born and raised on a farm that is
now part of Simbithi Eco-Estate

This is an inspirational and important book about hope, transformation, and engaging citizenship for the greater good! What Louise van Rhyn, her team at Symphonia, and all the PfP principals and business partners and supporters have done is to bring together the collective power of possibilities to elevate humanity. Grounded in sciences of complexity, sense-making, dialogic Organization Development, and more, they co-created and developed a program that has woven a social fabric from their heartfelt and authentic engagement with one another for the betterment of South Africa and for her children. For donors or investors who hesitate to support because of a desire for rigorous measures, I would encourage you to understand that human interaction, such as that found in the story of PfP, is not a system of discrete measurements, but a complex dynamic world that has and will continue to have impact that will emerge with time. Like the individuals in these stories, you sometimes must take a leap of faith, long before the measurable outcome can be known. This takes courage. These collective members have that courage and have, in the spirit of Meg Wheatley's calling, chosen who they wish to be in the world and live in the realm of possibilities as a way forward. Their story stands as an invitation as to who each one of us wants to be in relation to our humanity with one another!

Gary L. Mangiofico, Ph.D.
Academic Director, Master of Science in Organization Development
Executive Professor of Leadership, Organization Theory, and Management
Chair, Board of Trustees & President, Organization Development Network

I believe that education is the key to South Africa's economic development. We need an education revolution to empower all our people and to provide true redress. This can only be achieved through citizens from all sectors becoming actively involved and working together to strengthen our public education system. The stories in this book clearly illustrate how we can solve problems and make positive changes in our lives and our communities if we are willing to become active citizens. I applaud the Partners for Possibility movement and all the active citizens who have joined it and hope that these stories of nation-building relationships and win-win partnerships will encourage others to do the same.

Herman Mashaba
Entrepreneur, Former Mayor of Johannesburg & Founder of The People's Dialogue

We live in a society where it is easy to become paralyzed by despair. These stories of impact from around our country serve as a tonic to reawaken the soul.
Witnessing how partnerships with humble beginnings can have such far-reaching effects which change the trajectories of thousands of lives, fills me with hope and re-energizes me to keep going.

The knowledge that there are 1,300 plus active engines of change at work amongst our youth of today and leaders of tomorrow encourages me to keep doing my bit. I am inspired by the thought of how many Nelsons will come through the ranks amongst the many lives that have been touched and shaped as a result of these partnerships.

Irené Raubenheimer
Co-founder, ROGZ

Successful businesses rely on strong leaders who understand the needs of their organizations and the people in it. Schools are the same, except that their leaders are called principals and in SA their challenges are far bigger than those faced on a daily basis by any CEO or MD. PfP provides a platform where business people can contribute in a positive way to the education of our children, our future! The peer to peer learning creates benefits both ways and opens up resources and services to schools that are badly under-resourced. This provides the principal with the opportunity to be successful and gets our education on an upward trajectory.

Jean de Villiers
Former Springbok rugby captain and Citadel's Head of Philanthropy

Partners for Possibility provides a gateway to a world of strategic opportunities that schools and their communities can only dream of as they endeavour to build new ways of learning and working to ensure aspirational outcomes for each and every student.

Partners for Possibility, with the support of extraordinary organisations, helps schools translate positive and asset-based understandings of their learning environment into powerful models of school and teacher leadership that are grounded in both existing research and the complexities of life in organisations. Modelling draws on the strengths of relationships among staff and the broader school community to instil shared values and a common mission to pursue a relentless focus on achieving positive educational and social impact for each student, their school and their communities.

Partners for Possibility builds a compelling case for creating more inclusive, agile approaches to leading change that are designed to engage the hearts and minds of every student, parent and community member, teachers and school leaders and the businesses who together co-lead these new tomorrows.

Examples throughout this book highlight deep understandings regarding how high impact leaders continually build knowledge and capabilities to engage in inspirational ways with students and community, so that they can make a difference in complex, unfamiliar and changing contexts.

In a dynamic and changing world in which education and educational leadership matters more than ever, Partners for Possibility reminds practitioners, researchers, and policymakers that the centrepiece of any innovative change must fit with the moral purpose of education – to invest in every student to ensure they reach their full potential.

Dr Jenny Lewis
International education leadership expert and advisor on education systems

Educational research is equivocal on many issues except one – that the single most important factor in school change is the role of the principal leader. This is what one of the continent's foremost innovations in education has seized on: that by strengthening the role of the principal in difficult contexts (poverty, crime, unemployment etc.), entire schools can be transformed. *Partners for Possibility* has captured the public imagination with a simple idea – that by partnering resourceful business leaders with passionate school leaders, powerful learning happens. Unsurprisingly, the learning is bidirectional (principal leader and business executive) while the benefits also extend to teachers, learners and the communities in which the school is located. This book is a must-read for activists in non-governmental organisations, planners and policymakers in government and funders in the development business. Now, when corporates ask me the familiar question, 'what can we as business people do?' I have a simple answer: 'Here, read this amazing book.'

Professor Jonathan D Jansen
Distinguished Professor of Education, Stellenbosch University

In this book, readers are treated to a well-evidenced chronicle of Partnerships for Possibility's (PfP) innovative journey from an idea to a globally respected leadership organisation. PfP's commitment to the importance of nurturing relationships that foster mutual awareness and understanding is evident throughout. Commitment to acknowledging South Africa's history and commitment to its enormous potential are woven into the fabric of PfP's work. Throughout the book, corporate and education leaders, in their own words, share how PfP has changed their lives, work and perspectives. These vignettes bring PfP's mission to life and clearly demonstrate its influence on participating leaders and communities. Uniquely, readers also are privy to the learning and reflections of members of the PfP leadership and delivery team. Again, this additional layer of insight only serves to deepen our understanding of PfP's power. Almost as importantly, the book also provides a secondary roadmap for social entrepreneurs on designing and developing an organisation that creates sustainable social impact. The lessons gleaned from *Stories of Impact* will inspire social entrepreneurs and policy makers across South Africa and beyond.

Dr Karen Edge
London Centre for Leadership in Learning, UCL Institute of Education

This book is a brilliantly crafted narrative of how leadership ought to be. It explores the work of human beings both within themselves and in the ways in which they can influence those around them. PfP brings to light, through lived experiences and stories, the reality of what school leaders in South African schools face, especially those grappling with leading schools in poor socioeconomic situations, where school represents hope and the only mechanism through which the cycle of poverty can be broken. When a school leader takes on the challenge of uplifting the whole community (s)he has to become a catalyst for change, someone who can redirect deficit mindsets into funds of knowledge, one who respects agency and believes that all children can – and are capable of what Victor Frankl called "the last of the human freedoms" – the choice made to overcome any adversity so that learning and success are possible for all of South Africa's children. In this book, the partnership between school leaders and business leaders brings a dynamic relationship that gives and receives. In addition, the community is brought into the school gates to partner in the "business" of learning and school leaders extend themselves into a world where survival and prosperity require a shift in skills, mindset and attitude. These are relationships of equality, of combined hope for a better future by working together for and with each other. In this book PfP offers a model of hope and of possibilities needed more now than ever before.

Professor Kat Yassim
Faculty of Education, University of Johannesburg

What an opportune time for the publication of *Partners for Possibility, Stories of Impact,* by Louise van Rhyn with Theo Garrun, when we are faced with enormous challenges in our country, from deepening inequality to gender-based violence on an alarming scale. Within these pages, we read of passion, hope, resilience and the African spirit of perseverance and service to others. The Partners for Possibility programme is about ordinary people, doing extraordinary feats for the love of our children and country. These are citizens who are showing that change can be effected, not always by the powerful in lofty positions, but by people in community, ready to roll up their sleeves.

We know that our education challenges are systemic, and they require an overhaul of the entire system. However, this book demonstrates that we are able to influence and transform individual schools, to enable learners to receive high-quality education.
It is evident that the Partners for Possibility programme is not only about transforming schools: it has organically evolved into a project of nation-building. Citizens of all political persuasions, backgrounds and identities reaching out to each other in pursuance of a common goal. The testimonies illustrate that we foster belonging in 'struggle' and 'in action'. It is 'in the doing' that we discover that it is no longer about 'us' and 'them', but about our children, our communities, our country.

Salutations to the Partners for Possibility Team! You are helping us, not only to craft the new narrative of social and economic justice for all South Africans, but you are directly building the path as we walk it!

I yearn to see the love shining in the eyes of all our children. This book shows that it is possible… and in my lifetime!

Lucille Meyer
Chrysalis Academy Chief Executive Officer

The vision of South Africa's National Development Plan (NDP) is to eliminate poverty and reduce inequality by 2030. The World Bank noted that the link between access to quality education and economic and social development is direct and indisputable. South Africa's NDP recognises this and states clearly that strengthening the leadership capacity of school principals is a national priority. The heart-warming stories in this book illustrate how Partners for Possibility is empowering principals with new awareness, skills and confidence that are strengthening their capacity to manage their complex organisations and to lead with courage and determination in exceptionally challenging contexts. At the same time, the PfP programme is helping to break down cultural, racial and social barriers by providing participants with access and exposure to communities with whom they would not normally engage. This book serves as a reminder of what can be achieved when civil society, government and business work together to address their country's challenges.

Lynda, Baroness Chalker of Wallasey
Former UK Minister for Africa and Commonwealth (1986-1997) and Founder of Africa Matters Ltd.

Experiences that principals, learners and the school community gather through the PfP process are motivating, inspiring, re-energising and empowering. The list is endless. These experiences may fade over time as life situations change and other experiences come into play. However, documenting these experiences makes them live forever. This PfP book will make the experiences remain alive in the hearts and minds of those that have been through the programme and attract the interest of those who read about them. The simplicity and authenticity of the stories told will extend the reach of the PfP experience to millions.

Makgoshi Sindane
CSI Programme Manager, Development Bank of Southern Africa (DBSA)

Social transformation is complex, requires collaboration and takes time. Partners for Possibility understand these dynamics and has created an unparalleled model for civic leadership engagement. No doubt, the impact of PfP will ripple outward in the decades ahead. In South Africa, where class and racial divisions have precipitated a landscape of inequality, separation and low trust, PfP offers a signal of hope and a beacon of practical reconciliation. By building a bridge between leaders from disparate communities, embedded in the social institutional environment of the school system, the initiative strikes at the heart of all that is broken in South Africa. In this book, Louise and Theo draw on the collective experiences of their inspiring community of change-makers to paint a picture of how co-learning relationships can be the basis for skills-transfer and social cohesion. Anyone serious about social change should read this book.

Marius Oosthuizen
Lecturer in Strategic Foresight in the Centre for Leadership and Dialogue at the Gordon Institute of Business Science (GIBS)

A wise man once said: 'Purpose is the reason you journey. Passion is the fire that lights the way.'

This book relates stories about the possibility of possibility and the soul of change. It exposes the power within the collective diversity when we acknowledge each other as individuals bringing different worlds of reference to the same table. It teaches that when we synchronise our intentions by applying practical and mutually developed and supported ideas and strategies, all challenges move from being abstract obstacles to practical and successful outcomes.

The children of today are the leaders of tomorrow. The PfP model empowers participants to confront and address blinds spots so as to develop well – rounded, emotionally intelligent learners and leaders. It restores dignity.

Each one of these inspiring stories is the result of purpose-driven commitment to identify and simply do the work required – no matter the degree of effort it requires. Read between the lines and you will laugh, cry and be humbled. Above all, though, you will be inspired, because the soul of every story will touch you.

I conclude with a Jewish definition of humility: 'Humility is limiting oneself to an appropriate amount of space while leaving and creating space for others.'

The PfP story is about creating space – each one of these individual stories, experiences, and partnerships are creating space – now and for the future!

Matthys Ferreira
Motoring Editor, Lowveld Media

If you asked me to list the most crucial elements of any project aimed at making South Africa a stable, prosperous society, I would put education, leadership and active cooperation between government, civil society and the business community at the top of my list.

This is exactly the foundation of the remarkable PfP movement that has had such a profound impact on schools and communities it has touched.

If one analyses the failures and successes of the education system in South Africa, it quickly becomes clear that the quality of leadership of school principals is crucial. PfP addresses that by establishing partnerships between principals and business leaders.

It is a simple yet revolutionary idea and this book is proof that it really works.
The stories of those involved in the project make this book a compelling and inspirational read. It is more than a story of improved education outcomes; it is a story of how the interactions transformed human lives and attitudes.

I was particularly touched by the story of Upington business leader Freek Mulder, who says about his experience: "I have learned how to really listen to people." And by Rosie Chirongoma, a PfP facilitator, who says: "I cannot tell my life story without talking about PfP and not in a cursory by-the-way manner. It's shaped the person I am, the relationships I have and want to be in, the work I do, the conversations I have, and the way I choose to move through the world."

PfP is a beautiful example of how citizens can make a profound difference instead of waiting tor the state to run every facet of our lives.

Max du Preez
Author, Journalist, Political analyst & Public speaker

The work of genuine transformation happens over years and years, and this is a collection of stories of genuine transformation. These are real people achieving unreal change. Perfectly ordinary people building extraordinary partnerships. It's only when South Africans from different walks of life cross psychological and cultural borders, that things will really start to change, and my goodness, we are a country desperate for positive change. So read and share this wonderful book. Take courage, and take heart.

Mike Stopforth
Director, Beyond Binary

Partners for Possibility has been a true inspiration. This book demonstrates the power of working together to reform our education ecosystem; that if the idiom that the village can raise a child is true, it is through partnerships that we can educate our next generation of leaders. We have to partner to ensure change occurs for the future of our beautiful country and that it can truly never be said that the circumstances of your birth will determine your tomorrow. This book evoked hope in me for education as a transformative tool in our nation.

Mmusi Maimane
Politician and former leader of the Democratic Alliance

When a programme and intervention like PfP does so much for those helping as those being helped you know you have a successful programme. Reading the many success stories in this book reminds us all of the collective power of actually doing as opposed to talking about doing. Personal relationships do matter and make a difference.

The Mapula Trust has been privileged to have funded many partnerships over the years, and it has been rewarding to read about and see first-hand the positive outcomes that many have achieved.

In Louise's and PfP's mission to help, not just a small select group, but as wide and diverse a group as possible, the challenge of making a difference in South African education is a challenge which requires vision, stamina, guts and dedication. And for this PfP and all who work within and alongside it need to be applauded.

The Mapula Trust is especially touched by the incredible difference Ian Macdonald made in his time working with Gavin Alkana at Hillwood Primary. We are very proud of the collective support Ian's friends and family have given and continue to give as his living legacy at Hillwood Primary, and of being able to provide support for the Ian Macdonald Scholarship.

Michael Byron
Trustee, The Mapula Trust

Research shows that one defining feature of poverty is a deficit in access to social capital, which is the case in many of South Africa's under-resourced and under-performing schools. The good news is that providing social capital improves schools and student educational outcomes by providing resources, opportunities, and choices. Educational programs rarely consider this aspect of educational achievement. Partners for Possibility is a program that understands that poverty and disenfranchised schools and communities can be improved by gaining access to social capital by developing collaboration and networking. Using a bottom-up approach and sound pedagogical and leadership theories, PfP transforms communities and the lives of principals, business leaders, teachers, and students. The numerous stories in this book illustrate how PfP challenges the status quo and changes perspectives and thinking, leading to lasting school improvement. PfP and this book restore the hope and belief that all people can make a lasting impact in their communities.

Michael H. Romanowski, Ph.D.
Professor of Educational Leadership College of Education, Qatar University, Doha, Qatar

As I write this, the world is staggering as intelligently as possible towards survival in the face of a threat to every one of us. Whatever our histories and current contexts of oppression, whatever our bifurcated engagements between right and wrong, whatever the luxuries of the nuances in our values, today we are caring about each other as sentient beings, wanting each other to live.

At work right now, night and day, are people thinking, learning, rethinking, seeing, discovering, discarding, to develop ways to keep us alive. We are partnering. We will survive because we partnered.

And the quality of this partnering must be, and in many places right now is, the same quality of partnering PfP has pioneered in South Africa. These school principals and business leaders and all of the students they serve are engaging in a way of being that is our lifeline now.

This book tells part of that story. It is a story that will further inspire us and lift us, and that everyone needs to know. A story everyone will love. A story that will allow us to keep loving each other long into a calmer, safer time.

Nancy Kline
Founder and President of Time To Think and Published Author

Wow! Not only does this easy-to-read book tell the eye-opening story of Partners for Possibility and what the programme has so far achieved but, as you read the motivating individual stories and get introduced to the real-life players, it becomes an intense journey of self-awareness and leadership. It has been a long time since I have read a narrative that so succinctly makes the case that leadership development and personal development are so intertwined.

If you want to:
- Get your serotonin flowing and experience the high that a sense of possibility and hope gives
- Rebuild your faith in humanity and our individual and collective ability to rise above sometimes seemingly insurmountable challenges to build a better future
- Take some time to reflect on your own contribution to building a better tomorrow, not only for your own children, but for the whole community
- Become a better leader.

Then this book is for you!

If, despite your achievements, something is missing in your life, please take the time to read this book. It's a huge lesson on life.

Thank you Louise, and the all the Partners for Possibility team and participants for what you have created and the incredible difference you are making to so many lives.

Nick Christelis
Managing Partner, Nick Christelis and Associates Author, The Art of the Arrow: How Leaders Fly

Leadership in South African schools is generally conceived of as principals and other officials 'monitoring' the work of teachers. And for these 'leaders' this entails combing through the lesson plans and other mountains of paperwork which teachers are required to produce, using tickbox monitoring 'instruments' to score the teachers.

This activity does not help one bit in assisting teachers to be more effective: if a teacher doesn't know how to add fractions, getting a poor score on the state of her lesson plans will not help her to teach fractions effectively. But worse, the tickbox approach burdens teachers with hours of administration which has little to do with what actually happens in classrooms, and as a result in almost certainly detrimental to teaching and learning.

Into this depressing field Partners for Possibility (PfP) shines a brilliant new light on the concept of leadership, where the idea of 'mentoring' replaces the dead hand of monitoring. A simple change in spelling reveals a different world, in which seasoned leaders work with principals to solve the myriad of everyday glitches that hamper the work of teachers. PfP demonstrates to principals that leadership is as much about inspiration as it is about perspiration, and it is this twin approach which assists principals to lift the work of their schools to new heights.

Nick Taylor
Education Researcher, Joint Education Trust (JET)

Throughout the education value chain and ecosystem, there are certain points of leverage that properly unblocked would create the greatest opportunity for us to get the kind of quality throughput of students we deserve. However, first you have to believe that this is possible and be open to meeting others where they are at without bringing your own preconceived ideas of what a school environment is about!

Partners for Possibility is not only a leadership development programme for school principals but also a personal growth programme for business leaders. It is a model for nation-building where we can learn empathy and have a better appreciation for the resilience of our educators, who continue to thrive against great odds in the communities that they are part of.

More business leaders need this exposure and experience to make them even better decision-makers and help them use the immense resources they have at their disposal for better social impact.

I would urge more businesses to consider these partnerships as the mutual benefits are just too many to ignore. Louise and her team are giving us the workbook to guide us all in our commitment to building better school communities.

Nolitha Fakude
Chairperson, Anglo American South Africa

I takes a village to raise a child. Everyone knows that. But how does that apply to schools? *It takes an ecosystem to transform a school*. And the centerpiece of that ecosystem is the transformation of relationships between leaders in education and leaders in business. In this remarkable book, Louise van Rhyn shares how the much needed transformation of the education can actually work. Essential reading!

Otto Scharmer
Senior Lecturer, MIT; Co-founder, Presencing Institute; Author, Theory U

In difficult times, it is easy to be cynical about what is possible. It is also tempting to become fixated on initiatives where the impact can easily be proven with hard data and to assume that stories about individual experiences or changed human beings are not necessarily the truth. The stories in this book clearly demonstrate that the lives of thousands of children have been touched by PfP. Hundreds of principals and business leaders are thinking differently about their own capacity to make a difference with strangers who without this effort would never have met. I might be biased because I am over-credited with this story's origins, but the accomplishment of this project has the possibility to transform the world. All that is required is for each of us to decide to believe.

Peter Block
Author of bestselling books on leadership, empowerment and community

Research tells us that most partnerships to improve society fail. Start-up energy gives way to inertia. Key partners lose interest or pursue other priorities. Funding dries up. Successful ventures don't scale or replicate. Then frustration, fear, fire-fighting, fatigue, and collapse. So it goes. But sometimes not: Louise van Rhyn and her Partners for Possibility show how to beat the odds. Good ideas keep coming. Partners persevere and spread the word. Purpose and passion attract funds, talent, and set in motion a virtuous success cycle where, over a decade of refinement, the work gets better, motivation stronger and results more compelling. This book, chock-a-block with stories of trials and triumphs, speaks thoughtfully and practically to educators, business people, community leaders, social entrepreneurs, and change-makers alike. It celebrates both inspiration and perspiration, lofty visions and on-the-ground actions, hard work and the unbounded possibility of the collective human spirit.

Philip H Mirvis
Research Fellow, Global Network on Corporate Citizenship, Babson College Social Innovation Lab.

I have always maintained that most South Africans have interesting stories to tell. This is partly because of our unity in the struggle against one of the biggest modern-day crimes against humanity – apartheid – but also because of the almost in-bred tenacity and perseverance that we display. This, the second book about Partners for Possibility, tells the story of an amazing project that refused to accept the legacy of apartheid and instead decided to do something about it. Education has always been one of the key sites of struggle. During apartheid, it was used to subjugate the majority by offering them third-class education. In our democracy, education can play a different, and more uplifting, role. It can be the catalyst for the true liberation that we have been fighting for. Partners for Possibility and Symphonia for South Africa refused to accept the obstacles left behind in education after apartheid. Instead, through smart partnerships, they have taken those obstacles and turned them into opportunities for thousands of young people throughout South Africa. It is an achievement that should be celebrated.

Ryland Fisher
CEO, Ikusasa Lethu Media

Turning schools into vibrant places of learning and living examples of the democracies we aspire to become is more important than ever. Yet effective solutions will have to be very different from most of what has been tried so far to reform schools around the world: more movement building than program implementation; more collaborative cultures than compliance; more liberating learning than testing. As we strive to fundamentally transform schools and societies at large, we will be wise to look at and learn from powerful work already underway, especially in the

Global South. Enter Partners for Possibility (PfP), an initiative that has spread to over a thousand schools and their surrounding communities, reaching over a million people in South Africa in the last decade.

The idea behind PfP is elegantly simple: bring together business leaders and school principals to figure out solutions to the most pressing issued faced by schools in precarious circumstances. But ensure that business leaders come in NOT as experts, condescending donors, or patronizing bosses, but instead as learning partners. And this is where the magic happens: authentic partnerships where both business and school leaders grow, learn from, and change each other; where both face and figure out solutions to problems none of them has a clear answer for; where business leaders put their time, mind, and social capital in the service of genuine needs of schools. This infuses new life into the daily operations of the schools and society at large. It is much more than mere school improvement. It is nation-building at its best.

This book takes stock of the one-decade journey PfP has traveled so far and what it has accomplished, weaving through moving and compelling stories of those whose lives it's touched. A quarter century ago, South Africa ignited our hopes and invited us to imagine that social justice and the full realization of humanity were within our reach. This book will not only give you hope, but propel you to act on it.

Santiago Rincón-Gallardo,
Education Consultant and Author of Liberating Learning: Educational Change as Social Movement

Reading this book has taken me on a journey that started in 2015 when I became aware of Partners for Possibility by chance. An email from PfP landed on my computer inviting me to an information session somewhere in Sandton. Back then, the Gauteng Department of Education was in a process of restructuring and establishing circuits. I took responsibility for a circuit that was not performing well. Our year-end results then were a paltry 60% pass rate. Back from the information session, my first meeting with school principals was to talk about how PfP partnered principals with visionary business leaders. The response was tremendous. Our results improved year-on-year, and I am now proud to say that our results in 2019 stood at a comfortable 91% pass rate and our commitment to break the 95% target grows stronger by the day, thanks to Partners for Possibility.

This book will assist school managers to turn underperforming public township schools around and, in the process, narrow social inequalities by freeing the potential of ordinary South Africans. It's a concrete expression of making education a societal priority.

Selogamaano D Mogoane
Circuit Manager, Tshwane South District Office, Gauteng Department of Education

School leadership is one of the most important influences on student learning, and thus, a critical factor for improving the life and educational outcomes of children and the broader economic conditions of nations. However, there is limited evidence to suggest that strong school leadership exists in most of the world's schools. In many countries, improving the quality of school leadership will necessitate attention to professionalizing the role of the school leader as well as shifting the role from one that centers on management to one that emphasizes the leadership of learning. This, in turn, will necessitate widespread access to the kinds of school leader development programs like Partners for Possibility that are both informed by existing knowledge of robust leader learning designs and are also highly responsive to national and local contexts and context resources and needs. Documenting and disseminating lessons from this program to other similar settings are of critical importance, and this book, therefore, makes an important contribution.

Dr Shelby Cosner
Professor and Director of University of Illinois at Chicago (UIC) Center for Urban Education Leadership

PfP is advancing development through collaboration, partnerships and innovation with an ethos of Ubuntu which encapsulates and epitomises the rich tapestry of 56 million South Africans and a resilience that excite me. PfP raises our optimism and hope that our schools will become 'the central laboratory of holistic learning in communities'. It is the dream we must cherish.

Sharna Fernandez
Provincial Minister, Department of Social Development, Western Cape Government

The Dinokeng Scenarios Report of 2009 acknowledged that South Africa faces enormous challenges but also noted that we are a country of great possibility. It urged business, government and civil society to 'Walk Together' to address the critical social and economic issues that face our country. For the past decade, a diverse and increasingly sizeable group of citizens have been doing just that through Possibility for Possibility to address what is undoubtedly one of our most pressing challenges; the low levels of education attained in most of our public schools. One of PfP's key objectives is to strengthen a critical lever for school improvement, namely school leadership. The remarkable stories and testimonials in this new book vividly illustrate how school principals' confidence and capacity to lead their complex organisations are being transformed as a result of the peer learning and support, formal training, coaching, friendship and acknowledgement they receive through PfP. While critical, this is only one aspect of PfP's impact. The accounts in this book demonstrate how PfP schools and their students are benefitting from many different kinds of substantial practical support and resources, depending on their specific context and needs. In some instances, this support has completely transformed the lives of students from impoverished backgrounds. Perhaps most powerfully, these stories portray the change that is taking place in the hearts and minds of school principals and business leaders from vastly different backgrounds as they get to know each other as individuals and work together with a common purpose. I commend Louise van Rhyn and her PfP team for their exceptional and sustained achievement in facilitating reconciliation and building a more inclusive South Africa.

Simon Susman
Virgin Active Holdings Chairman, Former CEO and Chairman of Woolworths

Ten years is a big deal, especially for those whose vocation and witness is to help others and serve the greater good. Partners for Possibility is one rare organisation that believes in our inherent goodness and that within each of us there a God-given potential to maintain this goodness for people and God's creation. Over the last ten years, as attested by accounts from the field in this book, PfP has maintained and nurtured this goodness by challenging those who have them to share their skills, abilities and resources with the poor. The Letsitele valley is a valley of contrast. Contrast between very well-to-do farm owners who can get by with their self-sufficiency and others who are much less well off. PfP gave the farmers an opportunity to look to the 'others' and create equality of opportunity for rural school children. Well done and congratulations on this milestone! Do not tire to do good and especially for those in the household of faith, the Christian sacred texts urges you.

The Most Reverend Dr Thabo Makgoba
Archbishop of the Anglican Church of Southern Africa

I am a voracious reader. Reading is my success secret #1. I read and read ... and then read some more. I can honestly say that I may never have read a more exciting book than Partners for Possibility. Exciting? It's simple. By definition, there could not be anything on earth more important than the issues PfP has chosen to tackle head on. My career was made by a book called In Search of Excellence. It had one big difference from management books that had preceded it. It was 100% about success stories meant to inspire reflection—and action. This book, too, is about incredibly inspiring success stories about, as I said, the most important issues humanity faces. Bravo .. and keep up the good [make that "great"] work.

Tom Peters
Thought Leader and Author of In Search of Excellence

The preamble to our constitution commits us to 'free the potential of each person'. Education remains the only means to such freedom. We need to ensure that all people understand the process of education. Obviously, it involves eager learners and determined, engaged educators. In addition, it requires well organised and managed schools.

The overwhelming majority of school principals were highly successful teachers whose successes were recognised by moving them from the chalk-board into administration and management. We know that the training in pedagogical methods does not automatically translate into managerial skills. Yet, we must understand that, increasingly, the skills required as a principal are high-level managerial. The system allows for no pause between the classroom and administration. On the other hand, there are many people employed in the private sector who believe in the power of education, but whose daily lives take them away from formal education.

Partners for Possibility recognises the opportunity to bring these two groups together in order to cross-pollinate and strengthen both the system and outcomes of education; we may not understand enough of this. This book helps to fill our understanding of the interface between the people convened by Partners for Possibility. I know that understanding this draws us all closer and vests our collective interests in the power of education. These are the stories of hope in our future. Thanks to Partners for Possibility helping us see into the future.

Trevor Manuel
Chairman: Old Mutual

Copyright © KR Publishing and Louise van Rhyn and Theo Garrun

All reasonable steps have been taken to ensure that the contents of this book do not, directly or indirectly, infringe any existing copyright of any third person and, further, that all quotations or extracts taken from any other publication or work have been appropriately acknowledged and referenced. The publisher, editors and printers take no responsibility for any copyright infringement committed by an author of this work.

Copyright subsists in this work. No part of this work may be reproduced in any form or by any means without the written consent of the publisher or the author.

While the publisher, editors and printers have taken all reasonable steps to ensure the accuracy of the contents of this work, they take no responsibility for any loss or damage suffered by any person as a result of that person relying on the information contained in this work.

First published in 2020.

ISBN: 978-1-86922-846-0
eISBN: 978-1-86922-847-7

Published by KR Publishing
P O Box 3954
Randburg
2125

Republic of South Africa

Tel: (011) 706-6009
Fax: (011) 706-1127
E-mail: orders@knowres.co.za
Website: www.kr.co.za

Printed and bound: HartWood Digital Printing, 243 Alexandra Avenue, Halfway House, Midrand
Typesetting, layout and design: Cia Joubert, cia@knowres.co.za
Cover design: Miranda Capellino, design@miranda.co.za
Editing and Proofreading: Gail McMillan, gail@symphonia.net
Project management: Cia Joubert, cia@knowres.co.za

PARTNERS FOR POSSIBILITY

STORIES OF IMPACT

by

Louise van Rhyn with Theo Garrun

2020

Table of contents

Foreword by Professor Brian O'Connell _____ ii

Foreword by Ridwan Samodien _____ iii

Abbreviations _____ vi

Chapter 1: After 10 years: An opportunity to pause and reflect _____ 1

Chapter 2: PfP in Letsitele _____ 23

Chapter 3: Long-term partnerships with impact _____ 41

Chapter 4: Where it all started – Kannemeyer Primary School _____ 61

Chapter 5: Simbithi: At the heart of the community _____ 73

Chapter 6: Schools that have become a magnet for the gifts and contributions from people and organisations around the school _____ 95

Chapter 7: Hillwood Primary, Ian Macdonald and Fella's Army _____ 115

Chapter 8: Business as a force for good _____ 133

Chapter 9: Principals who have become 'symphonic leaders' at their schools ___ 163

Chapter 10: The School Pages Project _____ 171

Chapter 11: Youth@worK harnessing the power of collaboration _____ 175

Chapter 12: Principals who have been promoted since PfP _____ 189

Chapter 13: What happens when the 1:1 partnership does not work? _____ 197

Chapter 14: PfP as a consciousness-raising experience _____ 207

Chapter 15: Khumbul'ekhaya (Remember home) _____ 215

Chapter 16: Learning from being of service and in partnership _____ 225

Chapter 17: A few stories about the impact on the lives of individual children ___ 243

Chapter 18: Contributions from principals who have been part of PfP _____ 255

Chapter 19: Contributions from business leaders who have been part of PfP ____ 273

Chapter 20: The impact of PfP on the delivery team _____ 295

Chapter 21: Concluding thoughts _____ 339

Acknowledgements _____ 346

About the Authors _____ 348

Index _____ 350

Foreword by Professor Brian O'Connell[1]

It has been an honour and privilege to serve as patron of PfP. I have spent most of my life advocating for education. It is the foundation on which we must build our society as we pursue justice, equality and empowerment for all of our people. Louise is a champion for education and through PfP has taken up this mantle with determination and vigour, offering a creative and socially innovative programme that ultimately supports quality, accessible education for our children.

While South Africans continue to strive to overcome the legacy of apartheid, our nation and its citizens must also contend with new, unprecedented challenges that the 21st century has ushered in. Environmental degradation, water shortages and unsustainable business and industry are just some of the issues that we face today. Issues with global import where decisions made in one part of the world can have catastrophic impacts in another.

Governments around the world are beginning to acknowledge that their capacity to deal with this complexity and uncertainty is limited. Solutions are, therefore, likely to be dependent on a decentralised government that empowers and supports its citizenry in their efforts to develop and implement socially innovative policies and practices.

Crucially, empirical evidence consistently emphasises the critical role of education in overcoming social, environmental and economic challenges. For example, our nation's blueprint for development, the National Development Plan 2030, has likely been constrained by a lack of engagement with our youth as critical stakeholders. A recent study found that 94% of our Grade 12 pupils had no knowledge of the very plan on which we are basing their future. Education once again is vital. Building capacity and providing support to our principals, teachers and schools, in turn, is critical.

I believe that our future lies in local community-based solutions, implemented by an active and engaged citizenry, characterised by adaptability and flexibility, and offering opportunities for plurality in both local and national impacts and outcomes. PfP has provided just such a solution for our education system, underpinning both its success and continued relevance in these challenging times.

I want to commend Louise for her leadership, her team for their work and support, all the schools and principals for their courage and determination, and the business leaders and other partners for their time and expertise. You have all made PfP possible. Your contribution to building a sustainable future for our communities and our children is invaluable, and I thank you.

---

1 Former Rector and Vice-Chancellor of the University of the Western Cape and Superintendent-General, Western Cape Education Department.

Foreword by Ridwan Samodien

"If we carry on as normal, then the June 1976 Soweto uprisings are going to look like a Sunday afternoon picnic." – Professor Brian O'Connell, former Vice Chancellor of UWC.

'Our alternative,' he says, 'is to rally and enrol every single citizen to step into active citizenship, pay it forward, and do what is required to make a positive difference in the community – to give each and every South African a better chance at life. Go all the way and build that utopian society so that the pain of 1976 will RIP and never rear its painful head, ever again. '

It was these inspiring words by Professor O'Connell, my muse, my hero, a great believer in Partners for Possibility (PfP), and our confidant, that would become wedged in my mind, heart and soul. Words that would make me mindful of the enormity of our task and the profoundness of our purpose as citizens of this, our beloved country.

We are a society in deep pain; fragmented and broken, and his powerful words resonated and motivated me to contribute, for the rest of my life, towards building a positive collective future for all South Africans, especially the children. As Co-founder, I am immensely proud that PfP offers a generative solution to rebuilding our humanity and the capacity of our education system.

We need to understand what broke us, tore us apart and stripped us of our humanity and potential, so I will pause briefly to reflect on our country's history and then look to our future with a sense of hope and encouragement.

Our forefathers were traumatized by the colonization, theft and genocide carried out by Europeans, particularly Jan van Riebeeck, a ruthless proxy for the colonialist slavery of the Dutch East India Company (VOC). The unravelling of our identity and culture and the formation of a 'superior' separatist identity began in earnest from that time and haunts us to the present day.

The onslaught against our land, our culture, our dignity and sense of belonging was dealt another blow when our enslaved forebears were dehumanized through the commodifying of their lives into slavery. In 1658 the Dutch merchant ship Amersfoort anchored at Table Bay with 174 Angolan slaves in her hold. These slaves constituted the first shipment of many to arrive in South Africa from elsewhere on our continent and from Madagascar, India and South-East Asia. The VOC was forbidden from enslaving indigenous people in the Cape but subjected them to genocide and conditions as brutal as slavery. This continued, unabated, for 176 years.

With the advent of apartheid in 1948, we were dealt another severe blow through institutionalized racism and segregation, which divided South Africans into different racial and ethnic groups and classes. This period gave rise to the most barbaric land and resource theft in the history of our country, and it obliterated indigenous knowledge and practices.

The years between 1948 and 1994 are known as the 'dark years'. Never in our country's history had state resources been so thoroughly plundered and looted through institutionalized corruption and theft, propped up by erroneous policy, lies and brutal repression. Our children were starved of resources, inducted into a factory model of mass education and sold a story that they are inferior; in short, robbed of a bright future. The legacy of apartheid pervades every aspect of South African life and the culture of our present-day democracy. We have borne many body blows, and the effects of debilitating trauma are still visible in people of colour; researchers hold the view that it takes generations for the effects of trauma to disappear from people's DNA. No wonder the United Nations has classified apartheid as a crime against humanity.

Thankfully, a bright and shiny light emerged in the form of Dr Louise van Rhyn, and she gave birth to the Partners for Possibility (PfP) programme, which I refer to as a movement.

In *2015*, we published our first book: *Partners for Possibility: How business leaders and principals are igniting radical change in South African Schools,* which captured the essence of the work being done by this remarkable organisation.[1] This second book is a reflection on the journey of possibility that we have been on for the last 10 years. Through beautiful stories, it captures the energy and hope of the active citizens who have stepped forward to give us a fighting chance – as our beloved Professor O'Connell, among others, implored us to do.

The PfP programme has garnered many awards but, for me, the most important is the one bestowed by the Institute of Justice and Reconciliation in 2014 and presented to us by Archbishop Emeritus Desmond Tutu, for the programme's powerful impact in promoting social justice and reconciliation. This award bears testimony to the significance of the work being done across the length and breadth of our land. PfP is now providing the nation-building 'recipe' and the impetus for reconciliation among all races in every one of our nine provinces.

I am inspired and awed by the heroes featured in these pages, who have done so much to create a South Africa we can all be proud of. We celebrate each and every one for their tireless efforts. Let us all be inspired by their stories and set ourselves the task, so

---

1   Collins, M. (2015). *Partners for Possibility: How business leaders and principals are igniting radical change in South African schools*. Randburg: Knowres Publishing.

beautifully captured in the philosophy of the Indigenous American Indians, of restoring our sense of belonging, mastery, independence and of generosity.

This book, in my view, is a renewed clarion call for more citizens to step forward and join this extraordinary movement, pay it forward, and make a difference. Our country needs you now, more than ever, to sharpen your sense of generosity and give of yourself, give of your time to create a better future for all of our children. They deserve it.

Referring to every single child in South Africa, Peter Block once said to Louise, 'Aren't they *all* your children?' My question to you is 'Are they not all *our* children?'

Shouldn't we all play an active role in nurturing, motivating and inspiring them, so that our country has healthier more resilient children who are able to break the cycle of colonialist trauma? Are you willing to step into active citizenship, so that we can give them a good education that sharpens their skills and attitudes, and gives them the chance of living a fruitful life?

Abbreviations

CoP	Community of Practice
CTICC	Cape Town International Convention Centre
DBE	Department of Basic Education
DA	Democratic Alliance
FEM	Federated Employers Mutual Assurance Company
FC	Flawless Consulting
GDE	Gauteng Department of Education
HOD	Head of Department
ICT	Information and Communication Technology
KZN	KwaZulu-Natal
LPF	Learning Process Facilitator
PoE	Portfolio of Evidence
SACE	South African Council for Educators
SAODN	South African Organisational Development Network
SD	Skills Development
SGB	School Governing Body
SMT	School Management Team
SSA	Symphonia for South Africa
STEM	Science, Technology, Engineering and Maths
UFS	University of the Free State
UWC	University of the Western Cape
TTT	Time to Think
VUCA	Volatile, Uncertain, Complex, Ambiguous
WCED	Western Cape Education Department
WITS	University of the Witwatersrand

Chapter 1

After 10 years: An opportunity to pause and reflect

"Those who enjoyed the fruits of unjust privilege must be helped to find a new spirit of sharing." – Nelson Mandela

For the last 11 years I have been leading Symphonia for South Africa NPC (SSA), an organisation I founded in 2008. SSA's purpose is to inspire South Africans to work together to co-create a more just, equitable and joyful future for everyone.

In 2010 we launched Partners for Possibility (PfP), a nation-building and leadership development programme to mobilise active citizenship around one of the major crises faced by South Africa, namely public education, to create a better future for ALL children in the country.

To date, the programme has partnered the principals of over a thousand under-resourced schools across South Africa with business leaders in a year-long, collaborative and highly practical journey of growth for both members of the partnership.

Almost every day we receive feedback from people whose lives have been impacted by our work. We routinely hear from principals who tell us that they have developed new skills and networks that make them feel more energised, confident and hopeful. An exemplar is Principal Richard Sonkwala of Motherwell High School in Port Elizabeth.

In his ninth year as a principal, Richard was buckling under the pressure he felt from the education department and his community to improve his school's matric pass rate. Richard was anxious and depressed and contemplating resigning from his post. However, he took the decision to join PfP and started the programme in February of 2017, with Garth Löest of Sage as his business partner. A year later Richard said: 'I was experiencing a lot of emotional breakdowns and was on the brink of giving up, but PfP saved my life and my career. Thanks to PfP and the network of principals I was introduced to, I now have a safe haven to turn to for support and guidance. I am far happier and more energetic and will definitely complete my full term as a principal.'

Richard is one of hundreds of school principals who have told us that their lives have changed for the better as a result of their leadership growth and the acknowledgement and support they have received as members of the PfP community. From the business leaders who have partnered with principals through PfP we have heard countless stories of hearts, minds and lives transformed by the experience of moving out of their comfort zones and into communities where deprivation is the norm.

In addition to benefitting from strengthened leadership capacity, almost all of the schools whose principals have joined PfP are now also better resourced in a variety of other ways. Together, PfP principals and business partners have mobilised a wealth of financial, material and practical support for under-resourced schools in every one of South Africa's provinces. In some cases, additions and improvements to school infrastructure and facilities have transformed the institution, making it safer and better equipped to meet the needs of the learners and community it serves.

At hundreds of PfP events hosted across South Africa principals and business leaders have shared beautiful stories which powerfully demonstrate the profoundly positive impact that PfP is having in the lives of individuals and on under-resourced schools and communities across South Africa. Such stories are routinely documented and shared with funders in sponsorship reports. Many accounts of impact have been recorded by independent evaluators of the PfP programme. For its innovation and impact in education, leadership development and social justice, PfP has received recognition from organisations which include the Institute for Justice and Reconciliation (IJR) and the World Innovation Summit for Education (WISE).

However, many funders and other key stakeholders are not satisfied with these powerful outcome stories alone as indicators of the success of the programme. They also want quantitative data which shows that our work is having a sustainable impact on academic results in schools. Monitoring and Evaluation (M&E) practitioners tend to dismiss stories about impact (qualitative data) as anecdotal and want to focus on quantitative data to determine whether PfP has impacted academic achievement.

Throughout most of PfP's 10-year existence (particularly in the early years) it has been very difficult to produce the kind of learner-level impact data for multiple reasons, such as the time frame involved from the principal's engagement in the programme to changes at learner level and the myriad of factors influencing academic outcomes.

The purpose of PfP is to work with the adults in a school. We want to strengthen leadership capacity in and around the school so that the adults are in a better position to work together to improve the functionality of the school. Our theory of change is that principals who are more equipped for their leadership roles will, over time, engage their leadership teams, teachers and parents to strengthen the functionality of the school and that this will ultimately lead to improved academic outcomes.

We are working in a context where most principals have not taken part in any leadership development programmes. They were equipped with knowledge and skills to be classroom teachers but have not been prepared for the tough task of leading a complex and under-resourced organisation.

Given the time it takes for the effect of PfP's work with adults to reflect in the performance of learners, coupled with the challenges involved in assessing learner achievement in South Africa's public schools, we have only recently been able to provide robust quantitative evidence for PfP's impact on academic achievement. Around 80% of PfP schools are primary schools, and in 2019 an independent evaluation showed that in a group of Western Cape primary schools that joined PfP in 2014 the performance of Grade 3 and 6 learners in language and mathematics improved more than in non-PfP schools. Unfortunately, this research cannot currently be replicated elsewhere in South Africa because only Western Cape schools conduct standardised annual tests of learner performance.

At times, the difficulty in producing the impact evidence that some existing and potential sponsors want to see, and some of the feedback we receive from M&E professionals, has left me wondering about the *real* impact of our work. I have found myself oscillating between standing firm in my belief that our work has significant impact and wondering why we have not seen even greater impact and take-up.

I started to worry that we may have been listening selectively to what we wanted to hear and seeing what we wanted to see rather than confronting the possibility that our work may not be as impactful as we like to believe it is.

The PfP programme is designed to facilitate the following processes simultaneously:

- Nation-building
- Leadership development
- Support for school principals and leadership capacity building in schools
- Cross-sector collaboration (between business, government and civil society)
- Reducing inequality in education, *and*
- The opportunity for ordinary South Africans to contribute to a more just and equitable society.

Maybe this is the problem? – *that we are trying to do too many things*. The marketing people would certainly agree that we should focus on just one of the above rather than trying to achieve impact on so many levels.

And yet those of us who have committed our lives to this work are simply not willing to abandon any of these critical aspects of our work. We see all of them as *essential* aspects of our identity and mission. We think this is what makes PfP so special – that it aims to achieve all of the above.

Over the last 10 years, more than 2,300 leaders have experienced the 12-month leadership development process where business leaders and school principals are partnered in a facilitated co-action and co-learning partnership. More than a million people have been impacted by the leaders who have participated as Partners for Possibility. The PfP process is home-grown, developed by South Africans for our country's unique context, and informed by international best practice in capacity development for adults.

The programme is designed as a 70:20:10 development process, which means that around 70% of the learning happens 'on-the-job' (in our case 'at a school'), 20% occurs through peer learning, coaching and in communities of practice (social learning) and 10% through formal facilitated learning experiences. The programme's purpose is to develop the capacity to lead in a VUCA (Volatile, Uncertain, Complex and Ambiguous) world.

PfP did not start out as a leadership development programme. The original idea was to support school principals to mobilise support for their schools by using an Asset Based Community Development approach to tap into the gifts and contributions of the people and organisations around the school.

Peter Block and Community Building workshops

I was inspired by Peter Block's book *Community: The Structure of Belonging* and, in 2008, when I met him in San Francisco I invited Peter to come to South Africa to help build our capacity to develop community and heal our nation.[2] He said yes. Peter visited South Africa in 2009 and again in 2010 and became an 'excuse' for very diverse groups of South African citizens to gather for intimate conversations with each other. Those of us who were privileged to experience Peter's facilitation of the '6 Conversations of Community' found that it was a healing process and some of us grew committed to finding ways to use this methodology to build our nation.

In these workshops, Peter reminded us that communities have work to do: to raise children, care for the elders and keep people healthy. When I lamented the fact that *my* children had access to high-quality education and that it broke my heart that so many other children don't benefit from the same quality of education, he stopped me mid-sentence and said 'Louise, aren't they **all** *our* children?' We found ourselves talking about the idea of 'School at the centre of community' – where people around a school would bring their gifts and contributions to the school and work in partnership with the educators to 'raise *our* children'.

---

2   Block, P. (2008). *Community: The Structure of Belonging.* San Francisco: Berrett-Koehler Publishers.

Eugene Daniels (who was District Director of the Western Cape Education Department's Metro South District at the time) made it possible for members of his team to attend one of Peter's 2-day Community Building workshops in Cape Town.

Circuit Team Manager Thandi Jafta was one of those team members. After the workshop, she asked if I would be willing to contribute to an Education Indaba that she and her team were planning. The theme of the indaba was 'A new conversation' and its tagline was 'Our children, our hope, our responsibility.' Cross-functional teams from 18 schools in Thandi's district had been invited to attend.

Thandi asked me to bring some 'Peter Block thinking' to the indaba and to introduce the idea that citizens could choose to shift the narrative from a community's problems and deficiencies to its gifts and possibilities. Each of the 18 schools was represented by a multi-stakeholder delegation: the principal, two teachers, one current and one ex-learner, a non-teaching staff member and two parents. In total, 180 community members attended the event.

It was a wonderful day of connecting across boundaries. We ended the session in 'home groups' (groups of people representing the same school) and reflected on the experience of being in this conversation. One of the young men stood up and said:

'I don't think our school will be the same again. Something important happened today. It was the first time that all of us involved in the school talked with each other. We don't usually have the principal and the janitor and a parent in one conversation. We need more of this. We have many people and organisations working with teachers. And others working with principals. What we need is an organisation who can get us all together in one room and who can help to make conversations happen like the conversations we experienced here today. We need help to develop strong relationships with each other. Because if we can figure out how to do that, we will be able to create better schools for our children.'

I left that session on such a high. I thought that I had finally found a way to use what I had learnt from Peter Block. I felt 'called' to do exactly what this man had said. I wanted to be the facilitator that he described: the person who would facilitate Community Building workshops at schools and enrol all the stakeholders around a school to bring their gifts and contributions to the school. I saw this as an opportunity to mobilise active citizenship and inspire ordinary people to effect change by becoming actively involved in their local school.

I was so excited that I called Eugene Daniels. He knew that I was looking for a way to use what we had learnt from Peter Block to achieve the ambitious aim of 'School at the centre of community.' Eugene listened patiently and then he said: 'Louise, this sounds like an interesting idea. But you must know that you will be able to have very little impact as you will only be able to do this at a few schools a year.' Neither Eugene nor I knew it at the time but, with those words, he planted the seed that made it possible for us to reach more than 1,150 schools across South Africa during our first 10 years of doing this work.

I spent days wondering what to do with the curveball from Eugene, and then it dawned on me: we needed to find more people like me, train them in the Community Building methodology and mobilise them to work with principals to run Community Building workshops at schools.

Dinokeng Scenarios

The idea of business leaders working with principals was partly shaped by the *Dinokeng Scenarios Report*, which was published on 5 May 2009. A diverse group of South Africans had been working to develop possible scenarios for the future of the country and had developed these three scenarios:

- **Walk Apart**: business, government and civil society continuing on the path they were on – each group working to their own agenda with very little synergy or collaboration
- **Walk Behind**: a 'strongman' government and apathy from business and civil society
- **Walk Together**: business, government and civil society working together to address the critical issues facing South Africa.

The scenario team clearly illustrated the potential risks of the **Walk Apart** and **Walk Behind** scenarios and it was clear to anybody who read their report that we had to figure out a way to make **Walk Together** work. It was a call for active citizenship and leadership at all levels of society.

For me, this was a 'Road to Damascus' moment. I felt that I had been called to use my knowledge and skills to figure out a way to encourage people to work together across traditional boundaries to create a more cohesive, just and equitable South Africa. I remember how alive I felt after reading the report. I was so inspired that I wrote a note to about 3,000 people in our database to encourage them to read the report. I also publicly pledged to commit the next decade of my professional life to making the **Walk Together** scenario a reality.

Having made this commitment, I was a bit at sea. I had no idea how to do this work. I just knew that I needed to find a way to do it. I spoke with hundreds of people and finally developed a proposal that I called 'Create Our Future'. The idea was to mobilise citizens from all sectors to work together to develop proposals to deal with the significant issues identified in the *Dinokeng Scenarios* report. I realised that we needed to get leaders with gravitas involved in this work, so I took the idea to Dr Mamphela Ramphele who had been in the team that developed the three scenarios. I asked whether she would be willing to be the convenor for the Create Our Future initiative. I remember feeling very deflated when she rejected my proposal.

Walking Together in Education

A few months later I attended a talk by Professor Brian O'Connell. At the time he was Vice-Chancellor of the University of the Western Cape (UWC). He talked about the crisis in education and the need to prioritise education above everything else as it is the key to sustainable development. He also helped us see that the state of public education posed the single greatest risk to the country and that it needed our urgent attention. Hearing Prof O'Connell's talk in that small room in the Cape Town Library felt like another call to action. I realised that education could be the ideal arena for the nation-building work I was yearning to do. I decided to focus my attention on how to make **Walk Together** work in education.

Attending Thandi's Education Indaba in Philippi was the third call. I knew that I needed to harness all my energy and do something with these ideas. I asked Greg Vlotman (who was a Circuit Team Leader in the Metro South Education District at the time) to help me find a principal who would be willing to let me work with him or her to test the idea of business leaders like me working with school principals to achieve the **School at the Centre of Community** idea.

Greg kindly invited me to a meeting with a group of principals at Heathfield Primary School. When I think back on that gathering, I remember the spirit of generosity that came from all those principals. They were being very kind to this privileged middle-aged white woman who had an idea but clearly needed some help. They listened to my story and asked whether I would be open to their input. I am so grateful that I was genuinely willing to hear them as what they said made a massive difference to how I thought about this idea of business leader-principal partnerships.

Their feedback was positive. The principals liked the idea of business leaders working with them and saw that there was a possibility that their schools might benefit. But they also had strong caveats for the programme to consider before business leaders entered their schools which went something like this:

'We like the idea of business leaders working with school principals. We can see that there is a possibility that the schools may benefit. But we do think it will be important to provide some guidance to the business leaders before they come into our schools. Firstly: We don't need to be 'fixed'. We are fed-up with people coming into our schools with the idea to 'fix' us. We are not broken. We agree that we need support but we don't need to be fixed. Secondly: Please don't come into our schools with handouts. People bring their old Pentium computers to our schools that they can't use as they are too old. Then they expect us to be grateful. The reality is that we can't use those computers either. We also don't have storage space. Or they bring boxes of colouring-in books, but most of the pictures have already been coloured in. Or they bring old books, but when we go through the books there is peanut butter and jam between the pages. They will never take this stuff to Westerford[3]. Why do they think it is OK to bring this stuff to our schools? Thirdly: Please don't adopt us. You adopt puppies and babies, not schools and principals. It is patronising when well-resourced people and organisations want to 'adopt' schools. Can we change the language and talk about partnership rather than adoption? And lastly: We know that we will benefit from working with business leaders. But we don't want to just receive. We also want to give. We want the business leaders to consider the possibility that they will learn something from us too.'

Although we did not know it at the time, this conversation changed the trajectory of the PfP story. Because of the input from those principals, the idea of reciprocity and mutuality became a key organising principle for our work. Although they were willing to provide guidance, it is interesting to note that none of this group of principals was keen to work with me to pilot the idea.

Piloting an idea at Kannemeyer Primary School

Greg then introduced me to Ridwan Samodien, the principal at Kannemeyer Primary School (KPS) in Grassy Park. In April 2010 Ridwan and I started to work together. We did not really know what we were going to do, but we had a shared vision, and that was for KPS to become the centre of community. Ridwan and I arranged a Community Building event and invited parents and other stakeholders to join us.

We were blown away by what happened, and we were inspired to continue to work together. My 'day job' was to be a leadership and organisational development consultant to leaders in various organisations, so it felt very natural for me to have Ridwan as a pro bono 'client'. What I wasn't prepared for was the impact that this partnership and the experience of getting involved in KPS would have on me.

As predicted by the group of principals I had met with, I gained as much, if not more, from the experience of working with Ridwan as he got from working with me. Working with Ridwan at KPS created many opportunities for me to develop my capacity to lead in the VUCA world. Nothing worked quite as I had hoped. I had to learn to be flexible and to 'go

---

3   Westerford is a well-known well-resourced public high school in Cape Town.

with the flow'. I had no control or authority and could not 'make' anybody at KPS do what I wanted them to do. I had to hone my influencing skills.

Being welcomed into the KPS community was in itself transformational for me as a white woman who lived in a primarily-white affluent community in Cape Town. I discovered the joy of showing up 'warts and all' and how amazing it felt to be accepted for who I am rather than for the image I portray. I discovered that who I am is enough and that felt like a life-changing realisation.

I was so inspired by the experience that I enrolled eight other leaders in my network to do the same – to become partners to principals in under-resourced schools and to work with these principals to mobilise more community support for the principals and educators at the schools.

Leadership development through immersion and being of service

In October that year I attended a Women in Leadership breakfast at the Gordon Institute of Business Science (GIBS) in Johannesburg. One of the leaders of a 'Big 5' consultancy spoke about her organisation's leadership development programme which gives their leaders the opportunity to visit and work with a non-profit organisation in a Third World country. She talked about the value of crossing boundaries and working with leaders in under-resourced organisations in unfamiliar environments. I left the workshop thinking, 'Why do leaders need to travel to Third World countries? Why don't we just create the opportunity for them to work in under-resourced schools in South Africa on the other side of the highway?'

I realised that this may be the answer to 'How do we get more leaders interested in working with school principals to mobilise community support to the school?' If we made this 'work' part of a leadership development programme we may be able to attract more leaders to get involved, and we may even be able to get companies to pay for their leaders' participation in the programme. I realised that we could develop a structured leadership development programme with a significant 'action learning' component with the school as the site for action and learning.

In November 2010 we invited the eight 'pioneer' leaders who had been enrolled to partner with principals to a conversation, and it became clear that most of them genuinely had no idea how to approach the opportunity. We realised that we needed more than 'just' an invitation for people to work with principals.

At the same time I had a conversation with Professor Nick Binedell who was the Dean of GIBS at the time. He was very supportive of the idea of getting business leaders to work with school principals, but he was also clear that we needed to develop a process to support the business leaders. He recounted some of his experience of taking business leaders into under-resourced areas and said there was a real danger that business leaders may think they have answers for school principals. Nick knew how patronising it could feel to be at the receiving end of uninformed and unsolicited advice and did not want any principal to suffer that.

This idea of creating a process to support business leaders percolated, and in December 2010 I crafted a proposed design for a leadership development programme for business leaders and principals. I called it the **School at the Centre of Community Programme** and referred to the participants (business leaders and principals) as **Partners for Possibility**.

South Africa: Alive with Possibility

The story of my commitment to the idea of 'possibility' started in 2000. At the time my family and I were living in the UK, and I was terribly homesick. I read Rosamund and Benjamin Zander's book *The Art of Possibility* and was hugely inspired.[4] In the book they tell the story of a visit to South Africa where all the people they met were talking about their country. It was like 'a living breathing entity, a symphony of voices: Symphonia'. After reading the book I immediately asked my accountant to start the process to change the name of my consulting firm in South Africa from 'Shared Learning' to 'Symphonia Consulting'. I knew then that my family and I were going to return to South Africa and that I was being called to create opportunities for South Africans to talk together about the future that we envisaged for our beautiful and wounded country.

At the time I was busy with my doctorate, and I was exploring the transformational power of conversation and dialogue. I had a very strong sense that it was possible to potentially change the trajectory of South Africa's future if we could create opportunities for people to co-create the future they yearned for. Peter Block later introduced me to the idea that 'we change the world one room at a time'. This would become a core organising principle for our work.

Through my studies I had been introduced to the idea of social constructivism[5] and the power of narrative and stories. I had discovered that deep systemic change becomes possible when we disrupt the patterns that organise the experiences of the actors in the system.

---

4 Zander, R.S. & Zander, B. (2000). *The Art of Possibility: Transforming Professional and Personal Life.* New York: Penguin.
5 The central idea of **social constructivism** is that meaning is constructed through **social** interaction and is a shared rather than an individual experience.

I felt that I was being called to return to South Africa to help change the stories we tell about our country and about ourselves and that this could potentially lead to a better future for all of us. I finally returned with my family to South Africa in 2004, but it would be another three years before I felt ready to fully settle back in the country. I found it hard to be back in a country that I had no professional connection to after spending such a wonderful time working in the UK, Europe, Singapore and the USA. I chose the easy way out: I continued my work in the UK and Europe and commuted between there and South Africa.

In 2007 my daughters challenged me about the fact that I spent so little time in South Africa and I became determined to find a way to establish myself as a leadership and organisation development practitioner in South Africa.

At the same time I became aware of my own stories about South Africa. When we first returned to the country I was very excited about being part of the process to make democracy work. I was acutely aware of my privilege as an educated white person and had a powerful sense that I wanted to 'pay back' my privilege in some way.

During those first few years after returning, I was bombarded by negative stories about South Africa and regularly confronted by people who thought we had made a massive mistake in bringing our two beautiful daughters back to such a troubled country. While I was working in Europe it was relatively easy to just tune these stories out and focus on my work, but having made the decision to spend the majority of my time in South Africa I had to change my own story about the country.

I realised that I needed help to do this and decided to call on Rosamund and Benjamin Zander who had made such a big impact on my work with their book **The Art of Possibility**.[6] The couple had helped to craft Brand South Africa's tagline 'South Africa: Alive with Possibility,' and I had a very strong sense that we needed to find a way to reignite the story that South Africa was indeed 'Alive with Possibility'.

Ben Zander was due to speak at a conference in Sun City in May 2007, so after much effort I managed to get an agreement from his assistant that he would see me for 20 minutes. I used the opportunity to ask him whether he would be willing to work with me to engage large groups of people in a new conversation about our future. Ben was clearly intrigued by my suggestion but not ready to make any commitments. He said that if I was serious about this I would need to travel to Boston to enrol Roz as he was not going to do this without her.

---

6   Zander & Zander, 2000.

In August 2007 I travelled to Boston to meet with Ben and Roz. We met on Ben's boat on the Charles River, and miraculously both he and Roz said yes. As we left the vessel, Ben said, 'We are ready to be used as instruments of possibility.'

My team and I devoted most of 2008 preparing for their trip. In August of that year, the couple spent in 23 days in South Africa. We had arranged 97 engagements for them and, together, we engaged with more than 15,000 people. It was an amazing experience for all of us who had the opportunity to be in rooms with Ben and Roz. They became a catalyst for citizens to engage in conversations about the future we were committed to. Since working with Peter Block on the art and science of invitation, I have discovered how important it is to have the right 'attractor' to get people into the room. There is no doubt that Ben Zander is a wonderful attractor and he managed to get people from all over South Africa to say yes to our invitations.

Before their trip to South Africa the Zanders wrote a letter about their hopes and dreams for the trip:

> *Two shoe salesmen were sent to Africa from England in the 19th century to see if there was any opportunity to sell shoes.*
>
> *'SITUATION HOPELESS STOP' one of them cabled back, 'NO ONE WEARS SHOES'*
>
> *'GLORIOUS BUSINESS OPPORTUNITY STOP' wrote the other, 'THEY HAVE NO SHOES'*
>
> *This will be our fifth visit to South Africa – it is the country that we have visited together more than any other. Certainly we are drawn by the broad vistas and gentle sweep of hills and foliage, exquisite sweet-smelling flowers and balmy air, the long line of waves coming in from the South, as well as the views of vineyards and farmland (and, of course the opportunity to come up close to magnificent animals roaming in freedom).*
>
> *But most of all – by far most of all – it is the people who draw us back. The first time we came we were stunned and moved by the passion you South Africans have for the glorious, unprecedented political experiment that was born in 1994. We had never experienced anywhere else such excitement or such hope in virtually every conversation.*
>
> *On our first visit we spent an evening with Helen Suzmann and Madiba; we met future leaders and spoke with housekeepers and bellboys. Everyone talked the same way- with shining eyes! And every conversation centered on the dream.*

We came with a gift: The Art of Possibility. Possibility is not something you hope for – like good weather. It is a rigorous discipline rooted in the knowledge that we invent our own reality and can choose to frame our circumstances. We can either tell the story of the downward spiral (SITUATION HOPELESS) or speak in radiating possibility (GLORIOUS OPPORTUNITY).

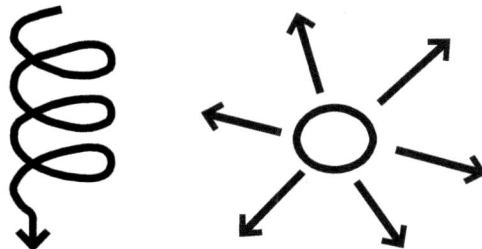

This is the Art of Possibility[7] and it lives in the way we speak and when we speak in possibility, our eyes shine. As a parent or teacher we are given this opportunity of leadership every time we open our mouths. Indeed, each interaction with another human being, or with any creature, is an opportunity for leadership. This is our message and the training we offer is to deepen the capacity for the adult conversation.

We believe that the practices of Possibility can be powerful tools for overcoming the challenges that could threaten Mandela's dream from becoming a reality. Of course, we are aware that South Africa faces many difficulties – increased crime, disease, mismanagement, and the frequent breakdown of systems, all contributors to anxiety and cynicism. We always say that a cynical person is a passionate person who doesn't want to be disappointed again. So we will always speak to the passion that is the birthright of every modern South African and not allow ourselves to be caught in the web of cynicism.

You are the warmest, most open-hearted people, generous beyond measure, always looking for opportunities where none appear to exist. Think of the many projects and institutions – schools, hospitals and clinics where you find the world's most spiritual and devoted people; the many companies that are dedicated to providing rapid training and advancement to those who a generation ago would never have dreamed of such a life.

The dream South Africa already exists. It has come so far. The cities glitter with modern industry; housing and infrastructure has sprung up everywhere, cafes and restaurants are vibrant as young people of all races take pleasure in each other's company and speak of the future.

---

7   Zander, R.S. & Zander, B. (2000). *The Art of Possibility: Transforming Professional and Personal Life.* New York: Penguin.

That is the story of South Africa. The world is watching, watching to see if the dream that Nelson Mandela harbored in prison for 27 years could be made real.

There is no need for despair, there is a need for faith – the faith that the strength and guidance of its citizens will enable South Africa to continue its amazing development.

What is called for is a story, a story already half-written, for the possibility of South Africa, a story alive with Possibility! A GLORIOUS OPPORTUNITY!

To put this story out into the world we need powerful and clear-headed leaders. We are coming to contribute to this venture. We believe that a true leader is the relentless architect of the possibility that others can be.

We are honored to be visitors once again to your country and privileged to join your song of Possibility.

Ben and Roz Zander

A few weeks before the trip I became worried that we may not be able to sell all the tickets to every event we had arranged, so I asked Roz and Ben to write a letter that we could use to enrol more people to attend the events we had planned:

All eyes will be turning again to South Africa on July 18th as Nelson Mandela celebrates his 90th birthday. We will be reminded that in 1992 not just South Africa, but the whole world, turned on its moral axis, as a visionary leader coaxed the human race back from the conflagration of the races towards a society, which Barack Obama now calls the post racial age.

It must seem sometimes to South Africans caught up as you are in the maelstrom of poverty, violence, HIV, and crime that now Madiba's dream is a far-off fantasy. But it is good to reflect at this time, how far human beings have come since 1992 and to take pride and comfort from the fact that the world community looks to South Africa and its legendary former President for inspiration and hope for all mankind.

I once had the opportunity to tell President Mandela that he was the first leader of Symphonia. 'Oh', he said, his eyebrows raised in amused interest, 'What is that?'. I explained that the word symphony is a combination of 'sym' – together, and 'phonae' – to sound – the sounding together of all the voices. 'You are', I said, 'the first leader of Symphonia, because instead of leading one party against another, you focused on allowing all the voices to be heard.' And then, with that inimitable broad smile that you all know so well, he said 'I like that!'

My partner Roz Zander and I will be returning for our fifth trip to South Africa this August. Louise van Rhyn, who named her company Symphonia, after hearing that story, has moved mountains to bring us back to speak to literally thousands of people in many different venues, because she believes passionately that it is vital at this time to realign South Africa with its vision: 'Alive with Possibility'.

The way we will do this is to first identify the ways in which despair, resignation and anger can take over and close down our energy and spirit. Then we will deliver practices to move into the open spaces of creativity, effectiveness and action by creating new stories.

Let me give you an example. A musician is about to perform for a large group. I ask, 'How are you feeling about performing for this audience?' 'Rather nervous' is the reply. I could say, 'Don't be nervous, you'll be fine', but it is unlikely to do much good. Instead I tell a story: Jackie DuPre, the greatest cellist of her generation, went in for her first competition when she was 5 years old. She was seen running through the corridor with her cello and a broad grin on her face. The porter at the door, says 'Well I can see that you have just played'. 'No!' Jackie shoots back, 'I am just about to!'

'Imagine', I say, 'she's 5 years old, and she already understands that to perform for people is a privilege and a joy!'

'Now, how are you feeling?', I ask the young musician, 'Much better' she beams. Everyone laughs and she is ready to play in a totally different mood and to an audience that has shifted into a state of complete receptivity.

It's a simple story, but full of lessons. The frightened performer cannot get access to her full capacities. Telling a story about a 5-year-old child unlocks that side of our nature which is playful, uncompetitive and expressive. The assumption that a child who is beaming from ear to ear must have completed the task and is expressing relief, is replaced by a much more powerful idea that we human beings are brought into the world to contribute and give joy and that it is thrilling and enlivening to do so. The audience, in turn, has changed from sitting in judgment (arms folded), to embracing the gift that is being offered. That in turn diminishes the pressure on the performer and the whole spirit in the room has changed.

The process I have just described is called transformation. It is partly intellectual, but just as importantly, it is molecular. The posture of the body is actually changed, from heaviness, tension and anxiety to joy and lightness. Endorphins, and with them our creative juices, are released. Barriers break down and we feel free to take risks. It doesn't mean that mistakes won't be made, but it gives us a more powerful relationship to failure. A mistake is not a judgment of worth, but a momentary lapse from which we can learn: 'How fascinating!' we shout as we toss our hands in the air and smile.

To say 'How fascinating!' when you make a mistake is a possibility practice. It shifts the attention away from blame (of self and others) and the paralysis which follows, onto: 'What went wrong?' What is next? What can I learn, so that I can avoid doing it again?' This practice, like all possibility practices, works at the molecular level. Try it next time you are out on the golf course! You make a lousy shot and instead of your body pulling down, accompanied by the usual swearing and cursing, you counter intuitively raise your hands and shout 'How Fascinating!' You will find to your amazement that there is a lightness, a buoyancy that comes into your being that sets you up beautifully to make the next shot. Try the same technique when you snap at your kid, or someone in your office.

If a father has an argument with his son and he wins, does he win? No, because in the world of possibility, which every parent recognises as the true domain of relationship, when the son loses the father loses too.

What has all this got to do with South Africa, you ask? Everything. A life lived in the discipline of the Art of Possibility is a life lived with grace, energy, joy and contribution. It is what we wish for ourselves, for our families, for our communities and for the world.

When I was a child I studied the cello with a very wise old man in his eighties: I tried to play a passage but I couldn't make it work. I tried again and it still didn't work, and a third time and I was no more successful. I remember making a frustrated grimace and putting down my bow. My teacher leaned over me and whispered, 'What? You've been practicing it for three minutes and you still can't play it?'

South Africa has often been tempted to put down its bow with a frustrated grimace in recent years. Roz and I are coming to remind you that you have only been 'practicing' for a mere 16 years! We are bursting with excitement to revisit a country we have come to love like our own. We can't wait to engage with the amazing people and to bring the clarity and expressiveness which are the natural by-products of the discipline called Possibility. I will have the additional joy of working with the Cape Town Symphony and performing several concerts, culminating in the ultimate hymn to possibility: Beethoven's Ninth Symphony with its incandescent Ode to Joy.

See you there!

Reading these letters from Ben and Roz now, more than 10 years later, I am noticing how they have shaped my thinking about leadership, active citizenship and what it means to let your light shine. Sharing those three weeks with the Zanders in August 2008, I realised that I wanted to continue to ignite possibility in South Africa.

Partners for Possibility

Fast forward to December 2010. I knew *what* we wanted to achieve at every school: **School at the Centre of Community**. The 'Partnerships for Possibility' structure became the *how*: business leaders and school principals would be working together in 1:1 cross-sector partnerships, guided through a carefully-designed 12-month leadership development process. The school and the domain of education would be their 'site of learning' and the 'arena' where they would practise and implement new ideas and learning.

A cluster of 8-10 partnerships for possibility (a leadership circle) would form a community of practice in which the individuals would learn from each other and from the experience of being in rooms and in conversations with a diverse group of fellow leaders from different industries, organisations, backgrounds, cultures and ethnicities, etc.

Based on the Harvard Graduate School of Education assertion that the best thing we can do for children is to support and develop the adults that interact with them[8], the programme would develop the capacity of the adults in a school community.

Importantly, it would be scalable to involve many schools all around the country, so I conceptualised the idea that every leadership circle would be supported by a local Learning Process Facilitator (LPF). This concept originally came from work that I had done at Ashridge Consulting where we facilitated leadership development programmes for large multinationals and had LPFs who accompanied each cohort of leaders on their development journey.

The role of the PfP LPF would be to support each partnership on its journey. We envisaged that business leaders would essentially act as development partners to principals, but the capacity to do that is not a generic skill, so we planned to set the partners up for success. Our intention was to equip the business leaders with the knowledge and skills needed to be organisational development consultants to the principals. We also wanted to ensure that they would not show up as 'know-it-all' consultants because that would alienate the principals.

In 2010 we started the process of recruiting business leaders for the first leadership circle, which we planned to launch in February 2011. That process turned out to be an important learning experience in itself. The first corporate leader who agreed to support PfP by sponsoring some business leaders to participate was Ayn Brown, who at the time was Head of Human Resources (HR) at Nedbank Business Banking. She

---

8 Center on the Developing Child at Harvard University. (2017). *Three Principles to Improve Outcomes for Children and Families. Retrieved from:* https://developingchild.harvard.edu/resources/three-early-childhood-development-principles-improve-child-family-outcomes/

was part of the team delivering Nedbank's 'Leading for Deep Green' leadership and organisational development programme and felt that what we were proposing was in line with the future of leadership development at Nedbank.

Ayn was particularly interested in the formal training modules that we planned to include in the programme, but she wanted to be confident that the five days of training would contribute sufficient depth and gravitas to the experience. I knew that many of the corporate leaders would also want to know more about the proposed formal learning, so I was comfortable to let Ayn and others know that participants would attend the following three courses during the facilitated year of PfP:

- **Time to Think essentials** – 1 day (designed by members of Nancy Kline's team and based on her book *Time to Think*)[9]

- **Flawless Consulting** – 2 days (a process designed by Peter Block, underpinned by his book *Flawless Consulting*)[10]

- **The Art of Community Building** – 2 days (a process designed by Peter Block, underpinned by his book *Community: The Structure of Belonging*).[11]

I have often been asked why these particular courses form the core of PfP's academic curriculum: I wanted the business leaders and principals to have the best possible chance to positively impact their schools, and I knew this meant they first needed to develop a strong and trusting relationship. We needed to consider the effect of power dynamics between business leaders and people who are not in business and felt that a workshop with an experienced Time to Think facilitator would be the right way for partners to start the journey.

I had met Nancy Kline when I attended her Time to Think foundational course in the UK. It was a life-changing experience for me, and I felt it would get a leadership circle off to the perfect start as a community of practice and help the partnerships make the transition from strangers to thinking partners. We felt that it was important to use this moment at the start of the journey to ensure that all participants were clear that they (business leaders and principals) had embarked on a leadership development voyage in which they would be learning from each other. Rather than the business leaders being seen as mentors or coaches, we envisaged that the pair would act as thinking partners to each other.

---

9 Kline, N.E. (1999). *Time to think*. London: Hachette Littlehampton.
10 Block, P. (1981). *Flawless Consulting: A guide to getting your expertise used*. San Francisco: Jossey Bass/Pheiffer.
11 Block, P. (2008). *Community: The Structure of Belonging*. San Francisco: Berrett-Koehler Publishers.

Many corporates in South Africa had been introduced to Nancy Kline's thinking and the concept of leaders being called to create thinking environments where their colleagues can think for themselves. A central idea of this work is that 'the person who holds the problem also holds the solution' and that we often just need a thinking partner to create an environment to think into.

In February 2011 we launched the first PfP leadership circle, consisting of nine partnerships, in Cape Town. Ridwan and I joined this circle and loved the experience of being in community with other leaders who were also committed to mobilising community support for their schools.

The National Development Plan

In November 2012 the National Planning Commission (NPC) published the National Development Plan 2030 (NDP) with a beautiful vision for South Africa. Trevor Manuel, who was the Chairperson of the NPC at the time, said that there were three key enablers to achieving Vision 2030 and the implementation of the NDP:

1. Active Citizenship
2. Leadership; and
3. A Capable State.

The NPC stressed that it would only be possible to implement the plan through cross-sectoral collaboration and that business, government and civil society would *have* to work together. We were encouraged by the publication of the NDP and the call to action by Minister Manuel and his colleagues at the NPC and hoped that this would inspire more business leaders to join PfP.

Reflecting on 10 years of PfP

Between February 2011 and November 2019 we launched 152 leadership circles across the country, and 1,150 business leaders have partnered with 1,150 principals in under-resourced schools. There are now partnerships for possibility in all nine of our provinces. More than a million people have been impacted by the leaders who have participated, over 350 organisations have sponsored our work, and the programme has received many accolades.

And yet, 10 years on, I am left with many questions: Why do so many people seem to believe that the only valid evidence for positive impact in under-resourced schools is learners' test scores?

Why, despite the way that PfP has benefitted principals and their schools and communities, has government not been more willing to fund our work? Other than one contract with the Gauteng Department of Education (GDE), which funded 66 principals to participate in the PfP process, we have not received any other funding from government.

Why, despite many stories of business leaders who feel they are better leaders as a result of being part of PfP, do only a few organisations offer PfP as a part of their leadership development programme? Is it valid to claim that PfP is genuinely an impactful leadership development process for business leaders as well as school principals?

We conceptualised PfP as a consciousness-raising experience. It gives privileged business leaders an opportunity to leave their corporate offices and work in under-resourced communities to facilitate change. It creates opportunities for leaders to be confronted with their own prejudices and generates greater compassion and understanding. Over the last 10 years we have heard many stories about leaders whose PfP journey has been life-changing. Yet I have wondered how typical these cases are. Do we just hear the stories we want to hear and not pay enough attention to those for whom PfP did not 'work' as we hoped it would?

The journey of this book

While grappling with these questions I found myself in a conversation with a group of senior leaders. One of them expressed doubt about the impact of the PfP programme on participating business leaders. She had participated in PfP as partner to a principal and was not entirely convinced of the methodology. She is a successful black leader with intimate knowledge of the township environment, so she did not feel that she was learning much by working with a principal in a township school.

After hearing her speak Brand Pretorius, retired head of the McCarthy Group and a good friend, responded to her doubts by saying 'I have just returned from Letsitele where my son Jan-Louis and a few other white farmers have been part of the PfP process. Being part of PfP has changed the fabric of their community and has had a big impact on the schools where the principals have been part of the process.'

Brand's comment touched me and made me think. Jan-Louis and the other leaders in his circle had joined the programme four years earlier (in September 2015). I started to wonder about the story of the Letsitele PfP leadership circle. What has the impact really been for the business leaders and principals in Letsitele?

The more I thought about it, the more I realised that it may be time for me to pause and reflect on the journey we have been on for the last 10 years. A few days later I received a text message from Jan-Louis with a photo of him and Juliet Shilubana, his principal-partner. Jan-Louis wanted to let me know that his partnership with Juliet has continued and they are still doing work together in their school.

I realised that I needed to visit them and the other partners for possibility (PfPs) in Letsitele to hear their stories first-hand and experience the level of impact of PfP for myself. In fact, I realised that I needed to visit PfPs across the country.

A few weeks later Theo Garrun and I visited Jan-Louis, Juliet and their fellow PfPs in Letsitele. We left inspired to visit more PfPs across the country, and we did that in the last few months of 2019. The process of writing this book has been a transformational experience in itself. It has changed how we think about and understand the impact of our work.

Our original plan with the second PfP book was to write a story that would make the case for PfP – we wanted to encourage people with an interest in education in Africa to rethink their assumptions about how to effect change in education. We felt that we had learnt so much and wanted to share our learning. My original idea for the book was that we should imagine writing it for Bill and Melinda Gates because their voices carry so much weight.

After the first few visits and conversations with principals and business leaders, I realised that we needed to shift direction and simply tell the stories of the people who have been touched by this work. As the designer of the process, I needed to hear their stories more than anybody else did. And I had to figure out how to share these beautiful stories – with people who are already in our community as well as those who will be joining our body of change-makers in the future.

I have often been asked how we made the decision about which stories to tell. The reality is that it has been an emergent process. I asked Theo to help me capture stories. Brand's comment led to a visit to Letsitele. And then I wondered about early partnerships that had excited me. I was interested to explore the impact of PfP at these schools several years on.

I started talking about the experience of writing the book and members of our team invited me to visit them and schools they are involved with. Theo and I went to Ballito and the Simbithi Eco-Estate in KwaZulu-Natal (KZN) and captured some beautiful stories of impact. This sparked an interest in other schools that have become magnets for the gifts and contributions from the people and organisations around schools. We loved capturing three stories about partnerships in rural KZN, Nelspruit and the Cape Winelands, and these led to the story about Ian Macdonald and Fella's Army. We were inundated with stories about business as a force for good, and it was difficult to decide which to tell.

Asking people in our community to identify stories worth sharing was like throwing a pebble into a pond – it generated many ripples and beautiful stories. We loved hearing about the transformation of individual principals and about initiatives like the School Pages Project and Youth@worK that have been sparked by PfP.

It was heart-warming to hear from principals who have been promoted to more senior roles and are convinced that their careers would have been very different if it weren't for PfP. We heard from principals who benefitted from PfP even though the partnerships with their business partners did not work as planned. We heard from business leaders for whom PfP was a transformational development experience and those who have heeded the call to 'khumbul'ekhaya'(remember home). We heard stories from individual learners whose lives have been changed because of PfP, and this generated dozens of further contributions from principals and business leaders who wanted to share their stories.

One of the most beautiful gifts of this process has been to hear from members of our team about the value they have gained from being part of PfP.

It has been an amazing privilege to hear these stories, and we hope that you will enjoy reading this book as much as we have enjoyed producing it. The stories serve as an invitation for you to think about your own practice as a leader and change-maker.

> "Many stories matter. Stories have been used to dispossess and to malign. But stories can also be used to empower, and to humanize. Stories can break the dignity of a people. But stories can also repair that broken dignity." – Chimamanda Adichie

Chapter 2

PfP in Letsitele

"Hope is not the same thing as optimism. It is not the conviction that something will turn out well, but the certainty that something makes sense, regardless of how it turns out." – Václav Havel

We regularly get feedback from principals and business leaders about the impact of the first year of the PfP programme, but we have not been able to connect with these leaders often enough later on to get a strong sense of its long-term impact.

Under the leadership of Jan-Louis Pretorius, the Commercial Director of Groep 91 Uitvoer, a large farming and export business in Letsitele, a PfP leadership circle was launched there in 2015. I decided to go back to Letsitele to find out more about the impact of the PfP process on those people who were involved.

Letsitele is in Limpopo and is part of the Greater Tzaneen Municipality, a farming community where most people live in rural villages and unemployment levels are high. According to Stats SA[12], 41% of the municipality's population have no source of income, and 45% of those with an income earn less than the minimum subsistence level of R1,600 per month.

Burgert van Rooyen is the Co-founder of Groep 91, a second-generation family farming business which manages 860 hectares of citrus orchards and Macadamia Nut trees to produce fruit exclusively for the export market. Burgert is 71 years old now but still works, albeit in a non-executive capacity. His son Henk and two sons-in-law, Jan-Louis Pretorius and Kobus van Wyk, now manage the farming business.

Burgert is married to Irma, an artist who is very much the heart of the Van Rooyen family. They live on the farm La Gratitude where they regularly accommodate business guests in their beautiful home. I stayed with Irma and Burgert when I first visited Letsitele in 2015 and was deeply touched by their warmth and hospitality. I looked forward to spending time with them again.

Groep 91's commitment to contributing to society began decades before their involvement in PfP. When I heard the story of Kaross, the embroidery project that Irma

---

12 Stats SA. November. (2019). Greater Tzaneen Municipality. Retrieved from: http://www.statssa.gov.za/?page_id=993&id=greater-tzaneen-municipality

started in the late '80s, I felt a strong resonance between her approach to development and the approach we were committed to in PfP.

After moving to the farm, Irma worked shoulder-to-shoulder with the women in the packing plant, but her artist's eye was a problem because she was rejecting far too many perfectly good oranges. However, while working with the Tsonga women, Irma was struck by the beauty of their self-embroidered mincekas (cloths worn over one shoulder). As a lover of embroidery, Irma recognised the women's talent for needlework and wondered about the possibility of collaborating with them in some way.

She invited the women to sit with her on a kaross (a traditional blanket) where they could embroider together. With Irma's gift as an artist and the women's talent for needlework they created something together that neither could have accomplished on their own.

Through their collaboration and ability to work together as innovative partners, Irma and the Tsonga women co-created a very successful business that now provides an income for more than 1,200 women in the community. Through Kaross, a business that she founded, Irma creates the designs and procures the fabric and embroidery yarn, then makes these available to her skilled Tsongan partners. Every finished item is purchased from them and then sold to a well-established clientele that is willing to pay for a high-quality product.

Irma's Tsongan partners feel that they have been empowered to do something that they would not have been able to achieve on their own. As a result of their talent for embroidery, coupled with Irma's creative flair and business acumen, Kaross products are now being sold online and in outlets to people all over the world, and Irma's partners are earning good money for their work.

Irma never saw this as an 'upliftment' project. She wanted to use her own skills and creativity, but also to work in community with the talented women who live on the farm. Her commitment to harnessing their gifts has brought a sense of reciprocity and mutuality to their endeavours.

This felt so similar to what we are doing with PfP. We create an opportunity for a business leader and a school principal to accomplish something together that neither could do alone. Principals bring their understanding of education and their knowledge of their local communities, while business leaders bring their business knowledge and skills; then they work together to achieve outcomes that would not have been feasible without each other.

About 20 years after establishing Kaross, Irma felt it was time to document her Tsonga partners' stories. She visited them in their homes, recorded their stories and took photographs of these extraordinary women. She turned the photos into sketches which, in turn, became superbly embroidered images. While capturing their stories, Irma asked each of the women to share their aspirations. Without fail, every one said that a good education for their children was one of their dreams.

At about the same time, Burgert was searching for a way in which Groep 91 could make a sustainable difference in the community.

'Opheffing is vir my 'n vloekwoord' (upliftment is a swearword to me) was one of the first things Burgert said to me when I arrived at the farm for my latest visit. His remark reminded me of the school principals who had said, 'Please don't adopt us. You adopt puppies and babies, not school principals.' I have come to realise that no one wants to be 'uplifted' because the notion that one person can uplift another carries so much judgement.

Commercial Director Jan-Louis is responsible for Groep 91's social development activities. He feels that it's important for the company's leaders to roll up their sleeves and get personally involved in efforts to achieve their social development goals, rather than simply donating money for projects. In 2014 he mentioned this to his father, Brand Pretorius, who then told him about PfP.

In October 2014, I received the following e-mail from Jan-Louis:

> *I came to hear of Partners for Possibility after my dad Brand forwarded me a copy of an e-mail conversation between himself and Bob Head a few months ago. After carefully studying your website today, I finally worked out why he sent it on to me, which I would summarise in 3 bullet points:*
>
> 1. *We share your belief in the cardinal role that schools (and notably school principals) play in the social and economic development of rural communities.*
> 2. *You currently have no footprint (from what I can see) in the Limpopo province.*
> 3. *We would like to make a difference.*
>
> *I'm a director of a medium-large citrus export farming business in the Letsitele district of Limpopo. A substantial part of our annual exports goes to big supermarket chains in continental Europe and the UK. With two of our primary receivers (Albert Heijn in Holland and Waitrose in the UK) we are active members of their Foundations, which means that every year, we receive money*

on a 'matched funding' basis, enabling us to establish suitable community development projects in our area.

There is no doubt that we would like to channel our investment in time, experience and money into strengthening of the primary and secondary schools in our area, but we struggle with finding a suitable (and sustainable) structure and programme through which to do so. It is for this reason that I decided to write to you, hoping that you perhaps have some thoughts on how we can support / partner with Partners for Possibility. I would be most grateful if you could let me know if you think there's an opportunity, and if so if you could point me towards the best person with whom I could flesh out the detail?

Jan-Louis and I met a few weeks later and agreed on a plan to set up a PfP leadership circle in Letsitele. After hearing that a circle ideally needs eight to 10 business leaders, each to partner with a principal, Jan-Louis started the process of gathering funding to enable the Letsitele partnerships and began mobilising business leaders to join the circle. He also initiated conversations with the circuit managers[13] and school principals in the area and found them to be very receptive to the idea of co-learning and co-action partnerships between business leaders and school principals.

Jan-Louis was surprised to hear from me that most principals would not have received any leadership or management training in preparation for their role as the leader of a complex organisation. We explored the possibility of offering a foundational management programme to the principals in Letsitele as we thought this would be useful in preparing them for the PfP journey. Jan-Louis realised that it might take some time to mobilise business leaders to join PfP, and a pre-PfP programme for the principals would give him breathing space.

I introduced Jan-Louis to Desmond Zeelie, a former principal who was running the Foundation of School Leadership and Management (FSLM). Desmond and Jan-Louis agreed on a 6-month foundation programme to be run for the principals, and this commenced early in 2015.

In the meantime, we started the process to recruit a local LPF. We knew we would need to find someone who lived in the area and who had the necessary skills to support a PfP leadership circle. The ideal LPF would be an accredited coach and experienced facilitator with good project management skills and would be able to fulfil the role on a part-time contract basis. It had been relatively easy to find suitably qualified LPFs in Cape Town and Johannesburg, but this was the first time we were having to recruit someone in a rural area.

13   Circuit manager: a Department of Education official who is essentially the 'line manager' for a certain number of principals.

Jan-Louis started looking for business leaders to join the circle and didn't think it would be difficult to find candidates in the area. In 2015, when he invited me for a recruitment visit I was delighted to accept and looked forward to engaging with the farmers in Letsitele and also to meeting a few potential LPFs.

After a few months, we were ready to launch PfP in Letsitele. We had appointed Tim Maake as LPF and Jan-Louis had recruited eight business leaders to join the programme. The principals who would be partnering with them had worked with Desmond for six months and were ready to be matched with their business partners.

On 31 September 2015, the Letsitele Leadership Circle was launched. It comprised the following eight partnerships:

Principal	Partner
Eric Tiba (Mapheto Secondary School)	Burgert van Rooyen (Groep 91)
Juliet Shilubana (Nyavana Primary School)	Jan-Louis Pretorius (Groep 91)
Vincent Mabunda (Gwambeni High School)	Henk van Rooyen (Groep 91)
Isaac Nkonwana (Hetiseka Secondary School)	Kobus van Wyk (Groep 91)
Nomsa Mhlongo (Manyunyu Primary School)	Andrew Jackson (Groep 91)
Suzzy Milazi (Nghwazana Primary School)	Gina Botha (Groep 91)
Obert Machimana (Mahwahwa High School)	Wimpie Mostert (Houers Kooperasie) – a Groep 91 supplier
Makhanani Shilote (Vhulakanjani Lower Primary School)	Felix Hacker (Du Roi) – a Groep 91 supplier

I was very excited about this circle and hoped to see sustainable impacts in the schools as a result of leadership capacity being strengthened. If I am completely honest though, I was more excited about the nation-building potential of eight white farmers working with eight black principals.

Jansie Rautenbach had just joined us as Manager of our inland region, and she attended the circle's launch. Afterwards, she shared her reflection on the event with me:

The circle's dynamics are quite different from any other I have seen:

- *The principals know each other and the Groep 91 Business partners really well as a result of the sessions they had with Desmond.*
- *It's clear that they are well prepared for our programme, thanks to Desmond, Tim and Jan-Louis. So they are almost on a different level than the other new*

> *circles, they know what to expect and are excited about it. They want to learn and are fully committed.*

- *The principals are totally different from my experience when we met them at Letsitele the last time. They stand proud, they are very vocal and know exactly what they want, without exception.*

We saw the Letsitele circle as an opportunity to learn from the experience of facilitating PfP in a fairly remote rural area, so I did my best to stay close to the group, albeit from a geographical distance. In January 2016, I returned to Letsitele to facilitate the circle's 2-day Flawless Consulting workshop. I arranged for my mother to accompany me because she adores embroidery and I knew she would love to meet Irma and the ladies at Kaross.

I relished the experience of being in the room with the members of this circle and remember being struck by the sense of possibility arising from leaders being in these kinds of co-action partnerships across traditional boundaries. I returned to Cape Town with a renewed sense of excitement about our work.

During the following year, Jansie, Dina Cramer (an LPF supervisor) and I remained involved with the circle through our interactions with Tim, who gave regular feedback about what was happening in the partnerships. In September 2016 the group held their celebration[14] event to mark the end of their 12-month journey. Unfortunately, I was unable to attend, but I watched the video recording and loved reading the report that our M&E team had produced.

I felt very privileged to have the opportunity to return to Letsitele in 2019 to hear first-hand from those who had been involved with the circle what had happened since 2016. I also saw this visit as an opportunity to learn more lessons from this experience of doing PfP in a rural area.

I invited Theo Garrun to join me. He has a gift for capturing stories, and I looked forward to working with him to compile stories of PfP's impact in Letsitele. Theo and I met Burgert and Jan-Louis for lunch on La Gratitude farm, and we asked Jan-Louis to share his thoughts on the experience of being part of PfP. He described it as an 'enlightenment' opportunity.

For Jan-Louis, Burgert and the Groep 91 leaders, PfP was never just a one-year capacity building programme. They saw PfP as a much longer development initiative in the eight schools.

---

14 At the end of the year-long facilitated process we arrange a celebration event. At this event the Partners for Possibility share their stories of impact and reflect on what they have gained from being part of the PfP process.

'It was clear from the start that PfP could be a long-term sustainable project for us,' Jan-Louis said. 'It had the potential to become the central activity around which we could develop other interventions to ultimately improve education outcomes in the schools in our area.'

'What appealed to me was the understanding that being part of the PfP programme did not mean we would be knights riding in on white horses to rescue poor failing schools. From the beginning, I was aware that the way the partnership worked was that we would be there to support the principal and that they would lead the change that happened in their schools,' said Jan-Louis.

'We also understood that we would need to first invest in our relationships. I remember you telling us that the magic will only come later,' he added. 'Over the last four years we have been able to roll out interventions to address some of the significant challenges in our schools. We have been able to address the urgent issues around infrastructure. We have also had many conversations with the local circuit manager and he helped us see that we needed to focus on language and early literacy. We have rolled out Brainboosters and have contracted Magri's Language Institute from WITS to help us with literacy,' he explained.

I also asked Jan-Louis and Burgert to share their current thoughts about the programme after being involved with their PfP partners for almost four years. 'It takes time to build relationships,' said Burgert. 'A year is not nearly long enough. Eric and I are only now getting to the point where we have a strong enough relationship to start to do some hard work together.'

'I have come to realise how unique every partnership is,' said Jan-Louis. 'We have had eight partnerships in our circle. They were all different and unique. Every partnership starts in a different place. They all progress at a different pace. The issues they have to deal with are so different.'

After lunch, we joined the circle's monthly Community of Practice (CoP) meeting. The facilitated PfP programme lasts for one year. Although it's expected that the partners will continue building their relationships and carry on with their work in the school and community, the PfP team's direct involvement and the monthly CoP meetings end once that facilitated 12-month period is over.

The partners in Letsitele elected to continue meeting as a leadership circle and to hold monthly CoP meetings without formal facilitation. By happy coincidence, their August CoP meeting was scheduled for the day we arrived in Letsitele. The meeting was attended by three principals and four of the business leaders. The other principals all had valid reasons for not being able to attend the session, while two of the Groep 91 business leaders were occupied with the orange harvest.

Although their CoP was no longer being run as a 'normal' PfP CoP session and was more of an operational and planning meeting, the group was demonstrating that the community of practice concept still has value for them four years on, and all of the partners who were present confirmed this.

It was a great opportunity to hear from principals Isaac Nkonwana, who is partnered with Kobus van Wyk and Eric Tiba, Burgert van Rooyen's partner. Both are high school principals, and, although it was clear that they found it incredibly valuable to be in relationship with their partners from Groep 91, not everything has run smoothly in their schools.

Kobus and Isaac's partnership at Hetiseka Secondary has not been an easy journey. Continued poor results have led to the school being downgraded to a junior secondary school and learner numbers have fallen. However, the partners have made infrastructure improvements at the school and Kobus is hanging in there and continuing to provide support.

Isaac believes he has become a better leader and that this has rubbed off on his school management team (SMT). 'I can leave the school to attend a meeting confident that the school will run smoothly in my absence now,' he says. 'I have learnt to lead and influence from being part of this process.'

Isaac feels that the growth in his leadership came about through his partnership with Kobus. 'We didn't get any training when I was appointed as a principal,' he told Theo and me. 'There was just a one-day induction programme. Kobus is a leader, so I was able to learn from him. Leaders are not born, they are made, and I am becoming a better leader.'

I asked Kobus about the impact that the programme has had on him. 'I was dumbstruck to see the difficulty and how alone and exposed teachers and principals are,' he said. 'I was blown away by how much is achieved by so little. I have been tempted to give up, but it is inspiring to see how educators continue to go the extra mile. It also made me sad. The teachers continue to put in so much effort despite the fact that the system is failing them on a daily basis,' remarked Kobus.

The school was so run down when Kobus first went there that he felt it was a health and safety risk. He and Isaac have managed to improve that situation though, and Kobus is convinced that starting at the bottom is still the way to go. 'I'm stubborn, so I'm sticking to the task, although I guess a call will have to be made by the education authorities on whether the school continues or not,' he says.

'For me, the exercise has been a valuable learning experience. I have been to and seen the areas where our colleagues live and the schools their children go to,' says Kobus. 'That has affected the way that I see them in the workplace. I certainly have empathy for Isaac, and I count my blessings. I think I have made a positive contribution to the CoP where my skills and experience have been useful.'

Burgert's partner Eric Tiba has also been through difficult times. His wife suffered a long illness and eventually passed away during 2019, so it has been hard for him to focus his attention on the school at all times. However, he is positive about the partnership with Burgert. 'At the beginning of our partnership I was uncomfortable,' Eric said. 'He was a white man and the boss of the farm. But he proved me wrong and the other farmers in the circle did too. He never said he is coming to help me and he wasn't there to judge me. It took a while, but we established a partnership based on trust and respect.'

Eric got a lot out of the formal PfP training sessions and has learnt to be more accepting. 'I found the workshops particularly useful,' he says. 'We need help with leadership and management because we don't learn about this anywhere else. I did not leave any of the workshops empty-handed. I have been able to share what I have learnt with my SMT and SGB[15].'

After hearing from Eric about his relationship with Burgert I was keen to hear what Burgert had learnt through being Eric's partner. 'I realised how hard principals and teachers work,' he told me. 'Being in education is definitely not a job for sissies. At Eric's school, Mapheto Secondary, more than 70% of the parents are illiterate and more than 50% are unemployed. I now have new respect for the principals and teachers who keep going under exceptionally difficult circumstances,' said Burgert. 'We have to face the challenges, and this is where farmers have something to contribute because they have learnt to be resilient.' Eric listened intently to Burgert and then responded: 'Hearing Burgert say this makes me want to work even harder.'

Later that evening, Burgert and Irma told us that they had been invited to the unveiling of Eric's late wife's tombstone. 'It was the first time we had attended a ceremony like that in one of the villages,' Burgert said. 'It was a unique situation for us, and we were humbled and honoured by being invited to attend the ceremony. That event was symbolic of a shift in our relationship. After four years in partnership, I feel we are

15   School Governing Body

now starting to find each other, and I'm sure we can achieve a lot more in the years to come.'

It had perhaps been over-optimistic of the partners to expect the backlog of challenges at the schools to be eliminated in just four years. The heavy emphasis on matric results has not helped. Magwaza Ngomana, the Circuit Manager in charge of the schools, knows that the narrow focus on achievement in the matric exams is a problem. 'We are painting the roof of the building when we should be building the foundations and the walls,' he says.

To bring about a meaningful improvement in matric results, the quality of teaching in the junior secondary classes has to improve, but overcrowding in classrooms, poor infrastructure and a lack of support for teachers is making that difficult.

The next morning Theo and I set out to visit some of the schools, starting with Nyavana Primary School. This is the school where Jan-Louis has partnered with Principal Juliet Shilubana. I'd been to the school before, but on the drive out there Jan-Louis warned me that I would not recognise the place. He was right. There were new ablution facilities, a new admin block, a large free-standing shelter providing shade from the sun and protection from the rain, and a flourishing vegetable garden that supplements the school's feeding scheme. The garden produces a surplus that is sold to the local community.

When we met Juliet in her office she reminded us that she used to work under a tree in the schoolyard after the old admin block had burned down. Jan-Louis had stood beside Juliet while she put pressure on officials from the Limpopo Department of Education to approve plans to construct new buildings. Jan-Louis speaks with a lot of pride in how she handled the situation and simply would not give up. 'I asked Jan-Louis to come with me for support and I think they assumed he was from the media,' Juliet told us jokingly. 'I managed to get them to build covered walkways between the buildings, which was more than they had initially planned to give us, but we have the new buildings now, and things are much better.'

Juliet began teaching in 1992 and quickly rose through the ranks to Head of Department (HOD), then Deputy Principal. In 2013 she was promoted to principal and was sent to Nyavana Primary School where she was given a brief induction and left to get on with it. 'I was young and the school was not in a good state,' she recounts. 'When we were approached to join with Groep 91 in the PfP programme I had my doubts. I knew we needed help, but I was afraid that those white farmers would judge us and label us as lazy and stupid. I agreed though, and looking back, I realise things would have been very different if I had not met Jan-Louis and joined PfP.

'The training with Desmond was valuable because it prepared me for what was to come. It was in the Time to Think training at the beginning of the PfP process when we had to sit down and talk to each other that I first made a connection with Jan-Louis and it was the start of the relationship that we now have.' Juliet now refers to Jan-Louis as her 'white brother,' and his wife Janine as her 'sister'.

Juliet says she is no longer lonely. 'When I have a problem I now have someone to turn to. When the school's numbers suddenly went up and we found we didn't have enough classroom furniture I called him,' she offers as an example. 'I remember that I cried over the phone to him and although he was in no position to get us more desks and chairs, he listened to me. We still don't have enough, but I know he is in my corner and the problem no longer overwhelms me.'

In her early days as a principal Juliet was, she admits, an autocratic leader. 'I gave orders and expected them to be followed,' she explains. 'There was no one I trusted to delegate any responsibility to and so I tried to do everything myself. One of the most valuable lessons I learnt from Jan-Louis was that teamwork is the key to success. Together we have developed my senior teachers and school management team and now I leave many things to them.'

This point was illustrated while we were at the school. A meeting of parents and teachers was on the go under the newly-built shelter. The parents were being told about a field trip that their children were taking later in the week, and Juliet told us that she had no involvement in planning the outing.

'I'm not really sure where that group is going,' she noted. 'I trust the HOD and the teachers involved to manage it, and my job is to sign it off when they explain it to me.'

When we had arrived at the school we'd found Juliet busy photographing, with a tablet computer, a bowl of cooked samp, cabbage and beans. This was, she told us, the morning meal – the only one of the day for many – that was going to be served to the learners later on. She explained that she had been selected to be part of a pilot quality control group of principals who report on various school matters to the Department of Education (DBE). Sending in a description and a photograph of the food that the learners will be eating is part of her daily duties.

I was to learn later that Circuit Manager Ngomana has appointed Juliet as Secretary of his circuit team. From what Mr Ngomana told us, her leadership has developed to a level where she is being recognised, and she is assuming wider responsibility.

Jan-Louis remembers Juliet's former authoritarian ways. 'When I met her, she wanted to be the leader in everything. I think the PfP journey taught her to step back and take a different approach. Now she embodies the best of the consultative approach to leading, but she is also prepared to take a firm stand when she has to,' he says.

There have been remarkable changes at the school Juliet tells us. 'The children know that we care about them, so they are disciplined and proud of themselves and the school. Importantly, they can all read, and that's due to a large extent to the projects that have been implemented as a result of our PfP involvement.'

Cami Maths and BrainBoosters are among the programmes now being run in Nyavana Primary, while Magri Genovese of Magri's Language Institute works with teachers on English language usage at every school in the circle.

Remarkably, there are no issues with getting the Nyavana teachers to attend these language workshops and courses. 'When spaces were limited at one of Magri's workshops the teachers told me that if they were not selected to attend, they would be going anyway,' says Juliet.

'I learnt that it's better to negotiate than to command,' she explains. 'The SGB weren't convinced about the PfP programme at first, but they have come around, and now the teachers come to me with ideas, and I find I am doing less and less around the school.'

Instead, Juliet is out in the community, hustling. 'So much of what we need can be got from the area around us, and as the school has grown I have found people more and more willing to give things to us,' she told us.

Jan-Louis, through his contacts, has lent a hand here. Wi-Fi networks have been installed at all the schools in the circle, courtesy of local communications company, Letaba Wireless.

It hasn't been a one-way street though. Jan-Louis sees his involvement with Juliet as an important step on his journey to becoming a better business leader and a better South African.

'Working with Juliet has been an almighty wake-up call. It has been very humbling, to say the least. I used to consider myself enlightened, caring and compassionate, but when I stepped out of my comfort zone into her world, I found myself facing a new reality. It was sometimes disheartening, but opportunities always abound. As a business leader, it taught me not to assume that what you perceive, is in fact reality. You need to get out there and see the real world – that makes you a more authentic leader,' observes Jan-Louis.

'Juliet is committed to a 'Good to Great' journey at this school. Watching her at work has reinforced my belief that the best mechanism to affect staff behaviour is by way of one's own example. She has also shown me the true meaning of resilience. She has faced challenges way beyond what I have experienced and come through them. That's a lesson every business leader can learn.'

On a more personal level, Jan-Louis believes he has grown as a responsible, contributing South African. 'I often take my own children along to activities at the school. They have been privileged to start their own education journeys at a different place to the children in Juliet's school and I think it has opened their eyes to that. I think it will make them better South Africans,' he contends.

Jan-Louis has discovered from Juliet and the other principals in the circle that working in education is not for the fainthearted. 'Neither is farming, of course,' he laughs. 'I think we have learnt that about each other, and it has made us more understanding, caring and compassionate.'

Juliet is proud and humbled that Jan-Louis believes he has learnt as much from her as she has from him. 'Jan-Louis is firm, with a soft touch,' she discloses. 'He dreams big, but is not divorced from reality, and he has taught me to celebrate the small victories along the way. My life would be very different now if I had never met him.'

As a result of the progress made by Juliet and Jan-Louis, Nyavana Primary has become the school of choice in the area. 'Parents want their children to come here,' asserts Juliet. 'They know that the education their children will receive will be good and they don't have the same confidence in the other schools in the area.'

As a result, enrolment at the school has increased dramatically in the past few years. There were 410 learners at Nyavana when Juliet's partnership with Jan-Louis began in 2015, but that number has mushroomed to over 800. The downside is that the school does not have adequate space for so many learners as it was designed to accommodate just 400. There are now more than 80 children in some of the classes and little prospect of new classrooms being added in the near future.

When I raised this matter with Circuit Manager Ngomana, he referred to it as a 'man-made problem'. 'Because parents are seeing that things are improving at the school, they want their children in this school,' he observed. 'There are other schools in my district that are not filled to capacity. Under the circumstances, we cannot supply more classrooms at Nyavana.'

From Nyavana, we travelled to Manyunyu Primary School to meet Principal Nomsa Mhlongo, whose school is another of the Letsitele circle's success stories.

When Nomsa was appointed as acting principal of the school in 1998 she could hardly have been more unprepared for the job. She started teaching in 1989 and nine years later was suddenly promoted to acting principal. A year later she became the permanent principal of Manyunyu Primary. 'I was never a head of department, or a deputy principal, so I knew nothing of school management,' she told us. 'And when I was made principal, a group of us attended an induction programme together. There was no one-on-one training and no one to ask for advice.'

Nomsa felt extreme pressure when she took on the job and her reaction, she acknowledges, was to be short-tempered and shout a lot. 'I didn't achieve much that way, but I didn't know what else to do. I was very frustrated.'

Under the circumstances, she welcomed the invitation to join the PfP programme. 'I was nervous about it, especially when I heard that Andrew Jackson would be my partner,' revealed Nomsa. 'He is the Manager of the packing plant at Groep 91, and he has a reputation as a strict boss. I was afraid that he would be racist and judgemental. Even though I was afraid, I decided to join the programme. I discovered that Andrew is not judgemental at all.'

'I learnt from Andrew that there are some situations where leaders have to take a firm stance,' she remarked.

Before her partnership with Andrew began, Nomsa did the 6-month course arranged by Desmond Zeelie. The PfP Time to Think training that followed was valuable in that it taught Nomsa to move step-by-step and not to rush into things. 'I realised that sometimes the journey is as important as the result and it has made me a better manager,' she says.

Nomsa is no longer so short-tempered and demanding and this has led to better outcomes she says. 'I now have a better relationship with the teachers, the SGB, the learners and even with my own family at home. The teachers are committed now and they call me mama or sister. Our relationship is a healthy one.'

At the end of the facilitated PfP year, Groep 91 asked Desmond Zeelie to do a baseline assessment at all the schools to help the partners determine where attention was needed. Nomsa confesses that she found Desmond's assessment of her and her school very upsetting. 'I thought that Desmond was quite harsh in his feedback. I felt judged and criticised. I felt like quitting there and then. But I thought about it that evening and decided that I was going to treat this as an opportunity to learn,' she says.

Andrew's role is a very busy one, and he hasn't been able to spend much time at the school but has always been available when Nomsa needs advice, and she still takes him up on it from time to time.

Between 2015 and 2019, the number of learners enrolled at the school doubled, and though this has brought challenges in terms of classroom space things are generally going well. Academically, things have improved, and the school won a tableful of trophies at the recent inter-district competitions in various academic subjects. The education department has provided a new kitchen, and a vegetable garden has been established with support from Groep 91 and the Kaross Foundation.

The foundation was established jointly in 2017 by Groep 91 and the Kaross embroidery business. Both had felt they needed someone who could focus on their social development activities and bring alignment and coherence to all of the work. Lidell Botha was appointed to manage the foundation's activities, and it is clear from listening to all the leaders involved that she has played a key role in building on and sustaining the impact of the partnerships in the Letsitele circle's schools.

In 2019 Groep 91 and the Kaross Foundation launched a 'Mandela Month' volunteering programme. Projects were run every Saturday throughout the month of July at each of the PfP schools. Lidell chose Manyunyu Primary for her project and created an opportunity for her own children and their teammates (who attended Tzaneen Primary School) to play cricket at Manyunyu.

Two teams were formed, each with players from both schools, and an exciting match was played. 'To have white children come to our village and play cricket with our boys was an historic moment. They will never forget it,' said Nomsa. Lidell told us that a team from Manyunyu will travel to Tzaneen Primary for the next game.

Andrew Jackson downplays his role in the partnership with Nomsa, but it's clear that he made an impact on her. 'We don't speak as often as we used to anymore, but Nomsa knows I am available, I sometimes wish she would take me up on it more often,' he says.

For Nomsa, her involvement in the programme has helped her to become more understanding and accepting of others. 'I realised that Andrew is just a person, he is not white or black, and that has had an impact in other areas of my life,' she said. 'For example, I got along much better with my SGB when I realised that they were just people with their own issues. I met them where they were and tried to understand them. We got along much better after that.'

Nomsa has found her involvement with the other principals and business leaders in the monthly CoP meetings to be invaluable. 'The ongoing commitment of everyone to the project means that it is sustainable and we are committed to continued improvement,' she says.

It is hard to spend time with Nomsa and Juliet and not be touched and inspired by their stories. A story that I was unfortunately not able to hear was that of Principal Makhanani Shilote of Vhulakanjani Lower Primary and her partner Felix Hacker. I had heard their partnership being described as the 'success story' of the Letsitele Circle. Sadly, however, Makhanani was in bed with flu during our visit, and I was disappointed that we would not be able to hear from her about her PfP experience.

I asked both Juliet and Nomsa whether they think things would have been different for them if they had not been in partnerships with Jan-Louis and Andrew. Both indicated that the picture would have been radically different.

'I was lonely in those early days and had no one to discuss my problems with,' says Juliet. 'That changed when Jan-Louis came along. We talk about many things, socially and about school. Through those discussions and through the programme, I got the skills needed to run the school more effectively. If I had never partnered with Jan-Louis things would have been a lot worse for us.'

Nomsa doesn't think she would have still been at Manyunyu Primary had it not been for her partnership with Andrew. 'I was inexperienced and there were many challenges. I thought of quitting more than once,' she admits. 'But there were changes that came about due to the partnership. There were improvements, thanks to Groep 91's involvement, and they were sustainable. I grew as a leader and the teachers are now committed. It would not have been that way without Andrew,' she concludes.

One of the challenges with assessing academic progress in primary schools is that external assessments are conducted in one province only; the Western Cape. So it is hard to know whether performances are actually improving as a result of PfP's involvement at these schools. We asked Circuit Manager Ngomana about this. 'We do run our own standardised tests and the schools involved definitely did improve in those. But the real difference is in the principals,' he told us.

'The education department has a big head, but little legs,' he said, meaning that there are too few officials on the ground. 'I'm in charge of 23 schools and they are widespread, so I can't go everywhere. To have principals who I know I don't have to worry about makes a big difference to me. I have that with Juliet and Nomsa.'

The performance of their schools in district competitions speak for themselves, and, Ngomana said, he counts on Juliet and Nomsa to help him with various tasks. 'It wasn't always that way. In the beginning, Juliet used to phone me for advice all the time. She called so often that I might as well have been running the school. Now she only calls to tell me about the things she has already done. It makes my life as a circuit manager so much easier.'

Reflections

It was clear that the two primary school principals had benefitted greatly from being part of the entire process – Desmond's programme, the PfP year, and the ongoing relationships and activities that followed the facilitated PfP year – so we could comfortably say that PfP was a successful intervention for these schools.

I found myself wondering about the definition of 'success'. Groep 91 had embarked on this programme because they wanted to see improvement in academic outcomes in the eight schools. They are delighted about the impact in the three primary schools but hugely frustrated by the lack of progress in the high schools. But is this all that matters? What about the impact on the individual leaders in this programme?

In my mind, there are so many indicators of the value of this process, including principals feeling more supported and business leaders having much more empathy and compassion and an understanding of the challenges faced by educators in local schools. The Groep 91 leaders now have first-hand knowledge and understanding of some of these challenges. They are frustrated by the complexity of the issues facing schools and have realised that it will take time to address these challenges; there are no silver bullet solutions.

While none of the white leaders wanted to discuss race, it was clear from our conversations with the principals that their stories about white people have changed. They talked about their initial fears of being in a relationship with a white person and how they have come to see these white people differently. When we spoke to Nomsa she said: 'Because of this programme I now get to hug and shake the hand of Burgert van Rooyen regularly. That is a big thing for me.'

While we were in Letsitele I was contacted about another agricultural company that is interested in launching a PfP leadership circle in the rural area in which they operate. I asked all the people we had spoken to in Letsitele if they had any advice to offer this company. They were very clear:

1. In rural areas, it is useful for PfP circles to have an 'anchor' organisation. Groep 91 was the anchor organisation in Letsitele. This enabled them to mobilise funding and support for further work in the schools (beyond the first year of PfP)
2. It is important to have one person who will take the lead. Jan-Louis' role was critical for the success of PfP in Letsitele. Every circle ideally needs someone like Jan-Louis to provide overall leadership
3. The work that Desmond did with the principals before the formal PfP year started was invaluable and definitely contributed to the success of PfP in Letsitele
4. The company has to be willing to make a long-term commitment. The facilitated PfP year is just the first year of a much longer process, and any organisation getting involved in this work must be willing to be involved for the long run. The ideal is to continue with facilitated CoP sessions for at least three years because one year is simply not long enough to effect transformational change in schools.

The Letsitele circle is unique and different from other PfP leadership circles. In many ways, its context is ideal for PfP. Groep 91 regarded the PfP year as part of a long-term programme of work. Through the Kaross Foundation, they have been able to mobilise additional funding to address some of the challenges in the schools. Their leaders care deeply and are committed to lead a long-term programme of development. Jan-Louis provided strong leadership, and Lidell is now leading the work of the Kaross Foundation. They know that there are no quick fixes and are committed to being involved for the long run.

Chapter 3

Long-term partnerships with impact

"What counts in life is not the mere fact that we have lived. It is what difference we have made to the lives of others that will determine the significance of the life we lead." – Nelson Mandela

After visiting the rural schools in Letsitele, I was keen to see what impact the programme had made under entirely different circumstances. So Theo and I paid a series of visits to a number of the urban schools that had participated in PfP during the early years and had been reporting ongoing partnership activities and growth.

Yeoville Boys' Primary School

Lindelani Singo is the principal of Yeoville Boys' Primary, an inner-city school in Johannesburg. His partnership with Anita Moerman van Blankenburg started in 2012, which was early days for PfP. Anita is a coach and facilitator with many years of leadership experience. Her participation in PfP was funded by one of her clients, the pharmaceutical company Lundbeck.

Yeoville Boys' Primary is more than 100 years old. For most of that time school catered only for white children, but it became a Model C[16] school in 1993. When Lindelani was appointed as principal in 2009 he was the only black person on the management team. Although the school's demographic profile had been changing rapidly, there was still a perception then within the surrounding community that this was a 'white' school catering for wealthy families. As a result, many families living in the nearby suburbs were reluctant to send their children to the school, and enrolment stagnated at around 400.

'Around 2005 and 2006 the suburb of Yeoville underwent dramatic changes,' Lindelani explained. 'It became the destination of many foreigners, and French became the most commonly language spoken in the streets around the school. The school was operating outside of the context of the area it was located in. The community did not see it as their school.'

---

16 Formerly whites-only schools that opted to admit black learners at the beginning of the process of integration started in 1991 were called Model C schools. The term 'former Model C school' is now commonly used to describe all schools that were once run as white schools by the provincial education departments in the Apartheid era.

As the first black principal of the school, Lindelani found himself trying to lead a divided team. 'Staff members did not mix in the staff room. There was a black area and a white one. I knew I had to close that gap, and I wanted us to become the school of choice in the community. I had dreams and a vision for the future, but I did not know how to achieve these dreams. I was frustrated. There was no one to talk to about what I had in mind, no one to bounce my ideas off. It was a lonely place to be,' he recalls.

Then, in 2012, Lindelani was introduced to the PfP programme and met Anita. 'Things began to change straight away. We went on training courses and attended Community of Practice sessions, but the thing I remember most is that she listened to me and I felt safe in opening up to her,' Lindelani told us. 'The only people who visited me in those early days were departmental officials, and I never felt that I could open up to them and discuss my issues. Anita was like a safety net. I felt I could talk without being judged and without being afraid of criticism.'

The idea of listening without judgement is central to the role of the partners in the PfP programme. I asked Lindelani whether it had made a difference that Anita came from outside education and didn't pretend to know how a school should be run – that she was able to listen without judging.

Lindelani confirmed that her absence of judgement had indeed made a huge difference. 'If I were to go to a struggling school in Soweto, say, I would walk in and compare what we do here with what I found there. I would be judging them, assuming that what we do is superior. I would not be in a position to offer good advice and they wouldn't be happy to receive it from me,' he observed.

Lindelani's remarks reminded me of our commitment to facilitate learning partnerships –where both parties are open to learning from each other. Many people have argued that we should be creating opportunities for retired school principals to mentor incumbent principals through PfP, but we have been conscious of the power dynamic that this would create. We chose instead to work with business leaders who would be willing to partner with principals from a perspective of *not knowing*. The role of the business leader in a PfP partnership is to be a thinking partner to the principal. These leaders don't need to know much about education to do this. In fact, as Lindelani pointed out, it is useful if they join a partnership without preconceived ideas of how things should be done.

'Anita came with a lot of experience of business and the corporate world. I know about education and how a school operates. I have also got to know Yeoville and the communities who live here. We put those two things together and as the partnership grew we were able to produce something good,' said Lindelani.

'Anita was not one of those people who wanted to get stuck in and do things at the school,' he explained. 'She knew that it was not her role to lead change at the school. That was my role. She wanted to hear about my vision, about the challenges I faced, and she wanted to know what I wanted to achieve and how she could support me.

'The big question was where do you start? We decided that getting the buy-in of the community, getting the parents involved and making the school the centre of the community should be the priorities,' recalls Lindelani.

The people living around the school did not see the school as theirs. And the parents of the children who were at the school were mostly disengaged.

In 2012 there were 400 learners enrolled at the school. By 2019 that number had tripled. Only 30 people attended Lindelani's first parents' evening. Now the hall is filled to capacity – with over 500 parents in attendance.

I asked Lindelani how he and Anita had contributed to this dramatic turnaround. 'We engaged with the community. We reached out to them and made it clear that they were welcome at the school. We also decided to become a source of information and advice for people in the community. It gave them a reason to come to the school,' he explained.

In the first year of their PfP partnership Lindelani and Anita worked on building those relationships. 'I was the one talking to people, but Anita was always beside me. Her knowledge and experience in business helped me to identify which doors to knock on, and she cheered me on. We drew up a plan, and she trusted me to execute it. She held me accountable and expected me to give feedback, but her role was to reassure me and celebrate the achievements with me. I knew she was behind me and supported me all the way.'

Lindelani remembers that they would talk for hours. 'She was in my corner. It was so different to my interaction with the department. They were there with a red pen, looking for what I did wrong. There was never any celebration of what I did right.'

Lindelani felt that the education department's Institutional Development and Support Officials (IDSOs) never quite got what he and Anita were trying to achieve. 'Anita saw potential in me. She did not come with a list of things she felt I should be doing. Instead, she let me do my thing and supported me.'

'Working with Anita made me see that there is a lot that we could learn from the world of business. I realised that we need to think of parents as our clients. You don't learn that as an educator.

'It was good to see that Anita was open to learning about my world too. Business people think they understand education because they were in a school once or because of what they read in the media. It is only when they spend time in our schools that they are able to find out what the real issues and challenges are.'

Looking back, Lindelani believes the person he was in 2012 and who he is now are two totally different people. 'Back then I did what the memo expected me to do,' he said. 'My relationship with the staff was strained and my leadership style was autocratic.

'After three years with Anita, I was a very different leader. I am more courageous. I stand up for myself. I find that sometimes I lead from the front, sometimes I lead from behind, and sometimes I'm in the middle, along with everyone else. I lead according to the situation.

'The contracting skills I learnt in the Flawless Consulting workshop have helped me to develop others. To give them space to do their best work. The confidence I have acquired and my willingness to delegate have led to changes in the management structure of the school.

'My school management team does not consist only of the deputy and the heads of department. Everyone who is in a leadership position is part of the team,' he explained. 'We have reached a stage now where I can hand over control to those running committees and activities and be confident that they can handle the situation.

'I have developed a relationship with them and I trust them. My job is to motivate and mentor those who are running the different areas of school life, and then to leave them alone.' Similarly, Lindelani said, he trusts the teachers to do their best in the classrooms and doesn't believe in looking over their shoulders.

The results have been impressive. From being something alien to the community, Yeoville Boys' Primary has become its school of choice, bursting at its seams. Eight years ago the overall academic average at the school was 22%. It is now 68%.

I asked Lindelani if he had confidence in those numbers, seeing that they were based on the school's internal assessments. 'Can your Grade 4s read for meaning?' I enquired.

His response was to send for nine-year-old Revdi Omba, a Grade 3 boy. Like more than 90% of learners at the school, his home language is French, but he uses English as a first language at school, with Zulu as a first additional language. Omba showed us a six-page illustrated story he had written in near-perfect English.

'Reading was one of the priorities Anita and I identified,' Lindelani explained. 'We got some sponsorship and re-opened the school library. The children read for 30 minutes every day of the week. Yes, our Grade 4s can read. I have confidence in these numbers.'

After visiting Lindelani I asked Anita whether she would be willing to share her thoughts about her partnership with Lindelani. Her response was an enthusiastic 'yes':

When I arrived at Lindelani's school for the launch meeting for the JHB3 Leadership Circle, I was both surprised and impressed from the moment I drove through the gate. I'm not sure what I expected, but driving through the suburb and noticing the conditions was quite depressing. What I experienced at the school was the opposite. I was greeted by neatly dressed, well-groomed prefects who escorted me to the library where we met with the other principals and business leaders. The children at the school were open, welcoming, engaging and I felt welcome and safe. They wore their uniforms with pride and their smiles reached out to me from their eyes. They treated visitors and staff with respect and I knew there was something special about the leadership of this school.

When I met Lindelani, I understood why the school was so different. Our first conversation was about his concern for two individual children, who needed psychological help because of abuse by a family member. His concern was not about himself or stuff needed for the school. He didn't complain about the Department of Education and being a victim of the system. He cared about the children and the community and had plans and dreams to address the issues that bothered him. I realised that we cared about the same things. When it came to the point where we had to choose our partners, I asked to be Lindelani's partner and he asked to be mine – and so it started.

I was truly curious about the school. As a coach, I knew that Lindelani knew his reality better than I could ever know it and if I wanted to add value I first had to learn. So, I asked lots of questions and I listened. I learnt that Lindelani cared about the individual child as much as he cared about the school as a whole. I learnt that he cared about his staff and approached their everyday challenges as if they mattered. He was practical, yet compassionate. He understood that each person, whether a learner or staff member, had an impact on the system and that the system, in turn, had an impact on each individual.

During the first few visits, I learnt about the changes that Lindelani had already brought about at the school, in the short period since he became the principal. Enrolments had doubled, he built new classrooms, bought a minibus and a car so that the learners could participate in events and so that teachers had a back-

up when transport was a challenge. I learnt about the vegetable garden that he planted to enable the school to feed more children, as for some of them the meal they got at school was the only meal they ate the whole day. There was also a holiday feeding programme for these children and an adult education programme that ran on Saturdays. My partner cared about the broader community and understood the impact of the bigger system on how the children showed up and performed at school.

I was on a sabbatical when I became Lindelani's partner and the cost for our partnership was covered by Lundbeck Pharmaceuticals, a former client of mine. At the time, I didn't have a big corporate with deep pockets backing me. All I had to offer was my time, experience, knowledge and training. I wanted to be relevant and I wanted my impact to survive my time as a partner, as I thought I might be moving to Cape Town the following year. As a coach, I knew that the best I could do for my partner was to be a sounding board, a thinking partner, the one to encourage him to go to places that might seem daunting, at times, and to be his accountability partner. He already had a vision and I was there to support him.

During that first year, I spent a lot of time with my partner. Sometimes we just talked about the application of what we learnt in the workshops; other times they were more coaching conversations and I also did some group coaching and workshops with his staff. The topics of the workshops focused on the staff needs and were aimed at addressing challenges and areas for growth.

Outside the school, I worked on introducing Lindelani to people in my network that could add value and address specific needs at the school. Some became long-term partners of the school and Lindelani continued with this practice, adding many supporters from the community that are still partners of the school, to this day, seven years later.

I was there to learn too, and I did, more than I thought I would. I grew as a human being. I was freed from many fears and could let go of some preconceived ideas as I became less fearful about our country and my survival in it. I was accepted and valued for who I was on the inside, regardless of my outer appearance. I felt valued and welcome, and I had a sense of belonging. In retrospect, I can also see how our partnership boosted both Lindelani's and my confidence. I guess knowing that you have a partner, someone who has your back, enables you to walk a little taller in the world.

I have remained involved with PfP because of my experience and a deep belief and love for what PfP does. As a result of my exposure to Flawless Consulting, one of the workshops offered in the programme, I became a facilitator as I could see the value it brought to the school and the value it could bring to every organisation. I later also became a Learning Process Facilitator for a group of seven PfP partnerships. I experienced successful partnerships and also a few that failed.

I have learnt that a successful PfP experience isn't a given, but that it depends on a few things. Both the principal and the business leader have to be eager, committed and energized, as it requires time and personal sacrifice. Both parties need to be open, humble and willing to learn from each other. There has to be self-respect and respect for one another and a celebration of one's differences, rather than seeing it as an obstacle. There has to be a love for children and passion for education. One cannot have a superiority complex or a victim mentality.

One has to have a sense of adventure and a preparedness to be surprised. There is so much beauty in the world, and all one has to do is to look up. One day I did look up, and thank God, there was PfP and Louise with her shining eyes and her big love for education. It changed my world.

Rembrandt Park Primary School

Our next stop was Rembrandt Park Primary School in Johannesburg.

Lizzie Seema applied for the deputy principal post at the school in 2008, and when she went to sign the contract for that role was told that she would immediately become the acting principal because the incumbent principal had resigned.

Lizzie was thrown in at the deep end with no preparation and little time to think. Rembrandt Park is a former Model C institution, and when she joined the staff team most of the members were white. 'I was the only black person on the school management team and one of only five black educators at the school,' she recollects.

Lizzie was apprehensive, and her fears were realised when some teachers and SMT members made it clear that they were not happy reporting to a black woman. 'We had a stakeholder meeting in those early days, facilitated by an outsider, and some staff members asked that I leave so that they could speak freely about me,' she remembers. 'I disagreed with them, and assured them that they could say what they wanted to, I would hold no grudges. I was firm and did my best to manage the changes we were undergoing, but it was a rough time for me, and it showed in my leadership style which was quite autocratic in those days.'

Then Lizzie met Thomas Holtz, Chief Executive of Multotec, an engineering company on the East Rand.

'I had been introduced to the PfP programme by a fellow parent at my daughter's school, and although I rejected the idea at first because I didn't think I would have the time, I was persuaded to join by Stephanie, the Learning Process Facilitator for the second PfP leadership circle in Johannesburg. I remember thinking at the time that things were going pretty well at the school and that maybe I could help some of the other principals by showing them how we did things. Little did I know that I was going to benefit greatly by being part of the programme,' she says.

At the launch meeting of her circle, Johannesburg 2 (JHB2), Lizzie recalls, the principals were on one side of the room, the business leaders were on the other. The principals were expected to choose a partner and approach him or her. 'I was very shy those days and I couldn't do it, so I stayed in my chair. At the same time, Thomas, a big white man was so intimidating that none of the other principals wanted to choose him. So, we were the only ones left at the end of the process and we had no choice; we were partnered and it was the start of a relationship that still continues today,' she said.

Lizzie was filled with pride, she says, to be partnered with the chief executive of a successful business and when she went to the Multotec offices every other month to meet with Thomas she was interested to see how the company did things. 'I realised that their success came from selling things and providing excellent service to their customers. I thought it could be the same with the school. We don't make products, but the learners and parents are our customers and we are measured by the quality of learning outcomes at the school.'

When she agreed to join the programme Lizzie thought it would be about receiving money and resources to address challenges that the school faced, but she discovered that it was 'really about bringing everyone together, in the school and the community, and working out how we can address those challenges ourselves.'

One of the projects she and Thomas ran in that first year was to organise some Mandela Day activities and to invite the school community to attend. 'It's still going on every year now, but it's changed,' she said. 'The community has taken some ownership of it. They come with ideas and help to organise and run the activities. Our most recent one was in August 2019, and Thomas was here to see how far we have come in bringing the community together.'

There were successes from early on. In the days of the Annual National Assessments (ANAs) the average marks began to improve and those improvements have continued. 'Together with Thomas, I thought of intervention strategies in areas where the learners were not performing. We met with the teachers and implemented our plans. The averages went up from 60% to more than 90%, and we sustain those levels by using the same strategies we developed all those years ago.'

The biggest changes, Lizzie believes, were those that she herself underwent. 'I used to be very quiet, but I joined the PfP programme and I changed. Thomas encouraged me. I was still nervous and not confident that I could manage the school, but Thomas would tell me repeatedly that he believed in me and that I can do it. "Go and do it," he would say to me.'

One of the things Lizzie learnt from Thomas was that she should have a clear picture of how she wanted the school to be. 'I became a visionary,' she said. 'I began to think ahead to what we needed, and then made plans to get those things.'

She gave us an example: in line with the call from the education department for schools to incorporate technology in the classroom, Lizzie decided to install whiteboards in the classrooms. 'I went to the SGB and sold the idea to them and then, with funds that Thomas and I raised through various projects, we began installing the whiteboards. Now we have a whiteboard in every classroom, and the department didn't pay for any of them.'

In her early days as the principal, Lizzie said, she would switch between democratic and autocratic leadership styles. 'I would listen when things were going smoothly, but when there were problems I would revert to ordering people around. Now I see myself as a collaborative leader. I have a clear direction and we have built constructive teams to perform tasks. Parents, teachers, department officials are all involved, depending on the situation and I trust them to run things.

'That has freed me to invest my time in improving the school. I spend more time building relationships, formulating strategies and sharing them with stakeholders. The confidence I got from my relationship with Thomas brought about these changes in me, and I have transferred them into making Rembrandt Park the school it is today.'

I asked Lizzie to elaborate on what it was about Thomas that led to her developing the way she has.

'Thomas is a special person,' she said. 'He is wise, humble and always prepared to listen. I know he says the same about me, which shows we have formed a bond. We are both very organised people and we are both critical thinkers, so we have become very alike.'

'He brings out the best in me. In the beginning I would undermine myself. I felt myself inferior and didn't believe there was anything he could learn from me. I worried about bothering him.'

I asked Lizzy whether she had any fears about working with a white man. 'His being white wasn't really a problem. I had white people as friends at my daughter's school and I had white teachers on my staff. It was more that he was a man and I'm a woman. I was worried about what my husband would think of us spending time together. I was worried about what his wife would say about me. We had to do some work to help our spouses understand that our relationship was all about work.'

Thomas didn't come to her with a list of instructions, Lizzie said, he came to listen, to share his opinion and to be available to help. 'There was no judgement. He recognised that I was shy and reserved and he encouraged me. He told me that I have the knowledge and the skills to be successful. He helped me to come out of my shell, and he would remind me that it's not about where you start, it's where you finish. He saw the potential in me and told me I could be the best.'

When others began to recognise Lizzie's potential, Thomas was available as a sounding board. 'Twice I was offered the opportunity to move to elite private schools, but Thomas helped me see that my place is here, that I am making a difference in a community that needs it most,' she says.

Lizzie thinks things would have been very different if she did not join PfP and Thomas had not come into her life. 'He is my cheerleader, always there to support me and help me deal with challenges,' she says. 'I am stronger because of him. I would not be able to make the decisions I do now. I am now a strong and confident leader because of him.'

The school would also have been very different. Lizzie has many stories of how Rembrandt Primary has benefitted from her involvement with PfP, but the story she is most proud of is how the school's music programme started. In 2013, PfP received the Reconciliation Award from the Institute for Justice and Reconciliation. The award ceremony was held at Steenberg High School in Cape Town and, because she heard that Archbishop Tutu was going to be at the event, Lizzie decided to travel to Cape Town to attend the ceremony.

That evening, she learned about Steenberg High's music programme. After a conversation with Steenberg's principal, Andre Kraak, Lizzie returned to Rembrandt Park with a mission to start a music programme at the school. 'Today we have a fully equipped music department with qualified teachers. We purchased string instruments (violin, viola, cello, double bass), brass (euphonium, alto horns, french horn, trumpets), percussion (marimbas, xylophones), woodwind (flute, clarinet) and recorders. We have a junior and senior choir. They compete in the ABC Motsepe SASCE Eisteddfod song prescribed by the Department of Education, the Segarona Arts and Culture Eisteddfod and Allegretto Eisteddfod. Learners learn music theory and practice. We hope that we will be able to erect a music studio sometime in the future.'

Lizzie also has fond memories of the courses she attended through PfP. 'Steph, our Learning Process Facilitator, made us understand what we were doing and reminded us that everything we did was for the children. From the Flawless Consulting course I learned about contracting. I called an SMT meeting and told the members of the SMT that if we wanted to be the best school we needed to contract with all our stakeholders. We started to contract our expectations with all the staff members, the children and the parents. We agreed what we wanted to achieve together and how we were going to achieve these goals. We still do it.'

'In Time to Think I learned to listen without interrupting and to really hear. That has helped me greatly, even with my own family.'

The key, Lizzie believes is that her relationship with Thomas has continued. 'One year is too short to make a real difference in the school. It was once our relationship had developed to a stage where I was able to take the lead and bring about the changes that things began to really improve. And Thomas was always there for me. I don't know how you can do it, but getting a longer-term commitment from the partners is really important.'

I was deeply touched by what Lizzie had told us and curious to hear what Thomas would say in response to reading what we had written. His response:

I had the privilege of getting to know Lizzie a little better, and her biography is a typical SA story growing up in a rural area with an absent father and two or three siblings. At an early age she made some choices that brought her to Gauteng and, with determination, led her to getting a post school teaching qualification. This may not seem like much in my world, but I think from that background this already needed some real discipline and determination. The path to becoming the principal at Rembrandt Park was not easy and when she finally got it she may have not been well prepared for it, but she persevered and has succeeded. She has real good leadership qualities, and by the time we met she may have been a little shy and reserved but I believe all the ingredients and the capabilities were already there. My time with her was more a case of being her devoted listening partner and the enabler for some of her latent abilities. It was tangible seeing her own perception of herself (glass ceiling) grow as we progressed through the year.

I have always been more inclined to try and empower others than take the limelight myself. I would consider my leadership style as democratic, consultative and as a facilitator of the latent potential that is possible when a group of people put their heads together and work towards a common goal. I had discovered story telling and Peter Block's Community Building before I even did PfP. I am also a huge fan of Otto Scharmer and Peter Senge and their work on generative thinking and systemic insight from the Fifth Discipline. So I was quite enthralled but not very certain about what I could do to support Louise's brainchild of leveraging into the government school system via the principals to make a difference.

The platform that PfP created was finding that shared DNA between two human beings, and the shared challenges between a business leader and a school principal. Take the time to get to know each other and learn from each other and accelerate the insights into action plans for the principal to implement. This very real partnership, when the chemistry is right, is where the magic happens.

I can honestly say that I have learned much through this process, the insights into how a black woman had a much harder struggle to 'make it' than I ever did in my career, the bridge-building into other communities and the faith that despite the bad press that the education department gets there are hard-working committed human beings doing their best to serve our children in their quest for an education and progress into adulthood. Lizzie had a real crisis situation during our partnership that she handled with real aplomb, and I could take a leaf out of her book on how to engage with all the stakeholders in these kinds of circumstances. The multiple levels at which this programme works is quite astounding and a real nation-building experience in South Africa.

I felt somewhat uncertain at signing up to this in the beginning, thinking that my pedagogical training is non-existent and realizing that all that was required of me was to show up as an engaged human being. Lizzie initially showed up with a list of objectives and I believe we probably did justice to most of those. It was a pleasure getting to know her and her wonderful family, in school, and at home. I have the utmost respect for her and what she continues to do every day. What could be more important than the work that happens in our schools?

Makgatho Primary School

Our next trip was to Saulsville in Atteridgeville, Pretoria to meet with Jane Tsharane, the principal at Makgatho Primary School. Her partnership with Bob Head began in 2013, and it's another partnership where the pair are still in contact six years after meeting each other.

When he met Jane, Bob Head was Special Advisor to the Commissioner and subsequently Chief Financial Officer (CFO) at the SA Revenue Service (SARS). He is British by nationality but had worked in South Africa for many years.

I remember meeting Bob at the SARS office in Pretoria early in 2013. I had been told that Bob was the driving force behind the Dinokeng Scenarios, and I wanted to let him know that PfP was a direct response to the call for the 'Walk Together' scenario. Bob was very interested to know more about PfP and quick to decide that he wanted to join the programme. He knew that SARS would not pay for his participation and decided that he would pay for it himself. I was very excited about having Bob as a partner to a principal and could not wait to see how he would experience the programme.

Bob and Jane were partnered in May 2013 in the second leadership circle to launch in Tshwane. Their Learning Process Facilitator was Francois Euvrard.

Jane's memory of meeting Bob was that he was quite scary. 'He operated at a very high level. He wasn't a South African, and I had my doubts when I realised he would be my partner in the PfP programme. I simply could not see how SARS, the UK and Atteridgeville could come together,' she recalls.

'I was still quite new at the job and was trying to do it in the way that the department expected of me. I didn't want to stick my neck out, and I was sure that because of Bob's stature he would draw attention to the school, and if he found things weren't right I would be in trouble!'

Jane had been involved with other school improvement projects and was very sceptical about the idea of business and education in partnership and that people from outside the education system could provide meaningful support. 'Our only experience with people from outside education was that we would get some visitors who acted like they were at the zoo. They would bring us a couple of things, smile, the kids would sing a song, they'd take a few pictures and disappear,' she told us.

'I was in no mood for another one of those. But I agreed. So when I Googled Bob and saw the level at which he operated I was intimidated; I was sure I wasn't important enough for him to spend his time on.'

Before she met Bob, Jane had never had a white friend. In fact, her experience of life and people outside Atteridgeville was very limited – she had hardly ever left the township and had only worked in schools within it.

'My experience of visitors to the school was that they came to judge us,' said Jane. 'I was worried that if Bob found things wrong and spoke about them, then, with his high profile, I would get in trouble with the department and there would be consequences for me and the school.'

Jane was, however, pleasantly surprised when she started to interact with Bob. 'From the first meeting, Bob and I connected. He told me that leadership is changing the future so we are all leaders, that we are all important, and he reminded me that I have a job to do.

'He wasn't judgemental. We were equals. He was prepared to listen to me and he clearly had an interest in education. I found that I could be myself with him. I could speak to him about everything and use him as a sounding board. It was all so different to my relationship with the educational authorities.'

When it came to the education department, Jane was expected to deliver their priorities, she said. 'There were expectations imposed on me and I had no say in them. With Bob it wasn't like that at all. There were no expectations at all. It was a two-way street with both of us listening to each other and learning all the time. It was a total partnership, not just about the work, but it was clear that the objective was to make me a better leader.'

If Jane could lead effectively, then the school would improve, they believed. And it did. When she became principal in 2009, after serving as acting principal in 2008, the school had nine staff members and an enrolment of 300 learners. Now, there are 34 educators and 1,200 learners.

'My job, I learned through the partnership, is not to manage those teachers and learners; it's to create an environment in which they can produce their best. To bring about improvement, you have to develop their skills, and that happens best in relationships where there is no fear.'

'On the Time to Think course I learned to listen. Through the PfP process, I learned that 'pressure' is not the only way to get things done. Bob often said that the art of diplomacy is letting other people have your way.'

I vividly remember the day that Bob and Jane attended Flawless Consulting together. The workshop was delivered at a training venue in Midrand, and Francois (the LPF) spent about forty minutes on the phone with Jane to guide her to the venue. This was the first time that she had travelled on her own out of Atteridgeville and it was a big deal for her to make it to Midrand. I sensed that Jane had crossed a boundary that day and remember saying to Francois that we need to remain aware of the significance of moments like this. Little did I realise that over the next few years Jane would become one of the most well-travelled people I know!

During the first year of Bob and Jane's partnership, I often stayed in Pretoria with Bob and his wife Mary. It was clear that Bob loved the experience of stepping outside of the corporate environment into Atteridgeville. Jane was clearly starting to feel like family rather than 'just' a partner on a leadership programme.

One of my favourite stories about Bob and Jane is about Bob arriving at the school for a meeting with Jane. Just as he stopped at the school Bob's phone rang; it was Finance Minister Pravin Gordhan's secretary. The minister needed to see Bob urgently, and his secretary wanted to know when Bob would be able to meet with him. Bob told her that he had an urgent appointment and would be able to meet Minister Gordhan in a few hours' time. When he saw Jane, Bob said: 'I'm sorry Jane. I can't stay as long as I had hoped to. Minister Gordhan wants to see me, but I told him I have a more important meeting and that I will see him afterwards.' Hearing Bob and Jane tell the story on more than one occasion has always reinforced my sense that this was another defining moment for Jane. For Bob, Jane Tsharane was more important than Minister Pravin Gordhan because he had made a commitment to meet with her.

Another favourite story is about Bob and Jane co-teaching an Economic and Management Science (EMS) class for Grade 7s. Jane gave Bob a copy of the learners' EMS handbook and he started to study it so he would know what to talk about with them. Then, he saw the following statement: 'You have to choose whether to work in the formal or informal sectors. The positive thing about the informal sector is that you don't have to pay tax.' It was an interesting experience for the CFO of SARS to read that in a Grade 7 handbook!

Bob's wife Mary is a researcher. So, when Bob wanted to understand why parents were not involved at the school he asked Mary and her team to do some research. The incentive for parents to participate in the research was that their names would go into a lucky draw and the winner would get an opportunity to fly over Atteridgeville in a plane belonging to Bob's friend, Pieter Senekal. Getting into Pieter's plane and then flying over Atteridgeville was a life-changing experience for a few of the families in the Makgatho Primary School community.

It has always been always a pleasure to see Bob and Jane together. It's clear that they enjoy each other's company and have loved the experience of being in partnership. I asked Jane to think back to who she was in 2013, before she met Bob, and to compare that person to who she was in 2015 after working with Bob.

'I had learned that it is OK not to do everything in one day,' she said. 'I realised that you need other people to help you achieve things and for that to happen you have to create a healthy working environment.

'I had learned to contract with myself. To achieve things within timeframes, and I set those timeframes for myself. That's something I learned from Bob's example. We kept lists of things we would do and were always clear on who, what and when.'

By 2015, Jane believes, she had begun to understand the value of teacher development and how to best do it. Her partnership with Bob had shown her the importance of building good relationships and that things can be achieved when you do. 'Teacher development is not just about the curriculum and performance in the classroom. It's about the whole person.'

As a result of Jane's leadership, Makgatho has become a school at the centre of the community. 'In the early days, we had little interaction with the people who live around us. Now they look up to us and come here with their requests and queries,' she explained. 'The community has become the eyes and ears of the school. If something happens at the school when there's no one around, they tell us about it. They keep us informed of any activities that are happening in the area. It's an atmosphere of trust and care.'

The level of parental involvement has increased greatly. Jane explained that parent meetings used to be held on Sundays, in accordance with departmental policy, and the turnout was usually low. 'Bob asked me how well I knew my parents,' Jane remembers, 'and the answer was "not very well at all". He organised a survey of the parent body, looking at how they found the school. The feedback of that survey led to a number of changes in the way we ran the school. One response was unhappiness with the way we scheduled things without consulting them, and, as a result, the parents' meetings were changed to Tuesday evenings. Their involvement in that decision led to greater commitment from the parents and the numbers attending those meetings increased rapidly.'

One of the things Jane learned from Bob was the importance of selling her vision to everyone. 'It began with us, then we went to the SMT, the teachers, the SGB and the learners. Through the teachers and learners, we communicated the vision to the parents and the community. Bob would meet everyone, but it was always in support of what I was doing. We also did staff incentives and talks together – including teaching – although Bob said he learned he could lecture but not teach,' she chuckled.

When she took over as principal in 2008, Makgatho Primary was classified as a nonperforming school. By 2014 they were in the top five in Tshwane, according to the

ANA results and were the top township school in the city. Now, Jane says, they are in the top five performers in the common evaluation results every year, and their averages are in the 90s.

'We reflect on our results continually and re-arrange things if necessary. We are doing well, but we don't accept things the way they are, we are committed to continual excellence. Parents want their children to attend Makgatho Primary. The school's brand is strong. It is seen as the school of choice in this community,' says Jane.

I have always seen Bob and Jane's partnership as special, and it was heart-warming to listen to Jane talk with such warmth and joy so many years after her introduction to Bob.

I asked her why she thought their relationship had become so strong and the PfP experience had worked so well for her and Bob. 'We had the right personalities,' she said. 'We both care, and we have a passion for education. We both talk a lot, so the structure of the programme and the Time to Think course helped us to listen to each other. Being part of the leadership circle helped as it kept us on track in the first year. Our Learning Process Facilitator also helped us to become a true partnership.

'This was all possible because Bob was genuinely interested in me. He was my sounding board. I could talk to him about everything. He gave me wings to fly.'

Working with a leader who operates at Bob's level was also important. 'He is a strategic thinker,' said Jane, 'he wants delivery, but he takes people along with him. Bob taught me that there is a difference between having a vision and the vision having you. I am still applying this.'

Bob also believed that exposure to the outside world would make Jane a better principal. He must have brought over 200 people to see the school, and that changed their perceptions about education in the townships, but he also arranged for her to travel to various events and places. 'He believes principals need to be elevated to the level where they belong. Quality exposure makes you take yourself seriously. You will pass what you experience on to the teachers, and they will talk to the learners about a wider world out there. The message is that "this is where we want our learners to go".'

The school is a very different place now. It has a well-stocked library because of Bob's efforts. His mother, who was 90 years old in 2019, has been collecting books for the school from the moment Bob got involved there. The library is managed by volunteer gap-year students from Germany, and the children are reading.

Teaching processes are benefitting from functional technology, and the school has been getting quite a lot of publicity. Makgatho has become the school of choice in Atteridgeville, with only 10% of its learners living in the school's immediate surroundings and the rest being bussed in from informal settlements, some quite far away.

The school is still benefitting from the ripple effects of Bob's involvement. Pieter Senekal, who offered flights over Atteridgeville as an incentive, is still actively involved at the school. He does career expos for the Grade 7s and recently arranged flights for children who want to become pilots. He arranged a manicure and pedicure for 40 young girls to expose them to entrepreneurship opportunities in the beauty industry.

In 2018 the school won an award in the National School Nutrition Programme Awards hosted by the DBE.

Jane's personal brand is growing all the time, and in 2019 she received a National Teachers Award for excellence in primary school leadership. She has been travelling the world and has come a long way from an uncertain principal who had never left the township.

And Bob and Jane have become life-long friends. Bob now lives in the UK, but he visits South Africa regularly, and when he does he always goes to the school. His friends know about his involvement in Makgatho Primary and send money to the school for stationery and food for the children.

Reflections

Having listened to the stories of these three partnerships, I am both humbled and frustrated.

It is impossible to listen to Lindelani, Lizzie and Jane without being inspired by the impact of the PfP process on their lives and by what is possible as a result of these kinds of cross-sector partnerships. And yet, when I tell these stories to external evaluators, they tend to dismiss them as 'anecdotes' as if to say 'anecdotes have no value'.

So how are we to think about the value and impact of PfP?

In my mind all three stories exemplify what we have been trying to achieve with PfP and why we started PfP:

1. **We were committed to reducing inequality**
   In all three cases, the schools are better off because of PfP than they would have been without PfP. The schools are better led and managed than before, and the children in them have more opportunities. Educators are more

energized and parents are more engaged. All the research shows that these are the enablers for improved education outcomes and, even though it took a few years, results are improving at these schools.

This ultimately means that we are reducing inequality. The children in these three schools receive the kind of education that I want for all our children.

2. **We wanted to strengthen the fabric of our society**
In each of these three partnerships, new relationships were formed, crossing traditional boundaries of race, geography, ethnicity, language, religion and gender. Leaders got to know each other as passionate and caring citizens who are committed to a better future for all our children. They developed life-long friendships with people they would not have met if they were not part of PfP.

3. **We wanted to mobilise the business community to contribute their gifts to education**
All three of these principals benefitted from being in partnership with a business leader. Their worlds expanded, and they gained something from the realm of business. I have always believed that the world's intractable problems will be addressed by cross-sector collaboration, and these three stories have strengthened this belief.

4. **We wanted to strengthen leadership capacity in our public sector**
It is clear from Lindelani, Lizzie and Jane's stories that they are better principals as a result of their PfP experience. They are more empowered and equipped than before to lead their schools. The educators and learners in their schools benefit from the fact that they are more skilled, confident and energized. All three of these principals have been able to lead a change process, and their schools function better because of their leadership.

> *"You can do what I cannot do. I can do what you cannot do.*
> *Together we can do great things."* – Mother Teresa

Chapter 4

Where it all started – Kannemeyer Primary School

"Relationships are based on four principles: respect, understanding, acceptance and appreciation." – Mahatma Gandhi

The legacy of the apartheid education framework, which was intentionally designed to provide an inferior education for black people in South Africa, still runs deep in the country's education system. Kannemeyer Primary School (KPS), which opened 1961 in the Grassy Park area of the Cape Flats, was built for coloured children and was therefore not set up to be a top-class learning institution.

The National Party won the South African general election of 1948 and, once in power, it quickly began enacting legislation aimed at enforcing its grand plans for an apartheid state.

Among the laws introduced was the Bantu Education Act of 1953. It was based on the principle that the education of black children should be inferior to that of white children. The ideology behind it was that black children should grow up to be manual and menial labourers, in service of an economy that was owned and controlled by the white minority.

At the time, there were quite a number of church-controlled missionary schools that were providing education to black children, with some financial aid from the state. In 1954 they were effectively abolished, which meant that government became the sole funders of education and was now able to introduce a racially discriminatory curriculum administered by a new Department of Bantu Education.

The objective of Bantu Education was to teach African learners to be subservient workers whose labour benefitted the white-run economy and society. Unequal provision of resources became the rule, with schools catering for white children receiving the bulk of the state's funding. So, apart from the intentionally inferior curriculum, the physical structures erected for black schools were of a low quality, and the funding for their maintenance was minimal.

Apartheid deliberately and systematically denied education to the majority of people in South Africa. Whites were ensured a better quality education than blacks, with black students receiving roughly a fifth of the funding spent on their white peers. The act imposed draconian restrictions on schools, teachers and the entire educational system available to black, coloured and Indian people who made up the majority of the population'.[17]

The educational disparities created by the Bantu Education Act were so massive that white children received a compulsory and free quality of education comparable to Western countries while black, coloured and Indian schools lacked basic necessities such as electricity and plumbing and school was not mandatory or free.

At the same time, there was a paternalistic element to Bantu education, with the development of black people seen as the responsibility of their white superiors. They needed guidance and supervision and that, inevitably, generated a limited life view and sense of inferiority, which was exactly the intention.

Bantu Education formally ended after 44 years with the introduction of the South African Schools Act of 1996. This was preceded by the National Education Policy Act of 1996, which set out the framework for the establishment of a single national department of education.

KPS faced the same challenges as its neighbouring schools: it was inadequately resourced and catered for only basic educational needs. The school could accurately have been described as 'dysfunctional'.

KPS was an institution that faced curriculum-related challenges on a daily basis. The education authorities and the educators at the school struggled to establish functional school systems that would achieve good academic outcomes. Graduates from KPS, and many other primary schools, proceeded to secondary school without the foundational skills to succeed.

The abolition of apartheid education in 1996 didn't change much at ground level in schools like KPS, and when Ridwan Samodien was appointed principal in 1990 he found himself in charge of an institution that, in his own words 'was not doing well'.

Like many other marginalised schools, KPS was floundering as it confronted an avalanche of policy and curriculum changes and different instructions as the DBE transitioned into a more democratic status. Every year it seemed that teachers had to learn, unlearn and relearn new policy prescripts. From implementing Outcome-Based Education (OBE) and Curriculum 2005, they switched to the National Curriculum Statement (NCS), and then to the Revised National Curriculum Statement (RNC) and, finally, to the current Curriculum Assessment Policy Statement (CAPS).

---

17   Collins, M. (2015). *Partners for Possibility: How business leaders and principals are igniting radical change in South African schools*. Randburg: Knowres Publishing, p9.

Amidst all these changes, the Western Cape Education Department (WCED) introduced its systemic evaluation in Grades 3 and 6, and the DBE brought in the countrywide Annual National Assessments (ANAs).

Ridwan faced an unhappy SMT, disengaged educators, discipline problems, poor academic performance by learners and a lack of parental support. Teachers were playing the blame game and criticising Ridwan for the miserable state the school found itself in. With a mountain of problems on his plate, Ridwan knew that he needed to find a way to turn things around.

'We were plagued by the things that affect schools of our kind: teacher and learner absenteeism, discipline problems, lack of parental interest and poor performance. The challenges were big, and there was little appetite from the staff to tackle them. I soon found myself slipping into despair.'

The principal, according to teachers who were there at the time, wasn't doing anything to help matters. Arnola Ross, now the deputy principal at KPS, says that when she first arrived there, the school was an unhappy, inefficient place.

'There were internal power struggles going on,' she said, 'and like so many other schools in the area, it was also the site for external political struggles.'

Ridwan, by nature a quiet, reserved person, found himself out of his depth, Arnola said. 'Things were not in place, and Ridwan wasn't confident in his decision-making. He was hesitant and couldn't implement his vision for the school.'

Ridwan soon became despondent. 'I couldn't get through to the staff and my ideas were not being implemented,' he said. 'I felt very alone and wasn't getting much support from the Western Cape Department of Education.'

The staff were not happy with Ridwan, and a number of complaints about how he was treating them had been lodged. It was particularly telling that none of the teachers on the staff at the time were prepared to send their own children to KPS.

'I was an art teacher who had been taken out of the classroom and I missed teaching. I realised that I genuinely did not know how to lead this organisation,' Ridwan recalls. 'I was out of my depth and desperately looking for solutions.

'I felt that everyone else was to blame for my unhappiness and was unable to take responsibility for the things that were going wrong. I felt myself ready to throw in the towel.'

This was the environment that I encountered when I first met Ridwan. I had been looking for a principal who would be willing to partner with me to test the idea that business leaders and school principals could work together in co-learning and co-action partnerships to strengthen leadership capacity and mobilise support for schools. My first visit to the school was in April 2010. It was a moment that would change the trajectory of my life.

Ridwan had said yes to the idea of a partnership, but he wasn't quite sure what he had agreed to. Neither was I. We had both been introduced to Peter Block and heard him talk about the idea of 'school at the centre of community'. This resonated with each of us, so at least we had that in common.

My offer to Ridwan was that I wanted to work with him to figure out a way to mobilise more support for the school. I asked him to allow me to be his partner in this endeavour, and he was keen.

At the time, we had no idea that we were piloting an idea that would reach thousands of people across the country. We did not think of ourselves as the first Partnership for Possibility, but that is essentially what we were.

On that first visit to the school, I was introduced to Davril Harmse, one of the foundation phase teachers. She was complaining about the forthcoming six-week-long winter school holiday (it was 2010 and schools were due to be closed for the period of the soccer World Cup) and that it would affect learners' performance in the provincial systemic tests they would write shortly after returning to school.

When I asked Davril what role the parents could play in helping during the holidays, she rolled her eyes and told me that parents in their community were not interested in their children's education; only in the well-resourced communities did parents support their children. I asked Ridwan if that was true and he confirmed it.

I have always believed that the way to change perceptions is to change the story that is told about a situation and that if you change the way people talk about a situation, then real change will follow from that. And in the case of Grassy Park, and many other low-income areas in South Africa, the dominant story told is that parents in disadvantaged communities do not get involved in the schools that their children attend.

I realised that we would need to be very practical, so I asked Ridwan if there was a particular issue they were grappling with. He told me that poor discipline in the Grade 4 classes was a big problem. He also said that he and the educators had run out of ideas for resolving it. They realised that they needed to get parents involved but didn't know how to persuade them to show up for a meeting to discuss the issue.

I asked what they would usually do when they wanted parents to attend a meeting. Ridwan said he would write a letter to the parents to tell them about a parents' meeting and send the letter home with the children. I wanted to know how many parents would then typically attend. He said 'maybe three or four parents'. We clearly needed to find a way to get more parents to the school; but I also did not know how to do that. So I suggested that we meet with the Grade 4s.

A few days later, Ridwan and I had a 'meeting' with the Grade 4s. I remember the two of us seated on small chairs at the front of the class with all the Grade 4s sitting on the floor around us. I asked them what they wanted to be one day, and they responded enthusiastically: 'I want to be a teacher one day,' 'Miss, I want to be a policeman,' 'I want to be a doctor.' One after the other, the children told us about their dreams and aspirations.

I asked the class if they would need to pass Grade 4 to be able to achieve their dreams. 'Yes Miss. We must pass Grade 4,' they told me. And then I asked if they thought this going to happen, given the way things were going in the class. 'No Miss. We aren't going to pass Grade 4. There are too many naughty children in the class Miss.' This was a great opening for what we wanted to achieve, so I asked: 'Do you think your parents would be able to help with this?' They were quick to answer 'Yes Miss. Our parents should come to the school for a meeting about this.'

I asked them how we could make that happen. I said that Mr Samodien had told me that it won't work to just send a letter to their parents because he's tried that many times and they usually don't come. After a while, one of the students made a suggestion: 'Miss, *we* should ask them to come to the meeting because when *we* ask our parents to do something they do it.'

We agreed on a date and time for the meeting and arranged for the learners to make invitation cards for their parents. We said that every learner who managed to get at least one adult to the meeting could have a 'civvie day'[18].

The next challenge was to get the Grade 4 teachers to agree to attend a meeting in the evening. They were very cynical and did not for a moment expect to see any parents show up.

Sixty parents and caregivers surprised them by turning up, and the teachers had a very productive conversation with these adults. This was the best-attended parents' meeting ever at the school, and it meant that the story about parents not being interested could no longer be told as the 'truth'.

---

18 Civvie Day: Learners are allowed to wear their normal clothes rather than school uniform.

In July 2010, we decided to host a 'Madiba Day' event at KPS. We wanted to bring parents and people from the surrounding community into the school. Ridwan and a pupil's grandmother walked the streets of Grassy Park handing out invitations to community members and to the owners of local businesses. The media were invited to attend, as were officials from the education department.

Because there wasn't a hall at the school, Ridwan and his team erected a blue and white marquee tent early on the morning of 17 July 2010. Over 100 people turned out to what would be the school's first Madiba Day event. Following the methodology we had learned from Peter Block, Ridwan and I facilitated a process in which we invited everyone to engage in conversations in small groups of 3-5 people – with a teacher, a learner and a parent in each group. By the end of it, the parents had held heart-to-heart conversations with the teachers and the principal. For many of them, this had been their first opportunity to do that.

The event also gave Ridwan and his team the opportunity to make parents and other community members aware of some of the school's needs. As a result, in the following days and weeks, the school received several donations and offers of help from members of the community. Some gave material items, while others offered their time and services.

That initial gathering was significant because it was the first step towards making parents and community members aware of the value of their role in the school. In the past, they had felt excluded and didn't think their participation was needed or wanted. Now though, parents realised that they needed to be involved in the education of their children.

Fast forward nine years and KPS has become the school of choice for parents in Grassy Park.

It's a success story in a South African community where success stories are rare. The school has a brand spanking new hall, a fully functional library and several specialised classrooms, including science and ICT labs, where effective teaching and learning are possible. The teaching staff are happy and motivated, and members of the parent body are interested and involved in the schooling of their children. Importantly, the teachers are now choosing to enrol their own children at KPS because it has become their school of choice.

KPS is a school at the centre of its community. During the Western Cape's water crisis of 2017/8, neighbours sent bottles of grey water[19] to the school to help keep its fields and gardens green.

The school, in turn, serves the community by making its facilities available for gatherings and events, and several community members work at the school; some on a voluntary basis but others as paid auxiliary staff members who assist the teachers in a variety of ways.

It wasn't that way in 2010 when I first went there. KPS used to be a school where children were sent because there was nowhere else to go. Now parents in the area are clamouring for admission. In the WCED's systemic tests – the only external academic assessment measures still happening in primary schools anywhere in the country – there has been a steady improvement over the years, and the most recent results show an average of 80% in both English and maths. This is way above the average for the province.

KPS is now a safe place for parents to send their children to each day, which isn't always the case at most schools on the Cape Flats. Drugs and gangsterism frequently rear their ugly heads at other schools in the area, and many have become sites of political contestation and are adversely affected by assertive union interference. KPS has risen above all of that.

While there have been many measurable improvements at the school, the most significant changes are those that the partnership brought about in Ridwan. He recently described his change journey in an essay about his experience as a Partner for Possibility.

> *Louise van Rhyn gave me an A when she first met me, in the sense that Ben Zander, as he explained in his book **The Art of Possibility**, gave his students As at the beginning of their studies. Then she enrolled me, gently nudging me to step into deserving that A.*
>
> *I have always thought of myself as a product of what was formerly 'gutter education'. I was very aware that I am the descendant of forefathers who had suffered the debilitating and brutalising effects of colonialism, slavery and apartheid. I was suffering from a poor self-esteem, lacked confidence and was overwhelmed by being the principal of an under-resourced school.*

---

19 Grey water is relatively clean waste water from baths, sinks and washing machines and it is now commonly used on gardens in the Western Cape to conserve fresh water.

According to Prof Brian O'Connell, being the principal of a former disadvantaged/ under-resourced school is one of the most challenging jobs in the country.

I was acutely aware that I was failing in my task and desperately seeking answers to turn the school around. I was in dire need of skills to build and inspire a demoralised team. I was trying to rally and shift a disinterested, disengaged parent body and community to become co-travellers on the journey and to get them to buy into a new paradigm; of taking responsibility and to share a 50:50 partnership in the process of educating all our kids. This later became a reality as a result of me being able to contract with people, a skill I gained from my Flawless Consulting process.

Apart from the other interventions – Time to Think and Community Building – Flawless Consulting is the one that enabled a life-changing 'Ah ha' moment for me, and the one intervention that galvanised my belief that I am worth the A my partner had given me.

Reflecting on that memorable, life-changing moment, I clearly remember listening to Louise, who happened to be the facilitator on the day, say that we were all going to be filmed having a very difficult conversation with somebody. The purpose of the exercise was to see yourself on video, ignoring all the negative voices in your head and to only look for or celebrate the positives. Those were the gems you were to unearth.

Being camera shy, and for years having escaped the camera or the lime light, I nervously went to Louise and informed her that I had met with an emergency, and that I had to leave.

Louise recognised that I wanted to chicken out and make a quick getaway. She put her hand on my shoulder, saying in a very reassuring voice, 'Ridwan, you are going to do this'. I resigned myself to my fate and braced myself for what I perceived was going to be a nightmarish experience.

We were five in the group, each getting a turn in front of the camera. Unfortunately, I don't remember the other participants, except Veronica Wantenaar, who at the time was my coach – a gift Louise granted me after I had earlier, directed such a request to her.

Veronica, who epitomises calmness and reassurance, was by my side, her demeanour and persona creating that space for me to have a greater sense of ease. When it was finally my turn, I stepped up, spoke my piece, and nervously waited for the playback and feedback. I was a ball of nerves, sweaty palms, lump in my throat, dry lips and wide eyes glued to the screen. I was struck by what I saw, not this shy timid person, the voice in my head kept telling me, but an amazing flower slowly opening, unfolding and reaching full bloom, like a glorious, radiating sunflower, spreading its light to all in its presence.

While my colleagues were giving feedback, I was caught up in the moment, wallowing in self-glory and a new-found self-esteem. After listening to all their comments it was finally my turn to reflect on what I had observed.

President Nelson Mandela's famous words were ringing in my head, in my ears and pounding my heart: 'You are powerful beyond imagination'. They resonated with me and in me that glorious, wonderful day. My heart was smiling with excitement and joy. A deep sense of relief entered my being. I had finally found my voice, a greater self-belief and a firm conviction that at last, I was able and blessed with the knowledge that I can put the negative voices in my head, to bed.

That moment changed my life forever. I now step into any public space, when called upon to do so, with Mandela's beautiful words ringing in my head, not as a sign of arrogance, but as a confidence booster to shut down the negative voices fighting violently to resurface and quell my confidence. I now confidently step into leadership, no matter how many people are seated and offer my voice as I believe I have a purpose, a contribution and a duty to all South Africa's children to speak on their behalf and to be a guardian of their future and a beacon of hope for all who enter my space.

I shall forever be grateful to Louise and Peter Block's **Flawless Consulting** for affording me this wonderful opportunity of self-discovery, confidence boosting and for healing me from my brutalised past and granting me an opportunity to finally shed the remnants of gutter education that was still part of my baggage. It is this self-belief that assisted me in tackling the many thorny issues at school and the Kannemeyer Community.

Today, because I have changed, we have a team of educators which has stepped out of despair and hopelessness and moved towards greater 'organisational health'. This as a result of me, being given an A and being able to reciprocate and give my team and our parents an A, in return. This has brought about the wonderful changes we have witnessed. My growth is inter-woven and inextricably linked to the growth experienced at Kannemeyer. As I have grown, so have I seen the growth at our beloved Kannemeyer and today can marvel at a school being 'Alive with Possibility'.

I have since been on many radio programmes, on national television, and I've been interviewed by a variety of NGOs to share my view and wisdom, and I am often asked to be the keynote speaker at events. Those are among the many beautiful accolades being bestowed upon me since I have found my voice. In my view this is a direct result of what I experienced at the Flawless Consulting session, the contribution of my partner Louise, and the inspiring PfP programme.

The following fabulous four, inspiring and most generous comments stand out.

One from my Life Coach Veronica, who once said to me... 'Ridwan you were reticent, but now you are bundle of energy'.

*Secondly Adi, who in my view conducted the most challenging, yet most rewarding interview with me for the video made for the **WISE Awards**, called me 'Mr Public Speaker'.*

Thirdly, Mrs Chotia, my Circuit Manager who, after requesting me to deliver a vote of thanks, said 'Thank you Mr Samodien, your beautiful personality lights up any event that you are part of. Your staff are truly blessed to have you as a leader!'

And finally from our IT teacher, Denise Beukes who, upon reflecting on my journey, said: 'Sir, it is so remarkable to see a person who at first was struggling, crawling along, straighten his back, and grow into this fabulous, flamboyant flamingo.'

In 2019, things are much changed at KPS. 'I believe the school is operating properly now because I am operating properly,' Ridwan said. 'I am much more open. I communicate far better, and that has led to more engagement from the teachers and an all-round improvement. There is far less tension and insincerity in the school now.'

Arnola puts the turnaround at the school down to changes in Ridwan. 'Things began to improve when Ridwan regained his confidence. His management style changed and he was transformed from a shy, unconfident and non-effective leader into a master networker and promoter of the school.'

'Clearly, he had learned new things about leadership and about school management, and he was keen to pass that on to everyone at the school – the SGB, management team and the teachers. He began to create space for all of us to become leaders and that made the real difference.'

'I can see the light now,' Ridwan said. 'Whereas I was ready to despair, seeing no hope that things could improve, I began to see that we can change things. By rediscovering my passion and care for the community, I was able to defeat some of the devils that were destroying education and my school.' In the context of the dysfunctional educational milieu in the country, the change in Ridwan Samodien and the turnaround of KPS qualify are minor miracles.

Given the decades of systematic neglect that KPS, and the community it is located in, had suffered and remembering that the inferior treatment was intentional and carefully planned, it was always obvious that things were never going to change on their own. Ridwan's willingness to partner with me got the ball rolling and, as the PfP model was refined in subsequent years, the situation at the school improved.

In the beginning, Ridwan and I were so committed to the idea that the school could be the centre of the community that we made the mistake of not doing enough to get the buy-in of the staff and SMT. So in 2011, we changed course and began to focus internally. We started by facilitating a full day of team development with the entire staff body. At this meeting, Denise Beukes, the IT teacher, came up with this vision statement: 'Kannemeyer Primary School should become the school of choice for the Grassy Park community.' This was significant because it became a rallying cry and created a sense of ownership.

'I had attended other principal development training courses,' Ridwan said. 'The difference here is that this was about personal connection. Louise was saying 'I am here, and I am interested'. That rubbed off on me and onto the school community. We were creating shining eyes, that's what I always wanted to do.'

At the same time, however, Ridwan insists that he wasn't 'fixed' through being part of the programme. 'That was never the intention. From the beginning, I insisted that I didn't want to be fixed. We were also not expecting to be given money to solve our problems. What Louise did was to show me the possibilities. She taught me that the quality of your thinking is going to impact on the quality of your actions. When I became more open and transparent towards the staff, our relationships changed, the school became a healthier organisation, and the quality of teaching in the school improved.'

Involving the community was a priority from the beginning, and many community members have become engaged at the school. 'We invited them to supervise substitute classes, to run our feeding scheme and do some work in the library,' Ridwan explains.

'Our results in the Western Cape Education Department's systemic tests have improved steadily over the years,' he said. But it's about more than just results. 'We wanted KPS to be the school of choice in the area, and there are signs that we are becoming that. Those decisions are made on the perception that the community holds of the school as a whole.'

Most importantly, Ridwan said, he was plucked out of despair. 'The poor education system is bedevilling South Africa,' he said, 'and our political leadership is losing its way. If a programme like Partners for Possibility can lift school principals out of the despair they are experiencing because of not being able to do anything to improve things, then those principals can, though their influence in the community, provide hope and things can begin to improve.'

Reflections

Being Ridwan's partner has changed my life. We have become life-long friends, and I often think that I have definitely benefitted more from our partnership than he has. Our partnership has shown us what is possible when ordinary people connect across traditional boundaries and commit to sharing their knowledge and skills with a spirit of generosity. I love listening to Ridwan talk about his and our nine-year journey because his words remind me that I can be a contribution simply by showing up – with an open heart, open mind and open will. Being Ridwan's partner and supporting him in his role as change leader at KPS has been one of the most rewarding and humbling experiences of my life.

Ridwan has been cultivating a strong sense of community at the school. Educators love working there, and parents and other community members feel wanted and welcome as partners. KPS regularly hosts volunteers from other countries to work at the school for one or more terms, and these supporters are usually very emotional when they leave as they recognise what a special experience it was for them to be part of the KPS community.

From one who was too shy to speak, Ridwan has become an orator of note. He is regularly invited to be the keynote speaker at events and routinely gets wonderful feedback from those present, many of whom say they were inspired by what he had to say. We often arrange visits to the school, and guests always leave feeling inspired and fired up to lead change in their own arenas. In my mind, Ridwan has become the kind of principal that we desperately need in all our schools.

Ridwan is approaching retirement and has recently been accredited as a Time to Think facilitator. He is on the board of SSA now, and we are hoping that he may join the PfP team as an LPF and member of the leadership team and also as a facilitator of Time to Think when he steps down as principal.

Chapter 5

Simbithi: At the heart of the Community

"We need our neighbors and community to stay healthy, produce jobs, raise our children, and care for those on the margin."
– Peter Block

PfP's leadership circles in the North Coast region of KwaZulu-Natal are, in many ways, quite remarkable.

So far, three groups of leaders have completed the one-year programme in three leadership circles. The fourth kicked off in late 2019. Each of these circles has been led by LPF Terry Dearling, a dynamic force of nature who has been the catalyst in an ongoing series of success stories.

Terry's involvement is one constant in these stories. The other is Simbithi, the eco-estate where Terry lives. Six of Simbithi's most senior managers have joined the programme as business partners, and more than half of the business leaders in the three circles launched so far either live on the estate or are associated with it. This, of course, means that Simbithi has an intrinsic connection to PfP. Malcolm Samuel, the general manager (GM) of Simbithi often refers to the estate as the 'anchor' of PfP on the North Coast – a position that is fondly held.

Simbithi has become the heartbeat of PfP in the region. The group's commitment to the programme falls under their community social investment (CSI) arm, as part of a uniquely formulated, community-driven strategy that focuses on education and engagement within, and beyond, the boundaries of the estate. Malcolm first learned about the programme at a presentation in Umhlanga organised by Ballito resident Clifton Smithers and his friend Peter Cameron, who were familiar with PfP's success in other parts of the country.

As he listened and began to recognise the programme's potential, a flame was lit in Malcolm's heart, and he knew that he needed to find a way to get Simbithi involved in the programme.

At the time, Malcolm recalls, there was restlessness within the homeowners' association that manages Simbithi (SEEHOA) concerning CSI. Of course, CSI is more commonly known as corporate social investment, but, by nature, SEEHOA is not a textbook example of a 'corporate'. At the very core of what SEEHOA, and its residents, stand for is community.

'At the time, our CSI programme was diverting attention from the core management functions of the organisation. There was no focus. We were doing things, but we didn't really understand what it was we should be doing, and I wondered about the impact we were making,' said Malcolm. 'I was aware of the fact that there were distasteful, largely misconceived, connotations attached to the term 'gated community'. I realised that existing in a bubble, isolated from the communities that surround Simbithi, was not right. I was looking for a way to use our CSI efforts to close the gap that existed, and PfP looked like something that could do that.'

Simbithi Eco-Estate is situated close to Ballito. Alongside the main road that splits the estate in two is the impoverished community of Shakashead. Many, if not most, of its members are employed in either Simbithi, Ballito, Salt Rock or Sheffield Beach. Malcolm's dream was to dismantle the perception of a 'them' and 'us' and to foster deeper engagement and understanding between the residents of Simbithi and those in the neighbouring communities.

'I liked that PfP was not about giving handouts. It was a process with reciprocal benefits: a way in which Simbithi could form partnerships with the communities around us and simultaneously contribute solutions to the serious issues in education. I firmly believe that to effect meaningful change one must begin with education.'

Malcolm was looking for a safe way to form those relationships. 'There are serious political tensions in this area. Rivalries between individuals and groups with differing political agendas are found in most community organisations. Education, I thought, was a safe gateway into the community. Schools had to include everyone, and everyone wanted good education for their children.'

So, through consultation with the Simbithi Board of Directors, it was decided that the estate would sponsor a few PfP partnerships.

At the time of Malcolm's appointment as GM, local newspaper *The North Coast Courier* published a congratulatory article. Malcolm saw this as an opportunity to share his vision about Simbithi becoming the heart of the community. The article was titled 'Taking Down Fences' and mentioned Simbithi's commitment to partner with two local schools.

When Terry Dearling launched her first PfP circle, North Coast 1 (NC1), in January 2017 Malcolm signed up as a business partner and was joined by Simbithi Board Director, Paul Sparks.

'I was partnered with Aleen Maharaj, principal of RA Padayachee Primary School in Shakas Head,' Malcolm explained. 'It was the beginning of a journey that challenged my thinking. Aleen taught me much about what it was to be an 'outsider' needing to break into the circle I was operating in. Our positions were very similar: she is an Indian woman leading a school of mainly Zulu children in a predominantly Zulu-speaking community. I am an Indian man leading a predominantly white organisation in an affluent, mainly white, community.'

The two were appointed to their positions at roughly the same time. 'We both felt we didn't really belong where we were,' Malcolm said. 'We were outsiders and each needed a way to become an insider.'

Terry's leadership and coaching played a big part in the success of their partnership, Malcolm said. 'She challenged me. She stretched my boundaries and asked the right questions. Aleen developed tremendously and is now so much a part of her community that she is invited to the war rooms and to council meetings where the elders of the community make pertinent decisions. She belongs in that community, and that has done wonders for the school.'

Malcolm's involvement convinced him that being a PfP partner would be a fitting developmental experience for members of his senior management team.

'It's a well organised, safe way to get to work in a community, and it is run by special people like Terry.'

Malcolm felt there would be great value in having the leaders in his organisation learning how to encourage high-quality independent thinking. 'We learned on the Time to Think course that the quality of your actions depends on the quality of the thinking you do beforehand. That is a valuable skill for any leader.

'There are some special people living in Simbithi,' Malcolm said, 'and of course Terry has been the 'yeast' in getting many of them involved. We have shared what we do through our own newsletter and local media outlets like the *Courier* and *Radio Life & Style*. So, our community is aware of our involvement and the response has been positive.

'I think we have been changing hearts and some minds. People are more aware of what is going on around us and are beginning to talk about it.'

Churches, well-resourced schools and other organisations in the community have all supported the schools and, again, Malcolm gives Terry the credit for getting them involved.

Simbithi's commitment to partnering with PfP stems largely from its brand: 'Welcome. You're Home,' which is authentically woven into everything the estate does. The partnership with PfP is no different, and the Simbithi Country Club and Fig Tree Restaurant have become the 'home' of PfP North Coast. Meetings and events are held there, and the principals have been welcomed in. 'We don't just invite them to come here; we try to make them feel welcome,' Malcolm said.

One way that Simbithi contributes to the schools is by sharing its expertise. Security is a specialist area for the estate, and it has helped the schools in that regard. The restaurant buys produce from the schools, particularly from North Coast Agricultural College, which supplies eggs and vegetables.

'Many of our staff's children attend the schools we have partnered with,' Malcolm said, 'so it's been a way of demonstrating our commitment to the community to them, and that has paid dividends.'

The people who live at Simbithi have demonstrated a willingness to contribute. There are 15 committees stemming from SEEHOA[20] involving an army of 123 volunteers who undertake various projects on the estate and in the community. 'We have willing hands, and we keep on going; it's important to not let up,' Malcolm said. 'A lot can be accomplished, one activity at a time.'

Four years later, Malcolm believes that much progress has been made. For Simbithi as a whole community involvement is now the norm, rather than an exception. 'The board doesn't question our involvement. I think we have softened people's hearts by exposing them to the need outside our boundaries. PfP has allowed us to contribute in a meaningful and sustainable way. This community now celebrates being South African, and by being a good neighbour to the communities around us, we have established solid relationships. We seem to be less affected by strikes and other political unrest, as people know about our involvement with the schools and children of the area.'

Malcolm would like to see Simbithi's success repeated in other gated communities around the country. 'I think communities like ours are well-suited to this task – to be agents of change – because of the people we have living within our boundaries and their levels of commitment,' he said. 'I would encourage them to use their gifts as many solutions can be found among them. Don't just open your gates to the principals you become involved with, invite them in. And, if at all possible, ensure that your LPF is also a homeowner, that's been the secret to our success!'

---

20 SEEHOA: Simbithi Eco-Estate Homeowners' Association

Chapter 5: Simbithi: At the heart of the Community

We were interested to hear the perspectives of other Simbithi residents and how their involvement in PfP has changed their experience of living in a gated community on the Natal North Coast.

I asked Tony Dearling, Terry's husband, to share his thoughts. 'The Ballito community is recognised as one of the most philanthropic and generous in the country, and Simbithi is part of it. The magic of the Partners for Possibility programme is that it allows Simbithi residents to contribute in so many different ways to an initiative they identify with intellectually, emotionally and spiritually. It is giving of self rather than a financial donation, and in this way it is rewarding, fulfilling, endearing, self-generating and sustainable,' said Tony.

Dysan Parasaraman is the security manager at Simbithi. He was partnered with Thami Mkhize, the principal of Emona Primary, and they were part of the NC3 Circle. Dysan has much to say about the benefits of PfP – for him personally and for the wider community.

'The PfP programme has been an eye-opener for me. There are opportunities and possibilities to produce change and to enrich the minds and lives of our learners, partners, family, educators, community members and friends. It comes down to the choices we make. I can decide to be disappointed in and negative towards the education system in our country, or I can choose to remain positive, be accountable and take responsibility. My amazing journey with PfP has evoked these two questions: Am I part of the problem? What am I doing to find a solution?

'Among the many benefits I have derived from being on the PfP programme is that my personal leadership skills have improved most. A standout point for me was discovering the art of leading through influence rather than authority. Motivating, supporting and being transparent with your team yields success. When you show your staff respect and treat them with dignity, they deliver results. Of course, I credit my peers from my wonderful North Coast 3 Leadership Circle who have inspired a change in my mindset. Because of them, I now focus on what is possible.

'Stepping out of my comfort zone also proved to be difficult at first, but the unwavering support shown by my leadership circle and my principal partner made it easy for me to make that transition.

'I could not have asked for a better partner than Thami. We understand each other and have always maintained an excellent, supportive relationship. Through my exposure to Emona Primary's operations and the roles that the different stakeholders play, I have learned about life in an under-resourced school. My objective is to continue to offer small gifts to my school with the aim of developing and enriching the minds of our learners and the SMT. My journey with Thami will definitely continue. I thoroughly enjoy working with him.

'PfP has inspired me to add more value, to always look at ways to improve service levels and to make an effort to impart my learnings from the programme to my colleagues and staff. By encouraging team members to be positive, respecting their suggestions and building a culture of efficiency in the workplace, I believe that we can do better in education and business.

'I unreservedly endorse the PfP programme. This is an impactful experience for business leaders who want to broaden their strategic perspectives, build collaborative relationships, take initiative and enhance their ability to lead people and lead change simultaneously. It's the simple things in life that matter—appreciation, integrity, empathy, encouragement, support, motivation, trust, positivity and the constant striving to serve as a leader. PfP has been, and continues to be, an inspiration to business leaders and school principals across South Africa.'

In the NC3 circle, there were two business leaders from the Netherlands – Cathalijne and Remco Bol. The couple lived in Simbithi during Remco's four-year stint as Managing Director of Unilever Food Solutions in Durban. Before they left South Africa, Cathalijne and Remco hosted a farewell party for 80 people. About half of the 80 people in the room were involved in PfP, and the others listened for more than 40 minutes while Cathalijne and Remco spoke about their experience of being part of PfP and how that has changed their lives.

Theo and I asked Remco to share a few highlights from his experience: 'At Unilever, we organised and attended inclusivity workshops. At one of these workshops, the facilitator explained to us that if you are not inclusive at home, you cannot be inclusive in the office: it would be fake.

'After four months living in Simbithi, we realised our weekends were only spent with white people who did not know what a 'shisa nyama' was.

'So, Cathalijne and I decided to change this, and we started to organise dinners for young, black Unilever colleagues at our place in Simbithi. Every two months we invited four people, and I prepared the best steak in town: Wagyu Ribeye from Taylor's Meat Company in Ballito. These dinners were a win-win situation: we learned about the struggles of our colleagues, the concept of 'Black Tax,' their views on politics and the future of South Africa. They, in turn, were exposed to life in a place like Simbithi. Furthermore, they received valuable advice from us, with our combined 37 years of experience in Unilever.

'Fast forward two years: we met Terry at a birthday party at one of the dams at Simbithi. I was hooked to her story about PfP; I decided at that moment that we had to be part of this awesome movement. I convinced Unilever to be a sponsor, and Cathalijne and I raised money in Holland from our friends and family.

'From the first introduction meeting until the last dinner, it was a fantastic journey. This journey opened my eyes and made me a more humble and inclusive person. Partners for Possibility brought the 'Real South Africa' through the gates of Simbithi. I strongly believe that many people who live in Simbithi want to contribute to a better South Africa, but they simply don't know how to do this or where to start. PfP is a great way for all these dormant supporters to wake up and get out of their comfort zone and start making impact.'

Remco was partnered with Busi Vilakazi, the principal of Simunye High School. I was privileged to meet Remco and Busi at the NC3 celebration event. During the presentation about their partnership, Busi affectionately referred to Remco as her brother. 'You are my brother because you came into our school, and into my life, and you made things easier for me. I was a newly appointed principal and I was actually clueless. Through the programme I have met experienced principals who were so willing to share their knowledge and expertise. Being on the programme has boosted my ego and has helped me to become more confident. I now feel ready for my job.'

Remco and Busi clearly enjoyed each other's company, and it was a joy to see them together. Remco told the story of the day that learners from Simunye High visited the Unilever offices in Durban. He described this as one of the highlights of their partnership: 'We had an honest conversation with them. We talked about their hopes, their dreams and their struggle. It was a tough conversation. It was difficult to hear all those stories. But, it was good to see the potential and to see that there is hope.'

Cathalijne was partnered with Joseph Taylor from Cottonlands Primary School. We asked her to share a few thoughts about what she had learned from being part of PfP. 'This programme taught me what volatile, uncertain, complex and ambiguous really mean – and how much do I admire the capacity of our school principals to deal with this every single day! It made me realise that 'control' is an illusion, and therefore, how important it is to always keep your mind and the possibilities open. For leaders, this means it requires a deflated ego, a positive outlook on the world we live in, a trust in people, and a solid amount of resilience,' she said.

'Also, it further deepened my belief that the only way to work on a better world and make a positive impact is by empowering every single person who is part of the possibilities. That includes me! Everyone has a gift, and I am responsible to ensure that mine is used. This programme gave me more core strength and a deeper trust in my own capabilities – they are more than good enough! It showed me there are lots of opportunities to make a difference. With the right relationships built, power arises in the room. People connect. Worlds apart and yet so similar. Diverse, but with the same longing to belong and add meaning to our lives. When people connect, things become possible. So look for people who support you, uplift you and have the same open mindset. Let go of people who keep pulling you back, or down.'

Andrew Thompson is a director of the eLan Property Group, one of the companies responsible for developing Simbithi Eco-Estate. Andrew's office is situated at Simbithi Country Club, and he was part of the NC2 Circle.

When Andrew made the decision to get involved in PfP, he asked to be partnered with Mavis Mpanza, the principal of New Guelderland Combined School as eLan was at the time conceptualizing a new development which would eventually house New Guelderland (an under-resourced government school) within the borders of the development.

Andrew loved the experience of working with Mavis. He describes PfP as a 'life-changing experience for my principal, Mavis Mpanza, and myself. It helped me to get a better understanding of the challenges within our schools and that which our educators are experiencing.' When talking to Andrew about his experience more than a year after their celebration event, I was excited to hear that his partnership with Mavis would still bear more fruit.

Mark Taylor, eLan's CEO and Founder, has been working for more than a decade on a blueprint for holistic community development for gated estates and what was happening through PfP at Simbithi resonated with him. Andrew's experience of being part of PfP contributed to the eLan team's thinking, and they have now incorporated some of these ideas into their plans for Blythedale Coastal Estate. A portion of the homeowners' levies will be used to upgrade and support New Guelderland Combined School. eLan's vision is for the school to become a well-resourced school of choice for the Blythedale residents and surrounding community members.

Listening to Andrew talk about the plans for Blythedale and New Guelderland got me very excited because I have seen photographs and a video of the school as it was before Andrew got involved. It was a typically under-resourced rural government school, with run-down infrastructure, poor sanitation facilities and no sports fields. I can only imagine how excited Mavis, her teachers and the children must be about becoming an integral part of Blythedale Coastal Estate!

Karenne Jo Bloomgarden is a Simbithi resident. She moved to South Africa from America in 2007. 'I had some preconceived ideas of living in a gated community,' she said. 'I was disappointed to find out that the population was not very racially integrated. I moved here as an idealistic former American thinking I could actually make a difference. I did, and still am, making a difference, just not how I expected.

'I pre-judged many of the people living in this gated community. I had a full-time job and started my own business in America, which provided the funds for my moving to a gated community. So, I am not at the financial level of comfort that most people living here are and I was jealous, envious and felt left out. Then I joined up with Partners for Possibility. I needed to feel part of a community, family, village to thrive.

'PfP has accepted me and provided support not just for our schools, but also for every individual in the group. For me, the best part has been the acceptance of similarities instead of differences among all the participants. The true emotional sharing at CoP sessions is the greatest gift.'

Frank Bradford is also a Simbithi homeowner. His partner is Principal Merryl Williamson from Stanger Primary, and they were in the NC2 Leadership Circle. Frank has noticed the impact of PfP in his conversations with Simbithi staff: 'The tangible benefits that PfP has extended to the less privileged communities is now well known among Simbithi staff who reside in these communities. The message of this positive work has no doubt got out to the broader communities where these staff members reside. This makes for a more cooperative and friendly relationship between the communities, as opposed to a 'them' and 'us' laager mentality,' says Frank.

We spent two days with Terry at Simbithi and were able to visit some of the schools. We first met Sunjay Bodasing and Marc McClure at North Coast Agricultural College.

North Coast Agricultural College

When Sunjay Bodasing reached the summit of Mount Kilimanjaro, he unfurled four flags: the flag of North Coast Agricultural College, the school where he is the principal; the dragonfly flag of the Simbithi Eco-Estate; the flag of the Linc Foundation and the flag of the Partners for Possibility programme.

The four flags, he told Theo and me, represent the school where he took over as principal in 2017 and the three organisations that have since then accompanied him on his quest to make it a great educational institution.

'We are recognised now as a leader in our community and an educational institution producing the next generation of leaders in agriculture. It wasn't that way when I started out and I wanted, when I reached the highest point on Earth that I have ever occupied, to acknowledge the role that those three bodies played in taking my school to its current height.'

North Coast Agricultural College used to be called Shakaskraal Secondary School. It was an agricultural school back in the apartheid education days but became purely academic in 1995 after the unification of the various education departments. In 2014 the education department began phasing in agricultural subjects again, and by 2018 Sunjay was ready to change the name of the school to North Coast Agricultural College.

'There was the piece of land that was used as a 'farm' in the beginning, but other than that nothing was left of the original school, and I was expected to oversee the transition pretty much from scratch,' Sunjay explained. 'The Departments of Basic Education and Agriculture contributed a lot towards the development of the land and the provision of infrastructure but there were many challenges.'

In 2017 Sunjay joined the PfP programme and was partnered with Marc McClure, the financial manager of Simbithi Eco-Estate.

'I was appointed as principal ahead of other senior staff members who had also applied for the post,' Sunjay said. 'They were still at the school and there was some resentment towards me. I also never got much support from the education department. I had been an acting deputy principal before, but I had no experience in leading a school. There was an induction programme from the department, but no training. The only support they gave was reactive, coming after something had gone wrong.'

The previous principal of the school had interacted with PfP and so, when Sunjay was asked if he was interested in joining, he said 'yes'. 'I knew I needed some personal support, and I was also keen to increase community support for the school,' he said.

The matchup with Marc was done by Terry Dearling, the LPF for the circle. 'I was a bit sceptical at first,' Sunjay said, 'there had been broken promises before, and missed appointments, but my mind was soon put at rest. Marc made me feel comfortable right away. The Time to Think training that we attended together early on helped with that, as did the fact that we were both new in our positions; Marc had only been at Simbithi for three months when we met.'

Sunjay's goal, he remembers, was to improve the economic status of the school and the community it was in, and he immediately realised that Marc could help with that. 'He was a financial expert and he represented a wealthy community. I spotted him as an asset and it did indeed translate into things at the school. I needed personal support as well: we were busy changing into an agricultural school and it wasn't easy.'

It struck Marc immediately that he might not be able to help Sunjay very much. 'He didn't need my help really; he was way more experienced than I was. He was confident and articulate. I thought, however, that he could do with someone to talk to, someone who was not connected with the school and who came from outside of the immediate community with its tensions and political rivalries. That would be my role, that of a thinking partner and that's where I could contribute.'

Simbithi and Shakaskraal are very different places, Sunjay said, but through the partnership he and Marc began to work together to improve things at the school. 'It was motivating, and we started introducing projects.' That is why Simbithi's flag fluttered at the top of Mount Kilimanjaro when Sunjay reached the summit.

Sunjay and Marc's first partnership project was an orchard of 200 fruit trees, supplied by the education department and supported by the Linc Foundation, the social upliftment arm of the Linc Church in neighbouring Salt Rock. It is because Linc contributes to the school in various ways that Sunjay took their flag to the top of Kilimanjaro.

The fruit trees are still small, but the potential is there for them to become a source of income for the school once they begin to bear fruit.

'We also rehabilitated the fields of the old farm with the help of an agricultural expert from the German organisation Senior Experten Service (SES) and have planted vegetables and crops there.'

Next were chickens. 'We are currently raising 1,500 chickens, 500 of which are laying hens,' Sunjay explained. 'The restaurant at Simbithi takes all the eggs, and we sell the chicken to the local community. We can't keep up with the demand,' Sunjay said.

'We also partner with the Linc Foundation in their One Million Strong programme, which is aimed at producing young leaders. They run their programmes at all the PfP partner schools in the area in an attempt to alleviate social ills.'

I asked Sunjay to imagine what it would have been like for him, and for North Coast Agricultural College if he had never met Marc and become part of PfP.

'I think the challenges I faced from senior staff members when I arrived might have got the better of me,' he said. 'It was something I would bring up at our CoP meetings, and the skills we learned on the Time to Think and Flawless Consulting courses certainly also helped. It took two years, but I think my SMT is better now. They are functioning and aligned. It has taken a lot of mine and Marc's focus, but I'd say it's operating at 95% now.'

Then there were the differences that came about through Marc's connections and with the help of Simbithi. 'Marc introduced us to the environmental experts at Simbithi who have helped us with managing the farm. We use ecobricks[21] (collected at the other PfP schools), for example, to prevent erosion and to build terraces in our nursery and vegetable gardens.'

Marc's expertise lies in finance, and he has made a huge difference at the school, Sunjay said. 'His financial and marketing strategies have been invaluable. I have the vision; Marc has made it possible and sound. He has energized my vision.'

Support for the school hasn't stopped with Marc, however. 'The entire PfP structure, led by Terry and the other partnerships in the circle have been behind us. That's how we got the SES expert to come here. He came on a pilot project, initially, but has been back since and will be returning in the new year. It was PfP who sourced him, and he has made a huge difference.'

Mark told us that Sunjay was building community, and this is why so many people and organisations showed up to make a difference at the school.

Sunjay believes he has grown through the partnership. 'Before I entered the programme my network was limited; PfP opened it up. I yearned to be a team player, but I was in a lonely position; that changed through the learning circle and our interactions. My story about white people changed. I never thought they would be prepared to work so hard for schools like ours, yet they have. The developments that have resulted have given me new hope for the public schooling system.

'My story about public education has changed. I realised that I used to stigmatise public education. I did not believe public education could inspire children. I used to encourage people to send their children to private schools. Through my experience with PfP I have realised the important role of public education to build our nation. I have realised that public education can also be excellent education.'

Marc said the partnership brought about changes for him too. 'I have benefitted from Sunjay's excellent communication skills. I have learned to listen and to speak up. I visited areas I normally wouldn't go to. I was taken out of my comfort zone and have learned to embrace discomfort. It has been a journey of personal growth for me. I've learned to embrace different cultures and it's changed the stories I tell myself. My stories of race, education and of South Africa have changed. I am no longer as judgemental as I was before. I am much more open-minded.'

---

21 An ecobrick is an empty plastic bottle that is packed tightly with non-recyclable materials, particularly soft plastic, until it becomes a strong and durable building block.

Chapter 5: Simbithi: At the heart of the Community

I was curious to know what role Terry, the LPF, played in their success. 'She is so committed to community. She made us feel so comfortable. Terry has amazing people skills. I would describe her as a catalyst and igniter. She sparked the flames for us,' said Sunjay.

The matric pass rate at North Coast Agricultural College has been rising steadily; from 53% in 2016 to 87% in 2018. The target for 2019 was 93%, and they are very proud that their pass rate for the agricultural subjects has been 100% for the last few years.

Produce from the farm is sold to the local community, and Simbithi has made a commitment to purchase any that is not sold locally.

We left the school inspired by what is possible through business-education partnerships. It is clear that PfP has been a reciprocal co-learning experience for both Sunjay and Marc, and it is also obvious that Sunjay and the school have benefitted from being part of the PfP community. We feel honoured that the PfP flag was unfurled at the top of Kilimanjaro.

A few weeks after visiting the school, we received a beautiful note from Sunjay:

> *I greet you with humility and love, my respected partners in education.*
>
> *Having successfully summited Uhuru Peak, Mount Kilimanjaro on 27 September 2019 at 8:40, I return with utmost respect and gratitude; the insignia of Partners for Possibility, mounted on 'the' flag.*
>
> **'The Flag'**
> *I am proud to say,*
> *greeted the mountain with pride and confidence,*
> *weathered the storms of the arduous 7 day ascent,*
> *on its journey from Macheme Camp to Shira Cave*
> *past the abominable Lava Tower*
> *through Barranco wall to Karanga Camp*
> *arriving at the infamous Barafu Base Camp.*
>
> *Having endured the slows of lush rainforests,*
> *through the lava-strewn rocky moorlands*
> *to the upper dry reaches of alpine desert and surviving glaciers,*
> *braving temperatures from a chilly 5*
> *to a summit night of sleet and snowfall at -18.*

Defying the odds of fatigue, loose gravel and unstable scree below,
and the endless trail of hikers' lights leading up, up, up
to the star-studded sky of the Milky Way
soon to be greeted by the awakening dawn,
the most fascinating sunrise on Earth.
Embracing its curvature with a brilliant halo of divine light
to set our team of 9 at Stella Point only 700 m away
from the roof of Africa.

If (the flag) had to be like its human accompaniment,
with hearts pounding,
and the altitude sucking out the last kilojoules of energy,
yearning to reach the ultimate destination – Zenith of Africa.

Uhuru welcomed it with perfect calm
displaying its valour with immense respect
and a gesture of modesty
a gentle whisper of prayer
under the weary breath of its bearer.

It deserves no less credit for the value it embraces
and the contribution it makes to our beloved planet.

Behold
A mountain conquered
Symbolically
by a mountain.

Hail **Partners for Possibility!**

Reflections

This story is such a beautiful example of what is possible when business leaders reach out to principals in their local community. It changes the fabric of the entire community.

During our visit, we talked about the possibility of retired farmers in the Simbithi community getting involved at the school to share their knowledge and skills with the teachers and the learners. We talked about a network of 'Friends of North Coast Agricultural College' and I am excited to see how this idea develops.

After our visit to North Coast Agricultural College, we visited Mshwati Memorial Primary School (their story will be told in Chapter 6), and Parkgate Primary (whose story will be told in Chapter 9). We ended our day by spending time with Sam Jooste and visiting Zilungisele Primary.

Sam Jooste and Zilungisele Primary

Before Sam became involved with Zilungisele Primary, she was part of a reading programme at Sizani Combined School in Salt Rock, where she and other adults would read with children once a week. Sam had been introduced to the school's Sizani Stars Reading programme by a friend, Hayley Browne, when she moved to Ballito from the Midlands.

The reading programme awakened something in Sam, and she realised that she wanted to do more. When Hayley told her about Partners for Possibility and the idea of business leaders being partnered with school principals, Sam initially did not think that as a full-time mother and 'trailing wife'[22] she had the necessary skills to partner with a principal. However, Terry helped her to see that she would be an ideal partner, and Sam finally said yes.

Sam was partnered with Sthe Shabalala, the principal of Zilungisele Primary School. She describes the first year of her partnership with Sthe as the best year of her life. 'It changed me completely. My husband says I am a better human being since my involvement with Partners for Possibility. Before I got involved in PfP my story about education was influenced by the media. Through my personal involvement in the programme, I have a far better understanding of the issues around education.'

After establishing her partnership with Sthe, Sam formally joined 'Terry's Angels,' a team that assists Terry with her PfP work. For the NC3 Leadership Circle, Sam took on the role of 'story catcher,' and has joined all of the circle's CoPs and training session to capture stories about their journey. 'The life of a principal of an under-resourced school is very tough. I love the fact that PfP gives principals a lifeline; someone who cares deeply. And, then, the partners get to shine a light on the incredible job they are doing every day.

'At Zilungisele Primary School, a deeply rural school, more than 70% of the 690 learners are orphans. They come to school because it is nicer to be at school than to be at home.'

---

22 The term trailing spouse is used to describe people who follow their life partners to different destinations because of work assignments.

When Sam and Sthe started their partnership, Sthe was the acting principal of the school. 'I later found out that it is unusual for PfP to take on an acting principal,' Sthe said, 'but it was good timing for me. The programme empowered me.

'I will never forget the Time to Think workshop. This was the first time in my life that I was in a close relationship with a white person. I wasn't sure how it was going to be. I was worried that she would be bossy. But I decided to open my heart to her,' said Sthe. 'I was born in this area and I wanted to prove myself. So, when Sam asked me how she could help me, I told that I wanted to make a mark at the school.'

Zilungisele Primary is in Cranbrook, a rural village in the Groutville District near Salt Rock. 'It's a very poor area. Some of our children are heads of families themselves,' Sthe said. 'Although I have since moved away from the area, I felt I had to come back and make a difference to these children. I wanted to show that, despite the poverty, Zilungisele could be a good school, producing competent, literate learners.

'That was my vision. I had lots of ideas, and becoming involved with Sam and PfP was an opportunity to turn that vision into reality. Three years later, we have started doing that.'

We met Sthe in the school's well-equipped library – a refurbished shipping container that Sam had acquired through the Zoë Carss Education Trust – surrounded by evidence of the school's very active reading and literacy programme. 'One of the first things we did was to sign up for the Linc Foundation's Gateway to Reading programme,' Sthe explained. 'It's a phonetic programme, and it had been offered to other schools who turned it down. We were impressed with Linc's commitment to providing this, so we agreed.'

The school's Grade 4s recently undertook a baseline literacy test through the programme and scored an impressive 62%. 'We are expecting an 80% success rate when they have completed the programme,' Sthe said. This impressive baseline test is due to the dedicated teachers, the DEAR time (Drop Everything And Read) and to the fact that the pupils now have access to a fully stocked library.

Sam is very proud of what the partnership has achieved with the library. It was one of the projects that she took the lead on. 'Getting the container donated was just the start of the project as we then had to get in good quality books to fill it. This was done by putting out requests on social media to friends, family and community and in our local newspapers. We also wrote many emails to NGOs and companies requesting books and were very generously assisted by Biblionef and Book Dash. Now that the Zilungisele library is well-stocked, we are able to send books to other PfP schools to grow their libraries. Even if the school does not have a library space, they can have a Book Box in each classroom with a selection of books and magazines for the pupils to read,' Sam explained.

Sam and Sthe told us that they always asked themselves two things when they were planning their projects at the school: 'Does it benefit the pupils?' and 'Is it sustainable?' If they could not say yes to both, then they would not do it.

I was interested in the differences Sthe saw in herself since she joined the programme. 'It's difficult to express in words,' she said. 'These ladies (Sam and Terry) interrupted my life in my darkest moments, when I wanted to cry out. They showed me that there are solutions. They taught me to celebrate our bad days and that it's always too early to say that we don't have answers. Sam has been committed to mobilising resources and we have achieved much.'

On a personal level, Sthe believes that she is now able to say yes or no. 'I can take a stand. I am firm and clear in my decisions. I wasn't always like that. I'm more capable of working with the parents, now. We invite them to become our partners instead of just asking them to come to meetings, and I find I can ask for help now.

'I have been empowered. I was reserved and withdrawn at first. I always tried to be non-confrontational. After attending the training programmes, I began to stand up for myself. That has helped with the tensions in the staff and with the functioning of the SMT and the SGB.

'The Time to Think programme helped a lot. It taught me to slow down amid the rush and to think before I act. That has made me a better principal,' she said.

'It is important,' said Sthe, 'to be a principal who is clear about the direction that she wants to go. Sam helped me with that. PfP are my supporters: they may not have money to give us, but they helped me to work with what I have to get what I need.

'Sam was with me all the way on that journey. There was no bossing around, we planned together and worked together. Without her support, I think it would have been too tough and I may not have been here.'

Sam has been very effective in mobilising resources and support. The school has a well-functioning computer room, although they suffered a recent setback when they were burgled and several machines were stolen. Through PfP, they attracted the services of an expert from the German organisation, SES, mentioned earlier, who helped them set up the computer room and will return early next year. Through the Youth@worK programme, the school now has an intern who works in the library and a volunteer who helps with the computers. A further three interns, who will provide valuable support to the school with sports, literacy and computer studies, have been promised for 2020.

Sam organised for surfing legend and motivational speaker Shaun Tomson to visit the school and inspire the pupils and staff to believe in themselves and to shape their own futures. Based on his best-selling book, *The Code: The Power of I Will,* Shaun encouraged them to write down a number of statements (codes) for their lives, each beginning with 'I will,' to serve as inspirational road-maps for their well-being and development. The learners and staff were mesmerized by the tall surfer, and afterwards Sthe said: 'Our learners need this, and we promise to support them to live their codes.'

Cell C KZN, where Sam's husband used to work, assisted with the painting of the school and installation of sinks, running water and lighting in the kitchen. They also donated a TV, two DVD players, crockery and cutlery and did a book drive for the library. 'We were also able to get our curtains replaced through donations and fundraising. A neighbour of Sam's at Simbithi donated their kitchen cupboards to Zilungisele to upgrade our school kitchen from where we serve our learners two meals a day,' Sthe told us.

'Sam has touched me in many ways,' says Sthe. 'Our initial year is over, but we have kept going. We speak all the time and I know she will support me. My world has been opened up. I can go to Simbithi now and feel welcome there. Our families are friends too. Sam's children have helped out at the school. It's been a wonderful journey.'

It is clear that Sam is touched to hear Sthe talk about the impact of the programme, but I could sense that this was just part of the story. 'She has done more for me than I have done for her,' said Sam. 'Sthe is a real friend. I don't ever have to pretend or act with Sthe. She accepts me fully for who I am. She sees the real me. She has no interest in the façade. I never feel judged by Sthe. She accepts me fully for who I am.'

Thanks to the relationship she has built with Union Tiles, Sthe has had the entire school tiled. The Santa Shoebox project supplied 690 gifts for the learners in 2018, and again in 2019.

Sam continued to work with Sthe and Zilungisele after the facilitated PfP year was over. 'You can't just stop a relationship or friendship. Sthe will always have my full support and friendship, even when she retires,' said Sam. Listening to Sam speak reminded me of my own experience of discovering how liberating it felt to be accepted, warts and all, when I went to Kannemeyer Primary School. It was so healing to not feel I had to dress up to be accepted and appreciated.

'I am constantly in awe of the principals I interact with on PfP as they have probably one of the hardest jobs on the planet. To try and put it into perspective: just imagine a parent, a nurse, a CEO, a CFO, a politician, a human resources officer, a security officer, a secretary and a teacher. Well, combine them, and you have the principal of an under-resourced rural school in KZN. Just stop for a minute and think about it. Every time I have a bad day I think about my principal partner, Sthe Shabalala, and I am motivated to put a smile on my face and keep going,' said Sam.

On the way to the next school, Sam told us a story that touched me on so many levels. 'I like to wear my red top and blue trousers when I go to the school because these are the PfP colours. But, my blue trousers have become a bit faded, so I recently went to Woolworths to buy a new pair. I discovered that it was going to cost R490, and, you know what? I just could not buy it. Do you have any idea how many books I could buy with R490?'

Reflections

For me, this story is a metaphor for what has happened in the lives of so many people in the community in and around the Simbithi Eco-Estate. Their sense of identity has changed. They are no longer 'just' Simbithi residents. They are part of a much larger movement of nation-building. They still meet at the clubhouse for a drink, but they don't talk about hair and make-up. They talk about 'their' schools and what they are planning to do at these schools.

Sam's husband, Dean, has also been impacted by PfP. He says he has been inspired by Sam's involvement in the programme and that it has opened his eyes to the real challenges in education. He has become an advocate and champion for the cause. 'At almost all my social gatherings with different groups of friends and colleagues, I look for opportunities to share what Sam has been doing and how PfP is making a huge difference in South Africa. People are usually shocked at the state of the schools but amazed at the difference being made countrywide. The fact that PfP can, and does, make such an impact gives me hope for South Africa as there are many people doing nothing to give back and not realizing that they have so much to offer and contribute if they just knew about the options available.'

Dean is not only a PfP supporter and advocate; he has also become the chief ecobrick maker on the estate. 'I went to North Coast Agricultural College with Sam to see how they use them, and I have that visual in my head every time I am stuffing another piece of plastic into a bottle. Our garage became an ecobrick warehouse, and we also have bi-weekly collections of ecobricks from one of the local businesses that has influenced their staff to get involved in the ecobricks movement here on the North Coast,' says Dean.

Dean has many stories about how Simbithi residents have become involved in schools in the neighbouring community – from kitchens being donated, to people getting involved in book drives and the furniture that was gifted by a local surfing club. He is excited about what is possible when people share the PfP story as his experience is that it inevitably results in some kind of engagement or donation to one of the schools.

One of the recent stories that touched him was when Sam gave a lift to a domestic worker from Simbithi to Ballito. The two mothers talked about their children. The lady told Sam that her dream was to get her child into North Coast Agricultural College, but that she did not think she would be successful. When Sam said that she knew Sunjay and would be willing to put in a good word for her, the lady could not believe what she heard. She never thought that a Simbithi resident would know anything about a government school in the neighbouring community.

Another Simbithi resident, Kim Blevin, has an interestingly honest take on life in Simbithi as she outlines her experience with PfP: 'The Simbithi Community, as I experience it, is a diverse, middle to upper-income group of people who have chosen to live in a safe, well managed, manicured world, separate and removed from anything that may be different. The general spirit is of living a happy, pristine, easy life; a pretty world inside a pretty bubble. On the upside, the above two points ensure a blissful, high-end social and uncomplicated life. On the downside, we see the toxic effects of a passive and privileged life on both the youth and parents. Dare I say, the devil finds work for idle hands.'

Kim acknowledges the yearning to make a difference, but also the uncertainty about where to begin. 'Enter PfP,' she says, 'a credible and established business that opens this door, offering a number of options: time, money, skills and connections. And then, the magic happens. The practical realities of sharing whatever it is you have to share that may be needed is put into place. It's the realisation of what goes on, on the other side of the N2 freeway. It's a window into the world of the people walking to work who we drive past in our single-occupant, high-end vehicles. It's the awakening to the realities of the different family life that happens. Consider just the 'Children going to and coming home from school' movie that unfolds each day…

'Then, slowly, things start to shift. The staff at the gate, who greet us each by name get noticed – interest is born. Never mind what goes on in our own homes – a simple understanding of the transport logistics facing our staff – of which one day's experience might send a manicured mama running for a double tot of her berried gin! And then, an interesting seed begins to sprout – that of comparison – and this time it is not odious! It is illuminating.'

For Kim, this brings to life the wisdom of Francis of Assisi that reminds us, 'For it is in giving that we receive.' 'And probably, the most powerful aspect of this is the legacy that we (the Simbithi Community) offer to our comparatively indulged children,' she says. 'Looking to the future, we need to understand what values and behaviours breed true success. I see PfP being a beacon of light and hope from which people can share what they have to offer and bring into their own homes that which they need, but perhaps did not even know it.'

Another resident of the estate, Tom Bassett, who also participated as a PfP business leader, commended the estate's former board of directors which, at the time, recognised the considerable synergy that existed between Simbithi's objectives of uplifting the less advantaged communities within the vicinity and PfP's impact. 'A direct spinoff from Simbithi hosting numerous PfP meetings and marketing functions at the Country Club's facilities led to a broader understanding by the Simbithi residents – a substantially group than just those who participated in the PfP programme. This also resulted in more Simbithi residents being prepared to sponsor or participate as business leaders in subsequent PfP circles,' he said.

Tom believes that PfP's impact has also boosted the resolve of residents to support the work to strengthen the management and leadership skills of school principals as a catalytic intervention to improve the education of pupils within the surrounding communities. Simbithi residents are committed to share their knowledge and skills with people in communities around the estate because they know that this will ultimately lead to a better future for all who live in and around Ballito.

Chapter 6

Schools that have become a magnet for the gifts and contributions from people and organisations around the school

"It is amazing what you can accomplish if you do not care who gets the credit." – Harry S Truman

When we first conceptualized PfP, we called the programme 'School at the Centre of Community' (S@CC) because the core idea was for business leaders to work with school principals to mobilise community support for the school. We advocated an Asset Based Community Development (ABCD) approach and envisaged that schools would become 'magnets for the gifts and contributions of the community around the school'. On our journey as partners, Ridwan and I had experienced this phenomenon at Kannemeyer Primary School, and I was keen to visit some other schools where this has occurred, to a lesser or greater extent.

Mshwati Memorial Primary School

Mshwati Memorial Primary School is situated in the deep rural area of Mthombesa in Upper Tongaat. The school serves a very poor community and has an enrolment of 278 learners.

Principal Bizie Magwaza was disappointed and hurt to hear that, initially, her application to join the PfP programme had been turned down. Other principals whom she had encouraged to apply were accepted, but Bizie was told that there was currently no funding available to enable her to join the programme.

Terry Dearling sympathised with Bizie's disappointment and committed to making a plan for her. Bizie was delighted when she heard from Terry that a sponsor had been found and that she was in. 'I had heard from a colleague who had gone through the programme that it had done wonders for her, and I was not prepared to take no for an answer,' said Bizie.

Bizie began her PfP journey alongside Gill Cox in January 2017. Gill is an entrepreneur who, with her husband, runs their family-owned industrial automation business, Numatics SA. Gill is also a keen mountain biker and belongs to the same cycling group as Terry.

Bizie was appointed as principal of the school in 2013. She is a foundation phase teacher by training but has taught all the primary school grades. Prior to her appointment as principal Bizie was an HOD and she had hardly been prepared at all for the role. 'We went to a two-day induction course, but that didn't teach us much. So when I heard about PfP and that it was about principal development, not about resources, I was very interested in it,' she recalls.

Gill and Bizie had met for coffee before the formal start of the programme and, Bizie remembers, Gill stressed that the idea was for them to learn together. 'She told me that she knows nothing about teaching and was not there to judge me, but that she would help me in whatever way she could.'

I asked Bizie about the impact of PfP on her as a leader. 'I am definitely a more confident leader now,' she said. 'The workshops we attended, and my interaction with Gill and the other principals in our circle, have made me more skillful and able to do the job as well.'

There are nine teachers at Bizie's school. They are supported by four interns who joined through the Youth@worK programme where young people are placed at schools to gain work experience[23]. The presence of these interns and how she manages them are among the positive changes that have occurred in Bizie and in the school as a result of her partnership with Gill. 'The interns make everything easier,' says Bizie. 'They assist with the learners, help with homework and just take the load off my shoulders. We also love the fact that we are able to provide employment to young people in our community.

'The teachers are more motivated too. They have gone on workshops to improve their teaching, and they have gained from the various benefits that PfP has brought to the school, including the interns and the other programmes.'

Theo and I visited Mshwati Primary on a Friday. This is the day when Glide and Ride visits the school to offer their cycling programme. I had heard about this programme and seen a video made by its founder, Ian Wilson, so it was wonderful to experience it first-hand.

Glide and Ride is a youth development programme that teaches children the fundamental skills of riding a mountain bike while focusing on boosting their self-confidence and growth through social and mental development.

Ian runs the programme in local private schools and as a holiday activity at the housing estates in the area, including Simbithi. He also coaches elite cyclists and runs

23 More about Youth@worK in Chapter 11

a mountain biking programme for women, which he calls the 'AMA Angels'. Gill and Terry are both members of that group.

'I've always believed in the concept of a 'business tithe' in giving back part of what we make to those less fortunate. I discussed the idea with my Simbithi angels and Gill came up with the idea of running the Glide and Ride programme at a school,' says Ian.

'So we came to see Bizie at Mshwati. I told her that I wasn't interested in giving a handout. I wanted the children to pay in some way as I knew they would then feel that it is valuable. I knew they did not have money, so we needed to find some other form of currency.'

At the time (almost three years ago), Mshwati Primary was challenged by learner absenteeism – a common problem at remote rural schools – and it was serious. In the Grade R class absenteeism had been 394 days per term, which translates into an average of 12 days per learner per term. 'I thought we could make attendance the currency,' said Ian. 'We could have an agreement that only learners who came to school every day during the week would be able to ride on Fridays.'

Ian remembers how close he came to walking away after introducing the programme in early 2017. 'On the first Friday, there were only two Grade R learners who qualified to participate. The next week there were four children. The third week we were down to two again. And this is when I thought it may not be worth it. But then we had eight children in the fourth week, and that grew to 26 in the second term.'

Ian and his team persevered. Now, nearly three years later, there is virtually no absenteeism in the grades that participate in Glide and Ride. Ian had started with the Grade R learners in 2017. In 2018, when those children went into Grade 1, he continued offering riding lessons to them on Fridays and brought the new Grade R children into the programme. By 2019 the Grade 2 learners were also participating.

When Ian started the programme he realised that children could not be expected to ride on empty stomachs and looked for a way to feed them. Keran Coetzer, who also cycles with Ian, Terry and Gill, heard about Glide and Ride and decided that in lieu of giving up something for Lent that year she would volunteer to feed the kids before they went for their riding lessons. In most cases, it would be their first meal of the day. Keran enlisted the help of her friend Lynette, and they prepared sandwiches and fruit for the children. These dedicated women still give the children a sandwich and some fruit every Friday before they Glide and Ride.

Ian was adamant that food shouldn't be withheld from the children who had been excluded from riding because of absenteeism, and now every child in the school gets a meal from Keran's network of donors, every Friday.

Meanwhile, since they were at the school every week to provide food, Keran and Lynette decided that they would like to get involved in some educational activities as well. They now source and bring educational games to the school, and on the day we were there learners were building model cranes.

I wanted to know from Bizie if the Glide and Ride programme had contributed to improved results in the lower grades. 'The lower absenteeism figures have definitely helped,' she said. 'Last year, for the first time, the entire Grade R group passed into Grade 1 in their own right, not a single one was 'progressed' to the next grade.'

Gill's involvement and Bizie's leadership have led to a number of other improvements at the school. Bizie wanted to establish a vegetable garden at the school. Gill asked her friend Nick Jordan from Living Earth for compost, and he arrived with a big truck and a team that helped to prepare the ground for planting. Ntombenhle Mtambo from the Mpophomeni Conservation Group came to the school to teach the children, and adults from the community, how to farm vegetables. She conducted a 4-day workshop at no cost.

Gail Stephano from Rotary helped with resources in the Grade R classroom and Gill's friend Adrian Legg from Kitchen Pro supplied kitchen cupboards and fittings. The Robin Hood Foundation provided shelves for the school library.

I asked Gill how she became involved in PfP. 'We were out riding, and I asked Terry a question that changed my life. I asked her whether she knew anything about Partners for Possibility. She was so excited to hear me ask this and immediately enrolled me to get involved.'

I wanted to know how PfP and her involvement in Mshwati had impacted Gill. 'I have loved the experience of working with Bizie. I have become a lot more collaborative. I have learned how to create a space for all the voices to contribute and to get the quiet voices to speak too,' she said. Gill told me that the reason she had decided to get involved with a second school in 2018 was because her experience with Bizie and Mshwati had been so fulfilling. 'For me, it is a social justice issue. We owe it to the children to raise the quality of education in the schools. I simply can't stand back anymore. I have to be involved. And I have realised that I have an amazing network. It is relatively easy for me to mobilise the resources we need in the schools.

'What I love about PfP is that it is so structured,' said Gill. 'It also helps to have Terry as a Learning Process Facilitator. Terry has such a gift to make everybody feel comfortable. When you are happy, you are at your best. I have loved working with Terry and being part of the PfP community.'

After writing this chapter, I decided to ask Keran for her thoughts about her and Lynette's involvement. I was deeply touched by her response and feel that her message is worth sharing in full:

Good morning Louise

My name is Keran – we met briefly at Mshwati in September when you visited the school with Gill and Terry. During that visit you asked why I keep going to Mshwati. I have thought so much about your question as there are so many incredible answers I could have given you! But with a bit more time to reflect on it and I really would like to share some of the amazing things that have happened since Lynette and I started visiting the school last year.

I think the most important lesson I have learned since visiting Mshwati is the value of treading gently and listening carefully. We have been going to the school for almost two years now and because we have been consistent about visiting every Friday, and tried to be respectful of the school and its teachers, we now feel like we are part of Mshwati's story. It took a few months for us to feel comfortable enough to make suggestions and I think going in quietly and observing and getting to know the teachers first has been really valuable in the long term. We have also noticed that the community now recognise my car and on Fridays we are always waved at and greeted enthusiastically on the drive into the school.

On our first trip to Mshwati Ian suggested we bring sandwiches to add to the loaves that his wife Derryn had been sending for the children each week. Lynette and I thought it would be a great idea to also take along marshmallow Easter eggs to give to the children. It was an eye-opener to see how they were far more excited and grateful for half a peanut butter sandwich than an Easter egg. This was our first reality check – these children were really hungry. We decided that on the next visit we would bring more sandwiches and substitute the sweets for fruit in future. We have since increased the number of loaves of bread we make sandwiches with to 10 loaves each. Along with the sandwiches Derryn sends, a few friends who contribute a loaf or two and we are now able to give all the children in the school a sandwich. Alison, another of the ladies from Ian's riding group, donates fruit every week.

One of the best parts of our visits to Mshwati is how warmly we are greeted by the children when we walk into the classrooms each Friday. Handing out the sandwiches and fruit each week has helped us get to know both the teachers and the children in the older grades who are not part of the Ian's cycling initiative. It has also allowed us into the classrooms during lessons, so we are able to see what they are working on. Neither Lynette nor I have any teaching experience, but we started recognising some of the syllabus from our own children's senior primary years.

Lynette is passionate about Maths and firmly believes that the more you practise maths, the easier it becomes. She started setting basic worksheets which she handed out on a Friday for the children in Grades 5 & 6 to do during the week. This was voluntary and they were all encouraged to take a worksheet home and complete it by the following Friday. When marking these worksheets she started to see some common errors that a lot of the children were making with multiplication. She discussed this with one of the teachers, Sipho, and he allowed her to join his class the following week and go through some of the basics. At first the children were reluctant to speak up, but by the end of the lesson they were lining up to come and do multiplication sums on the board in front of the class. On Fridays Lynette now moves from class to class shouting 'Maths is Fun' and setting problems for them to solve and they really enjoy engaging with her.

Doing this has highlighted how important it is to get the children to understand basic Maths concepts in the foundation years. Last year Gill Cox and Flick Holmes, the headmistress of the foundation phase of Ashton Ballito asked us to help put together a series of 'WhatsApp-able' videos for teachers from under-resourced schools which showed new ways to teach these very important basic concepts. The idea was that materials used in the videos should not cost anything and be able to be easily sourced by teachers. Flick was amazing and arranged for us to go and video her teachers at Ashton teaching Grade R pupils these basic concepts. The 18 videos were packaged as GIFTs – Good Ideas For Teachers.

From putting these videos together we picked up the importance of number value and number recognition in the foundation phase – for example asking the children to look at the number 5, and be able to count out 5 beans and understand what the 5 means. To help to teach this, Lynette designed a very simple game of Snakes & Ladders and the Grade 1 teacher allowed us to split the class up and play on a Friday morning. By rolling the dice, counting the dots on the dice, and then moving their counter the required number of spaces, the children quickly picked up the game and hopefully the concept of number recognition. The Grade 1 children don't speak much English, so we were fortunate that the two intern teachers joined us and helped to explain the game. We each supervised a group and played Snakes & Ladders with them which was a lot of fun. The Grade 1 teacher is wonderful but with over 30 children in her class, managing interactive teaching like this would not be possible without help. The best part of the morning was when she pointed out that the boy who picked the game up quickest and was the 'Snakes & Ladders Champion of the Class', was the same little boy who usually struggles with all of his classwork. His smile and excitement at being recognised as the 'best' at something was really special. Lynette has since designed an even simpler Snakes & Ladders board for the children and left laminated copies for them with the Grade 1 teacher in the hope that the children can now manage the game on their own.

Over the course of the nearly 2 years we have been visiting Mshwati, Lynette has put together a few more games for the teacher to use. Mica donated some wood offcuts and she painted a memory game with all sorts of shapes and colours for them. She also showed them how to play hopscotch and say the numbers as they jump.

In our first year at Mshwati, we noticed that the Grade 7 classes were learning about building an electromagnetic crane. Lynette remembered doing this project with her children in their Grade 7 year, so asked the teacher, Sipho, when they were going to build it. Sipho explained that they only learned about how to build the crane from the textbook as they didn't have the resources to actually build it themselves. Lynette contacted Mica and they donated 5 kits for the children to build the crane. She split the class into 5 groups and did a step-by-step lesson on how to build it. We were amazed at how good some of the children were with their hands and the quietest boy in the class became the glue gun specialist! At the end of the exercise, if the crane has been built correctly, it is able to pick up a paper clip. The teacher called Bizie in when all of the cranes were built and each group demonstrated how the crane worked to thunderous applause! The cranes were kept in the library so that the Grade 7 parents were able to come in and see them at the parent teachers meeting. This year Lynette approached the company that makes up the kits and they donated kits and she did the lesson once again.

My project for the second year running is to get the Grade R's to be able to recognise and write their names by the end of the year. The teacher has given me a class list which I have printed and then taken a 'class photo' of each child holding their name. The idea is that they each get a photo to take home and then copy their name over and over so that they know and recognise it by the time they start Grade 1. The parents also love getting a class photo of their child. Over our 2 years at Mshwati I have put together a number of videos of the children cycling, and how they have progressed, as well as thank you videos to Bata Toughees, Pick 'n Pay and Ashton International for the GIFT videos. I have loved doing these videos and it's a skill I never knew I had until I had beautiful stories to tell, like the ones that have come from Mshwati. These little video 'stories' seem to make such an impact when shared and I think for me personally the idea of doing more of this under the banner of 'Social Media for Social Change' really interests me.

Two of the unsung heroes of the cycling programme are the two cycling coaches – Wiseman and Gareth. They are both young men with no children of their own but they have incredible patience with the children during the cycling lesson. Because Wiseman understands and speaks Zulu, he is able to pick up on any issues that the children are having. A few months ago he noticed that one of the little girls had lost a lot of weight and had a strange rash on her hands. He noticed that a few of the other children had a similar rash on their arms and legs and showed it to us. Lynette's husband is a doctor and she took photos and sent them to him, and he recognised the rash as scabies. We were then able to download a treatment sheet for scabies written in Zulu and print copies to hand out to the children's parents. Bizie called the parents in and they took the children to the clinic to be treated.

Gareth and Wiseman also noticed that the children would bring their pencils with them when they came for their cycling lessons and put them in their pockets which was quite dangerous. They insisted they hand them in before the lesson started. Some of the pencils were so short there were barely able to write but were treated like treasure and at the end of the lesson each child knew exactly which stub of pencil was theirs! Jonathan is a young boy who is home-schooled and occasionally comes to Mshwati to help coach – he donated boxes of pencils and now Gareth and Wiseman hand out pencils as prizes to the children who listen or behave well during the cycling lessons.

I often send Gill photos and updates on what is going on after our Fridays at Mshwati and she is always so enthusiastic and encouraging. She recently asked me to do a video of Parkgate Primary for the end of year function and seeing my second Partnership for Possibility school has reinforced just how powerful this programme is. It seems like there really is a ripple effect of well-being that comes from this programme. I like to think that the role Lynette and I play in the PfP model is like an 'eyes on the ground' where we visit the school weekly and then feed back to Gill on any good news as well as issues that she may want to step in and deal with. It think it would be really beneficial if there were 'point people' in all of the PfP schools – people who want to get involved and help but don't feel ready to take on a business leader's role. We have realised that you don't need a teaching background to get involved and help children – just a genuine interest in listening and working out interesting ways to make learning fun and thereby unburdening some of the over-worked teachers in under-resourced schools.

I think I speak for both Lynette and myself when I say that being involved at Mshwati has been a really rewarding experience. Our children go to private schools and with the wealth of information we have gathered from that experience, as well as all of the resources on the internet, we are both excited about introducing new ideas at Mshwati.

There are days when the difference in the education that our children and the children at Mshwati are receiving is overwhelming. But we fall back on the proverb 'How do you eat an elephant? One bite at a time'.

And every Friday on the way home we always agree that you leave Mshwati feeling better for having visited.

I am only one, but I am one.

I cannot do everything, but I can do something.

And I will not let what I cannot do interfere with what I can do

EE Hale

Mthayiza Primary School

Mthayiza Primary School is located in Kabokweni, a rural area near White River in Mpumalanga. The principal is Elsie Chiloane, and she was partnered with Tersia Potgieter from Nedbank. They were in the Nelspruit 2 (NEL2) Leadership Circle with Mel Tomlinson as their LPF.

On the day that we visited Elsie, we were privileged to also have Tersia in the room. Tersia had invited Erika Human, her line manager, to join us. Erika had been a member of the Nelspruit 1 Leadership Circle and was the person who encouraged Tersia to join PfP.

Elsie told us that she has always been a confident and energized principal, but something shifted for her when she was partnered with Tersia. 'I have received unconditional love from Tersia and it has made me want to work harder. It has also given me more energy to keep going,' said Elsie.

'My relationship with Tersia was completely different to the one with my circuit manager. He supports me, but my school is just one of many that he has to look after. Tersia is like family, like a sister to me. We interact every week and I am able to talk to her about anything. She has time to listen to me and to ask incisive questions. She loves me and is committed to supporting me.

'Being a principal is a cold place. One feels so alone. Being on this programme with Tersia has shown me what is possible when you are supported.'

Elsie loved the programme structure and the regular CoP meetings with other principals and business leaders. 'You listen to the people around you, and you hear alternatives. Everyone is given a chance to express their ideas. I applied that in the school and in that way the load was spread, every stakeholder was involved and we were able to solve problems together.

'Since I have become involved in PfP we have seen more buy-in and more engagement at the school,' said Elsie.

One of the major issues at the school was security. The school is in a densely populated area, and it had been difficult to keep control of people coming into the grounds and to prevent learners from leaving.

One of Elsie and Tersia's first projects was to improve security. They realised that they would need to engage the parents and SGB, so they decided to arrange a fundraiser at the school and to use it as an opportunity to connect with parents. Nedbank staff from the local Kabokweni Branch attended and presented a session on 'financial fitness' aimed at empowering the parents. After the session, they engaged the parents in a conversation about the challenges at the school and asked whether they would be willing to make a financial contribution to enable the school to address the security issues. As a result of the parents' response, the school has been able to repair the fence and build a gatehouse which is now manned by a member of the community. This person receives a monthly stipend which is paid by the community.

The school had a massive issue with soil erosion and flooding, which created dangerous holes in its grounds and pathways. Tersia heard about some used bricks available from a local filling station, and Elsie arranged for them to be delivered to the school. Because parents were now more involved at the school, they were willing to help lay brick pathways. These have made it safer to walk around the school grounds, especially in the rainy season.

The Flawless Consulting training bore fruit when Elsie and her team applied the approach to the arrangements with the vendors who sell food in and around the school. 'We contracted with them and brought them from outside to inside the campus. Part of the agreement was that they would pay a small monthly rental which we are saving to be able to build permanent stalls once we have enough money. They have also agreed to keep an eye on the children, so they have become part of our security solution,' said Elsie.

'We did some of those things before we went on the Community Building training,' Elsie said. 'We did not even know it, but we were on the right track, and we are working hard at making the school the centre of the community.

'Most of the parent body are unemployed and many of them live off social welfare grants. After the Community Building workshop we were even more committed to focus on their gifts and what they are able to do at the school. We have been able to get many members of the community to come and help us improve things at the school.'

The school also had a big problem with regard to its furniture. They simply did not have enough desks and chairs for all the children. But they did have a storeroom full of broken desks and chairs, so Elsie decided to invite the parents to help. After a few weekends of work, they had repaired 75 chairs and 50 desks.

'The learners in our overcrowded classrooms no longer have to fight for a place to sit, which has made a big difference,' Elsie said.

The school has become a place where parents felt welcome. They have painted classrooms and offered to wash uniforms for children from child-headed households. Parents became aware of the plight of the children who have no adult caring for them and started providing extra support to those youngsters.

Parents also work in the school's vegetable garden, which is used to supplement the departmental feeding scheme, and they have tiled the Grade 3 classroom. Some parents have volunteered to clean the school, while others have offered to teach after-school craft classes.

A very successful project was the staging of a funfair at the school as a fundraising initiative. Elsie negotiated with a company in Gauteng to bring a funfair to the school. For most of the children in the area, this was the first time in their lives that they had seen anything like this. The event provided a colourful day of fun for the community and neighbouring schools and, in the end, made a profit of R8,000.

I asked Elsie how being in the partnership has impacted her leadership style.

'I am on a new road,' she said. 'The old road was a difficult one. I was doing things a different way. Before I met Tersia, I believed that because I was accountable I had to do everything myself. I never delegated anything. The load was very heavy and all on my shoulders.

'Through PfP I have grown. I have learned the value of working with others. My load is lighter and I feel empowered. I have learned the art of networking and how to grab opportunities, and I have grown in confidence. I have always been an implementer, but now I am able to implement faster.'

Throughout the conversation with Elsie I was acutely aware of Tersia and Erika's presence, so I asked Tersia to share the story of how she became involved with PfP. When Erika was in the NEL1 Leadership Circle, Tersia was supporting some of the partnerships, so she knew about PfP. When LPF Mel Tomlinson joined the programme and started to recruit business leaders to join the NEL2 circle, she contacted Erika, who suggested to Tersia that she may want to get involved.

Tersia wasn't sure. She had just lost her mother whom she was very close to, so it felt like a big ask to get involved in something as demanding as PfP. But Erika kept encouraging her. 'I knew from my own experience how valuable it is to be part of PfP, and I have always wondered who else we could gift this opportunity to. When I received the message that PfP was looking for business leaders in Nelspruit, I just felt the time was right for Tersia to get involved,' said Erika.

'After her mother's death, Tersia had a hole in her heart. I knew that contributing through PfP would bring healing for her, and I also knew that the principal would benefit from having Tersia as a partner,' said Erika.

'I met Elsie at a meeting that Mel arranged at the Kruger Mpumalanga International Airport before the programme got going. We ended up sitting next to each other, and I think the universe had a plan for us because we immediately connected,' said Tersia.

'I found out later that Elsie had also lost her mom the previous year, so we had a lot in common from the beginning. I went to see her school and she was so proud to show me around. It was also immediately apparent that she was a good listener, and I needed that.'

The training sessions, Tersia said, developed her and taught her skills which she has been able to implement in her role at work and in the communities that she interacts with, but they did more than that. 'The process gave me structure at a stage when I lost everything and I was able to find myself again,' she said.

'From Elsie I found no judgement, only acceptance. I was able to be in authentic relationship and that made me brave and confident. I made myself vulnerable in the process, but that led to me becoming stronger. I used to shy away from conflict; through the partnership, I found myself able to have courageous conversations. It has helped in my interactions with my clients at the bank.'

Klapmuts Primary School

Jessica Batts, a PfP LPF in the Winelands area, regularly shares stories about the principals in her circles and I had often heard about Mr Ronnie Frans, the principal at Klapmuts Primary School. In 2018 Principal Frans won the Lifetime Achievement Award at the DBE's National Teaching Awards.

From what I had heard through Jessica, it sounded as if this was a story worth capturing. I was particularly interested in the fact that so many funders have been contributing to the school, and I was curious to know how Ronnie had managed to secure so much support from different organisations.

Ronnie Frans has been in a PfP partnership with Stellenbosch business leader, Theo van den Berg, since 2016. Theo is an investment executive at Invenfin, Remgro's venture and growth capital division, and their partnership was funded by Remgro. In addition to Remgro, I knew that the school was also supported by the Cape Wine Auction (CWA), the Val de Vie Foundation and the Click Foundation. I was curious to know to what extent Ronnie's involvement in PfP has contributed to this situation.

Before going to the school, Theo and I met Andi Norton at a coffee shop in Stellenbosch. Andi is the Executive Director of CWA, which has funded projects at Klapmuts Primary. I wanted to know from Andi why CWA had decided to get involved with the school and why they remained involved.

Andi told us that Jessica Batts had invited her and Raymond Ndlovu, one of the CWA Trustees, to visit the school. They both loved meeting Ronnie and were inspired by his energy. They saw that the school was a beacon of hope in the community and listened to Ronnie talk about the challenge of large class numbers. This led to a decision by CWA to fund classroom assistants at the school. Andi is clear that CWA would probably not have become involved with Klapmuts Primary if it hadn't been for the introduction by Jessica.

The CWA funds projects in many schools, so I asked Andi what she thought was different or special about Ronnie and Klapmuts Primary. She described Ronnie as a 'gem' and said it has just been a joy to work with him. After hearing Andi speak, I was really looking forward to meeting Ronnie in person.

The town of Klapmuts is one of the poorest in the Western Cape. Klapmuts Primary School, which serves this community, has 1,500 learners, most of whom come from families who survive on social grants.

Klapmuts is a no-fee school, which means it depends solely on funding from the provincial education department and does not have the wherewithal to employ extra teachers in governing body posts.

When we arrived at the school, the secretary knew that Ronnie was expecting a visit from 'partners'. She took us to his office where he was waiting for us.

I asked Ronnie to start his story at the beginning. He told us that he had been appointed as principal of Klapmuts in 1994. He wanted the school to be a beacon of hope for the community, and he wanted to break down the barriers between school and community. To do this, he started his first two community projects that year: a gardening project and a sewing and needlework club. He began by inviting members of the community to make use of the school grounds and facilities. Then, for the sewing project, he attracted funding from a Swedish non-profit organisation and a donation of sewing machines and overlockers from the UK High Commission and made these available at the school to women from the community, who could then generate an income from the items they had made.

For his gardening project, Ronnie started by making allotments on the school grounds available to community members for the growing of vegetables. They started small, but later on he got the United Nations involved, and there are now greenhouse tunnels at the school which allow for winter cultivation.

In 2005 the WCED built a hall at the school. From the beginning, Ronnie and his team decided that the hall would be made available to the community. They valued the opportunity to use the facility and were therefore committed to protecting it.

They had a hall now, but the rest of the school was a problem. Learner numbers were increasing, and the buildings were literally falling apart. There was no response from the WCED to Ronnie's pleas for renovations and new classrooms. In 2006 he decided that he needed to do something drastic, so he circled the entire school grounds with hazard tape, refusing entrance to the learners because the existing buildings were unsafe.

'This got the department's attention,' Ronnie recalls. 'They arrived at the school with the people from the IDT [Independent Development Trust]. The IDT was looking for a school upgrade project in Cape Town, and they decided there and then that they were going to upgrade our school.

'The wonderful thing about this project was that we were able to design the school ourselves. We could design our dream school. We got them to include a library, a computer centre and planned for the entire school to be e-enabled. We did not have the computer equipment, but we wanted to be ready.'

The school was built with ducts for the wiring built into the walls and with plug points in the ceilings to accommodate data projectors. 'So,' Ronnie asked, 'we have a new building, now what?'

The new school design included a modern library and Ronnie immediately recognised an opportunity to serve the community by establishing a municipal library, rather than one catering only for the schoolchildren. 'I went to the Western Cape Library Service, and they agreed to provide all the books and the systems for the library. Stellenbosch Municipality agreed to fund two full-time librarians. This meant we were able to open the library to the community, from 10am to 5pm on weekdays and on Saturday mornings.'

Ronnie describes the library as the third building block which placed the school at the centre of its community. First came the gardening and needlework, then the hall as a community asset and now the library.

'By bringing community members onto the school grounds and allowing them to use our facilities, we were giving them a degree of ownership. The school belongs to the community and they are therefore committed to look after it. We have not had any vandalism or break-ins in recent years,' Ronnie said.

Ronnie's vision was that the school would be recognised as a leader in the area of e-learning. He knew that he needed to get more technology into the school.

The new school design included two computer rooms, but the school had just two data projectors and two classrooms with electronic whiteboards. Ronnie began working his contacts. He got local winegrower Michael Back to donate two more data projectors, then secured a donation of $5,000 from a US contributor, which enabled the school to buy another 14 projectors.

But then, in 2015, he hit a dip. 'We stalled. I still had my vision, but we were not making any progress. I became disillusioned and was ready to pack it in – my wife had just retired and I was contemplating joining her in 2017.' Ronnie said.

In 2016 Remgro invited principals from schools in their network to attend a course on management and leadership at the University of Stellenbosch. Ronnie was one of those who accepted the offer and, in turn, he invited 11 of his teachers to attend the course with him.

For their coursework assignment, the Klapmuts team designed a blueprint for the integration of ICT into teaching at their school. They received a mark of 87% for their efforts, and the document became the actual blueprint for what they wanted to do at the school.

'A number of things came together at just the right time then,' Ronnie remembers. 'Earlier that year Jessica Batts had asked whether I wanted to join Partners for Possibility. I did not know exactly what I was getting involved in, but it sounded interesting and I was looking forward to being part of the programme.'

Hearing Ronnie talk reminded me of the background to his partnership with Theo. I had spoken to my friend, Stuart Gast, about PfP and our need to find business leaders and funding to enable more business leader-principal partnerships. Stuart, Invenfin's CEO, spoke to Mariza Lubbe, the Director of Compliance and Corporate Social Investments at Remgro and she said they would be willing to fund Theo's participation on condition that he was partnered with Ronnie Frans at Klapmuts Primary.

Ronnie and Theo met each other in August 2016, and they joined the Winelands 5 Leadership Circle. Ronnie describes his partnership with Theo as the catalyst for change at Klapmuts Primary.

According to Ronnie, he and Theo just 'clicked' and he told us that he has heard Theo describe the start of their relationship as 'love at first sight'. Having Theo in his life was exactly what Ronnie needed. 'I was a bit flat and the partnership was the spark that I needed. By then, I was planning to retire the following year, but this helped me change my mind.

'Theo is a thorough gentleman, he is soft-spoken, and his willingness to give back to the community shone through,' Ronnie said. 'He understood my vision and saw there was no way of swaying me from it. Instead, he looked for ways in supporting me in making it happen.

'He was my cheerleader, and he spread the word. He brought people here with all sorts of offers, but I always told them about my vision: to make Klapmuts a full e-learning school.

'Theo was a sounding board for me. He created an opportunity for me to think through what I wanted to do and to become clear about what I needed to do next.'

One of the things that struck Ronnie was that the courses he did during the facilitated programme confirmed that he was on the right track. 'I had an idea that community involvement, partnership with other organisations and empowering my teachers to take initiative were the right things to do; now I found that there was theory to back that up. It was a boost to my confidence and I had new energy for the tasks ahead.'

He soon put this renewed energy to work to rally the Val de Vie Foundation behind his vision for e-learning. Theo had approached Lorraine Hadfield from the Foundation to ask for packets of sweets to give away at the Klapmuts Rugby Sevens Tournament. Lorraine came to the school and said that the Foundation wouldn't give sweets – it would, however, help with nutritious food for the players. When we met with Lorraine she told us that she had just loved meeting Ronnie, so their conversations continued.

Ronnie articulated his e-learning vision for the school and explained to Lorraine how he and his team were making the most of what they already had at the school. At the time, they had Wi-Fi connectivity in one of the buildings, and the teachers were encouraging learners to bring mobile phones to the school so that they could tap into it to access educational content.

'Lorraine saw that we were committed and had already taken the first steps in that direction, so she was prepared to help. We needed better Wi-Fi connectivity and she, with Theo, got the WCED here, along with other people, to discuss laying fibre lines,' Ronnie explained. 'The department initially said it was too expensive, but they somehow changed their minds and installed fibre at the school.' Val de Vie had planned to invest R100,000 to help install Wi-Fi but, since that had already happened, they used the money to buy tablets instead.

The following year, the WCED began to roll out e-learning in its schools. Klapmuts was designated as a 'Universal' school, which meant they would get 20 computers from the education department. Fourteen 'Model' schools acquired fully equipped e-classrooms, but Klapmuts wasn't one of them.

'I went with Theo, to see the Assistant Director and told him we didn't need the PCs because the school is e-learning ready and we already had a computer lab. After a few conversations they agreed to give us 14 smart classrooms.'

This meant that all of the classrooms now had data projectors and smartboards. In total, the school now boasted 27 e-classrooms, and this was when the CWA Trust agreed to pay for 24 teaching assistants. Their gesture has had a twofold positive impact: the teachers get help in the classrooms, and 24 unemployed young people from the community are given the dignity of a job and an income.

According to Ronnie, these classroom assistants contributed to a dramatic improvement in their Grade 3 systemic test results.

Referring to the school's relationship with the CWA, Ronnie said that it's all about trust. 'If you prove yourself to be trustworthy, people are prepared to trust you. And success breeds success; because we have made progress, people are prepared to become involved with us.'

A further example of the partnerships that Ronnie has been able to build is the one with Living Legends, a Stellenbosch-based youth development organisation that uses physical education and sport as a vehicle for improving the lives of young people. They run curriculum-based physical education programmes at schools and Remgro is one of their funders. The organisation was pointed in the direction of Klapmuts Primary by Remgro, and there is now a full-time Living Legends physical education instructor at the school.

We spoke to Le Roux Conradie, the CEO of Caylix Sport, who is a founding member of Living Legends NPO. He explained that the organisation aims to create moments of interaction with vulnerable children and a space where they can be nurtured and inspired through physical education, sports and life skills to become leaders that make a difference in their own lives and those of their families and communities, in South Africa and beyond. Through their specially designed programmes, Living Legends encourages its beneficiaries to embrace a healthy body-healthy mind mantra.

'We were familiar with Klapmuts Primary as we ran a pilot programme at the school before Remgro came on board and supported us by running the entire programme and placing a full-time instructor at the school. We were impressed with Ronnie's openness, his vision for the school and his passion for the children,' Le Roux said. 'It was the perfect place to get involved as we knew that we would get full support from Ronnie and his team.

'The instructors are recruited from the local communities. They then receive training and are happy to be giving back. They run and manage the physical education programme at the school and are also involved in sports coaching after school.

'Caylix Sport has become very involved with the Klapmuts Sevens Tournament to support Ronnie's vision of making it the premier primary schools sevens tournament in the Western Cape,' Le Roux said. 'In 2017 Ronnie approached us and asked us to help grow and promote the tournament. We leaned heavily on our current partners and through that could also get international sevens players to attend the tournament every year.'

In 2019 there were 16 under-13 teams playing in the tournament and increasing media interest in the event.

'We have partnered with the Val de Vie Foundation and the Stellenbosch Academy of Sport to ensure that the tournament is something special and that it continues to grow. The two teams in the final get to stay over at the Stellenbosch Academy of Sport (home of the Springbok Sevens) and also receive a sevens clinic presented by former international sevens player and captain, Frankie Horne,' Le Roux explained.

In Ronnie's mind, PfP has helped to strengthen the brand of Klapmuts Primary. It is because of PfP and Theo's involvement that Remgro was willing to make further investments in the school, and this led to CWA's involvement. Remgro has also sponsored Community Keepers to set up an office on the school premises, and they offer social work and counselling services to the learners, teachers and wider community.

Ronnie gives Theo a lot of credit for the things that have happened. 'He was beside me when we entered into many of those agreements and many of the people involved were his contacts,' Ronnie said. 'We are still in contact; in fact, he was with me when I received an e-Bosch Honorary Award yesterday evening.'

While he recognises that he was always determined and sure of his vision, Ronnie is aware of the assistance he gets. 'All of our successes are due to partnerships. There is no way the school could be the way it is now without them. The PfP programme, with its emphasis on community involvement and on building relationships, was an important part of our success.

'My involvement in a leadership circle and the CoP meetings was important because it gave me an insight into how things are at other schools. I got to experience what other schools have, and it taught me to tell my teachers not to underestimate themselves and what they have achieved at Klapmuts.

'I have learned to let the teachers shine. I am not an IT specialist; my job is to create champions and hope that they will spread the word and create the other champions that will make the vision work.'

I asked Ronnie what would have happened if he did not join PfP. 'I would have retired in 2017,' he said. 'None of this would have happened.

'I am now so much more confident than I was in 2016. Nothing will stop me. A lot of this confidence and energy is directly as a result of being part of PfP. PfP was the spark and has fired us up. And now we are just not stopping. We have implemented coding and robotics at the school and are waiting for programmable drones to arrive from America.

'I have experienced this idea of a positive self-enforcing loop. Success breeds success. People have been giving us positive feedback, and many articles have been written about what is happening at the school. This has led to teachers being proud and motivated and has given us all extra energy.'

I told Ronnie how inspired I was by his story. What he and Theo had achieved was exactly the kind of synergy that we are hoping for through PfP: for cross-sector partnerships to bring new energy to the school and that the school will become a magnet for the gifts and contributions from people and organisations around it.

However, the reality is that this does not always happen. There aren't many PfP partnerships where we have seen this kind of visible transformation in three years. I asked Ronnie why he thought that his and Theo's partnership led to so much impact at the school. 'When Theo arrived at the school we already had a vision. And we had started to walk towards that vision. We weren't waiting for things to happen.

'I am proud to say that I made the most of the opportunities provided to me by the PfP programme. I feel sad when I see principals who get the opportunity to be part of PfP, but they don't make the most of the opportunity.'

Ronnie and Theo's story exemplifies the power of cross-sector partnerships and what is possible when a 'man with a plan' is partnered with a well-connected and resourceful business partner.

Reflections

It is impossible to hear these stories and not be touched and inspired. These stories are such beautiful examples of what is possible through leadership and community engagement. When we dreamt about 'School at the Centre of Community,' these were the kinds of stories we envisaged – citizens offering their gifts and contributions because they know that 'it takes a village to raise a child'.

It warms my heart to know that children across the country are benefitting from adults getting involved in schools and that there are many more principals who have discovered their capacity to enrol parents and other adults to support the school. Imagine what would be possible if every school had a group of actively engaged citizens involved in it?

Chapter 7

Hillwood Primary, Ian Macdonald and Fella's Army

This chapter is written for Ian MacDonald's children

The story of the late Ian Macdonald and Hillwood Primary is one of the very special PfP stories that should be told.

It began in 2009 when Ian attended a Community Building workshop with Peter Block. At the time Ian was working as a member of the 'South Africa: The Good News' team. Here's what he wrote in the SA: The Good News newsletter on 16 October 2009:

Building communities one room at a time

This week I learnt that building a community is difficult. And I learnt that it is so very easy. I attended a workshop that was conducted by Peter Block, an American authority on the reconciliation of community.

Over two emotionally draining, yet invigorating days, I experienced how quickly a community can be formed. We were challenged to pour out our deepest fears, hopes, sadness and joy to people we had never met. It was so hard, yet we, as individuals and then as a collective, persisted. And as we did, it became easier and easier, deeper and deeper, until it was hard to believe that we don't communicate like this with everyone, all the time.

Peter Block believes that this is how social fabric is built, one room at a time, and that the small group is the unit of transformation. Large-scale transformation then occurs when enough small groups shift towards the larger change that we wish to experience in our societies

He maintains that the existing community context, in countries like the United States and within certain communities in South Africa (my presumption), is one that markets fear, assigns fault and worships self-interest and that this context supports the belief that the future will be improved with new laws, more oversight and stronger leadership.

The new context, one that restores community, is one of possibility, generosity and gifts.

Block challenged us to ask questions, instead of offering answers. He encouraged us to declare a possibility that we could create a future beyond reach, that has the power to transform our communities. He urged us to recognise our gifts and the gifts of others and to make use of these gifts in everything we do. He inspired us to open our hearts.

It is an incredibly hard process to describe, but it had immense power. In the space of two short days, a community formed out of a room of strangers from all walks of life. In hindsight, it was so easy.

The workshop was organised by the remarkable Louise van Rhyn of Symphonia. Louise is a phenomenon, a dynamo with a passion for this country that is quite beautiful.

When I emailed her to say thank you for making the workshop a reality, she replied by saying: 'When the **Dinokeng Scenarios** *were published, I had such a strong sense of being called – to do what I can to make the Walk Together scenario a reality.'*

'This week was a further refinement of that calling; walking together will only be possible if we are able to reclaim our humanity and become connected as human beings. So my commitment is to develop the capacity for community building in South Africa so that we can ignite communal possibility.

'Imagine if we can be a country where we are able to move away from a focus on individual achievement and truly live our Ubuntu heritage!'

She continued: '(Earlier this year) I expressed an intention to recruit a million South Africans to commit to walking together. This last week has made me rethink this. I think the task is to create opportunities for a million people to experience a deep sense of connection with fellow South Africans. I have no doubt that this will automatically lead to walking together but the starting point is connection and community rather than focusing on the work that needs to be done.'

Louise is striving to give a million South Africans the beautiful gift of connection and community. She is striving to make an immense positive difference in the land that she so loves.

She is doing it, one room at a time.

By Ian Macdonald

I was touched by Ian's article 10 years ago. Reading it today is still an emotional experience and a reminder of how privileged we were to have had the experience of being part of those first Community Building workshops with Peter Block.

I lost touch with Ian for a while and then he showed up in our community in 2016. At the time, Ian was working at Windlab, a Cape Town renewable energy company. Windlab's CEO, Peter Venn, had been a partner to Principal André Lamprecht at Levana Primary in Lavender Hill, so when Ian indicated to Peter that he was keen to join PfP, André was quick to suggest that he partnered with Gavin Alkana, the principal of Hillwood Primary, Levana's neighbouring school.

Ian and Gavin joined the Cape Town 17 (CPT17) Leadership Circle with Nadia Mason as their LPF. The partnership had a bit of a rocky start. Gavin and Ian met at the launch and Gavin was not entirely keen about the idea of working with a white man. They met for coffee at the McDonalds in Tokai and Gavin told Ian that he 'did not want a whitey who will try to tell me what to do at my school.'

When Theo and I met with Gavin at Hillwood Primary in September 2019, he remembered that conversation well. He said he was very firm with Ian and surprised when Ian did not walk away but rather responded by saying 'Gavin, this whitey doesn't know anything about education or about Lavender Hill. I will not try to tell you what to do. I want to learn from you.'

Gavin wasn't entirely convinced, but he decided that he would give it a go. But then, he said, 'the partnership became a friendship which became a brotherhood.'

'Ian and I had a shared history,' he said. 'We discovered that both our parents came from Old Place in Knysna. My mother was the domestic worker in Old Place and Ian's mother lived as a privileged white person in Old Place.

'Ian never tried to justify the past. He acknowledged that the past was wrong. He used to talk about the 'Lotto of Life' and how lucky he was to have won the Lotto because he was white in apartheid South Africa.

'I wasn't sure what to make of Ian. I initially thought he was going to give the school money and to be honest, that was all I was interested in. Ian showed up with no judgement and no expectations. He was just keen to support me as the leader of the school. This was a new experience for me.

'At first I worried that his lack of expectations was covering up for the fact that he thought I would fail, but I realised that he expected me to succeed and he was rooting for me.'

There was no money coming to the school as a result of the partnership, but Gavin says he got a lot more than money. 'I learned to listen. In the past I used to interrupt people because I thought that I was showing interest by interrupting people. I have discovered the power of beautiful listening.

'From attending the Community Building workshop I learned to work with organisations in our community. I used to be very narrowly focused on education, but through my involvement with PfP I realised that I have a role as a community leader. We moved from being a school **in** the community to being a community school.

'Before, we were operating in separate boxes – the school, the local businesses and the NGOs working in the area. We work together more now. It's baby steps at first, but we are all better off because of it.'

Hillwood Primary now offers 26 different extra-mural activities to its learners. 'I became open-minded about this, we used to only run the main codes [activities], but now, due to partnerships and with community involvement, we offer our learners a wide range of options.'

During the first year of Gavin and Ian's partnership, Gavin and the educators struggled to cope with the ongoing gang violence around the school. Nadia and the other partners in the circle rallied around them and started a social media campaign to raise awareness of what was going on in Lavender Hill.

They got the attention of Professor Jonathan Jansen who wrote the following article which was published in The Times on 1 June 2017:

The Big Read: The kids who dodge bullets

Cape Flats pupils risk their lives going to school — and the authorities don't seem to give a damn, writes Jonathan Jansen.

Imagine you send your son or daughter off to primary school and you do not know whether the child will come home alive at the end of the day. Throughout the day your child hears gunshots around the school. It is so bad that the school has to install bullet-proof walls to prevent injury or death as a stray bullet might hit one of the more than 1000 children on the inside. After all, children have been shot on their way to and from school, and sometimes even inside the schools of the area.

There are moments when the children have to duck, fall flat on the floor and stay there until another round of shooting nearby has stopped. Until the shooting restarts and the children drop to the floor again, some crying openly out of raw fear that their lives could end at any moment. Recently it got so bad that teachers were seriously traumatised. One had a heart attack and another a stroke for which they remain in hospital. Children plead with their teacher parents: 'Please do not go to school. I don't want you to die, mummy.'

Counsellors had to be counselled as they fell apart hearing story upon story of pupil and teacher trauma. Working-class parents had to take valuable time off from work to protest by shutting down the school until the police and the Education Department paid attention to a problem that will not go away.

The department says it is not responsible for managing the gangs and the deadly violence in the area; the local police do not have the resources or the capacity to deal with this problem short of national intervention. Officials from the Department of Education arrive with a police escort; more than one of these officials had to scurry to safety as gunfire broke out around them. Yet nothing changes. In the meantime, the schools are held hostage to sustained violence over the years.

Gavin Alkana is the kind of principal who restores my faith in the power of leadership to change the fate of the poorest child. Since he became principal of Hillwood Primary School in Lavender Hill on the southern Cape Flats, things started to change. A school hall was built after 40 years of waiting thanks to one of those unheralded change agents in poor communities, the Garden Cities Archway Foundation. Teachers who had long given up on hope started to express optimism with Alkana's appointment after a string of temporary principals who simply could not take the pressure of leading a school under duress.

Enrolments started to pick up again after parents once abandoned the school for its academic reputation on the inside and the mortal dangers on the outside. Suddenly there was order, predictability, direction and this elusive thing called educational leadership.

But even a good man has his limits. When I call Mr Alkana for this story, it is before 6am and he is already dressed to do a one-man picket on the main road connecting the fancy suburbs to the sandy beaches. He will be back at school by opening time, but he is desperate to be heard by the authorities in this devastating wasteland of lives and learning lost.

I write this column today because I am angry at the lack of effective response to a deadly situation that faces our children every day. Let me be blunt. Why is it that nobody gives a damn? Is it because these are the children of the working classes and the poor? Is it, department officials, because your children are safely ensconced in former white schools where a crisis is a child stumbling on the tartan track hockey pitch?

> *Is it, officials in national government, that these people of the Flats are voting fodder not deemed worthy of priority attention in black majoritarian politics? Or are you so callous as to leave a province that you do not control to the elements in order to make political advantage of this deadly situation? Or have all of you simply lost your humanity in your preoccupation with looting the state and staying in power? Does it matter at all that our children die?*
>
> *Of course it makes no sense to expect anything approximating education to happen under such conditions of duress. No child can concentrate and no teacher can offer the emotional calm and deliberation required for efficacious teaching and no principal can secure a school in the face of armed thugs.*
>
> *So what is to be done? Do not be fooled by politicking around this dangerous situation – like politicians going to Elsies River this week promising land, houses and more crime-fighting capacity. These kind of smooth-talking snap visits after the tragic death of children have happened before, and still nothing has changed.*
>
> *We need the co-ordinated response of national, provincial and local resources to attend to the crisis. In the short term, we need the army to secure the area and the police to end the gang wars. In the medium term we need to provide the schools and the community with the resources (such as social workers and psychologists) to strengthen the provision of education in safe zones. In the long term we need to rebuild these dangerous areas with job security and community rehabilitation that prevent young men from joining gangs.*

This article paints the picture of the challenges that Ian and Gavin had to deal with during the first year of their PfP partnership.

I asked Gavin to think back to the time before he met Ian and compare himself now to how he was then.

'The biggest difference is that I have a voice now. I used to see myself as a small little kitten. I have become confident and assertive. That came from being exposed to a different world to the one that I was used to. I felt intimidated at first, but through Ian that changed. The voice in my head that kept telling me that I was not good enough went quiet.

'Rich, powerful people came to the school and they treated me with respect. They listened to me when I spoke. Nobody ever talked down at me. It has changed my life to experience these equal partnerships of trust and to see that so many people genuinely care and want to create a South Africa that works for all.'

Ian very sadly died in a car accident on 20 February 2018. We were devastated to hear the news and knew that Gavin would be too.

Ian's death came as a massive shock to Gavin. 'I spoke to him the week before, and we were due to meet the day after he died. It was like losing a brother. We shared everything. I cried, the staff at the school cried, he was Hillwood's partner, not just mine,' said Gavin.

Ian's family and friends felt they needed to continue the work that Ian was so passionate about. Ian's father-in-law went to see Gavin and offered to step in as his partner in Ian's place. 'I told him that no one can take Ian's place. I told him that they could continue his work but they can't replace Ian. After Ian's death Rob Broster and Ian's family and friends became my support network,' said Gavin.

After visiting Gavin at the school I felt that I wanted to know more, so I watched the video of the presentation that Gavin and Ian gave at the celebration event which marked their circle's completion of the 12-month facilitated PfP programme. It was one of the celebration events that I had missed, and I wanted to know what they had said about their experience of being in a partnership. This is some of what they shared:

Gavin: 'My initial motive and expectation was to get money. Because we don't have a computer room. We don't have a library. We don't have resources. We don't have a science room. And I thought this is an opportunity for us to get money. The reality, however, was that I gained a friend.

'As somebody said 'When you are a principal it is a lonely position.' I was trained as an educator, not as a manager, not as a business leader. By speaking to my business partner I could gain that experience. I could gain that confidence. I had that safe space to share with Ian.

'Hillwood Primary benefitted from having Ian as a business partner.

'During the second term, our school was closed. The Lavender Hill schools were closed because of the shooting and the gangsterism. People were dying on a daily basis in Lavender Hill and educators felt unsafe. Learners felt unsafe. Parents kept their kids at home. Due to the support of PfP, we could put pressure on the education department and we met with the Premier and we met with the MEC. It is a wonderful day today because we had certain demands and these had been met. We wanted the police there, visible. We wanted the satellite station. We wanted security guards. We wanted a new fence because the fence exposed our learners to the shooting. This morning at twenty past ten I signed with the contractors for a new fence. That will be for 2018. That is because of the partnership and PfP's support and, for me, that was more valuable than the money I had anticipated.'

Ian: 'Our partnership was sponsored by Windlab and Piet van Zyl, a gentleman who lives overseas.

'The Partners for Possibility journey is an incredible journey. It's very profound and very well-structured. The courses that you do are extremely impressive and profound in terms of their realisations and the teachings that they teach us. How it is structured with the Community of Practice that gets together and creates opportunities for people to share experiences in an open and honest way where they can speak from the heart about matters that affect us all.

'Our CoP was very ably and beautifully and sensitively led by Nadia the whole time, so Nadia, thank you very much for all that you have done for our CoP for this year and to make this Partners for Possibility year truly spectacular, so thank you very much.

'As Gavin mentioned, one of the major challenges that Hillwood faced this year was the gang warfare. This year was one of the worst years in recent history. It just made me realise how incredibly challenging it is to run a school in these kinds of environments. My children go to a school in Sun Valley, and the principal in that school says the number one thing that is important for him is that his children feel safe. He says if you don't feel safe, you can't learn. To have gang warfare happening outside, to have automatic rifles going off outside of the school that you can hear, to have teachers having strokes and heart attacks because of the stress. These are the kind of challenging environments where Gavin and his remarkable team are able to deliver an amazing education to the children at Hillwood.

'We started off as a partnership. That partnership evolved into a relationship and it has indeed become a friendship. I've realised that even though we come from very different backgrounds we have much in common in terms of our family history, in terms of our age. We have three children of round about the same age. Two of our children even got the same name. It was a real realisation that we have so much in common even though we come from completely different backgrounds and completely different realities. There is so much more that binds us than what keeps us apart.

'A key focus of us this year has been acknowledging and appreciating the educators. These educators are operating under incredibly stressful situations and circumstances. Gavin is such a selfless leader. He is just always wanting to put his educators first. So a lot of our attention this year has been around appreciating these educators and letting them know that they are seen, that their work is valuable.

'Windlab, my company, hosted a Christmas party at the end of the year. I went out with the teachers and we bought all the goods and snacks and drinks and we had the most amazing morning. The next day they had a really fantastic party. We gave them all certificates acknowledging them for their amazing work. They each got a small gift.

'At the beginning of the year we hosted a staff development workshop which was facilitated by Lauren Ratcliffe who came on board and helped us out. She gave up her time and hosted a staff development workshop in a beautiful area of Constantia called Little Streams and it was just such a great start to the year to get together with all these educators in this beautiful environment and talk about what we can do to make the team stronger. Lauren also helped us with a website that she is developing and a video that we will show later.

'The other positive thing that came out of it was that we went into a partnership with the Shine Literacy programme who are pioneering a partnership with PfP to bring a love of reading to Grade 2s at Hillwood. This programme has really given me some profound realizations. I've learned so much about education. I've learned so much about Lavender Hill. I've learned so much about challenge. I've learned so much about resilience, about strength and I have learned about my privilege, and I recognise what a privileged life I've had. Instead of feeling guilty about my privilege I've realised that I can mobilise. And I can utilise my privilege for the benefit of others. And because of my privilege I have amazing networks. I have amazing people that I can tap into who have skills, who have resources, who have abilities. And I can mobilise them for the benefit of the school. People often say 'I really want to make a difference, but I just don't know how'. Partners for Possibility is an amazing programme that allows people to make a significant contribution to a school. And the school is such a powerful agent of change in this country. And it is a very inspiring process to be part of.'

I had so many mixed emotions after watching the video of Gavin and Ian's presentation at the celebration. I feel so sad to think that Ian is no longer with us, but, at the same time, I am so grateful for this video as I can only imagine how proud Ian's children must be when they watch their beautiful father speak with so much passion and commitment.

In April 2018 the following article was published on the IOL website:

R130K raised to help fix Cape Flats school

Cape Town – Children at a Cape Flats school have much to celebrate thanks to a recent crowdfunding campaign which raised more than R130 000 to fix their classrooms.

Principal Gavin Alkana, of Hillwood Primary School in Lavender Hill, says pupils are still using chairs given to the school when it first opened 41 years ago in 1977.

Several years ago, through a Partners for Possibility Programme (PfP), Alkana was introduced to Ian Macdonald, a father and businessman from Noordhoek.

'He partnered with us to help us improve school life for the teachers and learners. In 2017, he helped raise R35 000 to refurbish the staff room to improve morale among teachers,' Alkana says.

In February, Ian tragically died in a head-on collision, leaving the staff and learners devastated, Alkana says.

'We started out as partners, but we became friends and then brothers. His death was a blow for us because he did so much and he was a part of our family.'

Ian's friend, Rob Broster, then set up a campaign on crowd- funding platform, BackaBuddy, to continue Ian's work and to honour a friendship spanning more than 25 years.

'Ian didn't just talk about what must be done. He just did it. Besides his career he has always strongly argued for making a difference and for using privilege and network for positive change,' says Rob.

On 15 March, a campaign to raise R90 000 to refurbish four Grade 1 classrooms at Hillwood kicked off and within 24 hours, over R32 000 was raised.

In less than a month they raised over R130 000 with contributions from more than 60 donors.

Alkana says over the June school holidays, work will commence to repair broken windows, desks, chairs and flooring.

'Due to vandalism, many of the windows don't open and the door has to be open for ventilation. Some of the chairs the children are sitting on were here when the school first opened in 1977,' he says.

'This is a no-fees school and many of our children come from very poor backgrounds. They are raised in the dreary environment in Lavender Hill and then come to school and it is the same. We want to give them a chance to be inspired.'

In October 2018 the following story was published on the SA: Good News newsletter:

Chapter 7: Hillwood Primary, Ian Macdonald and Fella's Army

Cloudbox takes on the challenge

Cloudbox has accepted Carlyles 10,000 Charity Challenge together with a number of its business partners like Euphoria Telecom. The challenge is to do 10,000 push-ups during the month of November to help raise money for Fella's Army.

Fella's Army is a group of amazing humans that have taken on the mantle of Ian 'Fella' Macdonald in supporting the Lavender Hill community, and in particular Hillwood Primary School. Fella died tragically in a car accident earlier this year.

Cloudbox CEO Justin Trent says by continuing the amazing work he did supporting Hillwood is certainly the best way of remembering him. 'Ian believed passionately in improving the lives of others and as a tribute to him, his friends and family have grouped together to form Fella's Army in order to continue his mission.'

Hillwood Primary is a school in Lavender Hill run by a willing and dedicated team of educators, operating in a truly desperate environment. These are children that literally live with gunfire on a daily basis in one of the worst gang and criminal hotspots in the world.

'What makes this a cause worth supporting though is the principal and teaching body involved – they care deeply about giving these children a chance to break the cycle, and we know that the funding and charitable efforts provided by Fella's Army is spend wisely and diligently,' explains Trent.

Ian partnered with principal Gavin Alkana through the Partners For Possibility programme and grew to be a trusted friend and thinking partner. His positive spirit and friendly nature meant that he became a great friend of all the staff.

He assisted the teachers and school through several projects that he helped Gavin initiate, secure funding for and organise. These include a staff development day, staff room refurbishment, producing a video about the school and introducing new extramurals.

'I'm middle-aged, sedentary, and mildly overweight. Anyone who has ever asked me how long something will take will also know I'm prone to understatement. So, when I told the person next to me at a wedding that I'd signed up to do the Carlyles 10,000 Charity Challenge, you understand why the first response was hearty laughter,' adds Cloudbox CTO Oliver Potgieter.

'It's also nice to know that somewhere out there Fella's bellowing laugh is ringing out. 10,000 is a bloody big number,' he concludes.

I wanted to speak to the people behind the idea of 'Fella's Army', so we met with Ian's best friend, Rob Broster, and Suzie Allderman, his cousin, who were instrumental in its formation.

Rob had been friends with Ian for 20 years and remembers that when Ian was younger he was quite hedonistic and focused on having a good time. However, this changed after Ian lived overseas and returned to South Africa.

'When he came back he was much more aware of the world around him and his place in it. He had set up a group of friends who would meet regularly to explore what we could do to make things better. We wanted to figure out what role we could play and what we could practically do. Ian was action-orientated and wanted us to get things done,' said Rob.

'Ian kept searching. He had a conversation with his father-in-law and asked him the same question: 'What can we do?' This was quite a sobering experience for Ian because his father-in-law helped him see that he first needed to work on himself before telling other people what to do.

'Ian came back after the conversation with his father-in-law, and he told us that he had had a revelation. So the next few meetings were more about us and how we needed to change rather than how we change others,' Rob explained.

Later, Ian spoke to Peter Venn, his manager at Windlab and Peter suggested that he should consider getting involved in PfP. Afterwards, Ian told the group that he knew Peter had been able to mobilise a lot of funding for Levana Primary School and said he was worried that he would not be able to do that. Rob, who himself had been a business partner to a principal through PfP a few years before, told Ian that raising money is not what the programme is about, and the group helped Ian see that he had much to offer a principal. Ian asked them whether they would be willing to help him if he needed assistance, and they agreed.

Ian eventually partnered with Gavin and regularly gave feedback to the group about his experience. And then he was tragically killed. 'Ian was very gregarious. He had a large group of friends. His death really shocked us. We were devastated,' said Rob.

The day after Ian's death, a group of his friends gathered at the Club House in Constantia in an effort to process their grief. They talked about Ian and his commitment to 'do stuff' rather than talk about getting things done.

There were several other gatherings, and a WhatsApp group was started, initially to share pictures and memories. But then people started to talk about ways to honour

Ian's life. Someone asked 'How do we not let his legacy die? How can we continue to do the work he started?'

Ian's nickname was 'Fella', and at some point during the first week after his death, Rob asked 'What would Fella do?' Rob felt that the way to honour Ian (Fella) would be to DO something.

A week after Ian's death they celebrated his life and Gavin and most of the Hillwood educators attended. When Rob did the eulogy, he continued to challenge Ian's friends by asking 'What would Fella do?'

The following week Rob, Suzie, Clifford (Ian's father-in-law) and Michael Byron visited Gavin at Hillwood. Michael Byron became involved because he is the executive trustee of the Mapula Trust, the family charitable trust of Ian's good friend Charlie (Duncan) Parker who had asked Michael to see how Mapula Trust could support the process of honouring Ian.

They had no idea what to do. They just knew they wanted to do something. They also wanted to find out what Ian's plans for Hillwood Primary had been, thinking that they may be able to complete some of the work he had started.

What came out of that first meeting was that they would start a scholarship in Ian's name and that the school's eco-club would be supported (because the environment was one of Ian's passions).

'The four of us later visited the school and asked Gavin to show us around so that we could see what we could do to help. We met with him several times after that, and he told us the school needed equipment and that several of the classrooms were in poor condition and needed refurbishment,' Rob said.

Rob and Suzie then set up a Backabuddy campaign to collect funds to refurbish dilapidated classrooms. In the end, that project raised enough money to renovate ten classrooms.

The term 'Fella's Army' emerged as a metaphor for all of those doing good work in Ian's name, Suzie explained. Later it began to refer to an informal group of people who were involved in work at the school.

Two of Ian's friends who became part of Fella's Army are project managers. They took the lead in recruiting members of the Lavender Hill community to carry out renovations and oversaw the work being done at the school. They gave their time generously; doing everything from buying the materials, to supervising the workers and paying them. Justin Spreckley oversaw Phase 1, which involved the Grade 1 classrooms, while David Dugmore oversaw Phase 2 – the Grade 2 classrooms.

Suzie and Rob arranged two Saturday 'Paint-a-thons' at the school so that all the classroom furniture could be painted. For Rob and Suzie, it was important for the people who were part of Fella's Army to actually visit the school and spend time in Lavender Hill, rather than just donating money from afar.

People brought their kids to the first painting event in May 2018, but the second one later in was kept to adults only because there had been a lot of gunfire in the area. Gavin insisted that the volunteers leave the area by 1 pm.

Renee, Ian's wife, rallied support from her Fella's Army friends to make up a gift hamper for each member of the Hillwood Primary staff team for their end of year function. Continuing the tradition that Ian and Gavin had started, Renee also had certificates printed for every staff member.

Ian's friends have also rallied Fella's Army to link their MySchool cards to Hillwood Primary, which brings in about R1,200 per month. The school has also received donations of pre-loved, but fully serviceable, office furniture.

Rob and Suzie keep in contact with Gavin. He lets them know when a particular need arises, and they share the details with Fella's Army, who then make a request for support. For example, when a fire destroyed homes and property in Vrygrond, where many of the school's learners live, Fella's Army raised R10,000; when the school's bathrooms were badly damaged by vandals, they raised R5,000.

Clifford continues to work with the school's eco-club and has taken them on several excursions to Kirstenbosch Gardens.

I asked Rob and Suzie what it meant for them to be involved in honouring Ian's life in this way. Rob described it as a way of coping with his grief. 'It was very difficult for me to deal with Ian's death. My work was being affected and I needed an outlet,' he said. 'Ian and I shared the conviction that we needed to do something to make the country better. He was more vocal about it than I was, though. I felt that if I could get people to go and see the school and Lavender Hill they would be motivated to help us continue the work he did.'

Suzie's connection was a family one – Ian was her cousin. 'I lost my brother when he was 21 years old; he gave his life trying to save others who were drowning and was awarded posthumously for bravery. My parents set up a fund to donate books to his high school – there is now a section in the school library that is named after him and also an annual school award in his name. It's a great comfort to us that my brother has this kind of legacy, that people know who he was and what he did, and I wanted to help do the same for my incredible cousin Ian and for our family,' she said.

Fella's Army organised another 10,000 push-up challenge in November 2019, aimed at raising at least R150,000. The beauty of this group is that every single cent its raises goes towards projects at Hillwood Primary School because there are no overheads. This is an army that marches on love and love alone!

Ian touched thousands of lives while he was with us. He was an inspirational person to know. As a result of his involvement at Hillwood Primary, lives were and are still being changed for the better.

Peter Venn and the Mapula trustees have established the Ian Macdonald Memorial Scholarship, which will be awarded annually to a learner who displays academic excellence, all-round leadership qualities and a passion for environmental conservation. The award covers the cost of five years of high school and includes fees, uniforms, transport and stationery.

'The idea with the scholarship was not to simply donate the money required but to support the recipients along the way too. SAILI, an organisation that awards bursaries and manages students, was appointed to support the learners,' Rob explained.

Grade 7 learner Spokuhle Gcaxa was the worthy recipient for 2019, while Lolwethu Mjamba, a Grade 6 student, received the 2020 scholarship.

While we were busy writing this book, I joined the #ImStaying group on Facebook. Katherine Persson, who worked with Ian at Windlab, posted this message to the group on 28 September 2019:

> *A close friend, colleague, mentor (and so much more than words can say) wrote this in 2008. He passed away last year. Whenever I need a reminder of why #imstaying I read his poem.*
>
> *Ian Macdonald, you inspire me and guide me more than you know* ♥🐵☺
>
> ....

Why do I love South Africa? Ian Macdonald, 2008

I love her for the perfection of her days
The crisp karoo morning The joberg winter noon
The late summer Cape Town sunsets
The star-filled Free State night

I love her for her people
For our warm smiles
For our resilience
For our I-am-because-we-are

I love her because she delights my senses
Highveld thunderbolts
Jacarandas in bloom
Sunday braais
African sun
Icy sea

I love her raw power, her intensity, her strength
I love her because of how she makes me feel
Sometimes angry, sometimes joyous
Sometimes fearful, sometimes love-filled
Sometimes frustrated, sometimes hopeful
Always alive

I love her because she intrigues me
And challenges me
The Chinese have a curse: 'may you live in interesting times'
I see it as a blessing

I love her because she helps me keep things in perspective
By reminding me how privileged I am
Every day
I love her for being a microcosm of the world
A world in one country
For what we can teach the world
About compromise
And sharing

And forgiveness
And tolerance
And hope

I love her because she is imperfect
And full of opportunity
And potential unfulfilled

I love her because she has come so far
And has so much further to go
And whether we ever get there
Will depend on us

I love her because she's been good to me
And she inspires me to return the favour
I love her because she's my country
No matter what
I love her because she's my home
And where my soul is at rest

....

Miss you, Ian

Katherine's message is another reminder of the ripple effect of Ian's life.

> *"You cannot do a kindness too soon, for you never know how soon it will be too late."* – Ralph Waldo Emerson

Chapter 8

Business as a force for good

"Business should be a powerful force for social good."
– Adrian Gore, Discovery Founder and CEO

When we started PfP, we fantasised about the possibility that we could encourage every business unit leader in South Africa to make a commitment to supporting an under-resourced school with its improvement process. Our hope was that each of these leaders would partner with a principal and then mobilise their organisation's resources to assist the school. We dreamt of IT managers supporting IT in the schools, finance managers providing support with financial management and HR managers helping with HR issues. We envisaged that PfP business leaders would be the link between resources available in their business units and the schools. This vision has, sadly, not yet materialised in many places.

We have seen, for example, the power of this approach in the ROGZ-Sophakama Primary partnership, where many leaders from ROGZ have proactively used their unique talents and gifts to benefit the school. The IT manager helped to resolve computer-related challenges, while the production manager, who is a keen gardener, assisted with the establishment of a vegetable garden at the school. Irené Raubenheimer, the business partner, enrolled mothers from Elkanah House, a nearby private school, to set up a reading programme at the school.

I was interested in capturing more of those kinds of stories and also in finding out what had contributed to the generous sharing of resources in those instances.

Windlab and Levana Primary

In Chapter 7 we told the story of the PfP partnership at Hillwood Primary School. After our delightful visit with Gavin Alkana, I asked him whether it would be OK for Theo and I to walk from Hillwood to Levana Primary, which is close by. 'Well,' said Gavin, 'you are two white people, and this is Lavender Hill. I think I should rather take you with my car.'

After arriving at the school for our meeting with André Lamprecht, the principal, we had to wait a while before he joined us. When he finally did, André explained that he had needed to make some last-minute arrangements for the memorial service of a Grade R learner who had been shot the weekend before. This was yet another reminder of the kinds of challenges that principals like André have to deal with on a daily basis.

André joined PfP in 2014 and was partnered with Peter Venn, Managing Director of Windlab, a renewable energy company. When he started the programme on 30 October 2014, André had been a school principal for exactly one month. In those days, we had a 'rule' that principals were not allowed to join PfP in their first year of principalship, but somehow André had been invited to join.

Our thinking at the time was that new principals needed to 'get their feet under the table' at their schools before embarking on the programme. However, André says 'joining Partners for Possibility is the best thing that can happen to a young and inexperienced principal.'

Before he became principal of Levana Primary André was a course instructor at the Cape Teaching and Leadership Institute. 'I had all this head knowledge,' he explained, 'but I wanted to gain some experience as a principal. I wanted to work in the actual situations that we spoke about in our courses. If I was to maintain my post level and ranking at the education department I would have to become the principal of a school with more than 1,000 learners; that's how I ended up in Lavender Hill.'

When André joined Levana Primary he found that he would be leading a team of highly experienced teachers. 'I'd come into the school as a youngster from outside and into a situation where 20 of the 30 teachers were older than 50, and 12 were older than 55. Even though I had all the theory and policy, it didn't mean much when I got there,' he recalls.

The school was pretty set in its ways and André didn't know how he could change things. 'Peter brought a new dynamic, and discussing things with him made them clearer to me. I still bounce things off him now, four years later. What helped was that Peter did not arrive with a know-it-all attitude. He realised that even with his computer science, finance and MBA degrees there are no easy answers.'

A number of successes came out of the partnership, not least of which was stronger trust between André and his staff team. 'The courses we did certainly helped with that and Peter and I both learned a lot about human relationships. The older teachers began to accept me, and that brought about other improvements.'

There were practical issues that had to be dealt with. The school is located in an area that is blighted by crime and gangsterism and is often unsafe for schoolchildren. 'The fences around the school had just about all disappeared and security could not be guaranteed. We wrote letters to the Western Cape Education Department, without much effect, until, tragically, a two-year-old child was shot in the street outside. This was the catalyst to get the fences fixed.'

With no library at the school, the Levana Primary learners were having to cross a dangerously busy road to reach the nearest public library in a neighbouring suburb. The partners started raising funds to build a library at the school, and André, with support from his PA, initiated the '10,000 Books Challenge,' a project to collect 10 books for every child at the school.

'I told the school that if everyone reads 10 books, which means we will collectively have read 10,000 books, I will spend an entire day up on the school roof,' André said. 'They did it! I never did go up on the roof though – it would have been unsafe with the shootings that were going on in the area at that time – but I will keep my promise as soon as it's possible to do so.'

It's difficult to say how soon the effect of the book drive began to show up in improved literacy performances, but in 2016 Levana won the WCED's Growsmart Literacy competition, which 150 schools are selected to enter each year. One of the prizes Levana received was an iPad lab worth R250,000.

In 2018, with the help of a generous donation by the Albert Wessels Trust, a library was built at the school. It was named the Renee Roman Library in honour of a pupil who was murdered in 2017.

'Through other partnerships, we have added more books, a reading room and other facilities including Wi-Fi. There is no community library in Lavender Hill. The high school also uses our library, as do members of the community.'

Every time I hear André speak, I am reminded of our theory that a well-run school with an energetic principal tends to become a magnet for the gifts and contributions from people and organisations around the school.

As a result of support from Garden City Archways, coupled with the Albert Wessels Trust donation, a hall has been constructed at the school. Windlab staff got involved at the school, and instead of having an annual Christmas party they arranged for the Windlab staff team to paint the playground.

Through partnerships, the school has been able to develop its sports field, plant vegetable gardens and implement a variety of enrichment programmes for learners. 'Organisations are interested in us,' André said. 'I think they like to invest where they see other investments being made. Success breeds success. My commitment to partner with organisations and the community came from my involvement with the PfP programme.'

I asked André how things would have been different if he had not entered into the partnership with Peter.

'It would have taken much longer for me to get the trust of the staff,' he said. 'Those early successes helped me to gain the trust of my team. We don't have a problem with staff absenteeism, for example.

'Our results have gone up, but it isn't substantial yet. I don't believe that the systemic tests are the best measure of a school anyway, especially when they are written on the same day that a learner got shot directly outside the school gate.

'Levana has become an environment that is conducive to learning. We are proud to say that many of our learners are accepted into scholarship programmes that make it possible for them to go to schools outside Lavender Hill.

'Our relationships with parents have also improved,' said André. 'We now have more than 90% attendance at parents' meetings. Levana Primary is seen as a school of choice for parents in our community.'

A few weeks after visiting André, Theo and I got the chance to meet with Peter Venn. He spends a lot of time travelling, so I was delighted that we could make a face-to-face conversation happen.

I asked Peter why he had decided to get involved in PfP. 'I am a big believer in the idea that we need to use the skills available to move the country forward. I did not feel it should be all about money. I felt that there must be a way for me to share my time, skills and experience.

'Windlab is a small company, but we have amazing people working in the organisation. I wanted to figure out how to tap into this group of highly skilled and talented individuals.' There are only 55 people in the Windlab team. The majority of them are based in Australia, where the company is listed on the stock exchange.

'I was looking for a way to use what we have at Windlab to make a bigger contribution, and then I attended a PfP briefing. The concept made sense to me. I realised that there is a multiplier effect that comes from working with the leader of a school and that it would ultimately be more beneficial than just giving money to a school.'

Peter's gift is getting people to finance renewable energy projects. 'Every project we undertake at Windlab needs funding, and it's my job to go to funders and persuade them to invest in us,' he said. 'I felt that I could use those skills to help the school.'

Three Windlab leaders have joined PfP as business partners. Peter at Levana, Katherine Persson at Westlake Primary and Ian Macdonald, who was at Hillwood Primary.

'We all have different skill sets, and we brought these different skills to our partnerships,' said Peter. 'Ian's partnership with Gavin was very different from my partnership with André. In my case, I used my fundraising skills to contribute. I have probably mobilised about R12 million worth of investment to Levana through my network and connections.'

PfP provided a framework in which Peter could leverage his network. His Australian colleagues have been doing book drives at home for Levana Primary. The entire Windlab team felt that they were part of Levana, even holding their Christmas party at the school one year.

Peter appreciates the structure of the PfP process. 'As with most business leaders, time is a challenge for me. PfP is a professionally run project, and the schedule of activities is published in advance. That made it easy for me to participate.'

The match between himself and André was a good one. 'André was ready and keen to be in a partnership. My role was to build his confidence and provide a channel for him to talk to. I was able to use my privilege to make things happen for the school. For me, usually, all it needed was a couple of phone calls, but for him, it was often an impossible situation.'

Peter gave us an example: André had been battling to get the school's lawnmower repaired and was mired in departmental red tape. 'In the meantime, the field was becoming overgrown, so I called my office manager and asked her to have a new mower delivered the same day. It wasn't that expensive to us, but it made a big difference to André and to the school,' he said.

While Peter realises that his role in the partnership was not supposed to be about providing funding, that was the best use of his skills and time, he said. 'It was how I leveraged the time I was investing to make the most impact.'

That was not the only thing that happened in the partnership, Peter said. 'We were able to work together on many projects: we built a library and stocked it with books through partnerships, we got the Albert Wessels Foundation to fund a hall for the school, and we were able to make the school field suitable for sport to be played on.'

An experience that stands out for him, and one that he believes had a deep impact on the children involved, was the day they got Sporting Chance to take 50 learners from Levana to a rugby match at Newlands, using the official Stormers team bus.

'When we were walking along the outside of the stadium, one of the girls asked me where it was,' Peter told us. 'I realised that she had never seen the outside of a big stadium before, only TV pictures of what it looks like inside. It made me realise how limited the lives of many of these children are and how easy it is to broaden them.'

I asked Peter about the impact of PfP on his life. 'I guess I could use the old cliché of saying I received more than I gave in the process, and that would be true,' he said. 'But it went deeper than that. I began to understand issues and to see the challenges facing our country clearer. I am now much clearer about how SED[24] money should be spent and what business leaders could do to make a meaningful contribution.

'When I walk around the school with André and see the kids come up to him for a hug, I realise how important he is to them and how crucial his role is. Working with André at Levana helped me see what is possible when business leaders leave their corporate offices and cross the boundaries into communities like Lavender Hill.

'I have grown as a person. I moved out of my comfort zone and, for the first time, I saw the underbelly of the city that I had lived in all my life.'

I asked Peter what he wants his children to realise if they ever get to read this book. 'I want my children to know that I was committed to their future, and that is why I crossed the boundary into Lavender Hill.

'I am so humbled by what has happened at the school. Before our partnership, the school did not have a hall or a sports field. Now it has both. And it is having a massive impact on everybody in that community.

'I am a much richer person because of the PfP experience. I have friends who, like me, want to contribute to solutions to the problems in the country, but many of them are unwilling to step out of their current reality and get involved. I think they are missing out on an amazing experience to be part of the solution and to help create the future we want for our children.'

Nimble and St Agnes Primary School

Rowan Gordon is the CEO and founder of the Cape Town-based Nimble Group. Alfonso Louw is the principal at St Agnes Primary School in Woodstock. Rowan has not only shared Nimble's resources freely with St Agnes but has also been extremely generous in supporting SSA: for the last two years, Nimble has provided office space for our M&E team at its headquarters in Salt River.

Theo and I visited Rowan at his office. Rowan is acutely aware of his privileged background. He attended Rondebosch Boys' High and his children now go to top private schools. 'I wanted to do something to give back to society. I wanted to bridge the gap between those who have and those who don't. I wanted to do something with reach and scale,' he told us.

---

24   Socio-Economic Development (SED) contributions are monetary or non-monetary contributions that form part of the SA government's Broad-based Black Economic Empowerment (B-BBEE) policy.

Rowan had read the book *Judgement: How Winning Leaders Make Great Calls* by Noel Tichy and Warren Bennis. In it there is a chapter about the work Mayor Michael Bloomberg had done in New York City by partnering business leaders with school principals. 'The concept resonated with me, and I was wondering about doing something like this in South Africa. By coincidence, I met Irené Raubenheimer through an Elkanah House function and he told me about Partners for Possibility.

'I was initially a bit sceptical about the possibility of making an impact without strong support from government, but I saw how hard PfP was working to develop the relationship with the Western Cape Education Department and I decided to get involved.

'I had one requirement, and that was to work with a school close by to Nimble. I knew that it would help to be in close proximity to our partner school, and I also wanted to get my colleagues involved. I knew that would be easier to do if the school was close. In hindsight, I can say that proximity made a big difference to us. St Agnes is only five minutes away. From the start, Alfonso and I alternated our meeting venues. We meet at 12 noon on Tuesdays, and we meet one week at Nimble and the next at St Agnes.'

Alfsono and Rowan first met in October 2014. They were part of the Cape Town 12 (CPT12) Leadership Circle with Nicky Wilson-Harris as their LPF. 'I did not get involved for only one year,' said Rowan. 'I made a long-term commitment to Alfonso and to St Agnes. I am sorry that the facilitated part of PfP only ran for a year as I think it would have been good to stay more connected with other leaders who are working to improve schools.'

Rowan and Alfonso have been meeting weekly for almost five years. 'I spend 90% of the time just listening to Alfonso. He needs a sounding board, and I just let him speak. He is also keen to hear about my business challenges and solutions.'

Rowan believes that principals need more exposure to management, not just to leadership concepts, and he thinks that PfP needs to do more to expose principals to management practices. I explained to Rowan that our hope is that business leaders will share their knowledge about management with principals, and it turns out that this is exactly what Rowan has been doing. 'I have shared with Alfonso how I know what is happening in every corner of my business.'

I asked Rowan why he thinks that he and Alfonso have maintained their partnership, for five years now, after meeting through PfP. 'Alfonso is exceptional in how he recognises me,' he said. 'I don't want any recognition, but I have to admit that it does make a difference. You spend your time and money where there is an emotional connection. Alfonso is big on gestures; he always makes sure that I am invited to important events and occasions at the school. My whole office is full of gestures of recognition from Alfonso and his team. It has led to an emotional attachment for me. I love spending time at the school.'

The longevity of the partnership has been aided by the close proximity of the school, but also by Alfonso's careful use of Rowan's time. 'I never feel burdened by Alfonso. He is hesitant to ask for things, and he is almost apologetic when he does. We don't have daily contact, and when we do meet it is often simply to meander through ideas or challenges.'

Rowan said the interaction has definitely made a big difference to him personally. 'It's been gratifying to see the positive changes in the school. There are now almost double the number of children at the school since 2015. I have become part of the school community. It is a happy place, a safe environment and a sanctuary for the children.

'I think it is important to live a purposeful life. Being part of PfP contributes to that. My engagement has given me a better understanding of education and its challenges and I have found it goes far beyond the false stereotypes of union interference and lazy teachers. Being given the opportunity to help and share has been an enabling experience for me.'

While Alfonso's personal growth and development has been the most important outcome, there were also a number of practical things that came from the partnership. 'I work with a diverse team of professionals and they have much to offer.' Nimble's IT department was instrumental in equipping their computer room and setting up their systems. 'My guys managed to forge relationships with the ICT people in the education department and that has smoothed the way,' Rowan said.

'We have also done quite a bit of 'handyman' work around the school. We have helped with some sprucing up of the environment. We had the toilets fixed and repainted. We have facilitated the annual prize-giving to embrace and celebrate academic excellence. We have facilitated workshops with staff at Nimble to explore key challenges to improving educational outcomes.'

I wanted to know from Rowan if he thought his involvement has made a real lasting impact on the school. 'I think there has been a multiplier effect at work there,' he said. 'I work with Alfonso and he has a direct effect on 500 kids every year and 1,000 different children over a five year period. The children are flourishing, you see it in their schoolwork and in their activities.'

Supporting Alfonso is the key, though. 'It is so lonely to be a principal. He does not have people to talk to about the challenges he faces at school or the things he needs to make sense of. While there are various people I consult with before making a decision at work, and I can 'meander' before deciding, he doesn't have that kind of support. He admits to making rash decisions in his early years as a principal. Now he can use me as a sounding board before acting. I'd say that 60% of our time together is personal support.

'The rest of the time we talk about the school and the department, about our own kids and about his future and his career options.'

Evaluating the impact on the school's performance is more difficult, Rowan said. 'You can look at the results of the systemic tests, but they are skewed by the fact that, at a school like St Agnes, learners are often in classes where they simply don't have the foundational knowledge that is required.'

We left Rowan's office to drive to St Agnes. It took a little longer than five minutes to get there, but as we walked into the school we felt what Rowan meant when he referred to the school as a 'sanctuary in Woodstock'.

Alfonso assumed the role of principal in October 2002. He describes his appointment as 'being thrown in at the deep end being expected to just sink or swim.' He did not receive any training or support on how to be a principal and had to learn by trial and error.

'I'm a teacher,' he said, 'I was trained to teach children, in a classroom, but suddenly I found myself in the office, expected to lead a team and having to deal with administrative tasks that I didn't know how to do.

'I was operating by trial and error, and because I was under immense pressure I tended to make decisions in haste, some of which I came to regret later on.' Alfonso remembers feeling overwhelmed at times and admits that he considered leaving the profession more than once.

In 2014 St Agnes had 260 learners and its results in the Western Cape Education Department's (WCED) systemic tests were poor. Fast forward to 2019 and there are now 545 learners – which is all they have space for – and there has been a remarkable improvement in the Grade 3 and 6 systemic test results. Academic performances have also improved in other grades. Alfonso describes the progress as 'a steady increase of 7%, year-on-year.' In 2000 the school had only one class per grade; it now has two classes in every grade.

Parents recognise St Agnes as a good school and want their children to be there. Now though, demand is outstripping supply and there is a waiting list for entry into the school. Alfonso has been sent, more than once, by the education department, to help 'turn around' struggling schools in the area.

He believes that PfP made a massive difference to him and his school. 'It came at a time when I was feeling lonely and overwhelmed,' he said. 'The programme put me in touch with other principals and schools, and I realised I was not the only one facing those challenges. The training we received was great. It was invigorating to attend training and then be able to implement the ideas at the school. My wish is that the department officials had access to the same kind of training.'

Alfonso says that he hit it off with Rowan straight away. 'We have so much in common, the main thing being that we are both passionate about improving things for the children,' Alfonso said. 'Through my relationship with Rowan, I have realised the value of careful thought before making decisions. I have been able to bounce my ideas off Rowan and have come to see the value of looking at decisions from different perspectives.'

'Our relationship has grown beyond a principal-business leader relationship now,' Alfonso said. 'We have become friends and our families have got to know each other too. I don't always agree with him, but I listen because he speaks from a business perspective. At the same time, I think his eyes have been opened to what is going on in the world of education as well.'

Alfonso isn't sure that he would still be in education if he had not met Rowan. 'There have been times when I was so overwhelmed that I wanted to quit. I would call Rowan and we would meet. He would always cover my back and I know I can depend on his support.'

Alfonso told us about a recent incident where a teacher was falsely accused of physical assault. It ended up in the media and Alfonso had to accompany the teacher to the local police station. Alfonso was distraught and needed someone to talk to about it, so he turned to Rowan. Rowan enabled access to a lawyer who accompanied the teacher and Alfonso to court. The prosecutor dismissed the case as 'contrived'. Alfonso is convinced that if it wasn't for Rowan's support the case would have dragged on for months.

'I wouldn't be a thoughtful administrator if it wasn't for him. He has also helped me to be more confident; to the extent that I am not afraid to challenge the department if I believe what they are doing is not in the interests of the kids. I push back when the instructions I am given don't add value to the school; that's a business practice that I have learned from Rowan.

'I wouldn't be who I am if it were not for Rowan. He has opened the door for me and it's all about possibilities now. I try not to impose on him too much. I don't want our relationship to be based just on my needs. I think it's reciprocal now. We talk about his work too as his position is also a lonely one sometimes.'

It was such a privilege to hear Rowan and Alfonso speak about their experience. I wondered what Michael Bloomberg would say if he heard their story. This is the kind of business-school support system we had envisaged when we conceptualized PfP.

Mediclinic and Cloetesville High School

When Dorian Meyer, Principal of Cloetesville High School, was approached in 2017 by LPF Jessica Batts to enter into a PfP partnership, he was hesitant. 'I was only a principal for a few months, and I had already been approached by a few NGOs with offers of assistance. The school was already part of two other programmes and I was questioning their value,' he said.

'I wanted any association we entered into to have an impact on all the learners at the school. I did not want to do anything that would only benefit the teachers or a few selected learners, and I definitely did not want to do anything that would only benefit the principal,' said Dorian.

Dorian's history at Cloetesville High had complicated things a bit further. A few years earlier, he had been a not very popular HOD at the school before leaving to become a deputy principal at another school. Then he was appointed as Cloetesville's principal. 'I was quite aggressive and a bit mean when I was at the school before,' he admits, 'I knew I had to regain the trust of the staff, and I was not going to enter an arrangement that they would perceive as being for my benefit only.'

Jessica spoke with such passion about PfP that Dorian took notice and recognised that this might be a worthwhile project. 'I realised that this was not just about physical things for the school, but about a business that was distanced from the Cloetesville community wanting to get involved in our school. Jessica told me that there would be training involved, but much more too, depending on the business leader I would be partnered with.'

The first PfP meeting Dorian attended was an eye-opener. 'I met my business partner, Deon Myburgh, the ICT Operations Manager at Mediclinic, and I immediately realised that I was in the right place and it was happening at exactly the right time,' he said. 'I had already worked out a five-year plan for what I wanted to achieve at the school, and I realised that participating in PfP may help me achieve my plan – maybe even in a shorter time period,' he said.

'There was this white guy, who had not previously had any relationship with schools and communities like ours, now being prepared to come here and try to make a difference. That changed everything for me,' Dorian said.

Deon made it clear from the start that he had no intention of telling Dorian how to run his school. 'He said he wanted me to tell him how I run the school and to tell him how he can help me,' Dorian said. 'And he suggested that, at the same time, maybe he could show me some of the ways in which a business is run.'

Dorian had worked at a former Model C school and he didn't have any issues about working with a white man, but some of the teachers were sceptical. 'Dean overcame that challenge by telling the teachers, 'ek is hier vir julle,' (*I am here for you*) and then showing them that it was true. Everyone soon took to him. Irrespective of his race, his character won people over.'

Deon never showed any judgement, Dorian said. 'He never criticised; instead, he would say "speak to me, what are your needs?" He would tell me to list my needs, irrespective of whether I thought they were possible or not.'

Dorian's five-year plan was ambitious: he wanted improvements to the school's security; he wanted to assist children in need; he wanted the staff to see that he had changed from the person they knew before; he wanted the parents to get behind the school and he wanted to enter partnerships with businesses that could help the school.

'I already had a vision for the school. Deon bought into it. He didn't want to change a thing. Instead, he complemented it and added detail.'

In the early days of their partnership Deon facilitated a renovation at the school that Dorian describes as a 'game-changer'. The school's toilets were in very poor condition. They were so bad, Deon said, that some learners told him they were forced to wait until they went home after school to relieve themselves. 'There was no money to repair them, and the department didn't seem interested,' Dorian said. 'Yet I felt this was a human rights issue. It was degrading to the dignity of the kids, and it was a safety issue. Something had to be done, so I spoke to Deon about it.'

A day after Dorian had told Deon about the state of the school's toilets, Cathy Stodel, a supplier to Mediclinic, approached Deon and asked how she could help – she wanted to donate R10,000. 'Ten thousand rand wasn't that much, but we did what we could to stretch this money. We used our own labour at the school and tradesmen from the community, and we got further donations of equipment. In the end, the learners ablution facilities were completely transformed. It was early in our partnership and it set the tone for what was to follow,' recounts Dorian.

'Afterwards, I got a delegation of girls come to me and thank me. I realised how much it meant to the pupils, and it also led to them accepting Deon more easily.'

Safety and security was another high priority part of Dorian's plan. 'The fences were in disrepair and safety was an issue. We got sponsorship to have a good fence erected with CCTV cameras at the gate. Deon got ER24, a subsidiary of Mediclinic, to provide training to teachers and SGB members in what do to in case of emergencies, which was a valuable addition to our security plan.'

Mediclinic also sponsored a learner's participation in an interprovincial hockey tournament in Pietermaritzburg. Her mother had recently died and, without help, she would never have been able to go. One of their partner organisations also provided a female mentor to guide the girl. 'The thank you letter that kid wrote afterwards was moving and very rewarding,' Dorian said.

There were other practical improvements to Cloetesville High. Mediclinic donated their second-hand furniture to the school following an office upgrade, and that made a big difference to the staffroom and admin offices. In addition, 40 used but still very good laptop computers were given to the school. This meant that every teacher now had a laptop to prepare lessons on, and that was very good for morale.

'Those things may not have seemed like big investments,' Dorian said, 'but they showed that Deon was resourceful and that he was prepared to go to great lengths to help the school. It established a relationship of trust with everyone at the school. Deon became a part of the family. He is invited to all our functions and this year he was a guest at our annual derby soccer game.'

A major project is the annual 'Dare to Dream' careers fair that Deon and his Mediclinic colleagues hold at the school. Booths are provided and manned by people who work in various occupations within the organisation, and the learners engage with them, finding out about their jobs. Cloetesville learners from Grades 9, 11 and 12 attended the first event in 2018, and in 2019 learners from neighbouring schools and parents were also invited to participate.

'Our kids maybe cannot afford to see the world out there, but we can bring the world to them,' Dorian said. 'The difference it has made has been immeasurable. It means so much more to speak to someone who is actually doing a particular job, rather than them just reading about it in pamphlets. It's also important to show them that there are careers that do not require maths and science, contrary to what many are saying.'

Deon uses his network and relationships to encourage professionals at Mediclinic and at their partner organisations, to volunteer their time at Cloetesville. It was clear to me though that Dorian was already walking towards his vision for the school when he met Deon. He didn't need Deon to help him get going. I was keen to know what differences Dorian thought being in the partnership had made in his life and in Deon's.

'It's difficult to put in words the difference it has made,' Dorian said. 'It's been mainly a change in the heart. There have been many changes in me and the school. The staff work with me now. Going through the training and working with Deon has changed the way I lead. I had to show that I wasn't the same anymore; Deon helped me with that.

'We have developed strategies to improve parental involvement and are having some success with that. It had been very poor in the past. We used the things we learned in the Community Building training to get them more committed. We insisted that they come to the school to collect their children's reports and Deon was there that night, explaining his and Mediclinic's role in the school. It helped establish a relationship of trust with the parents.'

Dorian and Deon are trying to change perceptions about Cloetesville High. 'The feedback I am getting is that attitudes are changing. Our matric pass rate has gone up, and we have introduced a Grade 12 intervention to ensure that this continues. I am less stressed now, so I have more time to focus on academic improvements,' says Dorian.

When the partnership started, the SMT was not functioning well. 'It was a legacy of the past, and we had a few uncooperative members on the management team. Through Deon's interaction with the SMT there is a much more positive energy there now, and we are doing a lot better.'

Dorian believes that Deon has also grown in the process. 'We have identified the growth in each other. He tells me that he has changed the way he handles his staff now. They say he has changed; so much so that they asked him if he has taken medicine! He says he has become more compassionate and accepting, without becoming lackadaisical. I think the same can be said of me. I am still a strict principal, but I'm no longer a monster.'

Dorian loves working with Deon. 'We are partners for the long term. We still have a lot to do.'

We did not get a chance to see Deon while we were in Stellenbosch, so we arranged a telephonic interview a few weeks later. From our conversation, it was immediately obvious that his involvement with Dorian and Cloetesville High School has had a major impact on him.

As manager of Mediclinic's ICT operations, Deon says he works in a typical corporate environment. 'It's technical, solutions-orientated and results-driven,' he explained. 'Going to Cloetesville has softened me and opened up my heart. It has given me a different perspective on life in general, taught me to be grateful for what I have and to focus on the positives.'

This, in turn, has affected the way he shows up at work. 'My management style has changed. I learned how to influence people rather than to instruct them. I learned to be tenacious, to be creative in looking for solutions and to listen to and include the views of others,' he said.

'When I was first approached to join the programme I leapt at the opportunity. I think I always wanted to make some sort of contribution, but I wasn't sure how to do that. So when I heard about PfP I had no hesitation as I saw it as an exciting opportunity to do good.'

Deon wasn't afraid to approach his network of partners and vendors in the Mediclinic ICT ecosystem for assistance, and their contribution to his partnership and the school has been huge.

'I realised that people inherently want to help, but they don't know exactly how to do that,' he said. 'Many organisations have been scared off by stories of corruption and funds that have been misused. But once I was able to sell the PfP concept to our suppliers and partners they were willing to become involved.'

Deon knew that he needed to become a trusted member of the school community. 'When we first met, Dorian said to me that he would accept me when I could show him the value that I could add to the children, the teachers and the community. When I was able to do that, our partnership blossomed,' he said.

Deon realised early on that a school is a very complex organisation and that the challenges it faces are huge. But he also saw Dorian as a very intelligent, competent leader who was doing great things in the face of massive odds.

'From Dorian and the other principals at our CoP meetings, I got to realise that the problems I faced in my corporate role were minuscule in comparison. It was humbling to witness the graciousness, positivity and appreciation with which they accepted their challenges and approached their task,' he said. 'I left those meetings energised. I learned to go in to listen and understand and to focus on the good things first.

'The lesson was that it would be a mistake to think I could fix the school or that I needed to show Dorian how to run his school as a business.'

Once Dorian realised that his and Deon's core values are aligned, the ice was broken and they began to achieve some real success in the school.

'I knew we had to get the teachers on board. One of the things that made a big difference is that Dorian and I arranged a trip for the entire staff. I got two of my suppliers on board, and we arranged a bus trip for everyone to Hout Bay and to the V&A Waterfront for lunch. That excursion had a great effect on the morale of the teachers, and it got me to be accepted by them. From then on I found it easier to implement things. Now I am invited to just about all the school's functions and events and Dorian asks me to speak at many of them.

'Although the official first year of the partnership ended more than a year ago, Dorian and I still speak to each other at least once a week. We have become good friends. We meet socially as well.'

As Deon regularly shared what was happening at Cloetesville High with his colleagues, they began to ask what they could do to help. 'We now have two more Mediclinic staff members who have become PfP partners at other schools,' he said.

Because of the work that Deon had done at Cloetesville, he was asked to assist at other schools. 'My area of expertise is ICT, and it soon became apparent that this is an area that needs attention in many schools,' he said. 'Jessica, our LPF, told me about Groenberg Primary, a small farm school in the Wellington area. I went there and what I saw was heartbreaking and humbling. The school was very neglected; there was no technology and very little infrastructure. I was deeply moved and spoke to some of Mediclinic's partners. The upshot was that we got 25 laptops and five PCs for the school.'

Deon then went to Dorothea, a school for learners with special educational needs (LSEN) in Cloetesville, and to Rondeheuwel Primary, a small school in the Matroosberg area, where he found similar needs. 'Through our partners we were able to supply and install IT equipment at the schools.'

What was missing, however, was a working relationship with the IT team at the WCED. 'We supplied the hardware, but there was no connectivity, no network and no suitable educational programmes.'

Deon realised that he would need to find a way to develop a relationship with the WCED team. 'Through the Coalition for Quality Education,[25] I met Mr Brian Schreuder,

25 The Coalition for Quality Education in the Western Cape is a collaborative association for all education stakeholders (including government, private business, NPOs, civil society and funders). The initiative was launched by SSA and is being developed with a view to facilitating systemic change across South Africa's education system, so that all South Africa's children can receive quality learning.

the Head of Education in the Western Cape. He introduced me to Clinton Walker, the department's Head of ICT, and I am delighted to say that we are making good progress with regard to developing a strong working relationship.'

The key to making that happen, according to Deon, was that he applied some of the skills he had learned at PfP. 'When I met with Clinton and his team, I wasn't critical. I listened to them and tried to understand the challenges they faced. I told them that their vision for technology in schools was good and asked if we could help with the execution of it. That led to a generative conversation and laid the foundations for a productive relationship.'

And Mediclinic has also benefitted from Deon's involvement with the WCED ICT team. He was hugely impressed by the organisation that did the cabling at Cloetesville High and has since contracted them to handle some of Mediclinic's cabling at their hospitals.

I wanted to know from Deon how Mediclinic has benefitted from being involved in Cloetesville High School, given that the Cloetesville community is not part of the company's target market.

'It's been good for our brand and reputation, I think. This is an under-resourced community, and it's possible that a company like Mediclinic can be perceived as showing an interest in this community and supporting them. Our involvement has helped us live our values, which include respect, trust and partnership. I think we have built that. The people in the community know what we have been trying to do for them, and they appreciate it. Their perception of Mediclinic has changed.'

It was a privilege to spend time with Dorian and Deon and to hear them speak about their partnership and the work they have been doing together. Over the last few years I have had many conversations with Deon about his PfP experience, and I am inspired every time. I wish we could find more business leaders who are willing to get so wholeheartedly engaged at their PfP schools.

Famous Brands and John Mdluli Primary School

Sibongile Sibuyi, the principal of John Mdluli Primary School in Mataffin Township, Nelspruit, is partnered with Dennis Wevell, who owns two Mugg & Bean restaurants; one in Nelspruit and the other in White River. In June 2018 they joined the Nelspruit 2 (NEL2) Leadership Circle with Mel Tomlinson as their LPF.

Dennis had known Mel for some time when she approached him because she was short of a business leader for the NEL2 Circle. He agreed to get involved, but funding his participation was a problem. 'There was no sponsorship, and things weren't going that well in my business at the time, but I felt that I was being called to join PfP, so I was determined to push ahead in faith, confident that the money would come from somewhere,' Dennis recalls.

A few days later, Darren Hele and Graeme Morrison, Famous Brands executives, visited Nelspruit. They listened to Dennis talk about his interest in joining PfP and arranged for him to be included in a programme which funds Famous Brands franchisees to participate in PfP. Dennis speaks with huge appreciation for the support from Darren, Graeme and Famous Brands. 'It is so clear that Famous Brands is doing this for the right reasons. They care deeply about being a good corporate citizen and in impacting the communities in which they operate,' said Dennis.

Sibongile's participation was sponsored by the Federated Employers Mutual Assurance Company (FEM) Education Foundation. 'It was easy for me to say yes to the idea of a partnership,' said Sibongile. 'I had a vision for the school, but I felt overwhelmed by the circumstances. I was a bit nervous about the idea of working closely with a white man because of what I had experienced in the past. I thought he would be bossy and judgemental, but it wasn't like that at all.

'Before joining PfP I saw mostly challenges and problems, but now, thanks to being part of the PfP process, I see what is possible. I used to only see closed doors. Now I've learned to knock on those doors. Lots of things have happened at the school as a result.'

Sibongile told Theo and I about the developments that have taken place at the school. It's a great testimony to what can be achieved through partnership.

Right from the start, Sibongile and Dennis worked to establish a culture of 'munye ngamunye' (a commitment to developing the God-given potential of every person) at the school, and both were determined to do what they could for every child and every adult involved with the school.

The partners were committed to investing their time on things that would have a lasting impact on the school and the community, and they established five partnership principles that underpin their approach:

1. Through relationships, invest in people to improve their self-worth
2. Begin with the end in mind
3. Build to last – no quick fixes
4. If you want to go far, go together
5. Ensure a return on investment to investors, especially Famous Brands

An example of the issues that Dennis and Sibongile focused on is early childhood development (ECD). Teachers were concerned about the poor levels of school readiness among the Grade R learners coming into the school, and the partners realised that the problem stemmed from inadequate support in the township. So they set about organising some training for seven ECD practitioners in the area. Dennis enlisted the help of a Nelspruit occupational therapist, Gerda van Niekerk, who trains people to creatively use waste as educational material.

'Gerda had run a workshop with our staff at Mugg & Bean,' Dennis said. 'I made connections between the people involved, and we managed to engage local ECD practitioners in a process of learning and development.' Dennis also reached out to Penreach, an organisation that provides training for teachers and school leaders. In collaboration with Penreach, the John Mdluli ECD Partnership was established. Its aim is to improve the quality of education in the ECD centres around the school so that learners who enter Grade R will be more school-ready in future.

Sibongile and Dennis decided that they also needed to get children reading. They knew that Penreach was doing great work in the community, so they went to meet the team at their Nelspruit office. 'Ron Twala of Penreach introduced us to the idea of Book Banks: mobile libraries in crates that are placed at key points in the community. Community members are trained to manage them, and to establish reading programmes,' said Dennis.

Sibongile and her team managed to get 16 mothers in the community to sign up to be Book Bank volunteers. Penreach ran training for these moms, and they are now actively supporting children to read in their homes. The dream is to further 'infiltrate' the areas that feed John Mdluli Primary with more Book Bank volunteers, and the partners are hoping that some of these active citizens will establish ECD centres in their homes so that more children will have early learning opportunities.

A decision was made to rebrand the school library as an Info Hub. The school's leadership team wanted the facility to be about more than just books, even though it had no technical equipment. They visited the Ligbron Academy of Technology in Ermelo and returned feeling inspired and determined to find a way to make ICT more accessible to the learners and teachers at John Mdluli Primary.

Martin Tobias, a business partner in the NEL2 Circle, knew about Dennis and Sibongile's vision, so he grabbed the opportunity to reconnect with an old school friend who might be able to help. A WhatsApp group had been set up for the 40th reunion of Martin's matric class and, through this group, Martin contacted Albert van Jaarsveld, the MD of SmartLabs, a company that provides ICT equipment to schools. Martin told Albert about the work being done at John Mdluli and, a little while later, Albert called Martin to let him know that Diebold Nixdorf, a global technology company, was prepared to invest in the work being done in schools around Nelspruit. John Mdluli Primary was identified as an ideal recipient and received a massive gift of 25 tablets, three laptops, a smartboard, chairs, tables and a mobile science lab.

In acknowledging the generosity and implications of the donation, Sibongile said that Diebold Nixdorf probably had no idea how much their gift would change the lives of her learners, 'who will later become assets to their families and the community at large because of the skills they will gain from using this equipment.'

Both Sibongile and Dennis believe that discipline and character development are also key aspects of education, and Dennis set out to supplement what the school was already doing in this respect. 'The school had a prefect system, run by the teachers, but there were possibilities for growth,' he said. So, he asked Nico Grobler, the head of discipline at Hoërskool Nelspruit, to run a training session for the John Mdluli prefects.

Around that time, Dennis heard a radio interview with a teacher from Hoërskool Kuswag in Amanzimtoti who had implemented a programme at the school called Character Transformation. Dennis took a group of teachers to Hoërskool Kuswag to learn more about what they were doing. Character Transformation is a programme designed to imbed six particular positive values in a school (trustworthiness, respect, responsibility, fairness, caring and citizenship). After seeing how the Amanzimtoti school and its learners were benefitting, the John Mdluli educators became committed to implementing the programme at their school.

'Once the school has embedded the programme, the intention is to take it to the ECD centres and the Book Banks too,' Dennis said. The partners are also hoping to extend the programme to other schools across Nelspruit.

Sibongile and her team also want to restore pride in the Mataffin community, which used to be a very secure and stable farming area that produced many leaders. However, after the Mbombela stadium was built in the area for the 2010 Football World Cup there was an influx of people into the district, and it is now considered by the police to be a crime hotspot. The team enlisted the assistance of local storytellers Jennifer Schormann and Lenore Zietsman, who invited parents to share their stories.

This has now evolved into a school history club where learners practise story harvesting, and the hope is that some of these stories can be built into the curriculum followed at the ECD centres.

Another focus area for the partners was fundraising. Sibongile and her team wanted to appoint more foundation phase teachers, and the school needed to find a way to pay its water bill of R17,000 a month. Dennis and the fundraising committee brainstormed some ideas for addressing the water issue. They talked about the possibility of installing a borehole.

'Mr Charles[26] and I were travelling around the Lowveld looking for a venue to host a team building exercise for our SMT, and we discussed the funding challenge. Pastor Alfred Kariuki, who was to facilitate the team building session, was in the car and he overheard the discussion,' Dennis said.

'He knew Christan Barnett, the founder of an American organisation, 28Bold, which supplies boreholes to needy communities. He reached out to Christan, and she agreed to donate a borehole to the school.'

Getting the borehole as a gift was a big moment for the school. It meant that water could be used to grow vegetables to supplement the feeding scheme run by the education department. The school partnered with Working on Fire, a fire management agency, which established a vegetable garden at the school as part of the agency's food security programme. Through another partnership, with the school gardening and nutrition programme EduPlant, the school receives advice and support to manage the garden.

Sibongile will be retiring at the end of 2020, and part of her and Dennis's commitment to the future has been to ensure that the next principal will inherit a school that is poised for greatness. The pair are hoping that Deputy Principal Stanley Charles will become principal, and their partnership has morphed into a three-way collaboration, with Stanley being actively involved in all partnership activities.

Both Sibongile and Dennis feel they have undergone major changes as a result of being in the partnership.

'I see things differently now,' Sibongile says. 'Dennis is a kind man, but he is also dedicated and driven. He made me believe that anything is possible. My dream has been to leave my school in a better place than I found it. With Dennis, I think I will be doing that. God favoured me when he gave Dennis to me as a partner. I've told him about my dreams and what I wanted to achieve. We set a vision, and then we 'walked on water' believing it would happen.'

Dennis said that being part of PfP forced him to become involved in an uncertain human environment. 'I realised that if I wanted a prosperous future for my children in this country then I had to get involved.

---

26   Stanley Charles is the deputy principal of the school.

'I have always been a driven person, seeking recognition. It was when Pastor Alfred helped me see that I was using my Christianity to feed my need for recognition that everything changed. I have realised that I needed to make myself available as an instrument for God to use me. It has been a humbling experience to work with the teachers and to see the work they do under difficult circumstances.

'Sibongile and her staff have done the work; I have been able to see the possibilities and join the dots to make things happen.'

While listening to Dennis and Sibongile talking, I got a sense that Dennis had developed these massive invisible antennae that were 'tuned in' to catch possible opportunities to benefit the school. And then I experienced the 'Dennis Magic' in action...

When Dennis and Sibongile told me about the trip to Amanzimtoti, which HOD Pauline Thwala had joined, I made a throw-away comment that I wished Pauline could meet Principal Ridwan Samodien, my partner at Kannemeyer Primary School, who had been implementing the Character Transformation programme for years. I did not for a moment think that it was a 'real' possibility because Nelspruit is very far from Cape Town, and it just did not seem feasible to make such a visit work.

A week or so later, I heard that Dennis had been talking to a few people and that a group from John Mdluli was planning to visit Ridwan in Cape Town to learn more about what he and his team have been doing to imbed values in their school. At first, I did not think Dennis was serious, but I soon realised that this visit was happening – Pastor Alfred, three John Mdluli educators (Stanley Charles, Pauline Thwala and Thembi Mnisi) and Principal Glory Madonsela of Edwaleni Primary School, who is also part of the NEL2 Circle, were on their way to Cape Town.

Mel had helped to enrol Glory's business partner, Odie Latre, who works for Fedair and had been able to apply for sponsorships for all the flights. The next thing I knew, Dennis, Mel, Odie, Ridwan, Ronnie and myself were on a WhatsApp group and planning the trip. I suggested that we consider the possibility of the group also visiting Klapmuts Primary to hear Principal Ronnie Frans' inspirational story.

The explorers spent a day being wowed by Ridwan and his team at Kannemeyer Primary, and the next day they visited Klapmuts Primary where Ronnie and his educators had created an inspirational opportunity for them to experience the power and possibility of ICT and robotics.

I have a strong sense that this trip to Cape Town was a Damascus-like moment for these five 'explorers'. They returned to Nelspruit with a renewed sense of vision and purpose –inspired by leaders who have been on the PfP journey for a bit longer than they have.

I wish every school could have a Dennis – a person with a big antenna for opportunities that may benefit the school. During the last few years this is all I have done for Ridwan and Kannemeyer Primary School – just connect them to people and organisations who have gifts to share.

Dennis would not have been able to help make things happen at the school if he had not earned Sibongile and Stanley's trust. They know that everything he does comes from a place of deep care and commitment to being a contribution and making a difference. Because of the work that has been done to build trust between these leaders, they have become an unstoppable force for change.

Dennis would also not have been able to accomplish what he has done at the school without the unwavering support of Famous Brands. I have a vivid memory of my first visit to Darren Hele, Famous Brands CEO, to tell him about PfP. Afzal Seedat, an ex-banker and Famous Brands franchisee had made the introduction and asked Darren if he would meet with me. Darren generously said yes and we met in January 2016. He was immediately supportive and said that Famous Brands would sponsor Clive Ducasse, their regional manager in Nelspruit to get involved in PfP. Since then, many other leaders in the Famous Brands network have become partners to principals, and we regard the organisation as a key stakeholder.

Imagine if every school had a strong community of supporters around it? Imagine if every school had someone who saw possibility when others saw problems, who had a 'can-do' and 'make it happen' attitude and knew how to mobilise active citizenship? Imagine if every school could have a Dennis? And imagine if every organisation made the kind of commitment to public education that Famous Brands has been making for the last three years?

Sphere Holdings and Tlhatlogang Secondary School

The relationship between Itumeleng Kgaboesele of Sphere Holdings and Principal Khosi Ntuli of Tlhatlogang Secondary School stands out as something special and unique, even in the context of the extreme diversity that characterises the cohort of almost 1,200 partnerships for possibility that have been launched so far.

For a start, this wasn't the first PfP experience for either of them. Itumeleng had partnered with Bertha Motladile at Moetapele Primary School in 2015, while back in 2014 Khosi did a year in partnership with Martin Kingston.

Khosi's partnership with Martin was not ideal. Martin's work situation changed after they started and his availability became limited. As a result, Khosi found herself largely alone for most of the year, although she and Martin did find innovative ways to keep in touch via mobile technology and the internet.

As the Head of Sphere Investment Holdings, Itumeleng is also constantly challenged for time. He did, nonetheless, complete the PfP programme with Bertha at Moetapele Primary School in 2015 and said it was a 'natural progression' to get involved with a second partnership, at Tlhlatlogang Secondary, the following year.

His company, Itumeleng explains, identifies businesses with strong potential that have good management teams in place and then partners with them by providing capital and skills.

It's easy, therefore, he points out, to see the parallels between what he does at work and what he is trying to achieve through PfP. 'It's about drawing on my knowledge and experience to help my partners in the business meet their challenges; they build the effectiveness and profitability of their organisations in the process. In the case of PfP, it's about building the principal, the school and, through it, the community and the country.'

The second way in which their partnership was unusual was that Itumeleng and Khosi did not need to attend all of the courses that form part of the PfP programme to draw the full value from their partnership because both had done the training before. With Itumeleng's punishing work schedule, this was an advantage for them and they could focus on what they wanted to achieve at their school.

Itumeleng got involved in PfP because he wanted to make a contribution. He acknowledges his privilege and says it makes him even more committed to making a difference. 'My background and experience has meant that I am well placed to make a contribution by helping to build better schools, creating value for communities and eventually the country,' he says.

Itumeleng is well aware of the role that a good education has played in his own career journey and ultimate success. 'I would never have achieved what I have if I did not get the proper grounding,' he says. 'It's a tragedy that so many of our children are not receiving that kind of education now.'

At the same time, he is deeply aware of, and grateful for, the enabling environment created for individuals like himself in this country since 1994.

'My success in business, and that of my clients, is only possible because so much has been achieved in introducing policies that are designed to redress past injustices. I feel obligated to give something back. These things don't happen by themselves. The government needs the help of civil society to meet its challenges and I wanted to be part of that.'

And education, Itumeleng says, is where the rubber meets the road. 'You need proper leadership and committed teachers to have effective schools. Effective school leadership is an area that we are lacking in, so getting involved in a programme like Partners for Possibility was, for me, the ideal opportunity.'

Itumeleng admits, however, that his involvement is not purely altruistic. His business is all about identifying business opportunities, investing in them, and then supporting the resultant businesses so that they can make the most of the circumstances. Sphere Holdings has been involved in projects in the public sector that have taught the company how to tackle the challenges that exist, he explains. That has put them in the position of being able to make decisions about possible investments in the educational field.

'I am intrigued by the potential to do business in the world of education,' he says. 'In the process, of course, one would like to be doing good, not exploiting those who are suffering due to the dysfunctional system. So, through my involvement in the programme, I am always trying to identify potential business opportunities that are also developmental in nature.'

For example, Sphere Holdings has made an investment in Pearson South Africa, a subsidiary of the international education company Pearson plc. Sphere acquired a 22,5% holding in Pearson, increasing the company's black ownership share, and Sphere will add its expertise in managing projects in schools.

It's important, Itumeleng believes, for Sphere Holdings to become involved in more PfP partnerships. 'We have agreed in principle that it should happen, but in practice, it has not been easy. The time commitment is the big issue, and every executive's situation is different, and every partnership will involve different demands,' he says.

'In my case, time is the biggest challenge, but I believe this is so important that I make plans to give me the capacity to optimise my use of time and fit it in.'

As far as using involvement in a PfP partnership as a learning experience for the business executive is concerned, Itumeleng says that he can see how for some white business executives it can be a valuable 'opening up' experience. 'For me, however, it's been about aligning my actions to my personal values. South Africa has been good to me, and others before me have made big sacrifices so that I could get the opportunities that I have had. So, I see it as my responsibility to give back.'

If there has been a learning advantage for him, Itumeleng believes it's in gaining a better understanding of how the public education system works and about the frustrations and challenges facing principals.

Itumeleng says he has been shocked by the enormity of the problems that exist in the public education space. 'And it's clear that the solution does not lie in simply throwing resources at the problem.'

While he is aware of the size of the problem, he says he is not despondent about it. 'I am also encouraged. In my view, with better management we can achieve a lot more than what is being done at the moment.

'There are many excellent initiatives aimed at improving education, but not all of them are effective. With better management on the part of school principals, management teams and school governing bodies, we can turn that around.

'That's what the Partners for Possibility programme sets out to do, and why I am happy to be involved in it.'

The start of Khosi Ntuli's partnership with Martin Kingston coincided with her school merging with another bigger one and moving to different premises. That development dominated her time and attention during their year together and, she says, she will always be grateful to Martin for introducing her to the principles of managing major change.

'We were able to apply the principles of teamwork and collaboration; we drew up action plans and consulted with stakeholders. The result was that we pulled off the move to the new premises in two weeks, and when we opened on the first day of the new term we were up and running.'

Although that partnership ultimately fizzled out, Khosi thinks it was very valuable, and it set her up for the partnership with Itumeleng, which has made major differences in her own life and at the school.

'I enrolled for an MBA degree at the end of that first year,' she says, 'because I realised that a school principal has the same mandate and responsibilities as the CEO of a corporation and needs to take advantage of the principles and processes that successful businesses run on.'

Khosi's partnership with Itumeleng taught her the importance of strategy and of relating to people, she says. 'Everything we did, Itumeleng taught me, had to be aligned to strategy and vision. Then we had to ensure that we had the human resources required to put those things into practice. It's about capacitating the staff to operate strategically. Leadership development comes into it, and also consequence management,' Khosi says.

'We set targets and strategised about meeting those targets,' she explains. 'Then, we measured the extent to which those goals had been met or not and tried to understand the instances in which we have fallen short. After that, it was about taking action to ensure that we did better next time.'

There were many measurable successes during that first year, not the least of which was an increase in the overall matric pass rate from 52% to 80% at the end of the first year of the partnership. And in everything Khosi had the support of Itumeleng.

'Being a principal can be a lonely position,' she says, 'so it's valuable to have a partner you can talk to. Itumeleng and I are regularly in touch via Skype, e-mail and WhatsApp, and I find I can discuss everything that concerns me with him.'

When we spoke to Khosi in 2019, the partnership was still going strong. 'We are in touch all the time,' she said. 'I talk to Itumeleng on the phone, and we communicate electronically meet personally. Recently he invited us to the family fun day at his company.

'We are friends as well as partners now, and the foundation was laid during that initial year. PfP is all about the relationship between the partners,' she said.

There have been some great developments at Tlhatlogang Secondary School in the years that have followed, and Khosi explained that most of them, directly or indirectly, have flowed out of her partnership with Itumeleng. 'For example, we have learners on a Columba Leadership programme, an initiative suggested by Itumeleng,' she said.

In 2016 Itumeleng facilitated a workshop for the teachers, governing body, and other key individuals involved in the school, which enabled them to start putting into practice a culture of planning, execution and accountability.

In 2019 Sphere ran financial literacy training for the Grade 12s, and FNB came in and taught the Grade 8s the basics of budgeting and saving. Khosi also invited the younger teachers to attend.

Sphere regularly runs 'community days' at the school. In 2017 and 2018 they helped to improve the facilities used by learners at lunch and break times and built a netball court and a life-sized chessboard.

'I think the biggest lesson I learned about running my school was that it was my job to capacitate the teachers to do their jobs well,' she said. 'That's why I sent those teachers on that training. I realised that if they come to school with financial problems and worries they would not be at their best.'

Patience and a willingness to listen to others are important characteristics that she has acquired, according to Khosi. 'Getting the support of the SMT and the teachers is the key,' she said, 'and that comes from listening to everyone's views and taking them seriously. Dealing with issues and resolving conflicts are areas that I am much better at now.'

Looking back, Khosi would not have wanted to miss this journey. 'PfP is an exceptionally wonderful programme,' she said. 'Itumeleng has shown that he is committed to the school, and our partnership is one for life.'

'I believe sharing learnings and good practice is important,' Khosi says. 'Although we are talking about leadership craft and good practice, that's something that is learned over time. The real value of the PfP programme lies in the journey that the partners walk together. There are no short cuts; the key to sustainable success in addressing the crisis in schools lies in the establishment of more partnerships,' she concludes.

Reflections

I am so inspired by these stories. They are truly exemplars of the kind of business-school partnerships we had in mind when we envisaged what may be possible through PfP. Although there are many other stories like these, most PfP partnerships unfortunately don't maintain this level of activity for years after the facilitated 12-month programme period.

I've been wondering what the similarities are between these four stories. Peter, Rowan, Dennis and Itumeleng are all entrepreneurs who run businesses, so it may be that they entered their partnerships with a clear strategic view about mobilising the assets in their organisations. I am wondering whether there is something about how they were recruited? Peter heard me talk about the dream to mobilise this kind of comprehensive support from businesses to schools before he said yes.

Rowan's initial conversation was with Irené Raubenheimer, who represents another ideal school-business partnership. I suspect Deon and Dennis had been waiting for an opportunity to make a significant contribution, so for them PfP was simply the right initiative at the right time. Itumeleng had a strong sense of what may be possible because of his first experience of a partnership.

This is another reminder that there is simply no 'one size fits all' answer. Every PfP partnership is unique and shaped by the people involved. Each of these stories in this chapter are about individual leaders bringing their unique gifts and contributions to the partnership. We counsel leaders to 'meet their clients where they are'[27] and then to

27   A key idea in Organisational Development

plan the journeys from there. All four of these leaders did exactly that. They joined the principals with open minds, invested in the relationship before jumping into the 'work' and have made long-term commitments to support the principals and their schools.

Postscript: We have since heard that André Lamprecht has been promoted to a senior position in the WCED's Metro South District where he will be providing support to dozens of principals. I asked him whether he thought PfP had played any role in this promotion and he said 'Absolutely!' Peter is torn because he wants André to do well … *but* … there's no doubt that all the children and educators in Levana Primary will miss his enthusiastic leadership.

Chapter 9

Principals who have become 'symphonic leaders' at their schools

"The conductor of an orchestra doesn't make a sound. He depends, for his power, on his ability to make other people powerful." – Benjamin Zander

Through the PfP process, we encourage principals to move away from a 'heroic' leadership style of running a school, with a firm hand and an autocratic, hierarchical approach, to seeing themselves as 'conductors of an orchestra' – where their role is to create an environment in which every educator plays their 'best music' and all are encouraged to lead from where they are.

Ben Zander has said many times that conductors are the only musicians on stage who don't make a sound and that their power is dependent on their ability to make other people powerful. We often use the term 'symphonic leadership' when referring to leaders who know that their job is to create opportunities for others to shine.

There are many parallels between the role of a musical conductor and that of a principal. The principal is typically the only educator in a school who doesn't teach, but the quality of others' teaching depends on the principal's ability to engage and inspire them.

Many principals who have been part of PfP talk about how they now run their meetings differently. Before PfP, they would stand in front of a room full of teachers and talk 'at them' like an archetypal lecturer. After experiencing, through PfP, a different way of engaging, they now see themselves as facilitators who create opportunities for every educator to make a contribution – and they are excited to see the impact this has on them. Teachers who used to sit quietly when they were 'talked at' have become active contributors. They now experience **symphonia** at their schools – *the sounding of all voices*.

We have already shared a few stories about principals who have made this shift, and it was a joy to meet Ravi and Lukkie to hear how they too have become 'symphonic' leaders who ensure that every voice is heard and valued.

Lukkie Matsabe, Vulemehlo Primary School

Lukkie Matsabe joined PfP in June 2018 as a member of the Nelspruit 2 (NEL2) Leadership Circle. He was partnered with Martin Tobias, an accountant working in Nelspruit, and Mel Tomlinson was their LPF.

After hearing from Mel that Lukkie's PfP journey had been a transformational experience for him, and then speaking to Martin, I was particularly interested to hear from Lukkie himself about the programme's impact on him.

Before taking the drive to Vulemehlo Primary, Theo and I met Martin at his office in Nelspruit. He told us that working with Lukkie has been a special experience for him. He particularly appreciates Lukkie's willingness to be vulnerable and to share the challenges he is grappling with at the school.

Martin recounted his first visit to the school: Lukkie had invited the choir to his office to welcome Martin to the school. They sang a few songs and Martin's heart was immediately opened wide. He felt deeply touched by the opportunity and the responsibility of working with the school's principal. 'It was a heavy burden to accept,' said Martin.

Martin had been searching for a way to make a contribution to the country beyond his role as entrepreneur and accountant. He did not want to reinvent the wheel and was keen to join a programme in which there would be a reasonable chance of impact.

At the time of our visit to Martin, he and Lukkie had been working together for more than a year. The conversation with him left us in no doubt that Martin had benefitted from the experience of partnering with Lukkie through PfP. Martin discovered a world that he knew nothing about, and witnessing the dedication of the principals in the rural schools he encountered humbled him.

'I realised that I would not be able to be a principal in an under-resourced rural school,' Martin said. 'I am so inspired by the commitment and dedication of these principals. I discovered an entirely different reality to the stories I had read in the media.

'PfP took me out of my comfort zone. I was confronted with many things, and I appreciated the opportunity to work this through with Mel, our LPF. Working with Lukkie taught me about accountability. Working with Lukkie and being part of the NEL2 Leadership Circle changed my life.'

I am always touched to hear business leaders describing their PfP experience as life-changing, and I was eager to hear the story of Lukkie's journey.

We met Lukkie in his office at Vulemehlo Primary School in the Kabokweni Township, near White River. Kabokweni is more than an hour's drive from Nelspruit on a bad road that passes a sprawling township stretching for many kilometres.

Before getting down to business, we had to be welcomed: Lukkie called the school choir into his office. They sang beautifully and touched our hearts. I felt privileged and honoured by his gesture.

Lukkie told us that he had always been an ambitious person. Although he lacked confidence and always put other people first, he was determined to grow. He was committed to becoming more confident and learning how to stand his ground, so he read lots of motivational material and used every opportunity to network, hoping to draw strength from people he met.

Lukkie became Vulemehlo Primary's deputy principal in 2011 and was appointed as principal in January 2016. The previous principal had been in the role for 25 years and had a personality that was very different from Lukkie's. As a more soft-spoken person, Lukkie faced a lot of comparison and criticism. 'I was told that I wasn't a good leader because I was so different from the previous principal,' he said.

Lukkie heard about the PfP programme through a principal who had been in the first Nelspruit circle. He applied to join, and after being accepted he felt nervous. 'I was afraid that my weaknesses would be exposed and that my natural shyness would be a problem.'

Initially, as the programme got underway, Lukkie continued to feel a bit anxious but says his business partner, Martin, soon put him at ease. 'We became friends, we visited each other's homes and we would often work from my home near the school.'

Lukkie found that he learned a lot from the courses he and Martin attended together. 'From Time to Think we learned to listen and to create space for others to speak. Success is rooted in our thinking and everyone can contribute to finding solutions.

'I realised that it was different to the way in which the previous principal operated. His staff meetings would consist of him standing in the front and talking at people. I got to see that there was a different way. I realised that my role as a leader was to create a space where everybody can contribute and that solutions do not only come from me. I have discovered how powerful it is to treat all staff members as equal contributors and what becomes possible when you create a space for all the voices to be heard.

'We have changed the culture at the school. We don't just have one strong leader in the principal's office. We have a team of educators who are willing to lead from wherever they are.'

It has taken some time, but Lukkie has begun to feel comfortable and more confident in his role. 'Sharing my experience with the other principals and business leaders, and listening to theirs in our CoP meetings helped,' he said. 'I loved the CoP meetings. It was a safe space where we could speak freely without any fear.

'Martin has been a wonderful partner. He has attended events at the school. He has met with the parents. He has also introduced me to Toastmasters, an organisation he belongs to, and I am learning how to be a more eloquent speaker.

'My involvement with PfP has made me a better principal. I have matured, I have liberated the teachers from the old way the school was run. They speak up and they take more responsibility.

'They are taking a lot more ownership. This has made my life easier. I have realised that people can manage themselves. They don't need me to manage them. My job is to set the standards and be clear about expectations. And then I need to deal with the instances where people don't keep to our agreement. I don't have to micromanage anybody.

'PfP has taught me to focus on what is strong, rather than on what is wrong. In the past I experienced a lot of negativity from other principals and educators. I have discovered how we waste time when we focus on complaining and being negative. There is so much more power in being positive and having a solutions mindset.

'Because of the skills I have developed I have been appointed secretary of our circuit management team, and I have gained the confidence to speak up when I don't agree with things. It wasn't always that way. I can have the courageous conversations now. I'm no longer a people pleaser.'

And in the process, he says, the school has become a more caring, warm environment in which the learners feel free to approach him and the other educators. Lukkie is confident that this new culture will lead to improved academic outcomes as he is already seeing evidence of that.

The Saturday after our visit, Lukkie and his team hosted an event at the school for the parents whose children will join the school as Grade R learners in 2020. Martin was at the event, and afterwards he sent me a voicemail to say how blown away he was by the teamwork he saw and experienced. 'Every educator had a task, and they took full responsibility for what they were responsible for. Educators who were previously cynical about Lukkie and his leadership style were positively engaged, proud about what they were doing at the school.'

Receiving Martin's voicemail and hearing his enthusiastic account of witnessing 'symphonic' leadership in action was a beautiful moment of validation for the work we are doing through Partners for Possibility. Imagine if every principal could discover the power of distributed leadership, where all educators are invited and encouraged to step into a leadership role and to take co-responsibility for the well-being of the school?

When we encourage leaders to move from being 'heroic' to 'symphonic' leaders, who encourage every 'orchestra member' to play their most beautiful music, we help to create stories like Lukkie's.

Dr Ravi Perumal, Parkgate Primary School

Parkgate Primary is located in a town called Verulam on the KZN North Coast. When Dr Ravi Perumal was appointed as principal there in May 2018, his circuit manager, Mr Chetty, proposed that he join the PfP programme. Ravi was concerned that the time commitment would distract him from running the school.

'Mr Chetty told me that teaming up with a business leader could teach me about good management practices and that if I became involved it would help me and the school,' he said. 'Mr Chetty also told me that the possibilities of this programme are endless.'

Ravi was partnered with Gill Cox of Numatics SA, who has over 30 years of business experience, and they joined the North Coast 3 (NC3) Circle with Terry Dearling as their LPF. The circle was launched in October 2018.

'I quickly realised that I had made the right choice to join PfP. I was immediately taken by Gill's energy. She really cares and has an amazing ability to multi-task. I was excited to find out that there were so many privileged people who don't need to get involved with schools like ours, but are willing to do so.'

Joining the programme had a profound effect on him personally, Ravi said. When I asked him how his life would have been different without PfP, he said 'It's like chalk and cheese. It has been very impactful for me to be part of Partners for Possibility. It has been so valuable to have a partner I can talk to about anything. It is different from talking to a departmental official because you have to be careful about what you say in those conversations. That wasn't the case with Gill, we could talk about all things and often what we discussed was possibility; what could be done to improve things. That was a great help.

'Gill's connections and her expertise were very useful. For example, she helped us to get the assistance of a labour lawyer when we had a problem with our security providers. That made a huge difference to us. The other business leaders in our circle were all so generous and willing to share.'

Ravi says that the opportunity to be part of a learning community which included fellow principals was also extremely valuable. 'We had 10 principals in our circle and we created a great partnership. I benefitted from the experience of the other principals. It helped me to realise that we all faced similar challenges and we formed a close relationship.'

Ravi acquired many new skills from the training courses, he said. 'Looking back, I was quite an autocratic leader at first. The Time to Think course helped with that. I came to realise that autocratic leadership destroys creativity and that listening to others enables better decision-making.

'The Time to Think workshop encouraged me to open up my ears and close my mouth. To be a good leader one had to engage in delicious listening. Why stress when you can give people the opportunity to think and then harness the fruits of their thinking? I have learned to listen to those that don't normally talk and discovered that most of them have the most fabulous of ideas. I have learned to start meetings with positivity, as happy people always give off more than unhappy ones.

'The other courses were also valuable. Flawless Consulting taught me about transparency and about good contractual relationships based on knowing what people expect from each other. This is the basis of a good relationship.'

'We thoroughly enjoyed attending the Community Building workshop and have so many ideas with regard to how we want to mobilise community support for the school.'

I wanted to know what part PfP had played in the school during the 12 months since Ravi joined the programme. 'An enormous part,' he replied. 'And not just here. We have a chat group among the principals, and daily I read reports about the great things that are going on at the other schools. There are people and organisations who are willing to invest in our schools, and funders wouldn't do that if they didn't believe that good things were happening in the schools.

'It's working because the principals are prepared to work at it and because they grasp the opportunities that come their way. Through the partnerships, we are exposed to suitable opportunities and we are willing and able to run with them. That's the difference. I am confident in seeing the potential and in using the opportunities for the benefit of the school.

'And once you accomplish one thing you are energised to try others. One success leads to another.'

Mr Budram, the deputy principal of Parkgate Primary describes what has happened at the school as a massive change. 'The teachers have a new lease on life. The executive and the SMT support the teachers and they have embraced the changes,' he said. 'Our teachers go to workshops all the time, and the learnings have cascaded down to the others. It has made a big difference.'

Ravi says he has noticed a positive change in the school's culture. 'Teachers are now more willing to collaborate and take ownership of school initiatives. PfP has changed my way of thinking. I learned to harness the power of the group through various techniques I have learned. Challenges I face on a daily basis do not drive up my stress levels anymore as I do not have to think of all the solutions – but I am assured that the answer is always found in the room. The school management team feels rejuvenated and empowered to implement the school improvement plan.'

A member of Ravi's teaching team, Miss Moodley, has reported seeing several positive changes in the school since he joined the programme. 'Since Dr Perumal has joined the programme I've noticed educators being imparted with skills and knowledge needed, especially in the ECD. Through PfP, over 2,200 books – much needed – have been sponsored to our school. They have also imparted the skills on how to set up and run the library. Through PfP and Nal'ibali [a reading programme], our educators will have the skill to spark children's potential through storytelling and reading. It gives us the educators the courage and hope that we need to know that it is POSSIBLE to make the positive changes in the lives of our students. It has given me the courage to know it's possible for me to achieve the impossible,' says Miss Moodley.

On our way out of the school, Theo and I were told about some of the changes that have happened in the last few months. The litter problem had been addressed and the school is now completely litter-free. Food & Trees for Africa donated 56 trees. There is now a library stocked with 2,500 books from Biblionef and the Centre for the Advancement of Science and Mathematics Education.

Parkgate Primary's teachers have attended Nal'iBali literacy development workshops and, as part of a GOBY (Global Organisation 4 Brighter Youth) project, the school hosted a workshop about the recycling of plastic waste for 58 teachers in the area.

According to Ravi, 'PfP was the right thing at the right time' for Parkgate Primary School. 'It helped us move towards realising our vision for the school,' he said. 'The school has developed in leaps and bounds due to us exploring the possibilities presented by our business leader and the NC3 group members. This programme is a must for school principals to expand and sharpen their leadership as well as management skills.'

Being in the partnership with Ravi has been beneficial to Gill too. 'I have learned about the challenges faced in this environment and the wonderful committed people who are often ill-equipped for the challenges they face. I have learned to listen, and through listening to form a plan to get the best results for the school.'

Postscript

When we sent this chapter to the contributors for their sign-off, both Martin and Gill contacted me to say that it would be hard to do justice to the transformation they had witnessed in their partners.

Martin was blown away by what he saw on his last visit to the school. He says the difference at the school is palpable, with Lukkie standing taller and being more confident, and teachers stepping up to play their best 'music' as co-creators of a beautiful symphony at the school.

Gill recalls the first time she attended a meeting at Parkgate Primary; it felt like a very typical school meeting, with Ravi being in charge at the front of the room and little engagement from the other educators. She says that she has been astonished by the change that has occurred since that first meeting. 'Ravi has transformed the school just through listening and having collaborative conversations. He has learned to let every voice be heard, even the quiet ones. In a year, virtually every challenge at the school has been addressed. I cannot believe the sheer energy, optimism and outright joy of most of his staff.'

I love hearing these stories. I know what a difference it makes to employees when their leaders become conscious of the cost of autocratic leadership and committed to creating an environment where every voice and every contribution is actively sought, valued and welcomed.

Many scholars argue that this is the most important shift that needs to happen in education – a move from autocratic leadership, with one person expected to have the answers, to distributed leadership where all educators are invited to make their best contribution. I often hear from my peers how difficult they find it to facilitate these shifts, especially with more mature leaders. Perhaps I should introduce them to principals like Lukkie, Ravi and so many other principals in the PfP community who have made this shift so gracefully?

Chapter 10

The School Pages Project

"Generative journalism's goal is to build communities, not simply report on their wounds." – Peter Block

While we were sitting in principal Lukkie Matsabe's office at Vulemehlo Primary School in Kabokweni, he suddenly lunged into the bottom drawer of his desk and pulled out a pile of pages from the *Lowvelder* – the local newspaper for Nelspruit and White River. He searched through them until he found the page featuring a story about himself. The paper had profiled principals from schools participating in the PfP programme.

I had asked Lukkie if his PfP partnership has made a difference to his self-esteem, and he wanted to show me that he was now important enough to be profiled in the newspaper. 'People saw that article,' he said, 'I can hold my head up when I walk around in the community.'

While searching through the sheets, Lukkie found the double-page spread that the *Mpumalanga News* (the Lowvelder's sister paper) had published about his school. The pages were slightly dog-eared – clearly from being shown to every visitor to the school – and starting to yellow, but the pride he took in the recognition was palpable.

At the other schools we visited from the NEL2 Circle, we saw similar newspaper articles that had been published about them. In one case, stories had been laminated and framed; in another, they had been photocopied and pinned to the notice board, but all were clearly highly prized by the schools involved.

That Lowveld Media, the Nelspruit branch of Caxton Publishing, which owns the *Lowvelder* and *Mpumalanga News*, should be carrying stories about schools in the local townships at all is largely down to the initiative and vision of one man, Matthys Ferreira, and his School Pages Project.

Ferreira, a former policeman, is the motoring and features editor at Lowveld Media. When he joined the NEL2 Circle as a PfP business partner in 2018, he realised that the PfP model offered an opportunity to implement an idea that he had had for a long time.

'I believe the power of the media can be used to shine a spotlight on rural schools where the talent is as abundant as it is in the town schools. It can build self-esteem and write a new narrative about the schools in our community,' Matthys said. 'I thought that the School Pages Project, which we called Sikolo Setfu (Our School) could give exposure to the schools, the principals and the learners. It could be a win-win because it can increase our circulation as well as offer advertising opportunities.

'You have no idea what this opportunity and exposure means to these schools, principals and particularly the kids,' he says. 'As a community paper, we have the capacity to make a real difference to the lives of the people within our communities.'

Matthys invited all the principals and business leaders in his leadership circle to the Lowveld Media offices where he introduced the concept of profiling their schools in the local papers. There was immediate buy-in from everyone, including the Lowvelder's management, editorial and distribution teams.

The Sikolo Setfu project was launched in October 2018. The plan was to publish a double-page spread, featuring two schools, every second week in the *Mpumalanga News*. 'We established small editorial teams, made up of four or five learners and a teacher from each school. They were tasked with writing four or five stories and gathering a selection of suitable photographs. Then, on pre-determined dates, each team would come to the Lowveld Media offices to compile and be involved in the layout of their school page,' Matthys explained.

The brief to these editorial teams was that the stories must be light, positive and uplifting. It was suggested that the first time a school was featured, the article should include a brief summary of its history. The school's logo would appear prominently at the top of the page. 'We got one of the graphic artists at the newspaper to redesign their logos so that they could be used, which was a great service to the schools,' Matthys said.

Two school editorial teams visited the Lowvelder Media offices together, with Matthys hosting one team and Bongani Hlatshwayo, editor of the *Mpumalanga News*, hosting the other. The teams were familiarised with the entire publishing process and taken to see the printing press.

Each team was partnered with a layout artist and, together, they designed their school page. 'We used a basic template for the design,' Matthys explained, 'but the kids chose their lead story and had a say in the colours used and on other elements of the pages. It was amazing to observe their delight.'

Sub-editors suggested headlines for each story, corrections were done, and each team was then presented with an A3 black and white and an A4 colour print of their page to take with them.

'It was always a huge occasion when the newspaper featuring the school appeared,' Matthys said. 'It's highly emotional and a source of great pride for the school and its whole community.'

The principals and business leaders were interviewed by the Lowvelder's editorial team and profiled in separate articles. Business leaders were featured in the business section of the *Lowvelder*, while the principal's profiles were published in the *Mpumalanga News*.

Batches of the papers featuring the schools, principals and business leaders were delivered to the schools for them to distribute in their community and sell to raise funds. 'We also encouraged the schools to use those articles and newspapers as a teaching aid in the classroom. This led to the introduction of various reading programmes in the schools,' said Matthys.

Mthayiza Primary School made R400 by selling copies of the edition in which the school was profiled. 'The community showed more interest in reading because they read more about their own news that was written by their own kids,' said Elsie Chiloane, the school's principal.

Elsie reported that the learners who had visited the newspapers were now influencing others at the school, and more of them were showing an interest in writing as a result.

Lukkie told us that appearing in the newspaper had raised his both his profile and that of the school. 'Quite often our school communities, parents in particular, do not get to know us school principals very well,' he said. 'The profile has provided my school community – teachers, learners and parents – with a broader picture about me. Now they know me better. The profile enabled my community to appreciate my contribution towards crafting and shaping the future of their children.'

The School Pages Project, Lukkie said, benefitted the school in terms of exposure, career guidance and opportunities for learners to show their talents.

'As a provincial newspaper, *Mpumalanga News* exposed our schools to the Mpumalanga community,' he said. 'Our learners were taken on a tour of the different divisions at Lowveld Media and given information about subjects and qualifications needed to do certain jobs and job opportunities. They were also presented with the opportunity to showcase their literary skills and to display their knowledge about their experiences and issues affecting them in their day-to-day lives.'

The effect on the children involved has been profound. We were shown the project evaluation forms completed by the learners, and the consensus is that their involvement had led to great benefits for themselves, for the school, and the community.

'I learned that we have to be proud of our roots and culture,' wrote one learner. 'People became aware of the talent that we have in our school,' noted another, while a third pronounced that: 'The community should not lose hope in us and think their children are stupid. They can see that they can write in the newspaper.'

Martin Tobias, Lukkie's partner at Vulemehlo Primary, spoke to the learners who had been involved in the project and found that they all had a much clearer idea than before of what they want to become one day. 'The project encourages reading,' he said. 'All the learners are readers – although the library is far away from the school. They have all said that they want to carry on writing.

'This project keeps people updated and informed about the school.'

The schools profiled have benefitted in a variety of ways. 'Simanga Maloka, Principal of Mgwenyane Primary School, another of those featured on the pages, told me that the enrolment in his school has increased for the next year,' said Matthys. 'He puts this down to the impact that PfP is making in his school and especially the School Pages Project which has raised awareness about his school. The general interest amongst the community and parents is very heart-warming.'

Matthys describes the project as an emotional experience. 'I had a lot of fun with the kids. I remember the time when we were done with Vulemehlo's page, I spontaneously opened my arms and invited the kids for a hug – their response was immediate and complete. In that moment, I acknowledged and expressed gratitude because it is in these moments that miracles are born. The group hug has now become part of the standard operating procedure.'

Bongani Hlatshwayo is as excited about this project. 'I know that as we progress with this project, fireworks can be expected. Learners will be better prepared, and the quality of the stories will improve.'

Reflections

Peter Block speaks of the power of generative journalism, and it occurred to me that the Sikolo Setfu project is an example of this in action. Journalism is struggling because it does not report enough on local, cooperative things that are happening. Instead, it focuses on what is wrong. 'When you report on citizens coming together, that act widens the circle of connected citizens,' he said in a recent interview. 'Thereby, when you report on what is working in the world, the 'what is working' becomes the world in the experience of reading about it. If we only report on what is dying, then we die in the reading and the hearing.'

This School Pages Project in Nelspruit is an example of reporting on what is working. The direct involvement of the learners is unique and powerful. It creates mind shifts and restores dignity. It introduces possibilities. It encourages learners to explore and take ownership. It is powerful. It has the potential to create a tsunami of fundamental and authentic change within the minds of tomorrow's leaders.

Chapter 11

Youth@worK harnessing the power of collaboration

"This is a time for bold measures. This is the country, and you are the generation." — Bono

Erica Kempken joined the PfP programme in 2013 as partner to Victoria (Vicky) Mmuoe, principal of Zandspruit Primary School in Johannesburg. They were part of the Johannesburg 6 (JHB6) Leadership Circle.

The experience was a big wake-up call for Erica when she saw at first-hand the serious resource-related challenges that so many of our government schools face. After working together for a while, Erica and Vicky realised that some of the problems they were grappling with could be overcome by finding volunteers to assist with specific tasks or initiatives in the school; for example, Grade 6 and 7 learners could be paired with Grade 4s to create a 'buddy' reading programme and parents could assist in the kitchen or help to keep the school safe.

They recognised that the school could provide better services and education if there were more people to support the teachers and to assist with other functions like administration. At the time Erica was working with ProServ, a training provider that facilitates learnerships. In 2013 Erica convinced the ProServ management to place 90 young people who needed to gain workplace experience in IT into PfP schools in Gauteng. The candidates were placed at schools that had good IT infrastructure but lacked the manpower needed to use the technology effectively.

As a result of this intervention, each of the 90 schools involved had the support of an IT assistant in their computer lab. These young people prepared the lesson plans for IT classes, which gave the educators more time to teach and the learners more time to spend working on the computers. The retention rate for this school-based learnership project was 90%, and more than 80 eager young IT technicians left the schools having gained valuable work experience to seek jobs elsewhere.

The IT teachers, however, found themselves once again without support. Erica therefore worked hard to create more learnership opportunities and succeeded in placing more young people into PfP schools – each time learning a bit more about the potential for school-based opportunities as she sought to develop a sustainable model for employment in and through schools.

From 2013 to 2018 a total of 325 unemployed young people were placed into learnerships in PfP schools, where they gained a full year of paid work experience while boosting the operational effectiveness and efficiency of those schools. For these first-time job seekers, the principals and educators proved to be ideal mentors and role models who helped to build the young people's confidence in their abilities and to take pride in serving their community. This contributed to an outstanding overall retention rate of 93%.

The schools also offered a platform for young people to start businesses, such as private tuition in mathematics, coordination of recycling projects and, in one case, an internet café. Erica and her team recognised that the learnerships were not only benefitting the schools and the candidates themselves but were also facilitating the establishment of new businesses that would serve under-resourced communities around schools. During a five-year period this learnership initiative brought resources and training to the massive value of R9,802,500 into the public education system.

In October 2018 the establishment of the Youth Employment Service (YES) created a new form of youth deployment into workplaces as a means of earning B-BBEE points. Erica resigned from permanent employment and took on the challenge of establishing an organisation that could facilitate high-quality school-based work experiences through YES.

Erica was introduced by SSA's Stakeholder Engagement Lead, Robyn Whittaker, to Jacinta Roest-Tshidzumba, who has over 20 years' experience in various B2B (business to business) start-ups. Jacinta shares Erica's dream and recognised the potential of youth placements in schools. The pair soon partnered and spent a considerable amount of time visiting schools. They found that sponsors were donating resources like libraries and computer equipment but weren't providing any funding to pay someone to manage or assist teachers to manage a library or computer lab effectively.

'We knew that youth could provide valuable assistance that would enable schools to make the most of these donated facilities while benefitting from invaluable work experience and mentorship, and we were determined to find a way to make that happen. The YES initiative offers a platform for money to be channelled to young people working in schools. Its learning modules and ability to track progress via an app also support the development of each individual. The concept of placing youth into schools was becoming clearer,' said Erica.

YES recognises the critical role that young people play in shaping our economy and country. Those involved with the programme feel that the only way to reduce inequality is to get all South Africans into work and they are committed to supporting companies and communities to create one million jobs for young South Africans. YES believes in the power of cross-sectoral collaboration, coupled with innovation and technological best practice, to change South Africa's skewed economy. The programme is driven by business and fully supported by government and labour.

In February 2019, with support from Robyn and the SSA team, Youth@worK was accredited by YES as an Implementation Partner and was allocated the first 32 youth placements sponsored by Liquid Telecom. This meant that some young people who were about to complete a learnership at a PfP school and then seek jobs elsewhere, leaving learning facilities under-resourced once again, were able to continue working at those schools through the YES programme. In the following months, companies such as Sygnia, Gartner, Nedbank and Lightstone provided more funding for further placements.

In addition to exposing young people to the world of work and building their confidence as active citizens, the PfP schools have given them a sense of belonging. Erica has observed that 'school principals and heads of departments have a natural ability to manage new job starters and to build their skills gradually through clear guidance and patience, which is not always the case in other more corporate business environments'.

This positive impact on both the young people and schools involved in the initial deployment facilitated by Youth@worK led to an agreement between the organisation and SSA to continue and expand the provision of youth placement opportunities for young people in PfP schools.

Young people placed by Youth@worK in PfP schools have engaged in and supported a host of activities including administrative work, classroom assistance, aftercare support, fundraising, support for pupils to access services such as social workers, holiday sports programmes and many more.

'The schools have proven to be ideal centres in which youth can learn basic business principles. This is particularly important to change the perception that community establishments are not as important, sophisticated or valued as corporate employment is. Once youth understand this, they are more willing to engage with community businesses and to possibly form their own new enterprise based on the needs of the clients in the community. We have witnessed this positive blossoming of entrepreneurial mindset time and time again,' Jacinta explained.

The nature of the work they have become involved in at schools has helped young people to develop key work-readiness skills such as complex problem-solving, critical thinking, creativity, people management, coordination, communication, decision-making, service orientation, negotiation and business etiquette. With these skills, they will be better equipped to face the Fourth Industrial Revolution, to remain employable and create self-employment opportunities.

Shanice Aydapa was sponsored by Liquid Telecoms to work for 12 months at Zilungusele Primary School where she engaged in many different activities. She worked with the Santa Shoe Box project and helped to offer surprise gifts to 600 children. She designed a library programme to make reading cool and fun and to help young learners to recognise its importance and value. Shanice also spent time reading to Grade R and Grade 3 learners.

The exposure to new activities was building Shanice's confidence, and she decided to host and direct a beauty pageant at the school, for both boys and girls. The event, which involved parents and teachers, as well as the children, was a huge success. After the excitement of the pageant, Shanice received a letter from one of the girls who had participated, and this motivated her to enter the Miss KZN Ambassador competition (an initiative that gives a provincial platform to boys and girls who want to assist needy communities in KZN) In her October 2019 YES progress report Shanice wrote the following:

After the beauty pageant one of my students wrote me the sweetest letter saying: 'Ma'am you were the one who believed in me now it's time to believe in yourself and take part and make us proud' – so I did!

This pageant was beauty, heart and brain. It was a road I have already been walking on. Working with Youth@worK has opened up so many possibilities for me to have succeeded in this event. It has given me life fulfilment and purpose, and it has also humbled me as a person. Mahatma Gandhi once said, 'Be the change that you wish to see in the world'. Working for an organisation that brings about development and upliftment to the lives of many South Africans, I am so blessed to be a part of that change!

Youth@worK has also given me in the opportunity to work with the most incredible, inspirational, God fearing principal I have ever met. I have learned so much from her. Her encouragement, guidance, love and support was given to me by her. I enjoyed the best 9 months of my working career.

I am moving on to greater heights because of true passion, hard work and commitment to change.

I won the Miss Ambassador KZN 2019 title, Miss Charity Queen Title and best dressed award.

I didn't expect to win, however, it was in God's plan ☺

Thank you, Youth@worK for your support and commitment invested in me.

Shanice was offered permanent employment at Crawford North Coast as an aftercare supervisor on completion of her YES year.

To further the develop young people they had placed in PfP schools, Erica facilitated a workshop that she adapted from the Community Building course to share ideas on how to make a positive impact in schools and communities. She also invited the Africa Matters Initiative to run a 2-day leadership development workshop for 70 YES candidates during the July 2019 holidays.

Led by two young women, Farai Mubaiwa and Reanne Olivier, the Africa Matters Initiative is dedicated to empowering young Africans to change the African narrative and inspire change within their communities through leadership development, social entrepreneurship and community impact projects.

With Farai and her team, the young people discussed topics including: What is leadership? What is not leadership? Who is a leader? and What role can African youth play on the continent? They also explored social entrepreneurship and discussed approaches to community problems using a business model canvas and elements of design thinking. In groups, the young people were asked to deliver a pitch on a project they believe would make a positive difference in communities and could be developed into a business.

'The passion and creativity we saw during this session was pure magic!' exclaimed Erica. 'Needless to say, this course was very well received by our youth and allowed even the shy young people to find their voices, the outspoken to listen, and ordinary young people to be inspired and dream.' After the workshop, Erica received this letter:

> *I feel so humbled and blessed to be part of YES. Being part of Youth@worK has given me an opportunity to be part of a bigger 'change your country' movement. My journey has been amazing so far. This opportunity has given me a chance to do some deep self-introspection, as it has opened my eyes and shown me that I have more interests and skills to explore. Grooming, playing and teaching children makes me happy and pleased with myself. Waking up every day in a positive right state of mind, to inspire and motivate someone looking up to me is what keeps me going. I can say I have come a long way, although in a short space of time as there is so much I have learned, met so many influential and motivating great people from Nedbank, YES, YLED, Africa Matters, Fielding Dreams coaches. If I were to write each person by name, the list would be endless.*
>
> *My journey with YES has motivated me and given me a growth mindset. I am empowered and fully informed about how to be professional, how to succeed in the*

workplace, how to manage money wisely, how to prepare my CV and cover letter, entrepreneurship (Siyazakhela), customer service, SMART goals and how to plan.

Despite of all the information, knowledge and skills gained, I am able to take care of myself, be independent financially and also make an impact and influence good change in my community and country. There is also an opportunity of getting paid for what I'm actually supposed to do. Through Zlto I earn points for the good activities that are offered for me to do. I use my points to buy airtime, Shoprite's selected products, Uber rides, electricity and Ster-Kinekor; Pep Stores also coming soon.

After so many skills and experience I have gained thus far, beyond my YES journey, I am employable if not self-employed. I am highly motivated, full of positive attitude, mature and responsible. I am eternally thankful and humbled for being part of the winning team, Team YES.

Mpho Makhubo

Erica and Jacinta have been delighted that young people are gaining valuable work experience and skills, but they have wrestled with the fact that full-time employment is very seldom offered to them in government schools after they complete the YES programme. The pair have therefore looked for ways to sustain school-based employment opportunities beyond the 12-month YES programme.

'One of the ways we are attempting to do this is to train up keen sportsmen and women who will post-YES be able to seek employment or self-employment in sport. Through Robyn, we were fortunate to have met Vaughn Bishop, the former SuperSport presenter who runs GOBY.'

Vaughn's GOBY project promotes a healthy and active lifestyle and educates children about plastic waste while also developing their sporting skills through various activities in primary schools.

'The overall goal is to use sport as a vehicle to mitigate violence and transform schools and school communities into child-friendly environments. Through Vaughn, we managed to include some KZN PfP schools in the programme and met the leadership of Fielding Dreams who have since trained 54 of our YES youth funded by Toyota, Oracle, MMT Inland and Liquid Telecom on coaching skills and introduced them to the Amaven system which tracks their fitness and provides coaching lesson plans. It even informs the parents of the sports interventions and a lot more,' says Erica.

This initiative is having a tremendously positive impact on both the young people and the PfP schools involved. These young coaches are now creating training programmes, managing teams and teaching sport at the schools as part of the Life Orientation syllabus. They are learning about accountability and sustainability in sports programmes and being developed to run sports training academies. They are encouraged to charge for delivering sports clinics in the holidays.

One of the beneficiaries of Youth@Work's partnership with GOBY is Bonga Magwaza who gave this feedback:

> *I wake up every day with a smile now knowing that my coaching and sport career is of part the greatest sponsors I've ever been part of in the country, all thanks to Toyota who partnered with Youth@worK and the YES Programme. This programme will benefit me plus all the youth without jobs and those who are willing to learn more about their careers like myself.*
>
> *I found a school in Durban by the name of Hartley Road Primary School, one of the experienced coaches (Coach Stef Crasa) I was coaching with in my soccer club at Juventus (Durban North). Now he is my supervisor at the same school I work at. I am really enjoying my first week at HRPS. What's good here is that I'm active all day. During the week with physical education activities soccer and swimming and on Saturdays for school tournaments. I love these kids, they are super energetic and talented, all they need is for us to coach them on their developing stages both in football and swimming, and that's easy for me as a qualified coach in soccer under SAFA with my D Licence Course.*
>
> *I was coaching the past years as a volunteer. I got a chance to coach the under 15 soccer boys in a tournament in Italy in June and July 2019. We played well there in Italy. They invited us again 2020 April on Easter. I dream about running a rural development sports academy in Mbongolwane (Eshowe) where I grew up.*
>
> *Thanks for allowing me to dream and believe that this all is possible*
>
> *Coach Bonga Magwaza*

Bonga resigned from the YES programme as he was recognised by the Ethekwini Municipality and awarded an internship which has the potential to lead to permanent employment in sports management within the municipality.

Through a partnership they established with the Click Foundation, Youth@worK secured placements for 44 young people to work in Click Labs. The Click Foundation provides online English literacy and numeracy programmes in under-resourced primary schools and employs facilitators who support learners to work at their own pace through the 'reading eggs' programme.

As well as providing employment and development for 44 young people, the Youth@ worK- Clicks Foundation partnership has reached almost 9,000 children and improved their literacy skills, thereby reducing the risk that they will drop out of school.

To help young people placed through Youth@worK to gain additional skills Robyn introduced Erica to Alison, an internationally recognised free online learning platform that offers over 1,300 different certificated courses in languages, maths, IT, business and many other subject areas. Currently, 60% of the young people linked to schools are studying and adding to their qualifications, thus increasing their employability.

One young man, who was working as a Click Foundation youth facilitator at Ekurhuleni Primary School (which was part of the Johannesburg 27 Leadership Circle that launched in May 2017) resigned after five months as a result of securing a well-paying permanent job, that was in line with his qualifications and interests, at Impala Platinum. Below is an extract from his resignation letter:

I herewith submit my official resignation from my duties as a Lab Facilitator at Ekurhuleni Primary School, where I was deployed by my former host employers Youth@worK and the Click Foundation.

I am grateful for the opportunity which helped me to grow as a person and gain not only necessary experience but skills too. I thank you for your guidance and support and the knowledge about Alison Courses from which I acquired education on Occupational Health and Safety.

I thank Nedbank for believing in the youth and giving them financial support they need to get from one point to the next. I thank all stakeholders involved, and appreciate everyone's effort in making me a better person.

It would be a pleasure to work with you in the future and changing the youth, one person at a time, for the better.

Yours sincerely,
Dini Mnuka

The Youth@worK team has also collaborated with the Community Care Project (CCP) to help expand its HIV prevention and care work among vulnerable children and families through funded youth placements. In schools, each CCP facilitator interacts with around 400 vulnerable learners who get the chance to be tested and supported.

After discussing CCP with a group of young people in KZN Erica received this letter:

I am writing this letter to all at YES, VW Unlok'D and its members those who saw a need granting me an internship. You have made me a different person, one who views life in a positive way. I never saw hope in the future until you rescued me because I wouldn't have had this opportunity of working without you.

I am very interested in the course offered by CCP and would very much like to receive more details. I am pleased to tell you that I have completed my BBA at the UKZN PMB and next year I'll start a teaching degree at UNISA. I already accepted an offer, now I am waiting for a registration package.

Through the YES programme I benefitted a lot, though the journey isn't easy. I worked as an Admin Clerk at Umthombomuhle Intermediate School, but all that has been changed. Now I am a teacher who teaches Grade 7-9 Life Orientation and also assisting the mathematics teacher for the same grades. I also started the school garden and sports technical coaching and I motivate the learners to go further with their studies and try their best to follow the 4th Industrial Revolution change since technology is taking over in the Business Sector, everything now uses tech and I do the career guidance at school.

Please could you send me an application form and I look forward to hearing from you at your convenience.

BA Cele

Erica and Jacinta were looking for ways to encourage and support the young people they were placing in schools to deliver on their YES mandate and to easily track and monitor their work experience. Erica decided to meet with Allan van der Meulen, a member of the Zlto team in Mitchells Plain. Zlto is an award-winning digital platform that incentivises young people to gain work experience as a stepping stone towards employment by rewarding them for doing positive community activities with a digital rewards currency. With that currency, they can buy goods and services such as clothing, airtime, basic food supplies and Uber rides from a range of local vendors – including national retailers like Shoprite.

The young people keep track of their work experience by taking 'before' and' after' photos of the activities they engage in and uploading them onto the Zlto app. Their work experience is verified by Zlto 'validators' and recorded in a blockchain ledger, from where they can share it with potential employers. Organisations who are sponsoring the young people to participate in YES can also track their work experience via live data dashboards on Zlto.

Erica says that the Zlto platform 'has hugely impacted the way YES youth engage with technology'.

As well as providing them with access to employment opportunities, the Youth@worK team also encourage young people to think about entrepreneurship and services or products they could be providing to their community as a way of staying economically active after they complete the YES year.

One young person who has done this is Queeneth Nomkhosi, who was placed by Youth@worK at Ukukhanya Kwe Africa Primary School in KZN. Queeneth's sister is a keen seamstress, and Queeneth supports her to run a sewing business. While she was doing admin work at the school, Queeneth networked with a lot of people and told them about their family business. With the money she earned, Queeneth started buying sewing machines. The business has grown and the pair are now sometimes very busy. As a result, the reality of running a business has become much clearer to Queeneth and she now needs more entrepreneurial support to ensure that the business becomes sustainable.

Queeneth's experience is an example of how some guidance, skills, funds and a change in mindset can catapult young people from total dependence onto a path towards self-reliance and fulfilment of their potential in just a few months.

The Youth@worK team continue to look for ways of supporting Queeneth and others like her who have come through the YES programme to succeed in their new ventures. In Queeneth's case, they may be able to arrange for other young people to join her sewing business through a sponsored YES youth placement. To help other new entrepreneurs, Jacinta and Erica are raising funds to enable them to offer loans, small business development support and mentorship.

The impact of Youth@worK's support for entrepreneurship shines through in this letter:

> *I was hired to be an entrepreneur.*
>
> *With a loud excited shout of joy, the 25 employed youth at Ntuthuko Primary School cheered after being told in a thrilling and suspenseful wait by a lady from Youth@Work called Erica 'All of you have passed the interview and have been chosen to be employed under Youth@worK sponsored by Nedbank!!' she said enthusiastically.*
>
> *Six months in and the exciting and impactful YES programme has afforded me an opportunity to learn. I have learned about self-development to career development to what makes everything synchronise and prosper, Goal setting.*

The highs for me in the YES programme is when I recognised all the stakeholders involved in my career development, positively working together and using their resources to cultivate and harness an employable product and moreover an employing product beyond the YES program. I am very grateful. 'I was hired to be an entrepreneur'. I have partnered with my friends and we have started a learning institute which teaches about financial instruments. The name of this institute is Maqhawe Academy. Personally, I look forward to the day I get an FSB licence to be a Financial Adviser. One of the founders of Maqhawe Academy is an alumnus of Johannesburg Business School and they have to help us with our SMME development.

The most impactful intervention was the monthly report submission. Completely new to me. It taught me to diarise daily, journalise daily and keep tabs with my own personal development. I bought a bicycle end of July and it has been a joy ride. I have tackled indirectly my weight loss targets and I move with more vigour and energy. Most importantly also to that was positive self-talk that was taught. Telling myself for example 'I am the greatest click facilitator' 'I am joyful and content and I love myself'. That was a game-changer.

All the interventions were of superior quality. I walked out of every workshop having learned something new or just that one extra tool I could use to improve myself. I learned four questions which I use rigorously in my daily life; 1. Why, 2 Why Not, 3 Why Not Me, 4 Why Not Now?

Then the business development workshop whereby a random pig and fridge selection ended up being a team effort that harnessed all the creative juices out of my team members Ashley, Adwin, Precious and Lucky. The product thereof being a Cool Bank. Completely scalable.

The experience has afforded me be exposed on how I can go about that. This is a skill I will continue to pursue beyond the yes programme.

Lerato Twala

In yet another effort to create future self-employment opportunities for young people once their YES placement in PfP schools end, Erica has been collaborating with Seeds of Africa, a non-profit organisation that supports enterprise and supplier development and ECD in disadvantaged communities. They have offered to train and manage nine young people that Youth@worK has placed in PfP schools to deliver the Seriously Addictive Mathematics (S.A.M.) programme.

'Through this intervention we aim to not only develop more informed ECD practitioners in the Muldersdrift and Zandspruit area, but also to enhance the skills of foundation phase educators in maths. This initiative has the potential to empower young people to open their own ECD centres and strengthen the mathematical skills of young learners. We are cognisant of the gap between many ECD establishments and the foundation phase of public schools and this initiative will allow us to influence and manage the transfer of skills more effectively to increase impact on NGO funding,' explains Erica.

Through the collaboration between PfP and Youth@worK, our schools truly are becoming the centre of their communities, with entrepreneurship being encouraged, practised and refined so that it can flourish.

In October 2019 the Youth@worK team were informed that they had been allocated funding from Toyota for 229 placements and from Oracle for 45 placements. This caused great excitement! They immediately contacted our team and, together, we started a process to assess needs in PfP schools. Dina Cramer, a member of the PfP leadership team, was in Lephalale facilitating Time to Think training and heard about young people who needed work placements to complete their ECD and administration qualifications.

Dina contacted Erica who instantly agreed to earmark 70 placements in PfP schools on the condition that there was someone who could assist with the extensive paperwork required for the selection and recruitment process. Dina put Erica in contact with Annemie van Vuuren, a well-connected retired district education official who was willing to offer her services to bring opportunities to schools 'in the forgotten land'.

A group of motivated and passionate young people who are studying to become teachers have been selected for this opportunity, and the intention is to support these individuals to become teachers of the future, equipped with the technical skills they need, coupled with a 'possibility' mindset. The value of these placements to the young people and the PfP schools they will be working in is R3,000,000 and Erica is looking forward to reporting to YES about the number of permanent jobs, small businesses and future study opportunities that will be created with this money.

As a result of the partnership between PfP and Youth@worK Erica often receives messages like this:

What has made a great impact in my life is the fact that this year I completed my PGCE certificate and I'm now a qualified teacher.

Getting an opportunity to be in a school that has a lot of activities going on made my mind think broadly about what I can implement or influence the kids with. When I started in the school I gathered a group of girls and I joined them as girl guides. Now towards the end of this year I started a drum majorette group which made the girls really excited and wanting to engage.

There are more activities to be implemented and I hope next year will be indeed an exciting year.

Thenjiwe Mthembu

During 2019 Youth@worK placed 570 young people into PfP schools, collectively channelling an incredible R29,070,000 worth of services into these under-resourced institutions.

The support that these young people have been providing in PfP schools has positively impacted them in a variety of ways which include:

- Educators spending more time teaching through being freed from administrative tasks
- More efficient school administration processes, such as timeous reporting to education districts
- More extra mural activities being offered to learners
- Learners benefitting from mentorship and educational and emotional support
- Pupils becoming more engaged with their academic work and showing improved performance
- More participation by parents in some schools
- A reduction in learner absenteeism in most schools.

The school serves as a home for many children, who receive much-needed food, guidance, support and role modelling there – especially those who grow up in child-headed households. Together with teachers, young people placed by Youth@worK at PfP schools often fulfil some aspects of a parenting role.

In the final months of 2019, Youth@Work received further funding from Canon, Werksmans Attorneys, MacMillan Publishers, Vesuvius, MLC Quantity Surveyors,

Performanta, MtT Inland (Pty) Ltd, Entersekt, and Accounting and Financial Advisory to expand the YES programme into the Western and Eastern Cape. They have signed an agreement with LFP, an accredited training partner who will ensure that these YES sponsors receive the relevant B-BBEE points for their investment in young people.

Erica and Jacinta's dream is to develop a generation of young people who are empowered to fulfil their potential and become productive, self-sustaining members of society. Robyn has worked closely with this dedicated pair to help realise their vision and says:

Imagine if.......

...Our country's problems hold the seed of our greatest potential

- *We give our young people an opportunity to experience their first work as being in community, where they live*
- *Young people are mentored and become civic-minded*
- *Young people develop a deep sense of their ability to contribute meaningfully and impact upon others who recognise that a job entails being of value and being of service and who are rewarded and remunerated for this*
- *We can create micro-industry hubs born of in-community work with the development of key skills needed by that community, the opportunity to assess and meet the community's needs, and the development of trust within that community*
- *We can refine and develop a coherent, sustainable strategy to strengthen our youth, education system, and the economy in keeping with the demands of the Fourth Industrial Revolution.*

Chapter 12

Principals who have been promoted since PfP

"Any leader's greatest return is to develop other leaders." –
John C Maxwell

Our intention with PfP is to strengthen leaders' capacity to lead complex organisations. The idea is for these skills to be transferable and to stand the leaders in good stead for the rest of their careers. Many principals have been promoted to other roles since participating in PfP. I was keen to hear their thoughts on this and whether they felt their PfP experience had made any difference to their careers.

Belinda Petersen

Belinda Petersen was appointed as principal of Rustenburg Girls' Junior School in July 2019. It was a noteworthy appointment as she is the first black principal in the school's 125-year history, and it came at a time when the school was just starting to emerge from controversy following the resignation of its first black African teacher.

Belinda had previously been principal of Ottery Road Methodist Primary, a school with 280 pupils and 15 staff members. Rustenburg has 558 pupils and 40 teachers, so the post is quite a step up for her. In 2016, while at Ottery Road, Belinda joined the PfP programme and was partnered with Charmaine Matroos of the Nimble Group. I wanted to know what role the partnership played in her development as a leader and whether she felt it had contributed to her appointment to Rustenburg.

Her answer to my question was immediate. 'If I hadn't been part of PfP I would not have considered applying for this job,' she said. 'PfP defined who I am as a principal. I have been using the skills I learned through PfP from the moment I walked into the school. Having these skills gave me the confidence to have the difficult conversations.'

Belinda joined PfP in her first year as principal of Ottery Road. 'I learned to become a new type of principal,' she said. 'I became part of a new community of principals who listen to their people and who co-create with them.'

Reflecting on that PfP year, Belinda says it taught her to see things through the lens of possibility. 'Things fell in place for me and, through working with Charmaine and attending the CoP meetings, I grew in confidence. I learned to really listen and to engage unapologetically. I grew to believe in myself as a leader. I'm a better person, a better wife and a better mother. It's about listening, slowing down and focusing.

'When I joined PfP I needed help with figuring out how to move forward with regard to my vision. I knew what had to be done, but I didn't really know how to do it. Having Charmaine as a sounding board gave me extra strength. She didn't judge me and she never asked me to explain myself. Occasionally she would ask me 'have you thought of this, or that?' but mostly she would support me and assure me that she had my back.

'PfP has enabled me to engage with all people within the Rustenburg community irrespective of their background or status within the broader community.'

Belinda's husband persuaded her to apply for the head's post at Rustenburg. 'It was the only post I applied for. As the first black principal of the school, I am expected to lead the transformation process. I don't see transformation as only about race and the number of black learners or staff at the school; it's about everyone feeling that they belong.

'My PfP experience has helped me to take the first steps on the transformation journey,' she said. 'We had a community meeting based on the Community Building principles. People were anxious about that. They worried that we would be opening ourselves up too much, but I had confidence in the methodology. We did a community survey, and then we met in small groups with learners, parents and staff, to discuss the results. It worked well and we have started to make progress. I had confidence that we would.'

Belinda considers the challenges she is facing as the first black principal at Rustenburg to be part of her leadership journey. 'It's not just about academic performance; it's about connecting with the children and the teachers. We can become energised and confident through connection.

'I have started introducing Time to Think here by showing that you first have to get to really know each other. Then you can apply Flawless Consulting thinking and start contracting with each other. That's what I learned in PfP and it's what I'm applying here. I look forward to introducing my SMT to all the skills and concepts that I learned in Time to Think, Flawless Consulting and Community Building.

'Through PfP I have learned the importance of telling your story, to not be afraid to tell your positive story. I plan to do just that in my new role.'

Chapter 12: Principals who have been promoted since joining PfP

Lindiwe Ginya

In June 2019, Dr Lindiwe Ginya was appointed as Head of Programmes at the Matthew Goniwe School of Leadership and Governance, where she is now responsible for teacher development and ICT Programmes in Gauteng Province.

Lindiwe joined PfP in April 2016 when she was the principal of George Khosa Secondary School in Soweto. She was partnered with Frank Terblanche from Liberty, and Chantal Dawtrey was their LPF.

When I emailed Lindiwe to ask whether she would be willing to share the story of her leadership journey, she responded by saying 'Getting this role was not luck but rather an example of opportunity meeting preparedness. I was prepared for this role through my interaction with my business partner.'

Theo and I met Lindiwe in her corner office at Matthew Goniwe's regional premises in Benoni. I told her that I was interested to know whether her PfP experience had contributed to her career progression. Lindiwe smiled and told us her story.

She said that she had been quite comfortable as the principal of George Khosa Secondary. She had overseen improvements in academic performances (the matric pass rate rose from 69% in 2015, to 84% in 2016 and 94% in 2017), the school had forged partnerships with various organisations and was on the path towards becoming a fully-fledged e-school. Lindiwe had just finished a PhD focusing on women in leadership.

'I was comfortable and felt I deserved a reward for having completed my PhD. I decided that I was going to buy an expensive car,' she said. She told Frank about her plans and he advised her against doing that. He reminded her of their conversation in which she'd said that one of her goals was to become financially secure. An expensive car was not going to help her achieve that goal.

'Frank suggested that I should rather invest in property. I investigated a few options and bought some land in Soweto. I built 12 units that are now being rented out, which means that I am receiving passive income.'

Lindiwe used this story to demonstrate the impact that Frank and PfP had on her life. It is one of many such stories. At the time she met Frank Lindiwe was feeling that as a principal she had to take responsibility for most of the functions at the school.

'We had 1,285 learners, and I was swamped, trying to do too much myself. With Frank's help we put staff members on project management, financial management and secretarial skills training, so that I would have more support.'

Frank helped Lindiwe see that she needed to delegate some responsibility and strengthen leadership capacity within her team. He arranged for one of her HODs to go to Liberty for HR training. He encouraged Lindiwe to re-organise the administrative functions at the school, and when it was decided that one of the administrators would become Lindiwe's PA Frank arranged for her to be trained by some PAs at Liberty.

'His area of specialisation is financial management and he helped me in many ways,' said Lindiwe. 'One was in the area of budgeting. He gave me a crash course in budgeting and financial management. He taught me to align the available funds to our objectives. Instead of seeing shortfalls, we looked at possibilities. It's a skill I use now in my new job where I am responsible for a much bigger budget.

'I also developed as a leader. I got so much value from attending the Time to Think course. I developed a lot more empathy with my colleagues.'

For Lindiwe, her partnership with Frank was transformational. It turned out to be very different from what she had thought it would be. She had heard about PfP from a friend and went to an information session where Robyn Whittaker, our Stakeholder Engagement Lead, talked about the programme. Lindiwe decided that she would join PfP but admits that she felt a bit cynical and didn't expect a great deal from her participation – except that the school would perhaps get some money through her partnership with someone from the business community.

When Lindiwe heard that she would be partnered with Frank Terblanche, a white, middle-aged man with the same surname as the notorious leader of the Afrikaner Weerstandsbeweging (AWB), she was a bit apprehensive. But her discomfort soon disappeared when she met Frank and experienced him as a humble person who was committed to making a positive difference and had no intention of judging her.

Looking back on the experience Lindiwe recognises that she got so much more than money. She got to be in a partnership with Frank, and it changed the trajectory of her life. 'There was chemistry between Frank and I. We were able to talk freely about so many things. When I felt that he was being too pushy I could tell him. He challenged me to think big and to get out of my comfort zone.

'Frank was my cheerleader. He was committed to see me succeed at George Khosa. At the time I thought that I had reached a ceiling. I was a successful principal and things were going well at the school. Frank helped me see that I could influence a bigger landscape, and that is why I considered applying for this job.'

Lindiwe got so much value from her involvement with PfP and from being in partnership with Frank that she wanted to share it with others. She started a group with 12 other female principals with the purpose of sharing her learning with them.

Lindiwe doesn't believe she would have applied for her current role if it had not been for PfP and Frank. 'I was comfortable and prepared to stay on my path. I felt I had arrived. Then I met Frank and my horizons were widened. Through interacting with Frank and the other partners in our circle, I grew as a person and a leader. He helped me see that even though I have a PhD there was still much I could learn and much that I could offer on a bigger stage.

'I learned so much from Frank. Because of what I learned from him about human resource management and how to engage strategically, I am able to lead a team of directors. Because of Frank's assistance with managing a budget of R1.7 million, I am now comfortable with managing a budget of R157 million. I would not have known how to do this if it wasn't for Frank.'

Although she is no longer the principal at George Khosa, Lindiwe still regards Frank as her thinking partner. She knows that he wants her to succeed and that he still has her back.

I wanted to hear Frank's perspective, so I sent him the piece we had written after our conversation with Lindiwe and asked him for his response. This is what he wrote:

I was quite apprehensive before meeting Lindiwe the first time. I was expecting a career educator, set in her ways and formal by nature. Was I pleasantly surprised! Lindiwe (together with a good number of other principals I met through the PfP programme) completely broke the mould of my stereotypically understanding of what 'township' educators are like. She is a brilliant and dedicated public servant, in the true sense of the word. Her single focus was on improving the realities of the children in her school, whether it be by establishing a vegetable garden or a sporting programme at the school, or by driving to the homes of some kids after hours to ensure they were safe. During the months that followed Lindiwe exposed me first-hand to the challenges that many of our communities face. This has changed my perspective on life, making me a much more compassionate citizen.

During our very first meeting Lindiwe was quite open about her political and church affiliations. This took me by surprise and left me quite uncomfortable. In my culture these matters are considered private and are not to be mixed with business. It did, however, immediately allow me to understand Lindiwe's values, her passions and what motivated her. I now make a point of trying to get to know my business associates on a more personal level as it helps forge a closer and more trusting working relationship.

Lindiwe is very humble in crediting me for so many of her accolades. She has always been a hard-working self-starter with stakeholder management skills as good as I have ever come across in my professional career. Lindiwe shared with me how some of the male parents and grandparents refused to engage directly with her after her appointment as principal at the school, just because she is female. They would only talk to the male educators. Lindiwe overcame this cultural challenge by working hard to gain the trust and confidence of all her stakeholders. By the time she and her team had lifted the matric pass rate from 69% to 94%, the men were queueing up outside her office to spend time with her. This was a valuable lesson to me. Lindiwe put her own feelings and frustrations aside so that they would not interfere with what ultimately was in the best interest of her learners, a healthy working relationship between parents and school. I have become much more mindful of the altruistic goals in my life, ensuring that my ego does not come in the way of achieving them.

Finally, and possibly for me the most profound personal learning from my PfP experience, I have developed a deep appreciation for the feel-good benefits I get from being generous. After learning how small acts of kindness and thoughtfulness (as exhibited by the PfP partnerships in my circle) changed the lives of so many, I finally understood the true meaning of the saying, 'There is more joy in giving than in receiving.'

Lorraine Mgobhozi

We met Dr Lorraine Mgobhozi at the GDE's District Office in Meyersdal. Lorraine had recently been promoted to the role of Cluster Leader. In this role, she is responsible for 15 schools in the Ekhurhuleni District.

Lorraine participated in the PfP programme in 2014 and was partnered with Sean Hendey, a senior executive at Nedbank. I was curious to know whether she thought her experience with PfP and her partnership with Sean had contributed to her career progression. 'Oh yes!' she exclaimed.

'It was easy to establish and sustain a relationship with Sean,' Lorraine said. 'Our relationship went beyond work at the school. We became good friends and the relationship extended to our families as well. Sean's wife Louise also got involved with the school. I gained so much confidence through PfP and have been able to use much of what I have learned in the schools I am working with.'

When she joined PfP, Lorraine was principal of Ekurhuleni Primary School in Dukathole, Germiston. The school is located in an informal settlement where the unemployment rate is estimated to be 95%. The community, therefore, depends entirely on government funding and third-party sponsorship for its income. Unsurprisingly, the 1,000 plus children who attend the school routinely experience all sorts of social and economic problems. The school's fixed infrastructure is wholly inadequate for the number of pupils it serves and, for the most part, teaching takes place in temporary classrooms.

Because the number of classrooms is insufficient, the school operates on a 'platoon system', which means that there is a morning session for half the school and an afternoon session for the rest. To complicate matters further, the available classrooms are on two different sites.

'Whilst we were fortunate enough to receive support from multiple corporate partnerships, we recognised the need to build a holistic plan for transforming the school in a sustainable manner. Collectively, Sean and I developed a plan called 'Vision 2020' which was a 5-year transformation roadmap across six focal areas namely: ensuring Sustainable Academic Performance, creating a Safe and Secure Environment, involving the Community, developing Infrastructure, creating Financial Certainty and entrenching and expanding Partnerships.'

One of Lorraine and Sean's goals was a new school building. 'Our plan included getting a permanent site for the school and having a proper building,' Lorraine explained. 'I'm pleased to say that the school is well on its way to achieving that. PRASA[28] has donated a piece of land, and the education department will begin construction of the school building in 2020.' The pair had further successes by forging partnerships with a number of other organisations.

I remember attending the celebration event where Lorraine and Sean told the story of the first year of their partnership: Lorraine explained the difference between *commitment* and *involvement* using the analogy of a pig versus a chicken's role in breakfast. The pig is fully *committed* to breakfast as it has to die to provide the bacon. The chicken is merely *involved* in breakfast as it only has to provide the egg and continues to live. Lorraine likened Sean to the pig – fully *committed* to the partnership.

'He played a big role in developing my leadership skills. Working with Sean enabled me to articulate my vision and to get others to buy in to that. I also learned the value of working in partnership. My exposure to PfP also developed the art of copying in me. I saw the value of recognising things that work and duplicating them in other settings. That's another valuable skill I acquired.

---

28 PRASA is the Passenger Rail Agency of South Africa.

'The skills I'd learned on the programme, and the experience I'd gained by having Sean as a partner made the difference,' she said. 'I think I was always a confident person, but after my PfP experience I believed I could go into other schools and apply the principles I had learned and help them.'

In 2019 Lorraine was able to look back on the work she and Sean had started in 2014 with much pride. It was a different school and community. Results had improved, and in 2020 the infrastructure will be transformed.

'I felt I had it in me to take another step up. I could make a difference at a higher level,' she said. So, she applied and was selected for the position of Cluster Leader at the Ekuhurleni District office in Alberton. Lorraine is also the project manager of a leadership development programme in 38 schools in her circuit.

'I think the circuit manager spotted the skills I have acquired, mainly through PfP, and he asked me to lead the programme. I encouraged the principals involved to join the PfP programme, and some of them have shown an interest. It is just a pity that it isn't always possible to accommodate them all.

'I have used the Time to Think skills and the Flawless Consulting techniques in my job as a cluster leader and I think I am making a difference.'

Lorraine's passion for leadership development doesn't end with her work at the education department. She has written a book called *God has one more move* and has started her own leadership development consultancy which she calls Lavinah Consulting.

Reflection

It was heart-warming to hear Belinda, Lindiwe and Lorraine's stories, and I look forward to seeing more principals in the PfP community being promoted to roles where they will have an even bigger impact.

Chapter 13

What happens when the 1:1 partnership does not work?

"Life can still be beautiful, meaningful, fun, and fulfilling even if things don't turn out the way you planned." – Lori Deschene

Partners for Possibility is a multi-faceted leadership development process. A core aspect of the methodology is the fact that every participant is paired with a partner and that they work together to strengthen leadership capacity at the school. However, in about 6-8% of cases, the 1:1 partnership between the business leader and principal doesn't work as expected and the partnership is discontinued before the end of the 12-month programme. There are many reasons for this, but in most cases a partnership dissolves because the business leader is unable or unwilling to continue making the necessary commitment or because the principal disengages from the relationship for some reason.

When LPFs gets a sense that there is any risk to the partnership they typically invest a lot of effort and time exploring what can be done to salvage the relationship. Sometimes, however, we have no option but to accept that the pair will no longer benefit from being in a 1:1 partnership with each other. I was interested to hear first-hand from principals who lost their business partners.

Loretta Loggenberg (Attie van Wyk Primary School, Durbanville)

Loretta Loggenberg joined the PfP programme in 2018. She was partnered with a business leader from Durbanville, and they were part of the Cape Town 26 (CPT26) Leadership Circle. Nicky Bush was their LPF.

Unfortunately, Loretta's business partner left the programme during the first few months after being retrenched by the organisation he was working for at the time.

I was privileged to be able to attend the celebration event for CPT26 and was very pleasantly surprised to hear Debbie Horne, Loretta's circuit manager, speak about the impact of the PfP programme on her. Debbie described the changes she had witnessed in Loretta and her team following her involvement in PfP:

'After the workshop I could see the change in her. The way she managed her staff; and even the school in general. I think Time to Think equipped her to reflect on the practices at the school with the knowledge and skills she gained. She put structures and systems in place that had a huge impact on the ethos of the school,' said Debbie.

Debbie explained that she had made it a priority to support Loretta because she was a new principal and had been an HOD but did not get the chance to be a deputy principal before her promotion to principal.

Debbie had visited the school regularly and could see the changes happening. 'The exposure to Symphonia really enabled her to manage her school effectively and professionally. In a very short space of time she also convinced the parents about the importance of their involvement in the education of their children. For the first time, I could see many of the parents rock up for a parent meeting. Because they are a farm community, they are tired and they arrive at home late after harvesting, but they made time to come. Attendance to parent meetings increased significantly. This happened because Loretta created a belief in the parents that they can have a positive influence in the lives of the children.

'Since her appointment, the work ethic of the staff, the teachers and the support staff has improved. As a supervisor, I experienced a different ethos at the school.'

Debbie concluded by thanking PfP for our contribution to the development of the leadership skills of principals.

I loved the fact that Debbie had agreed to Loretta's request to be at the celebration event and to speak about the transformation she had seen. We have been committed to strengthening our relationship with WCED officials, but, because of general busyness, it has not always been possible for us to spend time together. Having Debbie at the celebration event was an important moment for us.

At the celebration event Loretta did not say much about her own experience of the PfP programme, so I was keen to hear more of her story.

Theo and I went to Durbanville to visit Attie van Wyk Primary School. We found an ageing, but immaculately clean little school building, surrounded by temporary classrooms and re-purposed shipping containers, nestled among the opulent wine estates of the Durbanville hills.

Attie van Wyk Primary is a farm school that is situated on a privately-owned wine estate. It serves the children who live on neighbouring farms and in the nearby Fisantekraal township. The school has 279 learners, nine teachers and one teaching assistant. The office where we met Loretta doubles as the school's admin office, and it was clear that space is a serious challenge.

Yet, Loretta told us, they have become the school of choice in the area. The walls of her small office are plastered with newspaper cuttings and certificates attesting to the achievements of the children. While we were there, a woman knocked on the door and announced that she had a bootfull of children's books that she wanted to donate to the school – something that happens quite regularly, Loretta said.

I wanted to know how she had become involved in the PfP programme, why she had remained on the programme after her partner withdrew, and how she had benefitted, despite the fact that she lost her business partner.

'I've taught at a number of schools,' Loretta explained, 'including Vissershok, where the principal was a PfP partner, so I was familiar with the programme. I had been a teacher at Attie van Wyk before, so I knew the school and the community. When I heard about the principal post I applied, even though I was only an HOD, but I was confident that I could fulfil the role.

'I was appointed as principal in 2017 and attended a 5-day course for new principals at the Cape Teaching and Leadership Institute. We were told that we had to go back to our schools to get the community involved in the school and to go out and find sponsorship from the surrounding businesses. We weren't told how to do that, however, and I had no experience of interacting with people outside of the school.'

The opportunity to gain stakeholder engagement skills through PfP was, therefore, something of a lifeline for Loretta.

'If it wasn't for PfP, I would never have had the opportunity to engage with CEOs and other senior business leaders. Being part of PfP was a wonderfully empowering experience – to be in conversation with other senior business leaders and to be treated as a leader who matters.

'I went on training with a phenomenal group of people who I would never have been in contact with otherwise. It changed my thinking,' Loretta said. 'I experienced their respect, and that was empowering and it built my self-confidence. I found I was no longer afraid to get into conversations.

'I applied the knowledge that I picked up on those courses. For example, Time to Think taught me to hear other people. Before that I prided myself on always being very well prepared for meetings. I thought I knew everything and I knew how people would respond to what I had to say. After Time to Think I changed my meeting agendas into a series of questions. I provided those questions beforehand and invited people to think about the questions. I listened to people's opinions. I learned to slow down and think before I speak. I discovered how important it is to take your time and think of the impact of what you are going to say before you say it.

'I found I was becoming calm and more aware of the impact of my words and the tone of my voice. It made a great difference. I don't raise my voice anymore. I treat my colleagues and the learners with respect and I look at them with soft eyes.

'I am a completely different person now. This also had an impact at home with my own children too. I realised that I don't need to have all the answers and that I'm not the only one who has an opinion. My children now enjoy their mother – not just the teacher with an answer. I have realised that our children often just want us to listen. They need our listening. Not our answers.'

Because of the growth she had seen in Loretta, Debbie told her about an opportunity to do the school leadership development programme offered by the Instructional Leadership Institute (ILI). While Loretta feels that she did draw value from the ILI course, she doesn't think she would have gained as much if she had not been part of PfP. 'PfP prepared me to get value from ILI,' she said.

'Through being part of PfP I got clear about my role as a leader. I learned how to articulate a vision and to get buy-in from others.'

As a member of a PfP learning community, there were people she could contact for advice and did not feel that she was facing her challenges alone. 'At the same time I knew that the leadership circle could benefit from my energy and experiences and that I could add value to them. That was empowering to me. I never missed a CoP meeting.'

The teachers at Attie van Wyk were a bit resistant to change at first, Loretta recalls. 'Many of them had been at the school for a long time and they knew me as an ordinary teacher during my earlier time at the school. I think my development as a person and the strong example I was able to set made them more eager to embrace change.

'Debbie had warned me that if I went through the PfP programme, but didn't apply it and live it, then it would be a waste of time. After every course I returned to the school and shared with the other educators what I had learned. I was committed to make the most of the opportunity because I had seen the difference that the programme made to the principal at Vissershok. I wanted to have a similar experience.

'For example, attending the Flawless Consulting workshop changed the way I held my staff meetings, I found I was becoming a facilitator, rather than a lecturer, and that was far more effective. I discovered that it is much more powerful for me to present a proposal and ask for input than to simply tell people what I had decided. I got a lot more buy-in and commitment from my colleagues.'

When I asked Loretta to compare her present self to how she was before her participation in the PfP she said she is a different person. 'My communication skills were poor. I didn't have people skills, and I had difficulty in presenting myself to the farming community and asking them to invest in us.

'Though PfP, I realised that I was not inferior to the CEO of a company. I had skills, I had self-confidence and felt comfortable in any company. My ability to communicate and network improved greatly. It broadened my horizons, and I went to places that I had never been to before. It made me realise that if you work at it you can broaden the horizons of the teachers too and that they can do things differently in the classroom.

'It also taught me how to communicate with the community, including the farms that surround us. PfP has a strong message to principals and that is that we as principals are equally important as CEOs and senior business leaders. This made me more confident to engage with other people who I previously may have been intimidated by.

'Because of my exposure to PfP I was able to talk to the farmers. I had learned how to contract with them and that I needed to first invest in the relationship before asking for something. I have learned how to recognise opportunities and grab them. It has been very valuable to the school.'

The community building side of the programme made a big difference to the way she dealt with parents, Loretta said.

'I now visit parents at their homes. And I know how to communicate with them. I show that I am interested in their children and that has led to them being more interested in the school. They have the confidence to interact with the principal now. They know I am approachable and available to them. That's because I am more confident and comfortable in myself. I can go to the houses in Fisantekraal and on the wine farms and that has made a big difference.'

The school's results in the systemic tests have improved, but it's too soon to assess the effect of the programme on the performance of the learners, Loretta said. 'We are hoping for better results next time, but we have had positive feedback from the Western Cape Education Department. The subject advisors who have visited us have been impressed with our organisation and processes and their expectations of us are up.'

The teachers have definitely benefitted from her involvement in the project, Loretta believes. 'Our technology teacher, for example, has been sent by the department to other schools to assist them in setting up their programmes,' she said.

There are improvements and achievements to be seen all over the school. We visited the library, located in a container. It's fully functional now, and manned by a volunteer from the community. The school has a full-time physical education teacher, courtesy of the neighbouring Diemersdal wine estate, and eight of the learners were awarded Western Province colours for cross-country earlier in the year.

On the wall of Loretta's office is the certificate awarded to Clinnica Anderson, a learner who won the 2019 Metro North District prize for the best story in English as an Additional Language (EAL). There are cuttings from the local newspaper celebrating that achievement and many others.

'I have built up a good relationship with the owner of the land that the school is built on and the wine estates around us are all very positive about the school,' Loretta said.

'The parents in the area realise that there is a special culture in our school; there is discipline here and children receive quality education. We have become the school of choice in the area.'

The school is succeeding and, as I have seen in other places, it has become a magnet for the gifts of the community. The lady with the books who visited while we were there is one example. The local wine farmers are always prepared to help, Loretta said, and there are businesses in Durbanville who support the school in various ways.

Felicity Sasman (Montagu Drive Primary School in Mitchell's Plain)

Felicity Sasman, principal of Montagu Drive Primary School in Mitchell's Plain, joined the PfP programme in 2015. She was partnered with a business leader from Bellville, but he had underestimated the amount of time he would need to invest in the partnership and withdrew from the programme after a few months.

Felicity decided to remain in the programme without him and, she said, it was the best decision she could have made.

'Looking back now, I realise that if I had left PfP then I would probably have given up on education. I was miserable and depressed. I was overwhelmed at the time, I was trying to cope by doing everything by myself, I never delegated much, and I wasn't managing.

'Now I'm getting ready to retire, and I can do so knowing that the school is in a good place and that I am handing it over to good hands. I just wish that I could have done something like PfP much earlier in my life.'

I wanted to know from Felicity about the value she had drawn from PfP in spite of completing the programme without a business partner.

'I was ready to give up on the school, but I didn't. Paul Abrams, our LPF, was a great help, as were the CoP meetings.

'At first I was reluctant to participate in the meetings. I was in a bad state, but later on the CoPs became a lifeline. I could share how I was feeling and hear the stories of the other principals. I made friends and I wasn't facing my problems alone anymore; and for the first time I wasn't feeling inferior any longer. I was encouraged to talk about why I was so upset after relating an incident, and that was a great help.'

Felicity attended the three formal training courses, and they were all very valuable, she said.

'Community Building was very meaningful to me, I learned that everyone has a story and that you shouldn't judge anyone until you knew what their story was. That helped me in my relationship with the teachers, and with the learners.

'Through Flawless Consulting I became more confident and assertive and able to have the difficult, courageous conversations. I was able to connect with people. I was able to get the teachers on my side. We reduced absenteeism and things began to improve.'

She has changed as a person, Felicity believes. 'I am not as stressed out. I am more approachable, and I don't take everything to heart anymore,' she said. 'I know who I am now and I know what I stand for, my values and principles are clearer.'

That has had a positive effect on the school, she said. The results of the systemic tests show that.

'Our Grade 3 and Grade 6 systemic results have improved. But it's not just about academic results. It's about the holistic education of the children. This has become a school that the parents want to send their kids to. The teachers are more committed and determined to get the children to learn.'

Felicity is convinced that it was her involvement in PfP that has made the difference. 'I am confident, assertive and brave, and I have been better able to lead the SMT and the teachers,' she said.

'I am proud of the way the SMT has grown. My post was advertised and all the internal people who applied for it were nominated. My deputy principal has been appointed to the post, and I know he will do a very good job. We have become a family and I can leave knowing that I have left a legacy and that the school is in safe hands.'

'I will definitely advise my successor to join PfP.'

Sihle Mdlalose (Prospect Farm School, Ballito)

During our visit to the KZN North Coast, we met with Sihle Mdlalose, principal of Prospect Farm School, at the Simbithi Eco-Estate clubhouse. Sihle joined PfP in January 2017 and his partnership started well. However, partway through the programme Sihle was promoted and moved to a larger school, which meant that his business partner had to travel a lot further than before to visit him at his school. Sihle's business partner also began to experience unexpected challenges in his company, and he stopped accompanying Sihle to CoP sessions and rarely visited the school. This meant that Sihle was essentially on the PfP journey alone.

'I realised that the partnership wasn't going to work as I had hoped it would, but I did not want to leave the programme,' Sihle explained. 'Terry, our LPF, was a great help and she encouraged me to keep going. I attended the CoP meetings on my own and Terry did a lot of one-on-one coaching with me, and other business leaders in the circle took me on and offered advice. Gill Leslie[29] also supported me. Bizie Magwaza at Mshwati Memorial Primary School became a close friend, and we worked together on many things.'

Sihle believes that he gained a great deal by remaining with the programme, even though his partnership with the business leader did not work as he had hoped. 'At my previous school, I was in charge of 140 learners and four teachers. At Prospect Farm School I have 560 learners and 18 teachers. There were immediate challenges, so the support I was getting from PfP came at the right time.'

A problem Sihle encountered as soon as joined the new school related to the SGB, where there was a conflict between the Chairman and Treasurer. 'We had just completed the Time to Think training then, and I decided to try out those skills to resolve it,' Sihle recalls. 'I set up a meeting and invited my deputy to join me. I insisted that the SGB members should talk and listen to each other without any retelling of the past issues that had led to the dispute. It worked. They made peace and we were able

---

29 Gill Leslie is one of three dedicated 'Terry's Angels' who provide assistance to LPF Terry Dearling and the partners for possibility she supports. The other two are Samantha Jooste and Karenne Bloomgarden.

to move forward. The communication and leadership skills I had learned on the course and the discussions we had in the CoP definitely contributed to that.'

Sihle believes that the programme has changed him as a person. 'I used to have confidence issues; I was shy and had difficulties in expressing myself,' he said.

That has changed and he has, for example, been asked to address all the principals in his district. Sihle is a talented ultra-marathon runner who has completed the Comrades Marathon seven times and run most of the long races around the country.

'Marathon running teaches you lessons about perseverance and about the value of planning and preparation. That's something I believe, but I never expressed it openly. Now I have made a presentation to the district on it. It's not something I would have done before.'

The negotiation skills that Sihle learned, coupled with the discussions in CoPs and information shared by other partners, have brought results for the school.

'There are many things needed at the school, and one of the most urgent, I felt, was to repair the floors in some of the classrooms which were in a very bad state,' he said. 'I had gone to the local tribal leader to pay my respects when I was first appointed and I told him about this. I told him that we also needed an admin block at the school and when he met with the leadership at Tongaat Hulett he passed that on.

'To my surprise, he arrived at the school with the Tongaat Hulett people, and they suggested that they build a new fence for the school. I disagreed and managed to persuade them to fix the classroom floors instead. I was able to do that because I had found my voice, and had learned some negotiating skills. I never had a partner to learn that from, but I learned it from being part of our circle of schools and partners.'

With the help of Terry and the other partners, Sihle was able to meet all the requirements for completing the PfP programme. He produced a school improvement plan, reflected on his achievements and built up a portfolio of evidence (PoE). After they moderated his PoE Sihle received a certificate of completion from UWC, which enabled him to receive 40 continuous professional development (CPD) points from the South African Council of Educators (SACE).

'It was the first time, really that I worked together with white people,' he said. 'It made me realise that all people are actually the same. If you get together and share experiences you will find other people just like you. I found people who were prepared to listen to me and to share their feelings. If you connect with other human beings, you learn their real stories. I grew and learned to see things differently.'

'In the end we are all mainly the same, we all have the same goals. Day by day, I continue to learn and grow.'

Reflections

I have always believed that there is a resilience inherent in the design of the PfP programme because 16 different leadership development processes have been woven into the year-long facilitated experience. The programme caters for many different learning styles, and if some aspects don't work exactly as expected the others will still generate learning and impact. It was humbling to hear Felicity, Loretta and Sihle's stories as they validate our theory about the built-in resilience of the PfP process.

Chapter 14

PfP as a consciousness-raising experience

> *"All progress takes place outside the comfort zone."*
> – Michael John Bobak

I have previously mentioned that while I was still playing with the idea of partnerships between business leaders and principals I was blessed with some wisdom from a few principals. They helped shape our thinking about the programme by saying: 'we know that we will learn from the business leaders, *and*…we want the business leaders to consider the possibility that they will learn from us too.' With hindsight, it is clear that this contribution has been part of the 'magic sauce' of PfP.

Much has been written about the value of mutuality and reciprocity in relationships and how that helps to shift patterns of patriarchy. I was aware of the work that Philip Mirvis and his colleagues at the Boston College Center for Corporate Citizenship had done around 'Executive development through consciousness-raising experiences'[30]. Phil and his colleagues studied examples of 'executives moving from the relative comfort of the corporate classroom into unfamiliar territory where they encountered people and problems seemingly far removed from the day-to-day scope and concerns of business life'. The researchers found that most of the executives come away having learned powerful and relevant lessons.

I met Phil when he was in South Africa in 2012. Following our conversation he wrote this endorsement of our programme:

> '**PfP** supercharges leaders with an extraordinary development experience. Engaging coursework, personal coaching, and a peer learning community set the stage for you to be immersed in a service learning assignment in schools where you must grapple with complex, multi-faceted issues and work with a multicultural mix of school leaders, faculty and students.
>
> Top global companies today develop their next generation leaders through service projects. **PfP** provides the guidance and support needed to promote real learning and to prepare you for challenges in your own organisation and community.'

---

30 Mirvis, P. H. (2008) Executive development through consciousness-raising experiences. *Academy of Management Learning & Education. 7 (2) 173–188.*

I wanted to meet with some business leaders who have experienced PfP as an 'extraordinary development experience'.

Clive Naicker, FirstRand

When I received a testimonial from Clive Naicker after his PfP year I was intrigued to know more about his experience. This is what he wrote:

> *PfP shaped me as an individual not just as a leader. It built part of my character that did not exist before. I am more rounded. I can relate to people different to me and to people at different levels.*
>
> *I found the Community of Practice valuable and meeting the other principals has helped me broaden my horizons of how to work with and interact with people.*
>
> *I feel like I belong to society now; before I felt isolated. I feel more socially accepted, I am better able to handle conflict, get people to deliver and ensure that I communicate in a way that my message gets across. I am better able to understand people and work better with them, it's not just about me it's about the team.*

Clive Naicker is the Head of Data Management and Architecture at FirstRand. Like many South Africans, he felt the need to make a difference in society. He had been looking for a way to do that, so when he heard about PfP the idea of partnership with a principal appealed to him.

Clive was partnered with Dalton Ramaoma, Principal of David Makhubo Secondary School in Kaalfontein, Midrand.

'My job at the bank is mainly about managing projects, so I believed it would be relatively easy: I would identify certain problems at the school and we could develop and implement some plans to address these,' he recalls.

'I discovered that life doesn't work in straight lines. I thought this was all about influencing the principals, but then I realised that the process was having an influence on me.

'I am very introverted, and my life used to be mostly confined to the corporate office. I have had little exposure to what is happening outside of Sandton. Through my involvement in PfP I got a much better understanding of the challenges in communities outside of my experience. It made me feel more connected to what it means to be South African.'

Clive found that experiencing a different side to the country from what he was familiar with had an impact on him. 'It is so different to see things in real life rather than on TV.'

David Makhubo Secondary is the poorest school in the circle of partnerships that he was part of, Clive said. 'Dalton was brilliant, but he did not have the funding to carry out his plans. It was not my role to raise funds for them; so when we discussed his challenges we agreed that he needed to develop more leadership capacity in the school management team and decided that we would arrange a team building session for them.

'In the bank we always work in teams, so I know how conflict and lack of alignment causes things to break down. I have been through many team building processes myself and know the value of team building, so I decided that I would facilitate the session.'

The plan was to get all the members of the SMT to agree to a vision and mission for the school. For the SMT members, this was the first team building session they would ever have attended. The experience pushed Clive out of his comfort zone as he had never done anything like this for a group of people he did not know well.

'I had done many team building sessions, but this one was for people that I did not know. I also had no knowledge of the subject matter or the tasks that the teams would have to carry out back in the workplace.'

The workshop took place at FirstRand's premises, which was a new experience for the SMT members. 'My aim was to get everyone to agree on that vision and mission. We achieved a lot through this session. When we returned to the school we had ground rules to implement, and people agreed to hold each other accountable. It was the basis for the work that we did during the year and it made an impact.'

I asked Clive how this experience had impacted him. 'I interacted with strangers and got them to interact with each other. Because I am so reserved, I rarely do things like this. It gave me more confidence in the organisation and outside. Before PfP I was quite timid. I have become more brave.

'PfP gave me a safe opportunity to cross boundaries and engage with people that I would previously never have engaged with.

'Before PfP, I found I struggled with my South African identity. My life was confined to home-work-home. I rarely left the bubble. Through PfP I had the opportunity to engage with people who live a very different life to mine. I found that I could relate to them. I realised that I belong.'

Clive discovered something that so many other leaders also grapple with. When he was at the school he did not have the identity of a senior manager in a large organisation. He had none of the power or authority that comes from being a senior leader. He had to use many other skills to influence Dalton and his team. 'It was a humanising experience to connect as human beings rather than titles on an organogram.'

The programme also had an influence Clive's parenting. 'I have become more tolerant of my children. I realised that I can't protect them in a bubble. And I realised that the bubble deprives my children of the full experience of living in South Africa.'

His PfP experience has also contributed to how Clive thinks about the role of business in society. He feels organisations should create more opportunities for business leaders to cross boundaries rather than to just give money.

We often hear people say they have become better listeners as a result of PfP. Clive's experience was a bit different. He has always been a good listener. Through his PfP journey he has learned how to ensure that he is being listened to and heard.

He has also discovered that he doesn't always need to have the answers. 'By creating an opportunity for others to find their own answers and solutions, I am showing them that I value their input and perspective. My team members seem to appreciate this.

'It has been humbling for me to discover the committed and passionate people in communities like Kaalfontein. It is so different to what we hear in the media. I am just sad we never hear about this. Having had this experience, I am now much less likely to just take things at face value.'

Among his qualifications, Clive has an MBA from Henley Business School. He believes his involvement with PfP has been a more valuable leadership development experience than an MBA leadership course in a classroom.

'PfP is a programme that crosses many different boundaries. You may not even know about your own boundaries until you push against one. This does not happen while you are in your comfort zone. You have to leave your comfort zone to be confronted with your own boundaries. When you cross a boundary in PfP you realise that you may be able to do it in other areas of your life.

'The MBA teaches you about leadership styles. You get to learn the things that other people know. My year of partnership taught me things you cannot learn in a classroom.'

Hearing Clive talk reminded me of the Nelson Mandela Lecture that President Obama gave in South Africa in 2018:

'As a community organiser, I learned as much from a laid-off steelworker in Chicago or a single mom in a poor neighbourhood that I visited as I learned from the finest economists in the Oval Office. Democracy means being in touch and in tune with life as it's lived in our communities, and that's what we should expect from our leaders, and it depends upon cultivating leaders at the grassroots who can help bring about change and implement it on the ground and can tell leaders in fancy buildings, "this isn't working down here".'

Grant Kelly, Nedbank

Grant Kelly is an Executive Head at Nedbank. He was partnered with Freddy Antwi, the principal of Summat College in Pretoria.

Grant's PfP partnership with Freddy was unusual because the school, under Freddy's leadership, was achieving excellent academic results, despite being poorly resourced. That meant the partners were freed from any emphasis on short-term goals and able to concentrate on their relationship and on opportunities for personal growth.

'For me, as a white male who is very aware of the advantages bestowed on me by the Apartheid system, my involvement in the programme was packed with learning opportunities, and it made a deep impression on me as a person and as a leader.

'Yes, some physical improvements to the school buildings and equipment were needed, and we did that, but the important thing is that those projects were delivered in an atmosphere of authenticity, with empathy and mutual respect. I certainly never went in there with a cheque book, looking for things to fix.'

Looking back, Grant believes his leadership style was profoundly changed as a result of his PfP experience. 'Freddy is not an imposing man, and younger than most of his staff, but he is a powerful leader. He has authority as the principal, and his achievements are due to the respect he has earned.

'I learned that you don't need rank to lead authentically. In a business there are certain management objectives that require levels of power. To evaluate KPIs[31] or to allocate resources, the manager needs a level of authority and control.'

But that's management, not leadership, says Grant. 'To be a real leader, you need humility and courage. You need the ability to influence people through relationships, not command. I realised that if I wanted to create better social outcomes I needed to lead through influence.

---

31   Key Performance Indicators.

'In an organisation like mine, it's very difficult to bring about large-scale change, but I certainly noticed a shift in my own thinking, away from emphasis on short-term business goals (which still have to be achieved) towards trying to create a greater awareness of the wider purpose of business, which has to be making a positive social impact.'

Grant believes his views on the South African corporate landscape are not the traditional ones. 'I don't believe the ongoing inequality we have in the country exists in a vacuum,' he said. 'As leaders, we all need to take a level of accountability for our current social predicament, both in the public and in the private sectors.

'The question I keep reflecting on is, 'as leaders in business, are we doing enough to drive the imperative of our purpose (positive social impact) through our operations?' There are high levels of social unconsciousness, still, in business leaders like me, who come from a privileged background and are often extremely unaware of what is going on around us – and that includes what happens in the lives of the majority of our fellow citizens, who don't live where we do.'

Being in partnership with Freddy definitely helped him in this regard, Grant believes. 'In my corporate role I increasingly ask myself how the decisions I take can lead to greater inclusivity,' he said. 'I have come to realise that we need more socially aware leaders. Any authentic response to the need for transformation requires that. At work, I'm starting to challenge what we do and how we do it, always bringing it back to our purpose.'

It meant, he said, less focus on himself and more on trying to influence the larger framework to focus on social outcomes. 'I have received some positive feedback within the organisation for my efforts in this regard, and given that Nedbank has been on a journey towards purpose-driven business for some time, I have had some successes.'

One of the challenges Grant faced in going into Summat College was that he found himself without any official standing and unable to act in any executive capacity, and yet he was eager to bring about change. 'That's where the work we did at the beginning of our journey together, establishing a level of trust between myself and Freddy, paid off.'

Grant cites the discipline problems at the school as an example. 'The system in place was traditional and old-fashioned, much like it was when I was at school myself,' he explained. 'It was punitive and authoritarian, with little interest in the learner's side of the story. Freddy and I discussed it at length, and I raised his awareness of issues like understanding, context and empathy, and trying to discover the root causes of misbehaviour. Together, we decided to try that approach.'

Freddy made the necessary changes to the disciplinary process and, as a result, there are fewer serious incidents now.

'That's bringing about change through influence, not rank, and it's a lesson I learned through becoming involved in real issues at the school. It required a mindset shift, away from providing answers and towards supporting my partner in his attempts to address issues.'

The programme forced Grant out of his comfort zone and took him into situations that he had never been in before, meeting people he would probably not have otherwise met. 'I'm a white male who has had a good education and who lives a comfortable life. Under those circumstances, it's easy to ignore the issues in our society that you know exist, to regard them as someone else's problem,' he said.

'The PfP programme supports you in getting to know a community intimately, and you gain insights that you would otherwise never have had. By getting involved in the issues in the school and its community, you soon build respect for the people involved and get a new perspective on the challenges.'

If a cohort of business leaders that understood these things was developed, Grant feels, it would go a long way towards building a more cohesive society. 'It was through personal experience that I gained new insights. That would never have happened if I had stayed in my office and never got involved with Summat College and met Freddy.'

The experience has been so profound that Grant continues to work with Freddy in terms of supporting the school and has started working more closely with the shareholders of Summat College.

'I am becoming part of that community and taking responsibility for the work that still needs to be done to keep the school on track in terms of meeting our long-term goals. It has taken on a new meaning for me,' he said.

Reflections

Hearing Clive and Grant talk about their learnings from participating in PfP made my heart sing. This is exactly the kind of value that we had hoped leaders would gain from being part of PfP. We envisaged that the process would create opportunities for leaders to 'bump up against' their own prejudices and blind spots and that they would discover something about themselves in relation to communities and environments so different from those they typically inhabit. There are many more Clive's and Grant's in our community. I just wish it was possible to capture all their stories for this book.

Chapter 15

Khumbul'ekhaya (Remember home)

"There is no power for change greater than a community discovering what it cares about." – Margaret J Wheatley

A while ago I received a call from one of the business leaders who was a partner in Johannesburg. He wanted our assistance to launch a 'Khumbul'ekhaya' (remember home) campaign – where business leaders go back to the schools that they attended to 'give back' to the community where they hail from.

This conversation prompted me to reach out to PfPs who have 'gone home' for their PfP partnership.

Pearl Nel (FNB)

Pearl Nel describes herself as 'proudly coloured and a product of the Immorality Act era'. She is the daughter of a Jewish father and a coloured mother, who met when the family lived in District Six. As their relationship was against the law at the time, and was reported in the newspapers, Pearl had to leave South Africa with her parents and live in Tel-Aviv during her early childhood. Pearl and her mom returned to South Africa during the 6-Day War in Israel. Pearl attended Zonnebloem Primary School until her family were ejected from their home as a result of the Forced Removals Act. Pearl, who was nine years old at the time, moved with her grandparents to the Cape Flats where she was enrolled at Vanguard Primary School.

She attended Bridgetown High School from 1976 to 1980 – difficult times in the townships of South Africa – and Bridgetown, like many similar schools, became a centre of resistance.

'I was an activist and a radical. Cheryl Carolus (who became a well-known South African politician) was my geography teacher in Grade 9. We were all very active in the struggle. My education was affected as a result of the unrest activities during the time of the State of Emergency, but that was a deeply formative time of my life.'

Pearl emerged from that background to become very successful in the corporate world. She is now FNB's Events and Volunteers Programme Manager for the Western Cape, and we met her in a boardroom in their beautiful Cape Town headquarters.

Pearl is the business partner to Andrew Windvogel, the principal of Bridgetown High School. I was interested to hear how it happened that she became the business partner at the school she had attended as a high school learner.

'Many of those who were involved in the struggle ended up in fields of study such as political studies and social work, to make a difference. Many of them went into government, but I felt that education was the area where I could make the greatest contribution. I studied to become a teacher, specialising in remedial teaching.

'I was deeply moved when I got the opportunity to participate in PfP, as only the second FNB business leader nominated from this province, and I insisted that I wanted to be partnered with the principal at Bridgetown High because of my long-term commitment to the school.'

Volunteering and mentoring are not new for Pearl. She has been involved in various community projects across Cape Town since her teenage days when she was a girl guide. 'In 2009, while the plans for Soccer World Cup were happening, I volunteered and was a board member for the 'Young in Prison' (YiP) programme, who were running Monday-to-Friday workshops at Pollsmoor Prison, including a soccer programme for imprisoned youth.

'In 2004, as the volunteer coordinator for the FirstRand Volunteers programme in the Western Cape, I had noticed that there was not an even focus between black and coloured communities. As a coloured person, supporting the marginalized coloured community was very important to me, and I insisted that if volunteers were school-based then Bridgetown High should always be considered. It was a way to give back to the community I came from.

'I wanted the learners at Bridgetown High to see me as a former learner who had been successful in the world of work. I was an example of someone who showed that you could be coloured, go to a government school, in a poor area, and still make something of your life.

'I look at young people who come from the same place I came from and realise I have a responsibility to show them what I've achieved. I want them to have high expectations and big dreams and hopefully be inspired by my journey.'

Pearl shared a beautiful example of a learner who was inspired by her story. In 2009 Bridgetown High was part of the 8-month Junior Achievement South Africa Life Skills and Mentorship programme for Grade 11s – for which FirstRand Volunteers received the Mail & Guardian Award for the Best Mentorship Programme of employee volunteers.

One of the Bridgetown participants, Yolokazi Jezile, was especially inspired by Pearl. After one of the Saturday morning workshops, in front of a group of parents and learners, she said: 'I want to be like Pearl one day.'

In 2017 Pearl was invited by Wesgro to speak at an event held at the Spier wine estate for Cape Peninsula University of Technology students who were studying event management – only to find that Yolokazi was one of the third-year students in the room – she had decided to study event management as a result of hearing Pearl's story in 2009.

When Andrew and Pearl were partnered in the Cape Town 27 (CPT27) Leadership Circle, funded by FNB and the FirstRand Volunteers programme, it enriched their relationship and enabled Pearl to make further investments into the school.

'I could come up with new initiatives according to the needs of the school and align it to the FirstRand Volunteers programme of matched giving and time,' Pearl said. She organised stress-relieving massages for the teachers and invited Bridgetown High girls to FNB to participate in the bank's 'Take a Girl-child to Work' initiative. She has also arranged for people in her network to visit the school to talk about different careers and organised financial literacy workshops at the school.

Through the FirstRand Volunteers programme and PfP, the school has also benefitted from donations of furniture for the school library and staffroom and funding for the renovation of the library.

As Events Manager, with the support of the FirstRand Volunteers programme, Pearl has also been able to create contract work opportunities for some Bridgetown High learners and they have recently launched a 3-year pilot mentoring programme for Grade 10 learners with FNB employees as mentors.

'We have also done a lot of good work in staff development with the SMT and with the learners. My biggest disappointment is that I've still not managed to get funding or endorsement for a hall for the school. It is one of the oldest schools in the Athlone area, but it doesn't have a school hall, and for various reasons I think that is totally unacceptable. We haven't given up on the idea. It is an ongoing project to achieve in the very near future and we encourage **all** that are able to contribute ideas and funding for this.'

I asked Pearl what it meant for her to be involved in Bridgetown High, the school that she attended as a high school learner. 'When your roots are from a disadvantaged background, you have a responsibility to help those kids to believe they have options. Because I come from the community, I have a strong connection to these children, and my purpose is to give them something to believe in. I want the learners at Bridgetown High, and in fact all learners in community schools, to know that they don't have to be shelf-packers and security guards; to not let their history define their destiny,' she said.

'I am grateful that Andrew said yes to being my partner. It is a great privilege for me to be partnered with him. It is so humbling to work with a school leader who is so passionate and committed about being the change, despite all the challenges he faces day-to-day at the school.'

Pearl's mantra is to 'be the change you want to see in the world'. She believes that, 'we as civil society are all being called to be the change. We have to stop thinking that someone else will address the issues we face or hope that the education department will improve education. We need to be that change, and EVERY ONE of us can make a difference'. Pearl has won numerous awards and recognition for her volunteer work.

One of Pearl's objectives is to send out a strong call for action among ex-students of Bridgetown High. 'Many of these past learners have ended up in hugely influential roles in corporate and government. I would like them to come on board and make a commitment to the school, to make it a better place for the learners and the teachers.'

A few of them, she suggests, can become PfP partners. 'Imagine a world where all, everywhere, nationally, who beat the status quo of being schooled in disadvantaged situations – and who made it despite that – can partner with a school leader and share how they overcame and made their mark – that would be **so** powerful,' she concluded.

Sharna Fernandez (Western Cape Government)

Sharna Fernandez is the Minister of Social Development in the Western Cape Provincial Government. Before that she was the Speaker of the Western Cape Provincial Parliament. She is also a partner to Principal Grant Paulsen of Square Hill Primary School in Retreat – the school she had attended as a learner 50 years ago.

Sharna was born in Diepriver and grew up in Retreat. In her second year of school, she moved to Square Hill Primary and still has fond memories of her first teacher there, Mrs Perez. Sharna loved reading. When she was eight years old, the librarian reluctantly allowed her to go into the adult section because she had read all the books in the children's section.

'My father was a simple man, a ship's carpenter, but he had higher expectations of us. He knew that education was the way to improve our lives. He wanted us to make the most of our opportunities and do well at school.

'The teachers at Square Hill Primary School made it fun for us to be there. They looked out for us and were like parent figures in our lives.'

After Square Hill Sharna attended South Peninsula High School, and then went to the University of Cape Town where she studied to become a teacher. During that time she became politically involved and unfortunately did not obtain her degree.

Sharna chose a career in banking, and in 1981 she joined Barclays Bank in Grassy Park at the bottom of the banking ladder. Over a 30-year period she worked her way up and held senior positions in three of South Africa's big four banks.

Career-wise Sharna was flying, but in 2009 she became very ill. 'Just days after my 50th birthday I was admitted to hospital and diagnosed with the H1N1 virus. I was put in an isolation ward and came close to death. I was completely burnt out.

'It took me two years to recover properly and, in the process, I learned the importance of finding balance in my life. Work had driven me at the cost of my family.

'I lost my memory at first, but it returned in 2010 and, at that stage, I had decided that I was going to pay it forward and become involved in service to my community. I served on a number of community structures in the Retreat, Steenberg and Lavender Hill areas and in 2011 Jan Burger of the DA came looking for 'that woman who is so passionate about the community'. I wasn't interested at first, but he persuaded me to go to a meeting, and I joined the party. That decision led to a career in politics.'

While she was Western Cape parliamentary speaker, Sharna was asked, as a prominent ex-pupil of the school, to speak at the Square Hill Primary School's valedictory assembly. 'The event was at Bergvliet High School because Square Hill didn't have a hall of its own,' she said.

'I was so taken with the potential that I saw in those children that I felt Square Hill should be the place where I wanted to pay it forward. That evening I made a commitment that I was going to help Square Hill get a hall.'

Sharna first became aware of PfP via Twitter. At the time, she was looking for a way to make a difference in the community and PfP seemed like a good idea.

'I applied to join the programme, on the condition that I could work at Square Hill. I was accepted but told that there was no funding available and that my involvement would cost R45,000. I agreed to pay the amount myself, in monthly instalments. It was well worth it. I spent R50,000, but I must have got R4 million worth of value out of it.

'It was important for me to go back to the community I came from. I wanted to show the children at Square Hill that it is possible to be successful even if you live on the Cape Flats.'

Sharna acquired skills on the PfP programme that have been valuable in her professional life and gained much from her interaction with Grant and the other partners in her learning circle. She particularly valued the opportunity to learn about the challenges faced by educators, learners and SGB members in under-resourced schools across the Cape Town Metropole.

'The Learning Process Facilitator, Siddeeq Railoun, is a gentle soul. His heart is in the right place. I related well to the other principals and business partners. I connected with Grant immediately. We took six months to cement the relationship, and then we worked very well together.

'The Time to Think workshop was of particular value,' Sharna said. 'I learned there to listen with intent, not to listen to respond. I use those techniques with my team now and they have helped us to gel.'

The Community Building workshop had obvious value to Sharna in her role as Social Development Minister. 'I have a much better understanding of the issues that educators and parents deal with because I spent time in community and in conversation with the learners and educators,' she said.

Because of her knowledge and understanding of the challenges in the community, Sharna arranged for Claudia Roodt[32] to do a workshop on trauma-informed education for the teachers. This made a big impact on the Square Hill team. Grant made a video with feedback from staff members about this workshop and played it at the circle's celebration event.

The educators talked about how useful the workshop had been and how it had changed their perspective on learner behaviour. With more understanding about the impact of trauma, the educators felt better equipped to work with learners who present behavioural challenges.

Sharna thinks that it definitely makes a difference if PfP business leaders come from the community in which their school is located because the learners and the educators can relate to them. It also gives legitimacy. We agree, but as Grant Kelly's journey shows, PfP business leaders who support schools in unfamiliar environments learn a great deal from that consciousness-raising opportunity.

---

32   Claudia Roodt is a qualified social worker, therapist and Trauma Informed Workshop Facilitator with extensive knowledge about the impact of trauma on brain development, behaviour and learning.

Chapter 15: Khumbul'ekhaya (Remember home)

Sharna also arranged for a group of people from the Western Cape Provincial Parliament to engage with the learners at Square Hill Primary. Grant arranged for feedback from the learners to be shown at the celebration event, and it was very clear that they had learned a lot about the workings of parliament.

She can deal with Square Hill differently now that she is a minister, Sharna said. 'I am looking forward to testing some of my ideas there. Schools are a key element of our whole of society approach to addressing social challenges.'

Sharna feels that 12 months is just not enough time for the programme and that it should ideally be longer. One of her and Grant's partnership goals was to acquire a school hall for Square Hill Primary. 'That valedictory service at another school made a deep impression on me. We never managed to get a hall during the initial year of our partnership, but we are still going and we haven't given up on the idea,' she said.

Joseph Kente (Vukani Musa Construction)

In the course of refining the PfP process we came to appreciate the importance of allowing the relationship between the principal and business leader to develop before expecting them to bring about change at the school.

As I have travelled around the country visiting schools, I have been blown away by the stories of personal connections that have been made. Speaking to Joseph Kente about his relationship with Principal Richard Okhaa at Sishen Intermediate School provided a different perspective, however.

Joseph is one of those business leaders who insisted that he be partnered with the principal of the school that he himself attended. He attended Sishen Intermediate as a learner from 1980 to 1988 and reconnected with the school in 2010 when the first of his own children entered Grade R as a learner there.

Soon after his first child enrolled at the school, Joseph was elected to the SGB and eventually became its chairman. When his children moved on to high school his link with the school was broken, but he picked it up again in June 2018 when he became the PfP partner to Richard.

'Richard and I were close friends before we became partners, actually,' said Joseph. 'I have known him for many years and we regularly play golf together. I served on the SGB while my kids were at his school, and over the years Richard has called on me if there was a special case of a child who was in need of something, and I would try to help.'

So, when a business associate at the Assmang Komani Iron Ore Mine recommended that he join the PfP programme, Richard agreed on the condition that he could go to Sishen Intermediate. 'I wanted to go back to the school as it was close to my heart. I knew it well because of my time on the SGB and I knew Richard, of course, but this was also my community and I wanted to give something back to it.

'I believe every responsible citizen should remember where they came from and should contribute towards the upliftment of the community where they were raised. Sishen Intermediate school gave me a sound foundation in life and I wanted to repay that in some way.'

When Joseph was a learner at the school, it had 130 learners and eight teachers. Now there are over 1,300 children and 35 teachers, so it is a very different place. Joseph's role as a PfP is also very different from what it was when he was Chairman of the SGB.

'Then it was about governance,' he said. 'I had a management role to play and some executive power. Now I have no authority – all I am is a partner to Richard. In a way, it was a continuation of the things I was already doing to help the school, using my skills as a businessman and my network to help. I got a real sense of what the school does and of the challenges it faces.'

The partnership between Joseph and Richard had a head-start on the others in their circle, seeing that they already knew each other so well. 'The other members of our CoP were surprised at the strong bond that existed between us,' Joseph explained. 'I think we served as an example and a motivation to the others as they were in the process of forming their own relationships with their partners.'

Joseph attended the training courses with Richard and they made an impact on him, he said. 'I learned things that I had never thought of before,' he said. 'In Time to Think I learned how to listen to people differently and that helped me with my leadership in my business. I apply that all the time now.'

Similarly, the Flawless Consulting training has been a great help. 'I learned that whatever you do has a ripple effect on others, so you should plan things carefully and consider the consequences.'

Joseph's background is a fascinating story of the rewards that come from hard work and perseverance. He has seven siblings in his immediate family, and his father had four more children in another relationship. 'My parents didn't place a high premium on education – if you could read and write, that was enough for them – so they weren't too interested in my schooling,' he recalls 'I worked on and off while I was in high school and eventually dropped out in Grade 9, at the age of 22 years.'

Joseph began working in maintenance, but studied and qualified as a carpenter, then later as a building inspector. In 1998 he decided to resume his schooling and get his matric. In that year he received the prize for the top adult education student in the Northern Cape, and in 2000 he matriculated, becoming among the first in his family to do so.

Joseph then went on to study business leadership at Unisa and project management at the University of Pretoria.

'I realised that you have to use your time fully and not let opportunities pass you by,' he said. 'I also realised that I have 300 employees working in the businesses that I run, and if I should fail I would be failing them too.

'That's the lesson that I have learned, and it's the message that I try to convey to young people. I tell them that I was a proud failure. I turned that around by working hard and it ultimately led to me succeeding.'

I asked Joseph how he sees his role at the school. 'I think Richard is proud of me as an ex-learner of the school who has been successful, a product of the school who made it despite coming from a difficult background. I believe I can serve as an example to the learners that through hard work and perseverance you can succeed no matter what your circumstances might be.

'Richard is a dedicated educator who has a passion for children. He is very proud of those who have gone on to be a success at high school and beyond.'

Joseph sees his primary role at the school as being a supporter of Richard and the teachers. 'Schools are under pressure in these times,' he said. 'They are under pressure financially, and the workload on principals and teachers is enormous. There is a lot of negativity around that, and they don't always get the recognition that they deserve.

'I see it as my role to recognise the role they play and to show them appreciation for it. By supporting Richard and being there for him I can help him to be more effective in his job, and that will affect the learners and the school positively.'

For Richard, partnering with Joseph was a very wise move. 'Joseph was a learner here and he became successful in the business world. He serves as a role model to the children, showing them that it's possible to succeed even if you come from a poor background,' he said.

'Richard is a leader who leads by example. Before he became my PfP partner he was always ready to help children who were in need. He was especially concerned that learners who have potential should have the opportunity to further themselves and not be held back by their family circumstances.'

Joseph's example didn't only impact the learners, Richard said. 'He has the ability to take people along with him and he got other parents, and members of the community, to follow his example and contribute to the school and the learners in whatever way they could.

'He has also got a movement going among other former learners; they contribute what they can to make their former school better, just as Richard is doing.'

I wanted to know from Richard what practical improvements had been introduced at the school through their partnership, and he gave the example of how they had improved the functioning of the SGB. 'There was not a lot of experience and expertise in our SGB, so Joseph and I decided to hold joint SGB-SMT meetings. That way we were able to get input from the people who were working in the school on a daily basis and we found we got a lot more done that way.'

Yolandi, their LPF, had told me about the golf programme that Richard and Joseph had implemented. 'We have introduced a 'Drive, Chip and Putt' programme at the school. More than 40 children from the school participate in it. The parents pay for their involvement, in part, but we have also made partnerships with other golfers in our association, with businesses in the town and even with the local golf professional to sponsor the children. We want them to learn the game of golf while they are young because we believe it will be valuable to them later on,' said Richard.

Reflections

Just imagine if all business people who 'made it' went back to the schools where they received their foundational education to **be** a contribution? Imagine if all children in under-resourced communities could have role models like Joseph? And imagine what a difference it would make if every principal had someone like Joseph to turn to when times are tough?

Chapter 16

Learning from being of service and in partnership

"The best way to find yourself is to lose yourself in the service of others." – Mahatma Gandhi

Marina Knox, Director: Human Capital at Citadel in partnership with Getrude Mafoko, Principal of Bona Lesedi Secondary School

In 2015 the Gauteng Department of Education (GDE) contracted us to support 66 school principals through the PfP process. The department funded the participation of the principals, which meant that we only had to source sponsorship for the business leaders.

Getrude Mafoko is the principal of Bona Lesedi Secondary School in Mamelodi. She was selected by the GDE to be part of the '66 schools programme' because her school had been classified as one that needed additional support.

One of Getrude's colleagues had told her about PfP but she was a bit sceptical. 'I couldn't see how someone who had no knowledge about schools and education could be helpful, and, in any case, I was new at the school, and there was so much to do that I really didn't think I would have the time for it,' she recalls.

At the same time, Marina Knox, Director: Human Capital at Citadel, was looking for a way to make a meaningful contribution to society. 'As Head of HR at Citadel, transformation, socio-economic development and outreach are part of my portfolio of responsibilities,' she said. 'Our policy is to get into direct contact with the communities where we are assisting, and I realised being involved with Partners for Possibility would do that.'

Marina heard that the programme was looking for business partners in the Pretoria area. 'I felt duty-bound to find out more about it, and what I learned appealed to the caring side of my nature. From a personal point of view, I was feeling at the time that I would like to do something that made a difference to people in need, and this looked like it could do that.'

She realised from the start that this was going to be a long-term commitment and that finding the time to do it justice would be a challenge, but she decided to go for it anyway.

Although both Marina and Getrude came into the partnership with some doubts and reservations, those disappeared soon after they met. 'The magic was there at our first meeting,' Marina says. 'I could see that Getrude was passionate about education, about the kids and the people at the school. I too have a passion for people, and so we connected immediately and built on that connection from there on.'

Getrude and Marina come from different worlds, but they soon realised that the school could benefit from their association. As the partners got to know each other, they discovered that they had two significant things in common: they were both operating in what are still male-dominated roles (only 36% of school principals in South Africa are women), and both came into their jobs as outsiders.

Getrude does not hail from Mamelodi. Her teaching and educational leadership background are rooted in the North West Province. She was appointed principal at Bona Lesedi ahead of a strong local candidate, and that presented an immediate challenge.

Marina's background is also rural – she grew up in Mokopane (formerly Potgietersrust) – and, as the only female director at Citadel, she also has to operate in a man's world. 'I'm a counselling psychologist by training,' she says. 'I'm not a financial person, but I find myself in a world dominated by financial facts and figures, so I could identify with some of the challenges that Getrude was facing.'

Marina's training and experience as a counsellor was, of course, to be of great value to her partnership with Getrude because, she says, her role was primarily to listen to Getrude talking about her task and the challenges she faced.

'I soon realised that the leadership issues and the challenges experienced at schools and in the business world were not all that different,' Getrude says. 'We share the same frustrations, and it seemed that we could discuss things from the point of view of a common understanding and, together, make plans to solve some of those problems.'

Getrude had found Bona Lesedi Secondary School in a poor state when she arrived there. 'It was basically a *laissez-faire* situation when I got there,' she remembers. 'The required policies and procedures were not being adhered to, absenteeism was rife among the teachers and the students, and there was actually very little teaching going on.

'There had been an acting principal in place for a year before I arrived, and the school had many challenges that needed immediate attention. I arrived at the end of year while examinations were running, and management of examinations was very chaotic.'

Getrude realised that to start with she had to get the school running along the lines required by the departmental regulations. She began implementing policies and procedures and insisting on compliance with them, a course of action that wasn't always popular.

'I insisted on the proper keeping of registers; for example, signing of the time book on arrival by all staff members and when knocking off. It took some time for all to toe the line, but there is a huge improvement thus far. The rate of absenteeism has dropped drastically, even though there are still some challenges that have to be addressed.'

By the time she joined PfP, Getrude had done much to get the school back onto the right track and things were a lot better.

'I came into the partnership with some misconceptions about the state of township schools,' Marina says. 'I was under the impression that they were a dead loss. Nothing worked in them, I thought, there were no systems in place, the teachers didn't work and the children were not being taught.

'After meeting Getrude and spending time at Bona Lesedi Secondary, I realised that I was wrong and that I had to shift my paradigm. I was humbled and greatly impressed by her. She was totally professional in all that she did. I could see that she was doing great work. The teachers were working and she was motivating them and raising levels of engagement. It was clear that she didn't need my help in the operation of the school – not that I had anything to offer her in that regard.

'My role, I saw, would be to act as a sounding board, to be there when she needed someone to talk to and to help her realise that she was valuable and doing a good job.

'I was a thinking partner, not someone who imparted knowledge. I re-confirmed her level of confidence and built her self-esteem through positive reinforcement. We connected as women. Although I was able, through my network of contacts, and with the help of the people in the Citadel office, to help the school in a number of different material ways, the connection between us was the essence of our partnership. That was my main contribution towards getting the school back on track.'

The facilitated partnership period came to an end in June of 2016, and at the end of that year the school's matric pass rate rose by an astonishing 30% on the year before – from 56.9% in 2015 to 87.7% in 2016. This was cause for great celebration at Citadel.

'I had drawn on the support and help of my team so often, and great matric results led to much pride in the office.

'The people in my team refer to Bona Lesedi Secondary as 'our school' and they were thrilled that the matric results had improved drastically. One hundred of them had been involved in the wrapping of 'good luck' presents for those kids ahead of the exams, and they saw that, in a small way, they had made a difference.'

Marina and Getrude agreed early on that their biggest task would be to get the staff team working well. 'We had to motivate and energise the staff,' Marina said, 'so that is what we set out to do.'

Getrude had already put the procedures in place and was busy talking to teams and individuals, Marina discovered. 'I saw my role as supporting her in that and encouraging her not to stray from a path that she knew was the right one.'

Looking back on where she was before PfP, Getrude is confident that she is a better principal, and person, now than she was before her partnerships with Marina commenced. 'I believe I was put into this position of leadership with a purpose. There are challenges of gambling, drugs and teenage pregnancies in our schools but we are addressing them accordingly, guided by the code of conduct for learners and supported by the department. Though a bit challenging, I am confident that as a school, with the support of all stakeholders, as well as Citadel, we will win this fight.'

For Marina, the partnership with Getrude has been life-changing. 'I would never have met someone like Getrude if it were not for the programme,' she says. 'and I would never have gotten a taste of the richness of township life.

'I have realigned my thinking as a result of working with Getrude. I learned so much about motivating individuals and about working with teams from Getrude. Those were valuable lessons that I took back to my own work situations.'

The community of practice component of the programme and the regular meetings with other principals in their circle was highly valuable to the partnership. 'Our thinking was expanded through those conversations with other principals and I made other connections there,' Marina says.

Facilitated CoP meetings cease when the 12-month programme ends, but Getrude told us that some of the alumni PfP principals in Mamelodi are keeping the concept going through mentorship circles. 'We hold monthly meetings at which we share good practices,' she says. 'We share our challenges and advise each other on the basis of our common experiences; that's been a legacy of the year with Partners for Possibility.'

'Getrude was already super when I arrived at the school and, I believe, she is even more super now after her experience of the PfP programme,' Marina said.

Getrude and Marina's relationship has continued way beyond the first, facilitated year of PfP. They are still in touch, and although they don't meet regularly anymore they remain connected. 'The magic of our relationship is still there. We still communicate through emails and WhatsApp most of the time; it's a way of saying "I'm thinking of you and I hope you are thinking of me?"' says Marina.

And Bona Lesedi Secondary is going from strength to strength. The school is now part of the University of Pretoria's new homework project on its Mamelodi campus, and this has contributed to big improvements in Grade 8 and 9 maths and science marks. There are now also Grade 11 and 12 learners from Bona Lesedi enrolled at the Kutlwanong Centre for Maths, Science and Technology where they receive high-quality maths and science tuition.

'We also have a teacher at the school every Saturday morning, and the parents pay a small amount to send their children for help and extra work,' Getrude said. 'We have moved a long way from being an under-performing school. I no longer feel like an outsider and our performance is continuing to improve.'

Johan Minnie, Group Executive at Liberty in partnership with Agnes Raboshakga, Principal of Olievenhoutsbosch Secondary School

In his own words, Johan Minnie, the Group Sales Director at Liberty, is a 'solution-driven, can-do sort of person'. So, when he started his PfP year at Olievenhoutsbosch Secondary School in partnership with Agnes Raboshakga in 2015 he thought it was going to be easy.

'I asked her for a list of the biggest challenges facing the school,' he recalls, 'so that I could start getting the money together to address these.

'Imagine how that approach of mine was blown out of the water when she told me the biggest problem facing the school was teenage pregnancy. It was something I had heard of but never really thought much about. To provide a solution to an issue like that was so far from my experience and capability that I realised, straight away, that this exercise was not going to go the way I had envisaged.'

By the end of the first year of Anges and Johan's partnership, the teenage pregnancy rate at the school had in fact dropped – but more about that later.

Johan told us the story of how the Liberty Group started and how it got its name. Apparently, the company's founder, the late Sir Donald Gordon, was appalled to discover that his father, after working hard all his life, was going to reap little financial reward for his efforts.

'It's a company legend now how, in 1957, at the age of 27 and with R100,000 in capital, Sir Donald founded the organisation, and he called it Liberty because his mission was to provide an advisory service that would guarantee freedom from financial woes for its clients when they stopped working,' Minnie related.

That philosophy has endured at Liberty and, in all it does, the company aim to help its clients to be financially independent. To do that, it needs to impart knowledge and give guidance, which, in essence, adds up to education. 'Our business is all about personal relationships with clients,' Johan said, 'and it's about guiding them along the path to financial freedom, and partnering with them at a deep level.'

At the same time, there was the belief that, as a company, Liberty had to make a contribution to the community it served, because it made good business sense to do so, but also because it was the right thing to do.

So, when it came to social responsibility involvement, it was natural that education was the area where the company was to be most prominent.

'For more than 20 years there has been a natural connection between who we are and what we do daily, and educating the nation,' Johan said. 'The Liberty Foundation was set up many years ago to help underprivileged children learn better. Long before corporate social investment became compulsory, we were active in educational programmes, to the extent that we came to see the education sphere as the Liberty space.'

The best-known of Liberty's corporate social investment ventures is their sponsorship of the Learning Channel, a high-quality curriculum compliant education programme that appears in print and on national television. The content is now broadcast to many other countries across Africa as well.

Through the Liberty Foundation, Liberty supports 17 schools in various parts of the country. In some cases, Johan explained, they built the schools from the ground up. In others, they supply furniture, equipment and learning materials.

'I always felt, however, that to be really effective, we had to be involved at a school leadership level as well,' Johan said. 'For the other programmes to be sustainable, there had to be good management in the schools.'

Chapter 16: Learning from being of service and in partnership

Johan remembers that the school he attended as a child was well-resourced and ran smoothly. He was aware that not all schools in South Africa were like that, but he didn't really know much else.

When Jay Naidoo, Director of Sales at Liberty, first spoke to him about Partners for Possibility, Johan was intrigued. 'She is an open-minded, systematic thinker, and she had decided that the leaders in the business need the tools to help us develop a sense of social responsibility and to meet the growing challenges we face.'

Jay had come across the PfP programme and, after attending a meeting at which there was a call for business leaders to become involved, she signed Johan, her boss, up for it.

'I think she would have loved to join the programme herself, but she was working in a highly pressured, target-driven area of the business and she was afraid that she would not have the time to commit herself to it.

'I guess she wanted me to go on the programme hoping that I would learn something of value that would help her in changing the way our sales force interacts with the communities that many of our customers come from.'

Johan was acutely aware that many of the schools in the country were battling, for all sorts of reasons, and he knew that he wanted to do something to make a difference.

'I was familiar with the various educational programmes that the company is involved in, and the successes that have been achieved. In most of those cases it involved, mainly, providing solutions to the financial needs of schools.

'I, however, knew that it should go further than that. It seemed to me that leadership was the key. If the school principal could make better decisions, then that would be amplified throughout the school and the community.'

Johan also immediately saw that there were potential benefits for the business leaders involved in PfP partnerships. 'I realised that this could be a way for our executives to gain a real understanding of the problems that are facing the country,' he says.

When he met Agnes at Olievenhoutsbosch Secondary School and asked her for that list of the biggest challenges facing the school, the idea was that it would form the basis of an action plan for the 12-month partnership they would be entering into and, one by one, they would tick off the items on it.

As already mentioned, teenage pregnancy was at the top of the list that Agnes provided.

That was followed by a lack of facilities, particularly sports fields and equipment, and the school's poor record in mathematics, both in the number of learners taking the subject to Grade 12 level and in the pass rate amongst those who took maths in matric.

'By far the greatest challenge was teenage pregnancy,' Johan said. 'The other two issues on the list were relatively easy to solve. The provision of sporting facilities was a matter of better management and of finding resources. Agnes was concerned that many talented boys and girls at the school were not being given the opportunity to reach their potential, sports-wise, and that was something we could work on.'

The poor standard of maths education in South Africa is well-known, and there have been many interventions designed to remedy this. Liberty has a good track record in remedial maths education through its other initiatives so, Johan said, this was an easy area in which to effect an improvement.

Teenage pregnancy was a different matter. 'I was clearly out of my depth as far as that was concerned, and it was immediately apparent that this was a serious issue at the school.'

Between seven and 14 girls at the school were falling pregnant every year, so it wasn't a one-off problem, and they were mainly in Grades nine and 10 – in the junior years – which meant there was little chance that they would be able to complete their schooling and their lives were, effectively, ruined.

'If ever there was a problem that throwing money at was not going to solve, this was it,' Johan realised. 'My financial background and management science approach wasn't going to cut it. Educational talks and the provision of free condoms hadn't worked in the past, so those alone were not going to be sufficient.'

The answer did not lie in the application of business acumen, and it was not going to come from Johan himself; it had to come from the school and the community. 'That's how we tackled it. Agnes knew that this was a social and economic issue. The girls were under intense pressure from men in the community and, at the same time, the money that a government child maintenance grant would bring in was important to the families.

'We decided to work to make the school a provider of a solution rather than a receiver of the problem. We reached out to the community, made the school's facilities available, and started involving the parents in school life. Through talking to the families, listening and having patience and involving the elders in the community we were able to formulate a plan. The problem of teenage pregnancy has not gone away, but we did make some progress in reducing it.'

In Johan's time at Olievenhoutsbosch Secondary School, Liberty never gave any direct funding to the school. 'In keeping with Liberty's philosophy of partnering for long-term financial stability, I tried to help the school to be entrepreneurial by facilitating partnerships with organisations that could help them,' he says

'Through my network, and the school's involvement with the community, and with the help of the network established through the community of practice meetings that we held with other principals and partners who were on the PfP programme, we were able to bring about some substantial, sustainable, material improvements to the school.'

That was important, but the biggest thing was the personal development that both Agnes and Johan experienced.

The PfP programme helps to meet the basic needs of a school through the formulation of an action plan and the implementation of that plan. 'In the process, there will be valuable lessons for the principal about how to manage projects and how to lead people to bring about positive change,' Johan said.

'And for the business leader there will be an emergence into a world that was unfamiliar, and lessons about how to find solutions with limited resources, and no direct authority.'

The PfP programme is undoubtedly successful as far as those goals are concerned. For Johan and Liberty, the leadership development of the executives that have been on the programme has been the big thing. Since Johan and Agnes joined PfP, eight other leaders from Liberty have become involved.

Being involved in the programme, Johan said, gives the business leader a real understanding of the challenges we face in the country. 'It keeps you humble and helps you develop a deep level of empathy for those who are less fortunate than you are.

'As a result, you wake up each morning more grateful and energised about your responsibility as a business leader in South Africa. That's a gift, one that every business leader can do with.

'This sort of exposure is particularly important for people working in financial institutions. We get so caught up in numbers, and in the 12-month reporting cycle, that we sometimes lose touch with the real world.

'Schools have problems that you cannot fix in 12 months. It requires a longer-term strategic approach, and being exposed to that kind of thinking can be very good for you.' Johan believes that the synergy with what Liberty does in obvious.

'The challenges our clients face are complex. It takes time and patience to gain a deep understanding of them. Based on that understanding, we, in partnership with the client, craft a life plan, not merely a financial solution to their retirement needs. There are clear parallels to be found in partnering a principal in a school.

'You are not just working to solve the financial problems that an under-resourced school faces by helping it to get better funding. You are helping to make plans that will sustain it in the long term.'

Putting its young managers on the PfP programme has helped Liberty to learn how to lead more effectively, and that's why Johan is sold on the idea of PfP as a leadership development programme.

When we spoke to Agnes in 2019 she told us that she learned a lot from being part of PfP. 'There is much from those days that I still apply in my leadership of the school,' she said. 'It was all about my personal growth and development. The important thing is that I now allow my SMT and the teachers an opinion. I discuss things before making demands. People are able to do their work without being afraid of being judged; that's important.'

Agnes and Johan have lost touch, but Liberty Life still plays an important part in the school. 'Johan's job changed, and he was no longer able to keep his side of the partnership going,' Agnes explained. 'But he didn't leave it at that. He found a new thinking partner for me – Peter Van der Merwe. We meet and talk regularly, and we have formed a bond that is working well.'

Dhiresh Ramdeen, Client Services Manager, Bestmed in partnership with Maud Langa, Principal of Esikhisini Primary School

When Dhiresh Ramdeen became Maud Langa's PfP partner at Esikhisini Primary School in Atteridgeville, he was the second manager from Bestmed to become involved in the programme.

The first was Michael Tsiane, who was partnered with Stephen Maboe of St Anne's Primary School in Atteridgeville. Chris Luyt, who was then the marketing executive at Bestmed, had suggested to Michael that he may want to get involved in the programme. Chris had hoped that becoming involved at a school and making a contribution to positive change might be meaningful for Michael.

Michael's involvement at the school turned out to be limited – he left Bestmed shortly after completing the 12-month programme – but Chris noticed that PfP had had an impact on Michael's demeanour and general positivity and that persuaded him to initiate a second PfP partnership. Dhiresh was to become that second partner.

Chris is a caring manager, always looking out for the people in his team, and felt that it was important for people in the organisation to be fully engaged.

At about this time, Chris had come across the story of Tony Hsieh, the CEO of Zappos who sold his internet shoe retailer to Amazon.com for $1.2 billion. Zappos had survived the dot-com crash, but the company was constantly struggling, and Hsieh was investing millions of his own money into the business.

Hsieh decided that the way to turn things around was to establish a culture that distinguished Zappos from its competitors and that one of their core values would be happiness. The people working there should be happy, and that would lead to happy customers and inevitably, profits.

Hsieh's book *Delivering Happiness: A Path to Profits, Passion and Purpose* describes how he turned Zappos around and eventually got Amazon to buy the company.

'Bestmed is a company that believes it has to make a contribution to the society it operates in,' Chris explained. 'We are in the business of healthcare, and realising that non-communicable diseases have become the major killers in society, it made sense that we should be doing things that contribute to education on health and well-being issues in communities.

'So, we developed what we call our five wellness pillars: be active; be safe; be nutri-wise; be financially fit, and be happy.'

If you can be those things, Chris reckons, stress will be reduced, good health will follow suit, and your ability to handle challenges will improve. If those five pillars became habits, lifestyle diseases like diabetes, hypertension and heart problems would be reduced.

'And, because our potential clients are generally parents – it's when you start a family that you begin to think of medical insurance – it was a short step for us to see schools as a good place to start in getting the message of the five pillars of wellness across,' he said.

'At the time we were toying with the idea of setting up a programme to facilitate partnerships between advantaged and disadvantaged schools, and at one time we were thinking of producing a book on the five pillars of wellness and distributing it to schools,' Chris said. 'But those ideas never found traction at Bestmed, so the project was shelved.'

And then, serendipity stepped in. Chris heard about PfP. 'It was a programme that suggested the way to improve the functionality at schools was to empower the principal via this partnership with a business leader, and I immediately saw the possibilities,' Chris recalls.

'I remember that I was influenced by two philosophical ideas at the time,' Chris said. 'I had heard a plea for assistance that went along the lines of 'hear me, know me, help me to prosper'. I also came across an adaptation of Maslow's hierarchy of needs, applied to levels of satisfaction that went – from bottom to top – security, excitement, belonging, growth and contribution.'

The implication was that people get the greatest satisfaction when they are making a contribution to others and are happiest when their contribution is meaningful, Chris realised.

'Michael, and the other young managers who formed part of Bestmed's Top People programme at the time, had clearly attained the bottom four levels on the hierarchy,' Chris said. 'I wondered if they would find fulfilment, and grow through it, if they could reach the fifth level.'

Pressed on whether the exercise had achieved its objectives, Chris said it was difficult to measure the long-term effects Michael's involvement had on him. 'During the year he was actively involved there, his levels of engagement clearly rose, and he involved himself in the programme with energy and enthusiasm.'

The next person to choose to join PfP was Dhiresh Ramdeen. 'One Saturday during his year at St Anne's, Michael organised a couple of combi loads of Bestmed head office staff to go through to the school for a day of gardening, painting, repairing and maintenance,' Chris explained.

'Dhiresh went along that day, and it was immediately apparent that this was something that he could be passionate about. He threw himself into the day's activities with gusto. I was reminded of Jack Welch's '4Es and a P' – Energy, Energising others, Edge, Execute and Passion. Dhiresh clearly had the energy and the passion. I was sure that he would be able to spread those qualities to those he came into contact with.'

Dhiresh works in Bestmed's client services division, so Chris had to persuade his colleagues in Dhiresh's division to allow him to get involved.

'Dhiresh himself didn't need much persuading. He immediately saw that he would be able to make a contribution and that's what he wanted to do. That he himself would grow from it was an added bonus.

'Dhiresh is all shiny-eyed passion. He believes you play the cards you have been dealt and good leadership will get you through,' Chris said.

For Dhiresh, his partnership with Maude was nothing less than life-changing, and the process began the first time he went to the school and met some of the learners.

'I was living in a comfortable house in the suburbs and had no experience of the areas in which schools like Esikhisini were located,' he said. 'My eyes were opened. I saw children who had no shoes, with torn and ragged clothing. There was so much potential, I was sure, but they were clearly neglected, and it touched me deeply. I knew then that I had to try to make a difference.'

An immediate problem was security. 'Maude told me that the school was plagued by burglaries and that anything of value would be stolen. I realised that we would not make progress under those circumstances, so I decided to do something about it. Fortunately, I had the support of Bestmed and of my team there, so we were able to mobilise resources and erect a security fence, with secure gates.'

Nutrition was another issue that needed to be addressed early on, and with the help of his team, Dhiresh helped the school establish a sustainable vegetable garden to supplement the daily meals that were provided to the children.

Maude has since moved on from Esikhisini – she is now principal of the new Curro School in Mamelodi – but Dhiresh still keeps in touch with her. 'I learned so much from her, and I think we both grew as a result of our partnership. I am thrilled that she has moved on into a high profile position.'

Dhiresh believes his own growth is reflected in his work and in the way he manages his team at Bestmed. 'Many of our staff members live in areas like Atteridgeville and being exposed to the reality of their lives changed my perspective and the way I operate,' he said. 'For example, I am far more understanding about late-coming and absenteeism now that I have seen for myself the challenges around the use of public transport and taxis to and from work each day.'

Working with Maude and attending the courses that are part of the PfP programme made Dhiresh take a new look at the way in which he manages people.

'My management style was a bit authoritarian before, I think. I have learned now to listen to the views of others and to take them into account. Exposure to new areas and different people has made me understand diversity better, and that has made me a better leader.'

Bestmed invests a lot in the development of their up and coming managers,' Chris said. 'Partners for Possibility is one of a bouquet of training programmes we offer our team members. Its alignment with our values and the connections that we have made with our customer base through working in the areas where they live has made it particularly valuable.'

Dave Morris, in partnership with Lebo Mokwele, Principal of Thopodi Primary School

By the time Dave Morris retired as Head of Business Improvement at Anglo American at the end of 2016, his path ahead, he believes, was pretty much mapped out – his retirement life would be one of community building and contribution, specifically in the field of education.

'Looking back, there were a number of things I had been involved with in my working years that nudged me in that direction,' he said. 'When I was working in the area of safety and sustainable development for the company, part of my role was interacting with the people living around our mines, and I became aware of the problems and challenges faced in poorly resourced communities. Before that, I had been involved with an Anglo project called the Young Communicators Awards, a public speaking competition for learners at schools in our mining communities, and I began to realise then that there is great potential in our young people, but that the quality of education that they receive at many schools was poor.

'In 2008 I was sent on a social management course by the company. It took us into communities in Chile and in South Africa, and I was immersed in a world that was foreign to me and got a real taste of the conditions that people have been forced to live under. It was about then that I asked myself the question 'when is enough, enough?' and I realised that I had to do something to help.'

Dave's daughter attended St Andrew's School for Girls in Bedfordview where he became actively involved, initially in their uBambiswano community partnership. This initiative sees 100 Grade 6 to 9 learners from Daveyton and Etwatwa attend St Andrew's on Saturdays over a four-year period. These disadvantaged learners receive tuition in literacy, numeracy and life skills, as well as enrichment activities such as music, swimming and cooking.

'I was then elected to the St Andrew's Board of Governors as the representative of uBambiswano and eventually became Chairman of the Board. Those experiences, again, served as a preparation for my later involvement in education,' he said.

Dave was introduced to the PfP programme by someone at Anglo American before he left there. He attended an information evening in October 2016 and soon signed up to be a partner. 'I think the thing that appealed to me most was that this was an opportunity to roll up my sleeves and get stuck into something,' he said. 'I had spent so much of my life sitting in meetings and serving on committees where we spoke about what needed to be done and then expected someone else to go out and do the work.

'I was looking for a way to make a real contribution, and PfP came along at exactly the right time. The beauty of the PfP programme is that it came with a structure and a sense of certainty. That was important to me as I found myself committed to making a difference but not really sure which direction to go into.

'I realise now that much of what I had been doing in mining, and in the projects I had been involved in my earlier life, was getting me ready for making that commitment.'

In 2017 Dave was paired with Lebo Mokwele, the principal of Thopodi Primary School in Old Etwatwa East, Springs. It was a partnership that lasted until the beginning of 2019 when Lebo retired (a few months later she was at the helm of a new independent school in a neighbouring area). 'I'm still I touch with Lebo, though. We speak regularly, and I have remained a thinking partner to her,' Dave said.

At the same time, Dave has maintained his ties with Thopodi Primary. He has continued his work there with the new principal, who was Lebo's deputy and is well versed with PfP and the relationship that existed between Lebo and him. 'The school is doing very well,' says Dave. 'I attended the opening of their new library recently, built with resources that the school itself obtained. I had no input at all, other than to offer encouragement along the way.'

The experience of being in partnership with Lebo changed Dave profoundly, he believes. 'I got to understand the value of first building a relationship before rushing in to try to do things,' he said. 'It took a full six months for Lebo and I to really get to know each other, and it was only after that we began to make real progress at the school.'

The courses they attended were also very important. 'I learned techniques there that I used at St Andrew's and that I still employ in the other things that I am involved in now,' Dave says.

At St Andrew's for example, he began to run board meetings according to Time to Think principles, and they used the Community Building methodology to craft a new strategic direction for the school. A new Executive Head, Ivanka Acquisto, was appointed to the school recently and Dave has become a thinking partner to her. 'We meet once a week and I, mainly, listen to her. She talks, and I offer very little by way of advice or direction.'

Dave has begun preparing to exit his role at the school as his term of office expires in 2021, but he has agreed to meet Ivanka fortnightly during 2020.

Among the other things that Dave is now involved in is a return to a role in mining. 'I was approached in 2017 to become a consultant to one or two mining companies and I agreed,' he said. 'My intended role was to provide technical advice and guidance to the management teams and, although it started off that way, it later changed. I found that I was beginning to serve as a PfP-type partner to those managers, and I found it interesting to see how easily the PfP 'way' could be transferred.

'Those mining managers were facing fundamentally the same challenges that school principals do. It's a lonely position, they have management teams who aren't always aligned and on the same page as them, and they are under pressure from above: from a board and the shareholders. They are in need of the same sort of support as principals, and so I again found myself providing the same type of support there that I had provided at Thopodi and at St Andrew's.

'We used Time to Think principles in our interactions, and I showed them how to use Flawless Consulting in formalising our relationship and in their interaction with their service providers, and there were positive results.'

Commercial partnerships don't last of course, and once the mining companies achieve what they were looking for they move on. 'That's OK,' Dave said, 'what I learned was that the theory of PfP can be adapted, with very little change, to other sectors.'

At the end of 2017 SSA found itself short of members for its own board and Dave agreed to join it. Once again, he believes, his experience in the programme has shaped the way he fulfils his role.

'I have my duties as a board member, but I have found that more and more I am in a support role to the management team,' he says. 'I am someone that they can talk to, I see myself as a one-man supporters club to the team. There's a potential conflict there, I think, a non-executive director does not get involved at that level, so we may have to look at the role of the board in the future. A supporters club is definitely needed as well.'

I asked Dave if he sees what he is doing as 'refirement'. Has he used the opportunity presented by his retirement to reignite, go in a different direction and find a new fulfilment?

'Definitely,' he replied. 'In some ways, I regard my previous working life as a preparation for this one. I have become part of a community, and I can see the good that we are doing. That's deeply fulfilling. I needed to be hands-on after sitting in an office for so long, and this was my opportunity to do that. It's spilled over to rest of my life, and I find myself doing all sorts of other creative things at home now.

'I'm the eternal optimist, I guess, but I am beginning to differentiate between optimism and hope. Optimism is often irrational and unrealistic. Hope is about having a real expectation and working towards achieving it. PfP has taught me that.'

Reflections

These stories are an extention of the stories in Chapter 14 (PfP as a Consciousness-raising experience). Marina, Johan, Dhiresh and Dave have learned more from leading in the VUCA world and from working with their principal-partners in under-resourced communities than they would have been able to learn from a traditional classroom-based leadership development programme. Their eyes have been opened to the significant challenges in under-resourced communities, and they have been called to share their knowledge, skills and experience in a spirit of contribution and humility. This has led to significant impact in these schools – exactly what we had hoped to achieve through the PfP process.

Chapter 17

A few stories about the impact on the lives of individual children

"Our children are the rock on which our future will be built, our greatest asset as a nation. They will be the leaders of our country, the creators of our national wealth, those who care for and protect our people." – Nelson Mandela

The PfP programme is specifically designed to strengthen leadership capacity in and around schools, but we regularly hear about individual learners who have benefitted from the involvement of business leaders in their schools.

Jaelyn Williams

Jaelyn Williams is in Grade 11 at the Cape Academy of Mathematics, Science and Technology (CAMST). The WCED established CAMST in Cape Town to provide specialised schooling for learners with the potential to excel in these areas.

We know about Jaelyn's story because a few years ago Kannemeyer Primary's Grade 7 teacher, Ms Morallie was invited to a tea for teachers from CAMST feeder primary schools. At this gathering, Ms Morallie heard about Jaelyn's achievements and how she came to choose medicine as a future career.

In 2015, while Jaelyn was a learner at Kannemeyer Primary with her sights on law as a career, she attended the school's annual career evening. Jaelyn remembers the event as a defining moment in her life.

'In my Grade 7 year, about five years ago, I attended a career evening. Although there was so much to see and experience, I fell in love with the idea of studying medicine and becoming a doctor,' she recalls.

'The reason I decided on medicine is because some of my role models, such as Dr Leila Denmark, Dr Elizabeth Blackwell, Dr Howard Atwood Kelly and Dr Irene Krawcyk (my GP) have all made a huge impact in the medical field. These are people who have inspired me, and that contributed to my decision.

'I was diagnosed at a very young age with asthma and have had to learn to cope in any environment with it. I would like to improve the treatment for asthma, or even find a cure. My passion is to help people, and my dream is to be able to assist as many people as I possibly can.'

It was so gratifying to hear this story. Ridwan and I started hosting these career evenings for Grade 7s in 2011. We saw this as an opportunity to introduce these learners to a variety of careers. During those evenings every Grade 7 learner would typically get an opportunity to speak to five or six adults about their careers. We had a sense that these interactions would have some impact, but this was the first time we had heard from a learner whose choice of career had changed as a direct result of attending a career evening.

Jaelyn's decision to study medicine took her to CAMST, where her horizons have been broadened even more. 'Being at CAMST has opened many doors for me. I recently applied for summer school at Yale University as part of the Yale Young Global Scholars. It's a lengthy process, but I am positive that I'll be chosen – fingers crossed,' she said.

'My mother is a hard-working woman, and she has had a big impact on my work ethic and how I should always work for what I want in life. She is a huge inspiration and has helped me develop into a strong young woman.

'I was privileged to have started my schooling career at Kannemeyer Primary. The teachers and the principal, Mr Samodien, played a massive role in my young life. I loved attending the school and being part of such a close-knit community.

'Being in Grade 11 is a whole different ball game. Now I'm at the point where I need to make huge life-changing decisions, and if I have not had the proper foundation at Kannemeyer, I would not be who I am today.'

Nkateko (Eddie) Manzini

Eddie Manzini went to Zonkizizwe Secondary School in Katlehong, near Johannesburg. The school's principal, Elizabeth Masemola, was partnered with Graham Haird of Polyoak Packaging in 2015.

'I come from humble beginnings. I grew up in an informal settlement on the East Rand, where I was raised by two courageous women; my mother, and my late grandmother who sadly passed away in a car accident in 2011,' Eddie explained.

After completing his matric at Zonkizizwe Secondary in 2015, he commenced his tertiary studies without any idea or plan as to how to fund his studies.

'Fortunately, my high school principal, Mrs Elizabeth Masemola, was able to see my potential. Together with her PfP business partner, Mr Graham Haird, they reached out to me and managed to assist me. Their intervention changed the course of my life.

'My fees were fully paid, and I was afforded an opportunity to gain some 'on-the-job' experience at Mr Haird's company, Polyoak Packaging. I was taught not only work ethics but invaluable interpersonal and life skills. This has undoubtedly shaped who I am today – I strive to be a team player, but I also bring something unique and dynamic to a team.'

Eddie graduated in 2018 with a Diploma in Accountancy from the University of Johannesburg, and in 2019 he completed an Advanced Diploma in Financial Management at the same institution. He has become a confident young man, ready to live a successful life of contribution.

Eddie has fond memories of other opportunities to participate in events and experiences that he would not ordinarily have had access to. 'In 2016, I was offered a prestigious opportunity to form part of a panel organised by the Nelson Mandela Foundation, under the theme 'Play your Part in Education'. On 25 October 2018, the day of my graduation ceremony, I was asked to be the MC at Symphonia for South Africa's inaugural Execs Back to School celebration event at the Inanda Club in Sandton.

'PfP has been a driving force that pushes me on a daily basis to wake up with the willingness to realise my true potential. It was a shelter from my struggles during my university years. The PfP partnership between Mrs Masemola and Mr Haird was truly a 'light at the end of the tunnel'.

'I believe that I am capable of academic excellence and that I am deserving in this life. I believe I have become somebody. I now understand that helping one person is a positive investment into someone's life. Individuals play the game, but a team beats the odds.'

Simbulele Mgengo

Simbulele was born in 2002 in the Eastern Cape village of Mhlopekazi. At the age of two she lost her mother, and her father was forced to relocate to the Western Cape, where he made the Dunoon township their new home. True to Simbulele's character, she embraced what life brought her way and made the most of every opportunity. At her school, Sophakama Primary, she excelled and established herself as a top performer.

The story of PfP's impact on Simbulele as a learner started in 2013 when her principal, Sabelo Makubalo, joined the programme and was partnered with Irené Raubenheimer, the co-founder of ROGZ and founder of the ROGZ Academy, which supports PfP.

In 2014 Simbulele was Head Girl of the school and its top performer. She was coming to the end of Grade 7 and knew she wouldn't be able to go to high school because her father couldn't afford the transport or other related costs. When her English teacher, Mr Jacob Funyura, found out about Simbulele's predicament, he made it his mission to find a solution.

Mr Funyura knew that she deserved a chance. He approached Irené, who in turn sought and managed to secure financial support from the ROGZ distributor in Belgium, Benelux NV. This became the first scholarship offered by the ROGZ Academy, and it enabled Simbulele to apply for entrance to a well-resourced school in Table View, Bloubergrant High School (BHS). The generous scholarship covered the annual cost of school fees, uniforms, stationery, transport and pocket money – thus providing Simbulele with a life-changing opportunity to expand her horizons.

Fast forward to 2019 and Simbulele has come to the end of Grade 12. She has worked hard over the past five years and had many successes. She was elected as a prefect in Grade 12, and at Bloubergrant's valedictory awards ceremony in 2019 she received the trophy for Best Senior Academic Achiever in Accounting and a certificate for first place in accounting in her grade. She also received a certificate for academic achievement in business studies.

Simbulele is now ready to begin the next chapter in her life – university or college, where she will be studying accounting with the aim of becoming a chartered accountant. At the time of writing, the university that she will be attending had not been confirmed, but members of the ROGZ Academy have no doubt that Simbulele will be very successful.

She recently wrote this letter of appreciation to the ROGZ Academy:

To the ROGZ Family

I do not know where I should start but I guess the beginning is the best place to.

I remember when the news was broken to me that they found someone who was willing to help me further with my studies. Not only was I able to go to the higher grades, but a school that was outside my area, a more privileged school. I was ecstatic. I still cannot believe it even today. I still shed a tear today whenever I look back or when I realise the environment I am in. Not only did ROGZ change my life but they gave my family hope and faith. And for that I will forever be grateful. I cannot even express how I feel in words.

Being in BHS has really changed the way I viewed life. I learned great lessons. The experience has really changed my life, from striving for the best to giving my all in order to achieve my goal. The hunger for success and knowing that there's people looking up to me is what pushes me every day to do the best.

From achieving academic achievement certificates to being elected as the member of the school's learner committee. It did not end there, I was acknowledged and given the responsibility to be part of the Prefects of 2019, and all that started because of ROGZ. They did not only support me financially but gave me moral support as well. I felt like I was part of the ROGZ Family.

To end on that note, I would really love to say Thank you for very much for all you have done for me.

Amahle Mngadi

We met Gill Cox during our trip to the KZN North Coast and visit to Mshwati Memorial Primary, where Gill is in partnership with Principal Bizie Magwaza. While we were travelling together, Gill told us about Amahle Mngadi.

Bizie had told Gill about Amahle in 2017 when she was a Grade 6 learner at Mshwati. Amahle was a brilliant student and regularly scored over 90% in all her subjects, but her parents were so poor that they would never be able to send her a fee-paying school. Bizie knew that Amahle deserved an opportunity to go to a high school where she could flourish.

Gill was hesitant to get involved. 'I knew where this was going and told Bizie that it was not my role to become involved in fund-raising and that I had no interest in taking on and raising another child,' she said. Gill avoided the Grade 6 classroom with a 'don't show me that child…it's not my problem' attitude.

But Bizie persisted and Gill agreed to see what may be possible. After many conversations with prospective well-resourced schools, Gill decided that the Inanda Seminary, an independent secondary school for girls would be the best option for Amahle. She spoke with Judy Tate, the school's Executive Head, to see if Amahle could possibly be offered the opportunity to give the entrance exam a bash.

Judy agreed, and Bizie drove Amahle to the school, which is over 70 kilometres from Mshwati Memorial. On the strength of her performance, Amahle was offered a scholarship that would cover 50% of the school fees. What to do now? – she had been accepted – but Gill had absolutely no idea how to go about raising the other R150,000 that would be needed.

I don't think Judy Tate thought it was possible. But incredible people unexpectedly came to Gill's aid. Her cousin, Kathy Arici, who lives in Australia, ran a crowdfunding campaign that covered Amahle's fees for the first year. Then the Rotary Club of Knights Pendragon in Johannesburg raised ALL the funds that would be needed to cover the remainder of her high school career.

Amahle started at Inanda at the beginning of 2019. It wasn't easy for her. She was homesick and worried that she would not be able to fit in. Then she contracted chickenpox and had to leave school before the end of the first term to recuperate at home

A few weeks after our visit in September 2019, Gill sent us Amahle's report card. In her 10 subjects, she had achieved 80-100% for eight of them and 70-79% for the other two. This is a girl whose mother can't speak English!

In November 2019 Amahle wrote this letter of gratitude to her sponsors:

Dear Sir / Madam

I appreciate the opportunity that has been offered to me. I am grateful for your financial support. I have embarked on a special journey and it has been possible because of you.

My life has been hectic over the past few months. Everything about it has changed. I have grown in many ways. Being a member of Inanda Seminary has changed me for the best. I am not the person I was in 2018. I have become more responsible. Being in a boarding school has been extremely hard but it has changed my resolve and prepared me for future challenges.

I have also developed an interest in reading books. The genre that I love most is mystery – I love the suspense and the possibilities of a mystery. My love for reading mysteries has contributed to my career choice. I want to be a forensic investigator, a career that my mother disapproves of because she fears that I am going to die at an early age. I find her fears hilarious because I know that I will be more than capable of protecting myself. I am going to be the best forensic investigator ever.

I have also developed a great relationship with God. I thought God was a myth. I never believed in Him but attending chapel services six days a week has changed my mindset and developed my faith. I thank God for introducing me to Gill – without

her support and devotion I would not have gotten the chance to study at Inanda Seminary.

I don't have any other way of showing my gratitude other than writing this letter. I promise to study really hard and pass with good results. I hope my achievements will make you proud.

Yours sincerely

Amahle Magadi

At the end of 2019 Gill received a message to say that Amahle was Inanda Seminary's top Grade 8 student. She got distinctions in nine out of 10 subjects and received beautiful notes of appreciation from all her teachers acknowledging her for her hard work, diligence, commitment and the extent to which she upholds the values of the school.

Amahle is the first learner from the Mthombisa community and Mshwati Primary School to receive a scholarship of this nature, and Bizie and all the other adults in the community are extremely proud of her. We all look forward to seeing how she will make the most of this opportunity.

Sphokuhle Gxagxa

We told the story of Hillwood Primary School, the late Ian Macdonald and Fella's Army in chapter 7.

One of the initiatives undertaken after Ian passed away was the establishment of the Ian Macdonald Scholarship. It is granted to a Grade 7 learner at the end of their primary schooling at Hillwood. The scholarship is financed by Windlab, Ian's former employer, and the Mapula Trust. Fella's Army helps to select the recipient from candidates put forward by the school and screened by the scholarship management organisation SAILI, and then presents the award at the school's annual prize-giving.

The scholarship is managed by SAILI, and it covers the expenses for all five years of secondary schooling, including school fees, stationery, textbooks and uniforms. The recipient attends quarterly sessions with a maths and science focus at SAILI and also workshops on study skills and career selection.

The first recipient of the Ian Macdonald Scholarship was Sphokuhle Gxagxa. He lives with his parents, older brother and two younger sisters in a shack in Overcome Heights, on the Cape Flats. His mom is a waitress at McDonalds and his dad is a gardener.

Sphokuhle was in the Enviro Club at Hillwood and also a member of the surfing club, which Ian helped start.

When we spoke to him in 2019, Sphokuhle was due to complete Grade 8 at Muizenberg High School. We asked him what being at Muizenberg High School on the Ian Macdonald scholarship meant to him, and his response highlighted the destructive effect that gangsterism has on schooling in Lavender Hill.

For him, being able to go to school without worrying about his safety has been the biggest thing. 'It's safe at Muizenberg,' he said. 'You can do your schoolwork and take part in extramurals freely. If it weren't for the scholarship, I would probably be at Heathfield High School where there's lots of gangsterism. I'm very glad about that.'

Spokuhle is thriving at Muizenberg High. He is in the school's under-15A basketball team and was expecting to get quite a few Code 7s (80% plus marks) at the end of his Grade 8 year. 'My favourite subject is mathematics and I'm on track for 80% in it this year,' he said. 'I want to be a doctor one day, and I know that means I need to do well in maths and science. I am definitely going for it.'

Playing basketball has been great for him. 'We had quite a good team, and we won most of our matches against other schools. I was the only learner from Hillview Primary in Grade 8, but I made a lot of friends through basketball.'

Spokuhle never met Ian Macdonald, but he knows that Ian did a lot for Hillview Primary. 'I am proud to have been chosen for his scholarship and grateful for the opportunity I've been given. The interest shown in me by Katherine, the teachers, my new friends, and the facilities at Muizenberg High have made a big difference in my life. I am very happy here and I want to show everyone that I deserve it.'

Spokhule Gxagxa is clearly an awesome young man – one Fella would have loved – and is a great ambassador for his scholarship.

Lwazi (Jetro) Nkuna

We spent some time with Mel Tomlinson when we visited the PfP schools in Nelspruit. She is the driving force behind some amazing projects, and a few of the inspirational stories coming out of her leadership circles are told in earlier chapters.

Just before I left for home, Mel told me about Jetro. He had appeared on her WhatsApp feed one day when Wiseman Nkambule, a principal in her Nelspruit 2 Leadership Circle, pointed out that one of the kids in a photo posted on the circle's chat group had been through a particularly difficult time after losing his mother.

Chapter 17: A few stories about the impact on the lives of individual children

'I initially saw this as a project we could throw money at,' said Mel. 'I rallied around, put a post on Facebook requesting donations and begun what initially appeared to be a reasonably easy to do, quick-fix. How difficult can it be to get a kid a school uniform, stationery and some civvies, top-up their cupboards with foodstuffs and throw some money at the problem?'

That notion changed after Mel met Jetro. She was deeply moved by him, and now, for want of a better word, she is co-parenting him with his great-grandmother Maureen. Jetro, now in Grade 9, spends every second weekend at the Tomlinson home. Mel's husband, Cobus, takes him to gym and he is learning to swim.

'We are sending him to extra maths lessons, and we visit the library, encouraging him to read books,' Mel said. 'I have been keeping a close eye on his schoolwork and there has been an improvement in his marks, although the school he is at is not great.'

Things are looking up. Mel helped Maureen to apply for one of the bursaries granted by the Innibos Lowveld National Arts Festival. The application was successful and Jetro will be attending Curro Meridian in White River in 2020.

Mel has no children of her own, so she hasn't lived through the experience of a child's schooling before. 'This has had a profound effect on me,' she said. 'The issues I have been dealing with in my work with PfP have suddenly become personal and real. My outlook has changed, and I have realised anew how important the work that we do is.'

Jetro recently wrote Mel a letter to express his gratitude:

> *I am grateful that I have you after my mother passed away.*
>
> *My life has changed. It is as if my mother had provided me with a second mother who will look after me when she is gone. I am not worried about school because I know you are here for me when she is gone. I am really grateful for that.*
>
> *Now I am going to the gym with Uncle Cobus and I am learning to swim, I play chess with Grandpa and you took me to the Kruger National Park. I am now attending extra maths extra classes on Saturdays and in the holidays.*
>
> *Now that I know that my granny will leave me one day, I will still have a mother and I will cry on her shoulder, I am really grateful, Mel, for everything you are doing for me.*
>
> *Thanks for everything,*
>
> *May God Bless you*
> *Jetro.*

Andy Mahlangu

Paul Marketos of IsoMetrix and Marcus Heradien, the principal of Malvern Primary School were in a PfP partnership on 2016. They were in the Johannesburg 18 Leadership Circle.

Gracia Lebepe, Principal of Paul Mosaka Primary School in Soweto, was in the same circle. Gracia told her fellow circle members about William Hlalele, a very bright Grade 7 boy who was living in a shack with his granny. The story touched Paul, so he arranged for William to attend the same school as his sons, King Edward VII School (KES), which is one of the top public schools in the country.

William started in boarding school, but that did not work out, so the Marketos family opened their home to him. He is now living with them and going home to his grandmother's about every second weekend.

Although William is a bright boy who had done very well at primary school, Paul noticed that he was struggling to cope at KES. It was clear that there is gap in standards between KES and the primary school that William attended in Soweto.

Paul had been toying with the idea of setting up a scholarship to give students at Yeoville Boys' Primary School the opportunity to do their high schooling at the nearby well-resourced KES. Paul's interaction with William made him realise that it would be better to enable boys to enrol at King Edward VII Preparatory School (KEPS) in Grade 6 so that they would have a solid grounding once they got to the high school.

So, Paul set up the Yeoville Boys' Endowment as part of the King Edward VII School Trust. (Yeoville Boys' Primary is also a PfP school – we told the story of the partnership between its principal, Lindelani Singo, and Anita Moerman van Blankenburg in Chapter 3). The idea is to raise enough funds to make the trust a self-sustaining venture, earning enough interest to add one beneficiary to the programme every year.

The endowment has been established with the initial funds raised, and the first scholarship has been awarded – to Andy Mhlangu, a student who came first in Grade 3 with an average of 83%.

Andy is a hard-working, confident and polite young man. His favourite subject at school is maths, and he loves reading. He plays tennis and soccer and participates in athletics. He lives with his mother Violet, a cleaner, and his father Gilbert, who is a security guard. Andy has three brothers and a sister who was awarded a scholarship to attend the Roedean Academy.

Andy says he is excited about going to KEPS because the school has good teachers and resources. He believes attending KEPS will create better opportunities for him going forward and feels that he can contribute to the school through his academic ability and sporting talent.

'We found Andy to be a confident, well-mannered young man, who is self-assured and independent,' said Paul. 'He has strong communication skills and has a great support structure. His mother believes in a well-balanced boy who does not focus solely on academics. His overall character aligns with the ethos of KEPS. Our decision in awarding him with the scholarship was based on all these factors as well as on the fact that he lives close to the school.'

Furqaan Jacobs

Furqaan Jacobs is at Portavue Primary School in Cape Town. He is an outstanding athlete – the South African record-holder in the U13 boys 200m hurdles. Like so many talented children who come from humble family backgrounds and attend schools with little or no sports facilities, Furqaan could well have been overlooked, disappearing into a different life with his talent wasted.

Portavue is a PfP school where Principal Trevor Da Rocha is partnered with Kelly April of Coronation Fund Managers. Trevor told us the story of Furqaan.

'At the start of the 2018 school year, we were hard at work selecting learners for our inter-school athletic competition in mid-February. Learners were trying their athletic ability in various events. At the time, we had no idea of the diamond we had in our midst. Our school field is a sand patch, our equipment practically kept together by glue and nails, and we had learners who were not really interested.

'Among them was Furqaan Jacobs, who had athletics in his legs, but no dream. However, in 2018 he found the 200m hurdles. It was like a fish taking to water. His potential was immediately noticed as he sailed effortlessly over the hurdles. Then, 2019, Furqaan seemed to fly while others were walking: the Western Province U13 boys 200m hurdles record broken and set at 27.85s. This allowed him the opportunity to compete at the South African Primary Schools Athletics Provincial competition and in the national event in Gauteng, Here our boy broke the SA junior record and set the time at 27.01 seconds.'

'It all started at school where I competed in the primary school athletics competition,' Furqaan remembers. 'We practised for the big day where I got to do 200m hurdles and 80m hurdles. I was a bit nervous, but I knew I had done it before, so I can do it again. I made it to the next round, the Western Province champs, where I came second in the

80m, but won the 200m, breaking the Western Province record. That took me to the nationals in Gauteng. As I made it to the final, I realised that it is time. As the gun went off and we came around the bend of the track where I was in second place, I pushed hard and dipped and broke the South African record, and that's basically it.'

'But we nearly did not have Furqaan at this event or have him achieve this lifetime achievement,' Trevor said. 'Financially, his parents were not able to support him. Kelly April and Coronation came in at the 11th hour to make this boy's dream and his achievement a reality. Kelly sourced some funding so that he could be kitted out with all of his athletic apparel. To any sportsman, the sense of pride the uniform gives adds energy to all your efforts.'

Furqaan is aware of the role Kelly played, and he is grateful to her. 'Thanks to Ms Kelly for helping me with my kit. I could only get the vest and the shorts, but she helped me with all of my kit. It really made me feel special when I walked around with my team. I am happy that she helped. Now I can go on to try even harder for new records in the future,' he said.

'Kelly's contribution cannot be minimised. Furqaan now has a dream: to become a full South African junior champion and then to represent our beautiful country at the Olympics one day,' Trevor concluded.

Chapter 18

Contributions from principals who have been part of PfP

"The single most important factor in school change is the role of the principal leader." – Professor Jonathan Jansen

For the purposes of this book, we could only visit a small percentage of the PfP schools and partnerships across the country, but we wanted to create a space for more principals to share their stories so we invited the other principals to send us their comments on the experience.

Here are their contributions:

Andre Engel, Principal of Wesley Methodist Practising School, Cape Town, Western Cape

PfP has been an invaluable journey for me. As a young and new principal, it has really set me up for a successful career.

The training has been immense and life-changing. From the manner in which meetings are conducted to the way in which I position myself in terms of the vocabulary I use; everything has contributed towards becoming more purposeful and effective.

Time to Think changed the way we conduct our meetings. Everyone must 'land' in the room and people's voices must be heard. Respectful listening is encouraged and only statements that are to the benefit of the speaker are allowed. This session also helped in finding solutions to problems more readily through formulating good questions. The quality of the question determines the quality of the answer!

The value of 'contracting' as part of the Flawless Consulting sessions cannot be overstated. This enabled me to negotiate more precise job descriptions with every member of staff, ensuring they understood their roles with greater clarity and knew exactly what the expectations were.

Through Community Building I really ventured on a private journey in terms of where I am in relation to the community I serve. This session sent me on a drive of finding just how I can serve this community in terms of its needs and not mine.

Apart from the workshops and training, the CoP was vital to my survival as a new principal. This forum immediately exposed me to a network of skilled and experienced principals and business partners with whom I could liaise and call up when the need arose. This helped me get through the nitty-gritty of being a principal and made my job so much easier.

Annemien Holtzhausen, Principal of Bokamoso Intermediate School, Potchefstroom, North West Province

2017 was a difficult year for me. I almost wanted to quit the education system.

Then a wonderful journey started in November 2018 when I was chosen as one of the 10 principals to take part in the PfP programme in Potchefstroom. I was not so sure what to expect from the programme.

Rina Vogler made a perfect match when she matched me with my partner (Dennis Coetzee). We both have very good leadership skills, but he just knew how to approach and work with me.

The partnership was like a jolly roller coaster ride. I involved Dennis in all the activities at school and also taught him a lot about the education system. I was one of the youngest principals, and Dennis was a mentor and life coach who added a lot to my personal development. He motivated and supported me in every possible way. With Dennis by my side, anything was possible because I knew my partner was there to catch and support me when I fell.

In 2018 I entered the school into a competition for the SQLTC (School Quality Teaching and Learning Campaign) Best Multi-grade Farm School: the school got position 1 (provincial Level). In 2019 I entered for the National Teachers Award and won sub-district level and came second in the district level. This was all possible because I had a Super Hero partner. He motivated me to overcome all the fears that crossed my path in 2017. I even ended up applying for a higher principal post.

We were both very busy at work, but we made sure we made time for the programme and for each other. We talked on a daily basis and decided not to end our partnership after the PfP course ended.

Dennis was an angel sent over my path when I needed someone the most, and that's all thanks to the PfP programme. I couldn't have asked for a better partner.

Carlin Symonds, Principal of Cedar Primary School Bonteheuwel, Cape Town, Western Cape

The value I received from being part of PfP:

Professionally

Assistance from a group when facing and dealing with challenges is valuable. It broadens your horizons; you get insight into challenges of other schools as well as businesses. You learn from the experiences of others.

Training Sessions
Practical role-play makes it easier to implement. We were exposed to a vast variety of expertise; it goes way beyond your imagination. It aims to develop participants holistically.

Personally
The partnership gave me more confidence to try out new ideas. It tends to motivate you to be more driven and passionate in daily execution of goals. It encourages personal growth, especially with leadership responsibilities.

Conclusion
We made a difference and an impact through the partnership in the school. New networks were formed. Some of the goals are long-term goals. I realised that it is not just a 12-month partnership, but it could be a life-long journey. Through the partnership, just when you think you have reached the end, new possibilities arise and you realise that the possibilities are actually endless.

Thank you to PfP for this valuable experience.

Dominic Raphahlelo, Principal of Mokone Primary
Cape Town, Western Cape

Taking part in the programme provided by PfP in leadership gave me the opportunity to understand how the business world approaches their day-to-day situations. Besides the corporate world, I got connected with a number of school principals and was able to network and learn from them. The workshops made me aware about experiences of life across the spectrum of Ubuntu.

I became aware of the need to listen to others qualitatively and avoid chipping in during conversations. I am on my journey to learn to work with the SMT as a team. The skills of contracting and Time to Think play out in my development and approach when dealing with people, both in the work situation and in my life generally.

The workshop with the SMT helped me to understand my colleagues and their experiences better and how they will react to life challenges and pressures in our working environment.

We weren't able to make all the changes we wanted to see during the 12 month period, but Liz (my partner) and I agreed that our partnership will continue beyond the 'celebration of PfP' event towards achieving what we set out in our plan.

In view of all, I know there are great possibilities to improve relationships, management, and the operations of the SMT to enhance Mokone Primary learners' achievement, both academically and in the extra curriculum activities that go towards enriching everyone's self-esteem.

Eunice Serine Manasse, Principal of Harmony Primary School, Cape Town, Western Cape

What an amazing and empowering programme!

I am fortunate and unreservedly grateful to be part of a PfP circle, and I am blessed to be partnered with Sullivan. I joined PfP in 2018 to acquire the necessary skills to manage our school like a corporate institution. Through leveraging off Sullivan and the rest of the PfP community during workshops, and sharing of relevant business management information, I have managed to improve my business skills a little bit at a time. I have applied these learnings together with my experience as an educator to grow our school's brand, develop its community (learners, educators and other stakeholders) holistically and improve the operations at our school.

Through consultation and the application of strategically focused leadership to drive achievement of our agreed-upon outcomes, I have also managed to attract good staff with the right fit to our school to support our quest for achieving our goals.

This programme assisted me in obtaining valuable skills that enabled me to involve the community and build healthy relationships between the school and community. It furthermore accelerated my development through networking with outside colleagues. It helped me to drive fruitful engagement with other schools in the immediate area and initiate and maintain internal collaboration with **all** the members of staff at our school and, critically, with the SGB and parents.

Our focus was on creating partnerships for holistic growth and on development that can be sustained at the right pace for all of us, for as long as it contributed to our collective goals.

The workshops I attended during my PfP journey assisted me in realising that the focus should be more on *people and relationships*. The CoP meetings evolved into a social gathering between the different principals and business partners, creating a platform of sharing our different, yet similar, worlds.

I value the regular meetings with Sullivan and his significant input that benefitted my leadership qualities to the advantage of the school and the achievement of our planned objectives. Sullivan's guidance and advice made me realise that a structured public-private partnership in the right framework can result in many constructive possibilities. The foundation for these partnerships were laid by the various facilitators who created a greater cohort of partnering school principals who otherwise would never have met and therefore not experienced each other's world of education.

I strongly recommend that this programme should be a requirement for all principals in the pursuit of meaningful collaboration and positive change in all schools.

Hasina Mahomed, Principal of Alpha Primary School
Lenasia, Gauteng

The PfP journey taught me that we are best when we are a part of a community that utilises different strengths, skills and abilities. My interaction with other principals and business partners during the Community of Practice meetings made me aware of the different leadership styles and the challenges that we principals face in our respective communities. I began to admire the strength that each principal possessed and the willingness that they had to continue to do their very best in leading the institutions tasked with educating our nation.

The developmental workshops Time to Think, Flawless Consulting and Community Building have made me a better leader and, most importantly, a better person. I am more empowered and confident to face the challenges that come my way. A special mention of Time to Think has to be made. This was a learning experience during which I acquired the skills of active listening and incisive questioning, and this has changed my relationship with people on a personal as well as professional level.

Imtiaz Adams, Principal of Surrey Primary School
Cape Town, Western Cape

My partnership with PfP has transformed me into a Principal of Change. One of the early take-home lessons was 'Listening to Lead Forward' by looking for the positive connections between myself and the other person(s). This action, and learning about partnership between me and my business partner, enabled social cohesion and me to become a change leader in our school and communities.

The business model of getting feedback from stakeholders was essential to growth and performance. This confirmed that we have a shared purpose and enabled us to rethink the why, what and how for delivering a good quality curriculum which is infused with hope and a vision for our communities.

The feedback I give is now anchored in fairness, focus, and frequency. This provides opportunities for teachers to have ownership and agency in their classroom management and seeing themselves as part of a larger purpose, namely equipping learners for the Fourth Industrial Revolution.

I've learned that we can move from good to great whilst in the active processes of leadership and creating possibilities in educational change; opportunities don't wait and 'done' is better than perfect.

PfP also taught me to look inward in order to move onward. If staff are not moving forward, do we focus on their resistance or our leadership? Someone with an external locus of control blames outside forces for everything, but with an internal locus of control I believe that I can influence events and outcomes. Teachers who believe this might decide to take some risks, try new strategies, or design an authentic project to meet the needs of learners.

John Matiso, Principal of Manzomthombo Senior Secondary School, Cape Town, Western Cape

Partners for Possibility was a very exciting experience in my life and an eye-opener as it gave me an opportunity to reflect on my role as a manager of an institution in relation to how I engage with myself, my management team, staff members and the community at large.

The most important learning came from being in a learning community with colleagues and peers. This enabled me to listen to others and then reflect, review and plan to improve.

The programme was of great benefit to me as it empowered me on how best one has to self-manage in order to improve and effectively coordinate team management as opposed to team control.

Kevin Velensky, Principal of Portia Primary School Lansdowne, Cape Town, Western Cape

My engagement with the PfP programme and my business partner, Lucille Meyer, CEO of the Chrysalis Academy, has influenced my leadership capabilities and my view on the power of partnerships. Lucille and I have forged a strong bond based on trust, accountability and authenticity.

I view myself as an influencer, a role-player in the redesign of the education landscape with the ultimate goal of producing value-adding citizens. The CoP has created opportunities for real educational and best practice conversations; this led me to become conscientious in my role as a reflective practitioner.

The many professional and personal development opportunities created through this programme have increased my awareness of the importance of quality relationships with people, whether directly or indirectly. Through these learnings, I have re-contracted more meaningfully with my own family. I am grounded and confident in who I am and what I represent.

Through Partners for Possibility, I have reaffirmed my Africanacity[33].

Lucille and I have committed to a sustained programme of support and intervention to ensure we influence the education system. We will continue to pursue collaboration with authentic partners. The journey has begun!

---

33 Africanicity is a term created by Absa Bank that means 'The distinctly African ability to always find ways to get things done.'

Mathipa Nelson Poopedi, Principal of Sinethemba Senior Secondary, Cape Town, Western Cape

There is a saying: 'If everyone is thinking the same, someone is not thinking.' Being a pracademic[34], I like to invest my time and energy into programmes or projects that apply solid practice underpinned by sound and relevant theory.

PfP helps to create an authentic relationship built on trust, respect and integrity. As a school leader and business partner, you are able to articulate your concerns and aspirations in a 'thinking space' without being judged. In this way, you are free to ask powerful questions and listen to answers. This thinking process allows you to realise that you already have the answers to your problems.

PfP brings possibility to impossibility. It encourages the power of positive thinking. At a time when the schools are engulfed with negative stories, I am grateful to have been accepted to the PfP community.

Matshedisho Pobe, Principal of Tebelelo Primary School, Bloemfontein, Free State

It is my second year as a principal at Tebelelo Primary School. The PfP programme came at the right time as I needed a partner and fresh ideas which would take the school forward.

The highlight of the year has been my partnership with Frank Makhabane, who is a lecturer in accounting at UFS (University of the Free State) and a business owner as well. He has become a valued friend in the long run. With his experience of how things are done in business, he helped empower me to knock on the door – which I had previously shunned.

As a result, our Career Day for 2019 was different as students from UFS visited the Grade 7 learners to talk about the various careers. Furthermore, a chess professional visited our school to hold a workshop for the chess players and encourage the other children who have never played chess before to enrol for chess in the school. This motivated the learners to do well in their academic work as well.

Our staff meetings have been revolutionized. All the teachers take part as we begin every meeting with a circle formation, and everyone must have their say. Thereafter, the items are discussed in smaller groups where the groups then go on to give feedback to the larger group. All the teachers at our school have expressed satisfaction with this new method of running the staff meetings.

I strongly recommend that more school principals should be given an opportunity to participate in this valuable experience.

---

34 Someone who is both an academic and an active practitioner in their subject area.

Peter Makgatho, Principal of Carter Primary School
Johannesburg, Gauteng

I had a tumultuous experience when I became a principal in 2015. Some of the staff members did not want to accept me as their principal. They made my life miserable and wrote a myriad of grievances to SACE, the MEC's office, our district director and our HOD. Investigations were done, and that resulted in me doubting my ability as a principal. My self-esteem was low and I wanted to please people so that they can accept me.

Then I joined the PfP project.

I had a business partner who listened attentively to my challenges and helped me to remove my defective assumptions. She was always there to lean on and to walk with me during the journey. The cherry on top is when we go through CoP meetings where we meet with other business partners who come up with business perspectives into our leadership and management. They are very objective and non-judgemental when listening to our challenges. They give us worthwhile perspectives and that helps us to be prudent in executing our duties.

In Flawless Consulting I was taught how to be assertive and set boundaries. Now I know that my yes means nothing if I cannot say no and I have bravely set boundaries with the SGB.

I attended all School Leadership Forums because I learn a lot of things that I can use in my school. I am a better principal since I joined PfP. If I had not, I think I would have crumbled based on the situation I was in. I wouldn't trade PfP for anything. I wish most principals could be part of this worthwhile project which makes a huge difference to us as principals.

Ronel Baker, Principal of Soneike High School
Cape Town, Western Cape

My journey started in 2017. I've grown as a leader and manager. PfP afforded me so many opportunities to grow my school into a centre of excellence.

Our STEM space programme through XinaBoX has been showcased on BBC and CNN. My school›s library and literacy programme benefitted tremendously with sponsors who blessed the school with mobile libraries.

My business partner, Yolanda Soobramoney from Metropolitan, introduced the Kickstarz Grade 11 financial literacy programme and our learners were taught entrepreneurship, budgeting and savings. They designed their own sneakers and had the chance to win a pair of the shoes they had designed.

We are a 'water-saving champion' school. Our school's greening project was given a boost when Trees4Schools planted grass and donated trees. My school is a Global Exploration[35]

---

35 Global Exploration is a Netherlands-based organisation that brings together young people from all over the world so that they can learn from each other.

school. We've hosted three groups of students from the Netherlands, and next year we will join their conference in the Netherlands.

These are a few of the many opportunities that I grabbed without hesitation when an e-mail came from Symphonia. The journey still continues.

Sally Mampa, Principal of Ipontshe Primary School Johannesburg, Gauteng

PfP has broadened my managerial skills as a principal. Partnering with different team members from other schools and from the business sector has widened my methods of operating and skills.

PfP has assisted me in being the best manager I could have ever imagined. My communication skills have improved. I have also learned to value other stakeholders and the inputs they present during meetings to make our school the best place for learners to learn and to maximise their potential. I am challenged to perform above the required standards because of the engagements we shared with my team members through PfP.

I wish PfP was an ongoing programme because I feel I still need to engage and learn more from my fellow members. Thanks a million PfP!

Samuel Skosana, Principal of Rosina Sedibane Modiba School, Ladium, Tshwane, Gauteng

My journey with PfP started in 2016 after being introduced by Mrs Carol Phasha. We are grateful to her for this has assisted our school greatly. Much appreciated.

PfP should be recommended to all principals of both primary and secondary schools because of its various advantages.

I am grateful to Marichen Mortimer, a workaholic and strong woman highly committed to improving performance, who co-ordinated all our meetings and introduced me to Mr Geoffrey Lee from Absa and his great team (Tina, Ability, Almarie and Thea). I am so grateful for their support.

Together we set up key objectives and goals for finances, infrastructure, sports and academics. He was so helpful because our school's finances have drastically improved.

Personally, I am now totally a different leader since I participated in PfP.

I learned a lot from the three courses (Time to Think, Flawless Consulting and Community Building). One of the things I have learned is that in life, challenges or problems should be regarded as possibilities. From other principals, I have learned that sharing good practices was the most valuable lesson in education. Thank you colleagues!

This also inspired and motivated me to know that I was not alone. I now listen to understand without interruption. I don't assume anymore but ensure that I have facts.

I hereby wish to express my sincere gratitude and appreciation for the opportunity to be a part of this wonderful and outstanding programme. May God continue to provide, protect and bless everyone.

Sandile Mzoneli, Principal of Bonela Primary School
Durban, Kwazulu-Natal

The PfP programme has sharpened my leadership skills and helped me identify areas for my teachers to benefit from the professional development workshops we've organised.

I'm aware of the importance of emotional wellness – that of my learners, teachers and parents/guardians.

It's so reassuring that support is available to the Bonela family.

My professional network and skills source has grown enormously. I pause for reflective practice and sound planning. Bonela Primary has joined the Governing Body Foundation and is benefitting from the expertise of this organisation.

As a leader and manager, I gained so much from the Flawless Consulting workshop. I deal with stakeholders more decisively, and I'm able to prioritise and articulate the needs of the school more efficiently. My resilience and EQ have increased enormously and I feel better equipped to 'keep my head when others are losing theirs'.

Networking with schools which are far less resourced than Bonela Primary has made me appreciative of our achievements: our short and medium-term planning; participation by many more stakeholders; enhanced academic programmes; improved infrastructure; an active fundraising committee and especially the support of our relatively new SGB. I'm delighted that other PfP principals and teachers are able to tap into our resources and utilize our learning spaces.

We're developing enrichment activities for above-average learners and identifying junior leaders. Mental health issues are being addressed timeously, and there are remedial lessons and small group tuition. We've upgraded the library and there are cheerful colours in the art room and Grade R areas. New co-curricular activities have been introduced and there's an attractive garden at the entrance of the school.

I express appreciation to Dr Louise van Rhyn, LPF Jackie Warner, the DBN9 Leadership Circle, business leader Yvonne Johnstone and the band of wonderful volunteers who have partnered with Bonela Primary School.

Thank you!
We continue to dream......

Shapule Modjadji, Principal of Makgongoana High School, Polokwane, Limpopo

I was appointed as a principal of Makgongoana High School in February 2017. It was difficult for me to cope with a secondary school environment because for 22 years I had been working as a primary teacher. The school was dysfunctional. Learners were ill-disciplined, educators' morale was low with no commitment to their work, the SGB did not know their responsibilities, there was a gap between the school and the parents (no parental involvement) and, actually, everybody did as they pleased.

As a perfectionist, I felt I had to change things around and this is when I was connected to PfP. Initially, I thought PfP's mandate was to give hand-outs, but no; PfP came into my life and empowered me. I do not regret getting involved with PfP.

When I became involved with PfP, I saw the opportunity of turning things around in our school. On 23 October 2017 I met the other business leaders and principals in my leadership circle. Amongst them was my business partner, Mapinini. This man became an inspiration to my journey. With him I was fortunate because he was the SGB chairperson of another school in Seshego. He came to my life, and we formed an amazing partnership.

When I joined the school, the pass rate was at 20% (2016). The year I joined the school we improved to 39.1% (2017).

The school has a serious problem with regard to infrastructure. The school has four blocks of three classrooms each. One of these classrooms has been converted into principal's office, staffroom and storeroom for the National School Nutrition Programme. The other three blocks accommodate learners. We also have four mobile classrooms which accommodate Grade 8 and 9 learners. In Grade 8, for example, there are 219 learners who share two mobile classes (112 learners in one mobile meant for 40 learners).

My business partner and I had to strategise in order to turn things around. This was 2018 when PfP was in full force, when we were attending CoP meetings. Things started to change bit by bit.

When I attended Flawless Consulting, I realised that I am capable. Flawless Consulting was an eye-opener to me because through this workshop I was able to grow as an individual and also in the work environment. Flawless Consulting taught me to establish and also maintain partnerships with the SGB, SMT, teachers and the learners as clients in the school environment. I have also learned to contract and negotiate and also give feedback. What is more important is to listen. In Flawless Consulting I also learned that in consulting we negotiate wants, deal with resistance, and close the meetings.

I have learned to understand and tackle different situations. It is not easy to lead as a woman. Even if I have many obligations, the PfP journey was helpful to both my family at home and my family at work. I am able to juggle work, family, social and my personal studies (I am currently making corrections to my PhD thesis). I can now listen, reflect, enquire and talk. I have learned to say no. There are people who want to take advantage of me as a woman, but it's not easy for them because of the way I deal with them. This is primarily because PfP made me a strong person inside and outside.

Together with Mapinini, we came up with a plan on how we should turn things around. Mapinini came to the school and we trained the SGB on their roles and responsibilities. The SGB, in turn, had to get parents to be involved in the education of their children.

I also emphasised the importance of teamwork, commitment and cohesion between the SMT, teachers and learners. Everybody had to take responsibility for their own actions. The SMT had to account for the performance of their departments, the educators had to account for the performance of their subject and learners had to account for their performance. This indeed yielded positive results because it's not an easy task to account.

Things started to improve when I attended the Community Building workshop with the SGB and SMT. It is when I realised that nobody shall fix Makgongoana's challenges except all the stakeholders in Makgongoana. This is when I actually realised that the SMT, SGB, parents and the community at large have the responsibility to fix their challenges; not PfP. PfP is actually there to bring cohesion between us as principals and business leaders and also to empower us to bring change in our schools and communities.

Through the 8 CoP meetings that I attended, I learned that it is important to share your thoughts, your ideas, your challenges, your weaknesses and your strengths. What an amazing experience I had with these principals and business leaders. They were and still are awesome. Initially, I wouldn't share my thoughts with anyone. But I learned that it is important to share our experiences so that we can learn from each other.

Having to do a SWOT analysis with Mapinini stood out for me. A leader is someone who is able to give direction and change situations. But what is important is that I am able to influence my colleagues so that we can make changes within this community.

When I came to this school, everybody did as they pleased. But since I have been here, educators' conduct is changing to realise the vision and mission of the school. This is very important to me as a leader. I am able to communicate with them through meetings, briefings, a WhatsApp group for both educators and SMT, and parents receive newsletters. These communication strategies are working for us as a school.

Some parents are able to come to school to discuss challenges with regard to their children's performance, and the SGB is fully involved in school governance issues.

The school is now the talk of the community. Teachers are committed, learners are disciplined and dedicated to their schoolwork, the SGB is fully involved and everybody is playing their role. Parents have started to take the school seriously because we report to them on a quarterly basis about their children's performance and conduct. Even those parents who took their children to other schools away from the

Makanye Village have started to bring their children to Makgongoana High School. Teachers, SGB and parents can see that I have brought changes to the school. It was very difficult, but I am trying.

There were instances where people were resisting change, even though it was for a good cause. But as a leader, I have to surround myself with all the stakeholders in order to fulfil the vision and mission of the school. Just to give an example; one SMT member once said to me 'Principal, your presence here has brought many changes. Learners used to get their first term results in mid-May and you have made history since you have been here. This is a positive change according to me.'

Because of our planning and the continued support of Mapinini, in 2018 we implemented a matric camp for a week at school. All Grade 12 learners and their teachers camped at the school. Our results improved from 39.1% to 69.7%. Our school received a provincial award for the most improved school in the province when results were released in 2019. This is as a result of the journey I had in PfP.

Our target for 2019 was 80%. But guess what? Our learners and educators worked beyond the call of duty and we are now at 88.2%. This performance was acknowledged yet again by Limpopo MEC of Education Polly Bishielo as the 2nd most improved school in the province on the 8th of January 2020. Watch the space... more is yet to come.

Because of our efforts as a school, and Mapinini's inputs, the Department of Education has approved our request for classrooms. In 2020 they will be building 10 classrooms, an admin block and nutrition centre. This will be our biggest achievement apart from learner performance. We also applied for sports equipment from the Lottery and this was approved. They gave us equipment and sports clothes worth R50,000.

The PfP journey will never stop. Mapinini and I have planned to source donations and funds for a library, laboratory, computer centre, school hall and functional ablution facilities. The journey is still long, but we will reach our destination as a school. This journey has been amazing so far. We still have challenges like gangsterism and drug abuse which makes it difficult for us to pursue our vision at times.

Our facilitator Marietjie, Oh!! What a beautiful soul she is. This lady is selfless, committed and loves what she is doing. I will always be indebted to her.

Thank you very much PfP. Because of you, my life has changed dramatically. There is a saying which goes: 'A bird sitting on a tree is never afraid of the branch breaking, because its trust is not on the branch, but on its own wings.' Because of PfP, I will always believe in myself, I can boldly say 'I am what I am today because of PfP.'

Snooky Msibi, Principal of Sekwati Primary School, Johannesburg, Gauteng

It was a blessing for me to attend the South African Principals' Association Conference in 2017 where Partners for Possibility was presented. I registered immediately without hesitation and I don't regret my decision. In September 2017, I was placed in the JHB29 Leadership Circle, led by Savanthika Pillay.

I partnered with Mr Mahmood Sonday. As thinking partners, we shared positive aspects and practices that make both our leadership effective. We contracted and related well and flawlessly, as per Peter Block's recommendations.

He introduced me to Shape of Emotion[36] which is led by Matthew Green and Chantal Dawtrey. Their life skills programme helped us to understand our inner being and relate better in our relationship with the school and business communities.

The young engineers from E-Squared in Sandton exposed learners to the world of robotics and technology. It was interesting to see learners being self-driven to build a robot by putting the logistics together – an experience required by today's youth to improve education in South Africa.

Thank you for exposing me to the world of reality. I met Reel Gardening, and together we promoted healthy living and school nutrition. I also met Wits[37] lecturer Mr Astonishment Mapurisa, who provides the school with social services. I met Vodacom and CNA. They provided learners with hygiene products and Christmas goodies. It was a great honour to be given a platform to speak on behalf of principals alongside the MEC, Mr Panyaza Lesufi. Mrs Sonday, Mahmood's wife, is currently busy with gifted learners and occupational therapy in our school. Thank you for making me who I am. I stand proud to be a partner and an alumnus.

Viva Partners for Possibility!

Thomas Hlongwane, Principal of Pretoria Central High School, Pretoria, Gauteng

Partners for Possibility was an eye-opener for me. My partner was Cassim Ibrahim, a well-established CA who was working for KPMG in Pretoria. Cassim has a strong passion for mathematics and his focus from day one was to improve our mathematics results. When we analysed our poor results in mathematics, we realised that the problem does not start in Grade 12; it starts somewhere along the line.

What we learned with this issue was that the problem of low mathematics passes starts way back in Grade 8 and 9. We therefore strategised to focus on Grade 8 and 9. This has impacted positively in my leadership of the school because I know that I need to allocate strong mathematics teachers in the lower grades. We are looking forward to 2020 when these learners who started with this focused area get to Grade 12.

---

36 Based on recent developments in neuroscience, Shape of Emotion is a model, process and tool for regulating inner feelings to release emotions that contribute to stress and physical illness.
37 University of the Witwatersrand, Johannesburg.

Working together, my business partner and I realised that a number of learners do not know what to do after passing matric. We decided to conduct career guidance workshops for learners and life orientation (LO) teachers. The involvement of KPMG career guidance personnel brought expert perspective. This impacted positively in my leadership because both learners and LO teachers knew that I am serious about the careers of our learners. The involvement of LO teachers also meant that the project would be sustainable.

But the biggest lesson I learned from PfP is problem-solving. I remember giving a case study in the Time to Think workshop which was eventually used by everyone for the day. There was an issue of a teacher who gossiped about another educator during a school trip. I mediated this issue by bringing all the parties involved, including the two teachers and all the learners that were present when the gossip happened.

I learned that issues of gossip can be very destructive to the running of the school. During the workshop, this issue was used as a case study and a lot of valuable approaches to solving it were explored. I liked the part when members in the circle asked probing questions to understand the issue better. This led to broad-based involvement of everyone. This has impacted positively on my leadership because problem-solving is now an activity which involves broad-based involvement of all parties.

In July 2017 my business partner unfortunately left South Africa to join KPMG Saudi Arabia, but the experience I gained through this programme will remain valuable.

Tracy Rae, Principal of Fairways Primary School, Johannesburg, Gauteng

I have been in education for 39 years and have been a principal in a primary school for the past 13 years. I was introduced to Partners for Possibility soon after I was appointed but felt that I was not equipped to join the programme at the time because I was so 'green'. I subsequently applied a number of times before being considered in 2018, and what a journey of possibilities it has been…

The journey provided me with a number of skills that I was able to put into practice to better assist in the day-to-day running of the school by spending hours reflecting on the manner in which I conduct myself in my relationships with colleagues, family, friends, parents and children. PfP helped me realise that no man is an island and that when you are able to voice concerns in an open and transparent climate, people know exactly where you are coming from and what is expected from them. In turn, they are able to express more openly what they expect from me.

The networking of principals and corporate company partners has provided us with a platform to obtain answers which in the past would not have been possible. Through the journey, I am no longer afraid to show my vulnerability, have faced challenges with greater confidence and am more open to ask for support when required.

My manner in dealing with the staff has changed. Where I am able to give of my time immediately I do so and give my colleagues the opportunity to speak without interruption, only asking for clarity when required. They, in turn, have come up with answers on their own.

I have also confidently said no when I am not able to do something, instead of breaking my neck to get things done and then feeling that it was not my best effort. This has afforded me some quality time to do what I chose to do without guilt. This has also been carried over in my private life. I allow life to happen and deal with it in my own time.

This partnership has improved my confidence in general and came about at a very trying time in my tenure as principal. The support received from my partner, Zeenat Harper-Valentine from Sun International, was invaluable. Without judging, the support provided was such that I knew I was not standing alone, that the team were there to support actions to improve the situation within the school in the best interest of all.

The staff, in turn, were included in the many training sessions offered to the school through Partners for Possibility – taking responsibility for their own personal development. I have been humbled by the experiences I have had along the way in our leadership circle and have witnessed the successes that have been made possible through this amazing programme.

My journey has been a positive one, and I would like to take the skills learned in the Community Building workshop to greater heights within the school to turn the parental and community involvement around to the point that every child has a parent or guardian at every function organised at the school. The value of this course has been based on social, emotional, educational and spiritual aspects, and no monetary value can equate to it.

Friendships have been forged for life, and the journey is sure to continue. I believe that all educators aspiring to lead would benefit from joining the programme.

Trevor DaRocha, Principal of Portavue Primary School, Cape Town, Western Cape

I am still a novice principal; 2018 was the third year of my principalship. When PfP came knocking the first time I was not ready, but the coordinator was persistent and I signed up. Somehow, I had to find time for workshops, meetings, lunches and a business partner.

I was paired with a ball of energy, totally the opposite of myself. But we had two things in common: love for education and a need to make a difference. Kelly, from the start, got me thinking, reflecting and rethinking. At first, far too many scattered ideas swam around in my head. Kelly would force me to focus on what do I want.

From a business perspective, the bottom-line always read results. My strategic leadership skills were severely challenged by this go-getter. She would constantly ask me, 'What do you need to make this difference?' For this reason, our first year was not very productive.

But, after a year of PfP, I suddenly realised what being a partnership means. It means you have the possibility of achieving that far out goal. This year I successfully oversaw the start of three projects, all because of my different mindset to business, partnerships and progress:

- a Learning Resources Centre – *completed*
- a boardroom for meeting – *in progress*, and
- a school hall – *in negotiation with local government*.

Educational progress is not just my responsibility anymore. Educational progress is tied in with a greater social revolution. Unfortunately, we are leaving many of our 'township' parents behind, but we cannot leave our 'township' children behind. As a principal, my business is education, but as a partner, our business is creating the South Africa we want our children to inherit. This is what I believe PfP made possible for me.

The greatest lesson I learned is that, as a leader and manager, I am constantly evolving: what I do at this grassroots level of education is instilling in my children a sense of pride and possibility.

Thank you PfP.
At Portavue Primary School this is my new mantra:
Positivity + Possibility = Success

Zamani Ngidi, Principal of Clernaville Primary School, Durban, Kwazulu-Natal

I was introduced to PfP in 2015, immediately after assuming my responsibility as the principal of Clernaville Primary School. I didn't think twice though I was a little bit reluctant given the handful of stakeholders (teachers and governing body- parent component) who criticised all my endeavours of changing the school for the better. It was difficult even to introduce a new project in the school. The union would demand that all the decisions be reversed.

While waiting for things to unfold, Jokkie (a business leader) was introduced to me as my partner and we had a series of interviews. I preferred to meet him outside the school premises because the working environment was polluted in such a way that I was suffocating. What I noticed about my partner was that he knew no barrier that will hinder one's success. Jokkie would sometimes give me some activities to perform at school, only to find that I would come back to him complaining. I even made several attempts to quit the profession or change schools.

Jokkie started a series of developmental meetings with the various school stakeholders. He presented the following workshops: Boundaries, Mind Sets and many more. He even assisted and taught the SGB to formulate a working school budget. After realising the rigidity of my stakeholders, Jokkie then understood my frustrations and assisted me in finding my strengths (StrengthsFinder 2.0 by Tom Rath). The following were discovered as my strengths: relator, individualisation, achiever, connectedness and empathy. My frustration was mainly caused by my failure to understand my strengths.

Eighteen months later there was a drastic change in my school management, governance and leadership. As a result, the office of the Durban North Circuit Management Centre tasked me with the responsibility to caretake a school that was dysfunctional. Within three months, with knowledge, skills and the strengths identified, I was able to bring stability in the school. I have also been requested by a handful of principals and SGB chairpersons to bridge the gap between management and governance. Clernaville Primary has become a fountain of knowledge for neighbouring schools.

Jokkie never minces words: seeing the condition of the ablution block in my school, he told me that if you cannot ablute properly, you cannot learn, and the academic performance of my school was in line with the statement presented. I then started working on renovations and an additional ablution blocks project, which has recently been completed.

Without PfP, I would have failed as a school principal.

Zelda Schonken, Principal of Nottingham Road Primary School, Nottingham Road, Kwazulu-Natal

I became a part of this programme filled with trepidation and wondering where this is going to lead to. What is required of me? How will this unfold?

The strange part of it all was that I had no expectations and only a limited idea of the programme.

But this all changed ten minutes into Karen McKenzie's presentation. Her warmth, enthusiasm and energy spelled it out loud and clear: this is going to be the year that I am nurtured and cared for, where I am going to be empowered to develop into a New Age leader.

Now I was starting to feel more comfortable...and then I was introduced to my business partner.

Amazing. Immediately one became two, and by now I was feeling a great sense of belonging.

Suddenly I had a person who was going to walk this journey with me.

A confidante. Someone who shares my love and vision for my school and special learners.

I was no longer an island. Three workshops were presented to us which made me realise things about myself that I did not know existed! Much like doing different exercises and using muscles that you did not know you had...and at times, it hurt!

The presenters were knowledgeable and their presentations were riveting.

My partner and I reached a comfortable platform where we now share more than just the school. My school is now my partner's school too.

We have set out goals and plans to improve various aspects of our school, and in our partnership we have achieved success.

We are now thinking bigger and better...and because of this empowering PfP programme I have grown into a confident leader, leading in a totally different way than I ever dreamed I would!

Thank you PfP for making me this person. The evidence lies in the positive relationships that I have with the parents, staff and community.

For me, every leader should have this privilege of living the PfP course - it would change the face of education.

Chapter 19

Contributions from business leaders who have been part of PfP

"Just as the good life is something beyond the pleasant life, the meaningful life is beyond the good life." – Martin Seligman

In the spirit of Symphonia (the sounding together of all the voices), we invited business leaders to share something about their experience of being part of PfP:

Andries Breytenbach, Marketing and Communications Consultant, Cape Town, Western Cape

In 2006 a friend handed me a copy of a book by Rosamund and Benjamin Zander, *The Art of Possibility: Transforming Professional and Personal Life*. My friend knew that the book would come in handy as I had just left a large ad agency group and was about to 'transform my own professional and personal life' into the scary world of a 'self-employed business consultant'.

In December of 2008, I attended a pre-concert talk held by none other than world-renowned conductor Benjamin Zander. He was about to conduct the Cape Town Philharmonic Orchestra's performance of Beethoven's 9th Symphony. Ben's pre-concert talks had built the reputation of 'taking the stuffy and dull traditional pre-concert talk and turning it into a message that is part motivational and part evangelical'. This talk was no exception.

A few days later I attended a lecture by Ben Zander in the CTICC[38] on his favourite topic *The Art of Possibility*, breathtakingly demonstrated through the on-stage coaching of three young classical musicians, including none other than the, then, young and unknown soprano Pretty Yende. Today Pretty Yende is South Africa's pride and joy as she is celebrated as one of the world's foremost sopranos and regularly performs on the world's most famous opera stages.

It was Louise van Rhyn's Symphonia Leadership Development who had invited Ben and Rosamund to South Africa. I didn't know Louise at the time but by pure chance happened to sit next to her father during Ben's lecture. Dr Meyer and I had such an intriguing conversation (about his daughter) that I simply couldn't resist emailing Louise, hoping that my encounter with her father would get me some time in the diary of this manically busy professional. Well, it did, and Louise and I finally met.

Since that meeting, I've attended all of Louise's condensed SAODN[39] training sessions, the full sessions with Peter Block on Community Building, Nancy Klein's Time To Think, Flawless

---

38 Cape Town International Convention Centre
39 South African Organisational Development Network

Consulting and several others. A few years later I joined Symphonia's PfP programme and became the business partner of the principal of Du Noon Primary. My partner and I did all the training together. I enjoyed the training even more the second time around as the learnings and shared experiences with my training partner, who faced completely different challenges to those typically faced by executives of large corporates, placed a completely new and fresh lens on everything.

It directly influenced and fundamentally changed the way I conducted my own business consulting. It changed everything: from how I listened to my clients, how they thought about their business challenges, creating platforms for management teams to have new and different conversations that would transform their businesses, change the cultures of their organisations, and change the way they valued their staff, forever.

So, my journey that started with Ben's book, then meeting Louise, joining SAODN, then Symphonia and PfP, all of it, changed the way I viewed everything and anything and created the 'missing link' between what I did for a living and that which I considered important about the life I live in South Africa.

The name 'Partners for Possibility' sums it up perfectly.

Arthur Collett, Director, Take Note Reputation Management, Durban, KwaZulu-Natal

I felt privileged and honoured to be part of this experience.

Constantly observing the state of South Africa (as we all do) I came to the realisation that if we really wanted to effect a change that it would have to be something more than legislation can do, more than quotas and B-BBEE and more than the window-dressing that is so often done. It had to be something far more profound than that.

These thoughts, coupled with my firm beliefs that relate to sustainable solutions (give the man a fish and you feed him for a day, teach a man to fish and you feed him for a lifetime), entitlement and the fact that with every right (that are so often demanded in today's world) there is a responsibility, led me to the conclusion that we needed to address the issue of the South African culture. South African culture, as opposed to Western, Indian, Zulu, Afrikaans and the myriad of other specific cultures that make up our wonderfully diverse nation. Where better to do this, than at grassroots or school level?

It was really rewarding to hear a principal in a CoP meeting advising some Grade 12 learners that had joined us for that session say, 'My advice to you is not to feel entitled.' I was witnessing what I believed was the solution taking place before my very eyes.

Partners for Possibility has allowed me to participate in this process of change, however minor, as opposed to being the 'armchair critic' who spends their time bemoaning all of our country's ills, without acknowledging the mountains of good that is being accomplished.

Ayesha Ismail, Business Executive, FEM, Johannesburg, Gauteng

The aspect of the programme that excited me was the opportunity to interact in situations which may be dire and to contribute to turnaround in the lives of young people, especially in deprived and disadvantaged communities. I believe that all children have immense potential, and all that is needed to unlock that potential is to create an opportunity for some timely intervention that makes all the difference for these future leaders. I see it as investing in our future and, at the same time, dealing with some of the social ills that plague our society.

I enjoyed and benefitted from the formal leadership development. I went in with an open mind and was inquisitive to learn as much as I could from this programme, and from my partner, and gave input into addressing some the needs of the school that I am partnered with.

Throughout the journey, my relationship with my principal evolved from being quite formal, at first, to a relationship based on friendship and trust. My partner and I discussed the usual topical issues but also some personal issues and challenges that had affected my partner. I was honoured that he felt comfortable to allow me into these aspects of his personal life.

What I learned from this is that my partner revealed little about his own vulnerabilities and had few opportunities to talk about the things that affect him emotionally. We shared stories of emotional events in our own lives and were comfortable to share, knowing that we would not judge each other. As the leader of a school, he was required daily to listen to others and to deal with and solve problems all the time. He is constantly bombarded with complaints of varying degree and urgency. Unfortunately, there is no one that he can talk to, or even act as a sounding board, to help him deal with his own issues. I found that it helped even just to be a good listener in these situations and allow him the opportunity to vent some of his thoughts and concerns.

Reflecting back, I believe that my partner has improved relationships with his SMT and teachers and the broader community, which was one of the areas he felt needed attention. Meetings are open, and everyone is afforded an opportunity to speak and give their perspective. These wonderful outcomes were achieved largely by the input of my partner himself. I found that during discussions the solutions to problems were easily grasped and that it was merely nudging my partner to implementation that closed out matters satisfactorily. Also, sometimes merely discussing the scenario presented simple, practical and common-sense solutions that were always within reach but needed merely verbalisation by my partner to become effective and tailored for implementation.

Our meetings involved time well spent and discussions that were meaningful. Above all, these meetings engendered positivity and confidence, whether it related to decision-making or implementation of small steps toward achieving an ultimate objective. Once again, I cannot stress just how far a mere discussion went in kick-starting a known solution, which, for whatever reason, had been relegated to the bottom of the 'to do' list.

Time to Think and Flawless Consulting helped me to rethink my own leadership role. I have had to give more of myself and demonstrate how I show up so that my team can also improve the way they show up. I now deal with matters and problems differently. We have real-time discussions about what's not working and how I can help resolve the issues that team members are faced with. This allows for more engagement, which has shown an improvement in how team members present themselves. I am mindful of my body language, which reveals more than I say. I have found, as with my partner, that the key is not to prescribe action or solutions, but rather to allow the discussion to yield the most desirable outcome. I appreciate each member of the team for their efforts and what they bring to the team. I have learned to be less judgemental and more concerned.

For me, this journey has been about mutual growth, understanding and empathy. At first, I felt overwhelmed by all the things that needed to be fixed and was intent on providing a solution at breakneck speed and implementing it at the same pace. As a result, I felt overwhelmed by everything that needed to be done. I was overly focused on the result rather than the important (small) steps that go to achieving that result. I now realise that learning the small steps that lead to confidence in making and ultimately implementing a solution is far more important than the end result. That is the most important experience that I have undergone during my time in the programme. That, for me, is what is meant by seeing the bigger picture and applying the lessons learned. Sometimes, just lending an ear is enough to spur an action or a sequence of events that lead to good things.

Community Building has taught us that if we share our methods and tools it can benefit so many. For example, sessions that were held by the Teddy Bear Clinic were extended to the broader community outside of the school. The school's computers were made available to all parents in the community who needed them to make online applications for school enrolment, regardless of the school they were applying to. This approach of sharing in abundance, I believe, will surely benefit our school.

Bernice Kotze, Cunningham Cottage Guest House, Kuruman, Northern Cape

Mother Teresa wrote these words in 1952: 'I never look at the masses as my responsibility. I look only at the individual. I can love only one person at a time, I can feed only one person at a time. Just one, one, one."

The power of one – one principal, one business leader, one school, one scholar, one person that put together this programme – can make a massive ripple effect in schools in South Africa.

Right at this moment, South Africans need good news in our current climate. PfP is the good news! Slowly but surely, one circle at a time, one school at a time, change is coming in like a rising tide!

I wanted to be part of the programme from the moment I was approached. When I enrolled, I was a 58-year-old guest house owner who had realised that ignorance was no longer bliss. I had a need to reach out to my neighbour and see how the other half lives. I was confronted first-hand with the challenges and difficulties that quintile 1 and 2 (no-fee) schools were battling with and the impact these have on scholars, educators and principals.

Personally, it was a year of immense growth and Copernican shifts. A totally new approach of being. What an awesome year and one that will have an influence on my day-to-day life for all my years to come. Thank you for giving me an opportunity to be part of this awesome journey.

Daniel Navazo, General Manager, Ramon Medina Arce Foundation RSA, Pofadder, Northern Cape

Humanity faces one of the greatest challenges in its history; learning to live with itself and in balance with the environment. We are at a decisive turning point. We suffer serious systemic problems: famine, poverty, wars, violence. We are suffering crises in all areas and around the world – crises of values, beliefs, crises in education, family, society and even the individuals themselves.

But that harmful model will be replaced by a fairer one based on human rights and the environment. This alternative is not made overnight but it is forming at the same time as the other system is falling.

The alternative – that world about which we dream – is not a distant idea but is already being, it is real. Many people in the world have realised that something is not working and we should start acting.

Partners for Possibility is a good example of this. It offers a platform for coexistence, reflection and transformation. Thanks PfP! The company and the school become gearshifts that transform themselves and the community as a whole.

Showing the way to work together for a more prosperous and enriching future for forthcoming generations.

Dave Wilson, Co-founder and CEO, National Mentorship Movement, Johannesburg, Gauteng

I have long been an admirer of Symphonia and Partners for Possibility and leapt at the chance to be a partner to Constance Maluleke of Mawila Primary in Meadowlands.

I gained huge personal experience of the challenges facing principals and educators in less privileged areas and the courage and commitment they need to show every day to do what is right for their learners, schools and communities. I was forced to confront my own privilege relative to Constance and those she serves and to recognise how much I had to learn about the lived reality of the vast majority of South Africans.

As the co-founder and CEO of the National Mentorship Movement, I also gained immensely from exposure to the philosophies underlying the programme, such as Time to Think, Flawless Consulting and Community Building, and have applied them in both my professional and my personal lives. I would recommend the programme to anyone who cares about this country and who wants to grow and learn while giving back

Dennis Coetzee, Group Executive: Human Capital, NWK Limited, Potchefstroom, North West Province

When I was contacted by Rina Vogler to get involved with the PfP programme, I had no idea what to expect from it. The framework that I saw intrigued me as I had seen the name Symphonia before. Rina said she had a specific principal in mind for to partner with for this journey. Reflecting back on the journey so far, as we near the end of the first year of our partnership, Rina made a perfect match with Annemien Holtzhausen.

I am a believer that you, as an individual, will always need to develop yourself. The business environment is continually changing and puts new pressures on you to cope with. This could be pressure to learn new skills or knowledge, to change the way you do things, both as a manager and as a leader, or changing work procedures due to stakeholder shifts and expectancies.

When I read through the programme, the three main skills development courses that you need to go through are not ones that I would have chosen for myself. But, they are extremely powerful courses on their own as well. Time to Think, Flawless Consulting and Community Building – each has its purpose in the programme, and each builds foundational knowledge for the way we interact with our different stakeholders and how we handle our partnerships as well. These principles were discussed at the COPs as well thus strengthening our understanding and application thereof. We also shared how we applied the principles or practices learned in each course within our different environments.

The one-on-one coaching, received from Rina, also assisted in forming a framework on how to assist and be there for our partners. Her guidance and questions solidified what we did in our partnerships. I was privileged to implement a lot of the learnings and practices in my day-to-day work and changed the way I facilitated some processes (group strategy sessions meetings). I got a lot of positive feedback from this as well.

The partnership – I would not have come to know the inner workings of the current education system if it were not for this programme and the heroic principal I was partnered with. Annemien is a goal-orientated, purposeful, driven individual who wants to make a difference. Her passion for what she does is evident in the way she performs as a principal in the type of school and community she works in. Every time I get there, the school is busy with one or other project that involves the communities Annemien operates within. I got a lot of insight into what principals face on a daily basis and more respect for how they get to do things, as this is not so easy as it seems from the outside.

The programme, which exposes you to different schools (as each CoP is held at a different school), gives one a great sense of what is happening in the school system. I have a lot of respect for all the principals that are involved in this programme, but especially my POTCH1 group. The reflections shared during these sessions were insightful and also an eye-opener.

Annemien's innovative way of using available resources and getting stakeholders on board is commendable. All the prizes she has received throughout this journey show the quality of the leadership she has demonstrated on a daily basis. I am extremely proud of my partner.

She also involved me in all the school's activities and events. When I could not attend she kept me up-to-date, with pictures and WhatsApps. The success of our partnership was built on mutual respect for one another's work and accomplishments and a clear understanding that we are there to support one another.

We set clear guidelines for how we interact with one another in monthly face-to-face meetings, and we were always available to reflect on the best way moving forward with a specific problem or challenge. I could not have asked for a better, more dynamic partner than Annemien. We have also decided to keep on going with our partnership after the facilitated programme is finished.

Thank you Symphonia for a wonderful programme. South Africa is better off because of this programme!

Felix Hacker, Director, Du Roi Agritech, Letsitele, Limpopo Province

Since its inception in January 2016, the partnership between Vhulakanjhani Primary School and Du Roi has progressed into a sustainable and growing interaction, based on the strong foundation created by the initial PfP programme. Within the first year of formal training we identified many of our strengths and weaknesses which, in turn, led to the development of new skills which I could add to my management 'toolbox' of life skills.

Patience, learning to listen and to appreciate others were some of the direct initial benefits. My knowledge and understanding is expanding daily as I am exposed to the complex issues facing our rural communities and our rural schools. Racial barriers have and are still being broken down through the forming of friendships based on trust, respect and appreciating our diverse cultures in South Africa. Working together to reach our common goal of improving the education of our young learners has been most uplifting, and celebrating the small and big victories, after the implementation of various learning interventions, has brought great joy and energy.

The widening of our various networks across racial barriers has been most liberating within my business environment, and I look forward to the continuation of our relationships and friendships and the formation of new ones as we increase the area of influence.

Florence van Rensburg, Sales Head, FNB Business, Cape Town, Western Cape

For me, the PfP programme has been a very profound experience; not just learning from the various books, courses and fellow partners, but also at a personal growth level.

This was a very humbling journey for me which opened my eyes to the reality of our education and the struggles faced in our schools. The principals in our circle shared with us their day-to-day challenges, but we also dealt with burglaries, repeated theft, drugs, violence, weapons on school grounds, vandalism, threats, bullet holes in classrooms, protests, setting property alight, withholding the delivery of bread and even a hostage situation. And somewhere in between all of this, they do the amazing job of managing their schools and educating our future leaders.

My partnership with Astrid Barreiro (Accordion Street Primary School in Belhar) really started deepening when we attended the Flawless Consulting workshop which gave us the opportunity to share experiences and reveal some of our personal vulnerabilities (Astrid and I share a lot of similarities albeit that we work in two different worlds). In this process, we developed a deep friendship which is based on mutual respect and understanding and growing together in our respective leadership roles. I learned so much from Astrid, benefitting more than I ever expected, and for that I am truly grateful. Our journey has not ended, and I am looking forward to what we can still achieve together.

Participating in this programme was a privilege, and it had so many positive aspects, but the highlight has been the realisation of how small steps and changes can lead to massive change and how reaching out to your community and building new networks can have long-term impact.

I would highly recommend this programme to anyone looking for a challenge to make a real difference in the world around us.

Freek Mulder, Director, Nel en Vennote, Upington, Northern Cape

The PfP programme changes people! Through building new relationships with school principals, other business leaders and facilitators, my mind has been renewed...opened to possibilities...and my actions have followed suit. I have learned how to really listen to people and empower them to find the solution that lies dormant inside of themselves. Even in my personal relationships I have seen the fruit of this change in me. I have seen my 6-year-old daughter's spirit light up when she is able to tell her daddy everything going on inside her beautiful little mind. I have seen my marriage thrive on beautiful attention. I have experienced more peace and joy in my working life as I have learned to say no when need be.

Above all else, I have learned that I never know the full story. This has created in me an inquisitive mind that I believe is an absolute necessity in order to take that 'walk in someone else's shoes'. I have started to ask, 'What if?' and this has shown me that indeed hope is alive and well in our country.

Where there is hope, possibilities can grow into reality. Indeed, life can be beautiful!

Geoff Lee, Managing Executive, Absa Home Loans
Tshwane, Gauteng

For me, the PfP journey can be captured in two ways:

- My initial appreciation for the hard work that principals who are part of the system put in was non-existent before PfP. This incredible work, against all the odds, was an eye-opener for me. Every day, they battle budget constraints, lack of community and family involvement in the learners' education and resource challenges. However, they show up with energy and commitment to make a difference, and I found this inspirational.

- The work that PfP as an organisation and the PfP leaders and coaches put in is incredible. They are dedicated to improving and transforming education in SA one school at a time. I was humbled by this selfless dedication, and it had a profound impact on me as a person.

Greg March, Economic Development Officer, Atlantica Sustainable Infrastructure
Upington, Northern Cape

I've come to recognise my most hidden weaknesses and unknown strengths over the past few months. PfP highlighted my biggest fears and turned them into outright tools for my professional and personal life. I'm grateful for being part of this group and programme since I've also noticed and experienced a sense of spiritual growth, maturity beyond recognition, and a greater understanding of my role in other people's lives. I'm a proud advocate and marketer of this and similar programmes in our communities and country at large. 'Thank you to my circle members, LPF and PfP!'

Heidi Edson, Group Socio-economic Development Specialist, Sun International, Cape Town, Western Cape

Upon commencing my PfP journey in 2018 with Mrs Berry, principal at Lantana Primary, the sense of knowing it all quickly dissipated as I stepped into her world, and I now have even more respect the educators in our society today.

Our relationship has developed into an understanding of each other's personalities and goals and, ultimately, into an atmosphere of two-way knowledge sharing. I realised very early in the partnership that I had to take one day at a time, and the Time to think workshop helped me hone that skill; I was not in the corporate environment, and I had to quickly adjust.

The partnership impacted not only on my current career at Sun International but also my personal journey at home. Flawless Consulting was an epic eye-opener, and to this day I recontract with each and everyone be it at work or at home.

My most memorable moment, thus far, was the 1st day I walked into Lantana Primary with an attitude that I knew and understood the challenges – after all, I grew up in the area. However, that mindset quickly changed when I sat outside Mrs Berry's office and witnessed 'A Day in the Life of a Principal' dealing with many facets of school life.

The Art of Community Building has led me to practise the rare skill called 'listening with intent and engaging with your target market first'. We'll be amazed at the power and knowledge a community has.

PfP has changed my life.

Irma Jacobsz, Regional Manager, Symphonia for South Africa, Johannesburg, Gauteng

Throughout all the years I worked in corporate companies, I was privileged to work with the entry-level market. I saw the hardships that people who live in disadvantaged areas are going through. When it came to the choice of 'should I pay my funeral insurance, or should I feed my children?' their choice was always the latter. They cared so deeply about family and even in the poorest areas that was always their most valuable asset.

I knew that I wanted to give back. I just didn't know how. Partners for Possibility miraculously crossed my path the month after I retired, and I just had to become a business partner.

The experience cured me of being afraid and taught me how to deeply appreciate what learners in orphaned families are going through. I learned how to trust and to instil trust. The deep sense of someone relying on me to be a friend, a supporter, a thinker and a shoulder to cry on humbled me.

The fact that I was able to engage openly with a person from a different background and a different culture assisted me in doing my work at Partners for Possibility.

Working with people in corporate is far from the real experience of truly 'getting your hands dirty'.

I appreciate the opportunity.

**Kamentha Pillay, Director, Humanised Innovation
Durban, KwaZulu-Natal**

My PfP journey started at a time when I had just stepped off the corporate path. Whilst it was a time of discovery and excitement, it was also incredibly scary! I questioned my self-worth, which had somehow become intertwined with the corporate identity I had developed over the years.

I remember the first meeting with Zanele; she exclaimed, 'You're so young!' and whilst I had an awareness around this, she did not diminish my presence or my suggestions during this journey.

Our life experiences, age and race are different; yet there are so many more commonalities. We are both strong women who have each claimed our own space (in education and engineering respectively). We are passionate about our country, our families, young eager minds and the value of education.

We have each gained confidence through our interactions with the principals and partners whom we've had the honour to walk this path with during the last 12 months. For me, being a PfP partner means embracing the idea of active citizenship. It is a journey to realising that human compassion and collaboration is often equally, if not, more useful to solving some of the most complex challenges facing our school principals.

Kate Baynes, Millford Nguni Stud and B&B, Pietermaritzburg, KwaZulu-Natal

I am a proud South African. I love my county and all its idiosyncrasies. It is what makes living here so colourful and vibrant. Born amidst the apartheid era, into a supportive upper/middle-income family, I was sheltered from the horrors that became so much a part of the '80s and early '90s. Fortunately, I had very progressive and liberal parents who tried to enforce respect, egalitarianism and an understanding of the unique cultures in our country.

I am grateful that by the time I was able to be independent and in charge of my own path, apartheid had come to an end and I was able to forge ahead into my adult life with the morals and values my family had instilled in me. Although my journey has been slow, doing what I could when I could, I knew I needed to help, and I wanted to make a difference.

Years later and well into my 40s, children behind me and two successful business later, I found myself with time to give and a need to do more. So began my journey with PfP.

A journey of self-discovery and a new understanding of myself, my family, friends and the community I live amongst.

A journey of equality where I have felt at ease and affirmed
A journey of independent thinking and problem-solving
A journey of leadership with integrity, thought and equal appreciation
A journey that has no guilt but welcomed help with no assumptions
A journey that has forged new friendships and like-minded people
A journey that will continue into the future long after my PfP year

I am a proud South African, and I am proud to be a part of PfP.

My PfP journey is how I have been able to show my love and appreciation for my country by being part of an organisation that is able to make a difference in the future of our children and our country.

Ken McKenzie, Founder and former co-owner of McKenzie Rudolphe Film Services, Cape Town, Western Cape

Many years ago, I went to a talk about a student's journey across the M5 in Cape Town and her journey from one side of the road to the other side and the challenges and difficulties she experienced in the pursuit of a better education (for those who don't know, the M5 divides Cape Town pretty much between well-resourced schools and under-resourced schools). PfP took me towards the latter side.

It all started with a conversation with a friend at my sons' school who said I should enrol for PfP. A couple of months later I met my principal, Aneez Manuels, at his school, the CAFDA School of Skills. His warm smile and complete passion for his work instantly won me over. During the year, we worked together closely and formed a very strong bond that has kept us trying to make the school a better place.

Over the first year we identified four core areas that we wanted to address. These were learner retention, staff morale, parent and community participation and, lastly, rebranding the school. We constantly evaluated these issues and refined them as we went. At this stage, two years later, we slowly seem to be attaining the various goals we have set. We have a more focused and interested base of learners and staff, we have painted various areas of the school and put in a mini 5-a-side multi-purpose astro field, and we have engaged more with community and parents. We constantly reassess and have added new and more relevant goals to our existing list.

When I reflect on where we are and how we doing, I look not only at the school but how we have advanced as individuals in the space of two years. PfP has bought the good in us to the fore. We have been honest with each other, realistic, goal-orientated, passionate, and we tackle our various issues with pride and humility.

I only wish I had crossed the M5 earlier.

Komala Pillay, Senior Manager Retail Strategy, Sasol Johannesburg, Gauteng

As human beings we are moulded by all our life experiences. Aside from our parents, there is arguably no bigger influencer on shaping humanity than our schools. I was fortunate to have received quality education as a child, albeit in modest surroundings. It is heartbreaking to see how we are failing so many young people today by not providing them with the standard of learning that they deserve and that is needed for this country to thrive.

It was within this context that I started looking for opportunities to give back in the education space. Through a series of fortunate events, I stumbled upon the PfP programme and, after some consideration, threw my hat into the ring and embarked on what would turn out to be a life-changing journey.

The details of this journey will vary for everyone, but I suspect that there are a few common outcomes for business leaders. The first is an increased connection to the country and to our fellow countrymen; the second, an increased optimism for what is possible, even in the most dire of circumstances; and the third, a better understanding of one's role as a leader.

It is the last aspect that has most impressed me about the PfP programme. Participants in the programme are exposed to a year of honest, open communication in an environment without performance ratings, bonuses and company politics. It is a unique setting, and out of it arise unique insights and learnings. Any company considering a culture-change journey to enhance their leadership approach should consider making the PfP programme a part of the change intervention.

Of course, there was also the technical part of the PfP experience where my business skills were applied to various projects, including a new literacy centre at the school. It has been wonderful to have met and built a friendship with Ilana Heradien, the dynamic principal of St Ives Primary School. We have committed to continuing our partnership and I look forward to our future successes!

Lerato Lotlhare, Entrepreneur, Kuruman, Northern Cape

Just hearing the name Partners for Possibility ignited something inside of me. As a businesswoman and philanthropist, I just wanted to be part of it.

As a wife, a mother and an entrepreneur, I was previously so caught up in daily responsibilities; attending to business, meeting the next deadline, rushing to the next commitment and managing everything in between, that I had lost touch with many of the things that matter most.

Before my PfP journey, I thought making a meaningful difference meant giving away money, or buying things worth a lot of money, or rendering a service and not asking for money in return. But I have now experienced that time, presence and just creating a safe space for someone to think and to feel heard make a difference that no amount of money can buy.

Through Partners for Possibility I got an opportunity to get to know and interact with some of the most incredible people in our Kuruman community. I got to experience the harsh realities faced in our schools by principals, teachers and our beautiful children, and am left feeling that the first year of our partnership is just the beginning.

Liz Dewing, Magnetic North Facilitation, Cape Town, Western Cape

I circled the periphery of PfP for years – literally – after being profoundly affected by the visit of the Zanders in 2008 when I was still working for Old Mutual.

It took until 2018, and an accidentally established connection to Principal Dominic Raphahlelo of Mokone Primary in Langa, before I signed up. In October 2018 when the CPT30 Leadership Circle started, I travelled a distance of about 3km as the crow flies every two weeks and entered a different universe.

It has upset me, inspired me, challenged me and grown me immeasurably. I have developed a deep respect for the educators in these hard places who achieve so much with so little and whose work is easily as demanding as any role in the corporate jungle. I have learned to listen even more deeply, to keep an open mind and reflect before I offer an opinion. I have learned to take time and question my own assumptions. I have been awed by the strength in community and really seen the gift of diversity in action within the range of races, ages and personalities in my circle. I have laughed, cried and discovered riches both in myself and in others. It has been a gift.

Lucille Meyer, CEO, Chrysalis Academy, Cape Town, Western Cape

Words are inadequate to describe my year-long journey within the Partners for Possibility family. Not only have I enriched my leadership capability and enhanced my network of associates, but I have come to appreciate the complexity of the school ecosystem. This means that as a leader who prides herself in disrupting inequality and injustice, I have become an advocate for effecting transformation at a local level despite the constraints within the larger system.

A year into the journey, I am decidedly more reflective and capable of engaging in compassionate listening without interruption, whether with peers or direct reports. Flawless Consulting was a profound learning experience that has enabled me to contract and recontract more meaningfully with staff, family members and partners. My role as a thinking partner to the principal of Portia Primary school, Kevin Velensky, has reaffirmed the value of forging authentic partnerships based on equality, honesty and commitment. PfP has made me a better South African and African and, above all, a more open-hearted human being! My gratitude is immense and I am proud to say that my PfP journey has just begun!

Marina Bidoli, Partner and Office Head, Brunswick, Johannesburg, Gauteng

Undoubtedly, the business leaders and principals in my group learned a lot from each other – in our individual engagements and at the community of practice meetings.

By sharing lived experiences and creating respectful, thinking environments, we were better able to understand each other and often also able to come up with solutions to what initially seemed like intractable problems.

Moral encouragement, too, can go a long way. Simply by acting as sounding boards and actively listening to the principals' daily challenges (which involved numerous issues including assault, drug abuse, low teacher morale, absenteeism, disempowered leadership and limited resources) made a difference.

On joining the programme, I heard several principals questioning whether they would be better off leaving education for the private sector or retiring. By the end of my year, only one principal had left. The remainder said they had been re-energised – and it was clear that their senior leadership teams, at SMT and SGB level too, were inspired to make a positive difference. Most encouraging were those committed principals who, despite the odds, continue to lead high-performing schools, transforming young lives in the process. They are the role models who must be encouraged and lauded as they are critical to the success of our country and sustainability of our businesses. Ultimately, we all share the same country, and it is in all our interests that our children are able to fulfil their potential. It's for this reason that the PfP programme is so important.

Mike Stopforth, Director, Beyond Binary, Johannesburg, Gauteng

When you want to get fit and strong, you go to gym. You go to gym, because you can use machines and weights to create resistance, and that resistance gets your muscles working harder and, hopefully, amounts to better physical conditioning. Or so I've heard!

Where do you go if you want to have the same effect on your mind? The mind is like a muscle, in many ways. It needs to be exercised. It needs to be fed. To be developed, it needs to be moved and manipulated in new ways. It needs resistance. The best type of mental resistance is fresh perspectives.

My PfP experience was one of new experiences, new perspectives and, ultimately, a deeper appreciation for the notion of value creation in a society as complex as ours. Businesses all too often have the luxury of being preoccupied only with their own success: growth and profit. Never mind the cost(s). PfP taught me that we are all linked. We are part of a complex and intricate ecosystem, and no self-respecting leader can consider his or her decisions in isolation from that system. We can't win when someone else is losing.

My principal, Ruth, taught me about the power of conviction and that the kind of leadership that survives and thrives in the absence of a multitude of resources is the kind of leadership that will see our country succeed. She taught me about the importance of perseverance. She taught me, without wanting to sound like a motivational poster, how powerful a force love can be. I am an immeasurably more complete person because of my journey with her.

This programme achieves what very few comparable programmes can: genuine equity, powerful perspective shifts, and significant long-term social impact. It is worth your time and energy.

Petra Snyman, Author, motivational speaker, former social worker, Upington, Northern Cape

Everybody has got a diamond of potential that lies dormant inside of them that we often overlook. It may not look like much but, if you cultivate and nourish it, it can amount to much. Pupils must take time and be guided to look inside of themselves and find their own miracle, value and worth and do something great with it! Often our potential is clouded by the circumstances and the environment that we are operating in.

As a business partner, I had the opportunity to connect with people. I learned to look at people from a different perspective. Not mere meeting of needs but the developing of the person's potential. We should look into the heart of people and discover their real-life story and legacy.

PfP ignited the awareness in me that we can do better, and we can raise the standard. We do not only have to have material outcomes; we must enlarge our thinking and dream big. We can start by shifting the boundaries and the barriers in our mind. Much more should be done to motivate our learners by way of motivational speaking. We must never stop dreaming. The dream becomes the drive to transform the challenge into a purpose. Without a vision the people perish!

Phinias Gololo, Director, Keyskill, Polokwane, Limpopo

From beginning to finish, PfP was a remarkable act of kindness, a privilege; first for the deprived hopeless learner, then for the PfP partners. For the partners, it stirred up hitherto dormant adroitness and strength of character, a blend which, during workshops and community of practice sessions, got skilfully marinated with essential learnings.

It is worth noting that programme kick-off coincided with my wife undergoing spinal surgery and getting summarily dismissed from work whilst on sick leave; she could neither drive nor take care of herself and the family as she had been doing. Also, her medical aid was immediately terminated. With five children below the age of thirteen, household responsibilities inevitably increased and, throughout, hefty legal battles and protracted financial distress plagued my journey.

Buoyed by stories of resilience; such as one partner's miraculous recovery from intensive care and another's multiple triumphs over serious illness, I stayed the course, and it paid dividends.

Nancy Kline's techniques for drawing the best actions out of people, such as those for creating the optimal thinking environment, found immediate application in my life before transforming the school, my work situation and the surrounding community. The impact on my family was decisive; understanding and respectful relationships supplanted coerced responses and fearful expectations. Kind, sacrificial and collaborative gestures, among others, became a key distinctive of family life.

Peter Block's pearls of wisdom, such as cultivating authentic behaviour and a capacity for deeper relatedness and partnership, came in handy as well. Predictably, the school's vision and attitude underwent a paradigm shift, with strategic planning workshops transforming the school's leadership. In addition, emboldened fundraising campaigns changed the fortunes of the school with a private sector donation of at least R1 million. Learners also shook off the cobwebs, notching a 75% Grade 12 pass rate after the previous 50%.

Sarita Phillander, SIM Train, Kuruman, Northern Cape

Let me start by saying that this was a journey that I was very reluctant to go on because I was in a very bad space – personally and in business. I didn't feel that I could add much value to this programme. But because PfP had appointed an excellent LPF (Yolandi Strydom), I was convinced to at least give it a try.

Well, after our first CoP, I was convinced to be part of this great journey. I have benefitted from my coaching sessions with Yolandi more than I could've imagined.

I was privileged to get to know someone from a different culture than mine, very intimately. Someone who reminded me that, as females, we too can make a difference within our sphere of influence, without losing the kind-hearted softness of a woman. That person is my principal partner, Grace Pitse. Grace taught me that no matter what life throws at you, you just have to face it and, with the help of our gracious Father God, we can do all things.

I most certainly also cherish the new friendships that were formed with all the partners in the circle I was a part of. The PfP Kuruman1 Leadership Circle taught me that we can overcome the borders of race, culture and socio-economic circumstances if we all take a stance, join hands and work together to make our world a better place.

Stephen Goddard, Retired businessman, Durban, KwaZulu-Natal

I don't believe, Louise, you can comprehend the wonderful gift you have given to us and the people of this country. As business leaders, we have been part of giving children a better education with future possibilities.

We have seen headmasters being given support, guidance, funding and an injection of hope and opportunities for schools they try so hard to run and improve for their children. We have been exposed to the poverty and the hardships at schools, the uncomplaining attitude of many of the teachers and headmasters, the incredible help and generosity of wealthier schools and businesses and the love and support shown by the public; and then…

The unbelievable, unexpected gift that comes from giving of your time, money and soul to try and improve the lives of others less fortunate than yourself. This gift only comes with unconditional love and giving and is totally unexpected. How many celebrations have I been to where the business leader is given his opportunity to talk and says to the principal, 'Well if you think that you and your school have benefitted, you have no idea, what this experience has done for me'? It is a God-given gift, and this is what makes this experience for business leaders so incredible.

EVERYBODY benefits – what a gift for all of us. As a business leader, I can only say thank you!

Thandi Puoane, Emeritus Professor, School of Public Health, University of the Western Cape, Cape Town

I am grateful that I participated in the Partners and Possibility programme during 2019. I have grown in many aspects related to my work and family. I will organise my experience and benefits into three aspects as follows:

Broadened my knowledge and skills

After attending each of the following workshops: Time to Think, Flawless Consulting and Community Building, I applied the knowledge and skills learned from the workshops. If it were not for PfP, I would not have attended these workshops, nor even been aware of them. I received several books and videos to help enrich my knowledge

I have learned that each and every person has a story to tell, and this story may affect his/her current activities, so it is very important to listen without interrupting. I am now a good listener and I am able to apply this skill at work, with friends and within my family. I am now able to convey the message of appreciation, especially to my grandchildren and to my friends.

I have also realised that, even though I may be in a leadership position in working with communities, I have to recognise that the success of any project/work is based on partnership but not on dictatorship.

Met new people

I met and interacted with several people that I would not have met if I was not part of this initiative. These include teachers and business partners from several companies. I visited schools and areas that I have never visited. This enabled me to learn about several school environments

Because of PfP, I was invited to attend several principal leadership forums. I met people such as Prof Thuli Madonsela and Trevor Manuel, attended their talks and learned from them.

Understood the challenges faced by the public education system

I had the benefit of understanding the challenges faced by the principals and teachers at the schools, including barriers faced by learners and parents to achieve good quality education. I realised that as citizens of this country, we have a role to play to ensure good quality education and better future for all children in South Africa.

Tom Bassett, Retired construction company MD
Durban, Kwazulu-Natal

When I joined the PfP programme as a business partner, from what I had previously heard in the media, I already had negative perceptions about what I expected to find in the school in which I was to be involved and also in respect to the competency of the school's principal. However, I soon realised that my negative perceptions were largely unjustified as the dedication and passion with which the principal, deputy principals, senior teachers and administration staff manage their school was astounding.

In the community of practice sessions, with a total of 10 principals, I also found that these positive attributes were clearly fairly common across all of the participating schools. This is despite the fact that the principals and teachers were trying to execute their duties and educate their pupils, without any significant formal management training, in the face of daunting, insurmountable obstacles caused by the lack of physical infrastructure, insufficient qualified teachers and other logistical problems resulting from the significant underfunding by the ministry of education.

Rather than with principals and senior teachers, the problem generally lies with the various departments within the ministry of education and within the provincial branches in which the teachers union have undue influence at all levels of the ministry of education in trying to impose and place unqualified teachers and principals into senior positions in schools. This clearly undermines the whole future success of the schools and is thereby definitely detrimental to the education system as a whole.

As a managing director, I had already benefitted from various business school management programmes, some of which are common to the PfP programme. However, I believe that many business leaders will undoubtedly enhance their management skills by attending the formal PfP training; to the ultimate benefit of their future management careers and the companies for which they work.

My PfP experience has strengthened my belief that schools and principals need as much help and management training as possible; hence the necessity for business at large to assist the PfP programme with sponsorship and to provide business leaders to partner with principals. This will enable companies and managers to play their vital role in positively influencing the communities and society at large and, as a result, make South Africa a better country for all in our society to live in successfully in the future.

We have recently entered a new chapter in our country's history; hence it is even more important for the private sector to enhance the effectiveness of the PfP programme. There has never been a more important time for companies and business leaders to step up to the plate and make their vital contribution towards the management training of school principals and teachers and the successful education of their future employees!

Yolandi Strydom, Learning Process Facilitator, Symphonia for South Africa, Kuruman, Northern Cape

Through Partners for Possibility I have grown from an insecure, anxious person, who did not believe I really had the ability to move mountains, into someone who is anchored on the ground, and I walk now with ease in my shoes – which were once too big – leaving a footprint of love.

In my first year at PfP, I grew more in my self-awareness than in 50 years of my existence. I am loving myself more, and my capacity to share that love has grown far beyond what I expected.

PfP changed my whole life and shifted my focus from myself to the community around me. I have developed a hunger just to plough more and more back into my community. I used to plant only one seed at a time, but PfP empowered me and gave me a whole bag of seed so that there will be an abundant harvest.

I believe with all my heart that love can change the world, and PfP has given me a platform where I can share love in abundance. Being a partner in this programme gave me more energy than it took from me. My door of destiny is opening in this opportunity to serve. Thank you PfP for the incredible opportunity I got to be part of the family!

**Yvonne Johnstone, Retired School Principal
Durban, KwaZulu-Natal**

When Rudyard Kipling wrote the poem 'If—' he surely was thinking of school principals...

'If you can keep your head when all about you are losing theirs and blaming it on you,
If you can trust yourself when all men doubt you, but make allowance for their doubting too;
If you can wait and not be tired of waiting,
If you can dream and not make dreams your master...'

Sandile Mzoneli is the principal of Bonela Primary School in Sherwood, Durban, and after reading the poem he said, 'Wow!'

I'm sure we'd have had many other principals nodding in agreement!

When Sandile walked me around his school in February 2018, his kindly sense of humour, friendly professional demeanour and what proved to be his unflagging enthusiasm soon unfolded.

I listened with gentle eyes to all he had to say and was totally captivated by the opportunities that lay ahead!

A few months later Sandile joined the PfP programme, and I was excited to fill the role as business partner.

In 2017 Sandile had inherited an under-resourced school that had suffered from vandalism, lack of planning, declining academic results and the absence of a school governing body. EVERY aspect of the school required his earnest attention.

Dr Jonathan Griffiths wrote about choosing to be a 'Jack of All Trades'. Indeed, the principals of many state schools fill that role admirably, and Sandile is busy championing the title every day. When faced with so many challenges, it requires great resilience to 'keep one's head'.

I have felt as if he's struggling to 'climb a ladder' of improvement and achievement for his school. His ladder has 'questionable rungs'. Some are missing completely. My place has been to hold fast and 'prop up' the ladder when necessary. This has, and continues to be, great fun and a huge privilege!

I believe the principal and his team espouse Rudyard Kipling's words:

'Yours is the earth and everything in it.'

Sandile Mzoneli, his staff and school community are building a legacy at Bonela Primary School, and they deserve every support.

I thank Dr Louise van Rhyn and a hugely supportive Jackie Warner. I have sincere admiration and respect for the PfP programme.

Zeenat Harper-Valentine, Senior Audit Manager, Sun International, Johannesburg, Gauteng

I was selected by my director to represent Sun International and become a part of Partners for Possibility. At first, it all seemed quite daunting because I was up to my eyeballs in deadlines and deliverables at the office. I took a deep breath and began this beautiful journey with the fellow business leaders, principals and my leadership circle leader, Paula Quinsee.

It was a phenomenal journey and, when I look back, I wish I could do it over and over again. The camaraderie and support that I was able to provide, both to my principal and others, and using my knowledge and expertise to assist her in the school warmed my heart. It finally felt like I was putting everything I had acquired (i.e. all the accolades and qualifications) to the best use. I was making a difference in the lives of children, teachers and principals.

Once upon a time I was also a learner, and if it wasn't for the dedication and commitment of those few teachers and, of course, the grace of the Lord, I wouldn't be where I am today.

So what am I trying to say? The best thing we could do as a nation, as we climb our mountains and reach the peaks, is to extend a hand and pull as many people up as possible. It could be something as simple to us as business leaders as developing a performance contract that makes the ultimate difference for a principal or teacher whose main focus is shining a light and raising our future generation.

Zuko Mlonyeni, HR Executive, RCL Foods
Durban, KwaZulu-Natal

Partnering with Mrs Thandeka Luthuli-Mpanza, on behalf of RCL Foods Limited, to lead Ukukhanya Kwe Afrika Primary as a progressive school, was in pursuit of my authentic leadership development plan. It brought my philosophy of making the difference in others, in the best possible way I can, closer to reality.

Seeing the little hands adorning the canvas donated by the school, displayed on the company's wall, in appreciation of its contribution through PfP is a constant reminder that every act of kindness counts. Imagining the smiling faces of the Grade 1 learners enjoying their daily provision of porridge, in their beautifully painted classes, courtesy of the RCL Foods' Do More Foundation, gives one a sense of fulfilment.

Ongoing collaboration with partners like SSS, which provides security to the school, and the Methodist Church of Southern Africa volunteers, who read English with Grade 2 learners, fulfils our calling to go, not only to those who want us, but to those who need us the most.

'Getting closer, being sensitive to the needs of the school community, doing the least one can,' would be my message to whoever is keen to make a difference in the life of South African education system.

May PfP's efforts be multiplied; true to the saying that 'the more, the merrier'.

Chapter 20

The impact of PfP on the delivery team

> *"Never doubt that a small group of committed citizens can change the word. Indeed it is the only thing that ever has."* –
> Margaret Mead

Paulo Freire was one of the most influential philosophers of education of the twentieth century. One of the core tenets of his *Pedagogy of the Oppressed* (1968) is that both the teacher and the student have to be willing to learn from each other. He was vehemently opposed to the 'banking method of education', where students passively receive and store information 'deposited' by a teacher, as he believed that a hierarchical student-teacher relationship creates an oppressive environment in which students do not learn how to think critically or to feel confident about thinking for themselves.

Freire advocated a reciprocal relationship between teacher and students in a democratic environment where everyone would learn from each other. The concept of reciprocal learning is foundational for PfP, so I wanted to hear from our LPFs and the other members of the team about the extent to which they have learned from others during their PfP journey and how this has impacted them.

The impact of facilitating the PfP process on Learning Process Facilitators

> *"Holding space for another person means that we are willing to walk alongside another person in whatever journey they're on, without judging them, making them feel inadequate, trying to fix them, or trying to impact the outcome. When we hold space for other people, we open our hearts, offer unconditional support, and let go of judgement and control."* – Heather Plett

Anita Moerman van Blankenberg
Partner for Possibility, Learning Process Facilitator in Johannesburg and Facilitator of Flawless Consulting

Symphonia and PfP came into my life when I was not in a good place personally. I was low on hope. When I was first introduced to PfP, in Cape Town, what I saw was something that worked with the future and worked in the space of hope. And that is what I have experienced.

In short, what I got was more than I could ever imagine. I became connected to the bigger South Africa, to people I would otherwise never have been connected to. For the first time, I felt that I was part of something really important and that I, in my small way, could have a positive impact on the lives of so many more people than I ever imagined. I also realised the responsibility that came with it and that I had to be a good steward of being a partner to my principal.

I have been inspired, accepted and loved by so many more people than I could ever imagine. In my partnership with Lindelani, with his staff and his school, in every CoP, at every Flawless Consulting workshop I have facilitated, at every workshop and get-together I attended, I could love and I was loved. I am a whole person because of that. The healing it brought into my life cannot be described in words.

Brenda Scrooby
Learning Process Facilitator in Modimolle

Before signing up in 2019 to become an LPF, I was confronted with the reality that I had to commit to the learning processes of the programme. I had retired from the corporate world with numerous business and leadership awards but knew I would need to transform my own leadership style of pioneer and front runner into one that balances the key elements of coaching and project management and to become an almost invisible role model. Observing Louise and others in the PfP leadership team and experiencing first-hand their humility, perseverance and commitment to living the values of PfP and listening to all the voices in the room has helped me to do this.

I was privileged to start my journey of transformation by attending the Time to Think and Flawless Consulting workshops. I found the 10 components of the thinking environment to be simplistic, yet revolutionary. The hard work of learning to become an effective listener had started and will remain a work in progress that impacts all areas of my life.

The full understanding that, 'the vehicle for my contribution is my humanity' struck me in my gut during the Flawless Consulting workshop. For me, this was on the mark because my heart is infused with love for the children of South Africa and the desire to develop the adults who lead them, so that all can attain their calling and destiny. I realised that I can simply give myself and be authentic and sincere, with no need to wear a mask, or follow any philosophy or textbook.

So, as an LPF, surrounded by inspiring role models and equipped through coaching and the PfP workshops, I learnt to facilitate the programme as a role model myself. I contracted with my partners by clearly communicating my own and the programme's 'wants' and allowed them to express their fears and concerns which helped to ensure that they were committed to their deliverables. In meetings with them I practised my listening skills and created and held a space in which every voice could be heard. Time to Think tools such as "the circle" and "thinking council" made my work as facilitator easy and enabled the engagement between partners and increased their respect and support for each other. This has helped them to find their own best answers and freed me from having to give advice, guidance or my opinion.

My learning and hands-on experience have totally transformed my leadership style and liberated me from a sense of responsibility for the partnerships' performance. I know that as long as I remain true to my true role as Learning Process Facilitator who holds the space and cheers the partners on from within the circle, they will progress in their own time as transformational leaders and change agents.

I will forever be thankful to PfP, our CEO Louise, and our leadership team for this wonderful opportunity to live my passion out with such joy, knowing that every day my life and my partners' lives are being changed, somehow, for the better. I am humbled that I can play a tiny part in this and feel so grateful to the DBSA which stepped in with funding for the partnerships in these eight outlying schools.

Coba Röhm
Learning Process Facilitator in the Northern Cape and Stakeholder Engagement Lead for the Northern Cape

During October 2017 I was invited into the beautiful world of PfP to help grow the programme's presence in the Northern Cape. This made me very happy and created an opportunity for me to make a contribution in the beautiful 'land of the big orange mountains'.

Communities from Vioolsdrift to Kuruman, De Aar to Upington, Onsseepkans to Kimberley have opened up their hearts, their worlds and are taking hands to support School Principals in this vast, arid region.

As a coach, I have grown through being part of the PfP leadership team and I keep discovering triggers which I am learning to control in this nurturing space.

As some of them prepare to immigrate, family and friends frown upon what I do, jokingly telling me to 'get a REAL job'. But hey, there is nothing more REAL than healing our country by developing responsible citizens.

Jackie Warner
Learning Process Facilitator in Durban

I am currently facilitating my fourth leadership circle and, as I look back on the last three years, I almost have to pinch myself that my everyday reality is being deeply immersed in this work. My heart and soul are filled with love, deep care, compassion and respect for being a part of this very special community.

I can't begin to adequately express how much I have grown as an individual – I feel I have grown from a little seedling into a steady and well-grounded palm tree, able to explore ongoing learning and growth with curiosity. I not only feel, I know that I am a much better citizen and individual than I was three years ago.

Being in this space has allowed me to heal myself and move towards being a more wholehearted individual and, in turn, I've been afforded the opportunity to create the space for others to do the same. To move from brokenness to feeling complete has been one of my life's best gifts – a gift that keeps on giving so generously and abundantly.

Knowing that I'm part of a movement and way of daily being that are filled with opportunities and possibilities makes my heart smile broadly and my eyes shine brightly, with laughter coming from so deep within my belly that it can only be infectious.

What an honour and privilege to be a part of this magical and beautiful community – thank you, thank you, thank you.

Jo Monson
Learning Process Facilitator in Cape Town

In South Africa, so many of us are called every day to stand up and do something. As human beings we just can't look away from the poverty and potential around us and do nothing. I was grateful to find PfP as a way to do this and a way that has the possibility for a high impact. School principals have the ability to influence not just their school and the life of every learner there, but also to make an impression on the parents and the whole school community. In working directly with the principal there is a lot of leverage for social change. For me who had spent years working in smaller spaces, with groups of young adults or else writing public education materials, this was irresistible. The potential for high impact was the first thing that attracted me to PfP.

When I started as an LPF in 2016 it was hard. Here was a principal and a business leader, two people from utterly different places, different perspectives, different everything and now suddenly they had to be partners, to get on and get something going. And the primary part of my role was to facilitate this relationship! It was hard and it was awkward, and yet my partners taught me so much. They really did open up the space of possibility. Not all, but most of them stuck it out.

Sometimes they seemed to start out as 'shut down', but they kept showing up and being present with each other and, little by little, things shifted; they started to trust each other, and things started to happen at the school. The big hearts of these partners and their ability to keep coming back changed my life. I realised that actually most people have big hearts and that this is the norm, it just needs some space to show itself.

LPFs at PfP are professional coaches and we learn during coach training how to prepare ourselves and hold the space for a generative conversation. We learn how to let go of judging and how to show up with compassion and curiosity. We know that within a coaching relationship whatever happens is a microcosm of the macrocosm of their life and that everything that happens is an opportunity for development and growth.

At PfP we are expected to be "leaders as coaches". We meet regularly with other LPFs and support each other. We also have a supervisory coach, and all of this has allowed me to live myself out as a coach and as a leader; to really sit in that place of not knowing and of possibility and to be with people. To get this quality of support for my chosen practices of coaching and facilitation has been tremendous.

One particular business partner taught me so much about not giving up on someone. She was partnered with a school principal who had been in an accident and had spent a lot of time away from school. His matric results had dropped and he was very stressed. Again and again, he missed meetings, didn't communicate and didn't turn up. But she kept holding a space for him. She said his willingness was still there and, therefore, so was hers. She said if the situation were reversed, "I would want someone who wouldn't give up on me." Incredibly, she was able to find a way with that principal and into the school and there began to be ripples into the school community. The last time I saw the principal his whole body was different. His face was open and his body was relaxed. He was joking and able to show up as himself rather than the stressed person he had been. That business partner stretched my limits way beyond where they were because, the truth is, I would have given up on that principal. I realised that sometimes all it takes is someone else to hold a space for us and not give up on us.

I am enormously grateful to PfP for holding the space for me, and for all of us, to build our nation, to be there for each other with big hearts, to practice our leadership, to come again and again out of possibility and to not give up on each other.

Karen McKenzie
Learning Process Facilitator, Kwazulu-Natal Midlands

In retrospect, it was the magnitude of saying yes to this journey, knowing that it is what was destined to be, what a lifetime of experiences, beliefs, strengths, networks and relationships have prepared me for, that daunted me. My usual personal sabotage suspects of bravery, a bit of self-doubt, you're an "all or nothing" girl told me that when I say yes to this PfP journey, that is it, it will become a life mission and slightly overwhelm.

It has, in essence, been a journey of alignment and resonance, a homecoming to self, an acceptance of responsibility in my community and stepping into my light. In PfP terms we might call this saying yes to active citizenship and conscious capitalism, but if I am honest, I was still a bit tentative as to what I said yes to. I know now in the words of Marianne Williamson, what I was trying to resist –

'Our deepest fear is not that we are inadequate. Our deepest fear is that we are powerful beyond measure. It is our light, not our darkness that most frightens us. We ask ourselves, 'Who am I to be brilliant, gorgeous, talented, and fabulous?' Actually, who are you not to be? You are a child of God. Your playing small does not serve the world. There is nothing enlightened about shrinking so that other people won't feel insecure around you. We are all meant to shine, as children do. We were born to make manifest the glory of God that is within us. It's not just in some of us; it's in everyone. And as we let our own light shine, we unconsciously give other people permission to do the same. As we are liberated from our own fear, our presence automatically liberates others.'

This journey of YES included my personal alignment of 'Roots and Wings', hippy heart with boardroom head, allowed me my idolised job of conductor and warmly welcomed the words of 'gurus' that shaped my thinking – Dr Angeles Arrien, Patti Digh, Elizabeth Kubler-Ross, Nancy Kline, Ben and Rosamund Stone Zander – as treasured seeds of wisdom on my PfP path.

I am by nature quite a grounded person, a solid citizen if you wish, I like to feel rooted in facts, patterns and research. The roots that I found in the PfP process is the strong foundation in scholarship, in theories of change, backed up by world-class monitoring and evaluation.

For years in my coaching practise I used a very simple "check-in" process, a quick alignment between head, heart and feet. When head and heart have not found each other in acceptance and forgiveness, we incapacitate our feet…taking that next step becomes tentative, making a decision difficult, moving in authenticity tough. What I have absolutely loved about my PfP journey is the alignment that I have found between my **"hippy heart" and "boardroom head."** My "hippy heart" always believed that all our social demands and ills could be solved with a coming in peace, in conversation, in detaching ourselves for a moment from the detail of the brokenness and focus on how we wanted this to end.

My 'boardroom' head argued, but Karen, how were you going to measure, evaluate and framework this progress? What will let you know that there is success? Again on a very practical level an example in our circle. At Bruntville Primary, partners Protus Sokhela, the principal and Kim McNally, business owner of Select International, decided that one of their first strategic interventions was going to be the creating of a compelling vision for their school. A big vision indeed – to be the best township school in the country! A key pillar to the vision was to re-write their values. A vision of joy. Oh how content this made my 'hippy heart' and so a series of workshops rolled out with the SMT, SGB, educators, parents and learners to write a new school song, add some groovy moves, create a compelling new logo, t-shirts and if we could but measure the energy shift in that school ! Where ever you look and listen, you will notice reminders at Bruntville:

> *We grow learners who read, write, think and communicate. We care and respect ourselves, others and the Earth. We are committed, disciplined and we always work hard. This is our vision and values of joy!*

Each parent and teacher have a laminated A4 to help them with modelling the values for their children. To extract from the Bruntville parent in action poster…we show care and respect for ourselves, others and the Earth, by stopping and greeting, by picking up litter, switching off the lights, hug, smile or 'high five' to show joy to others and we read to our children every day. More than 20 parents volunteered to 'do stuff' at the school…feed learners for breakfast, support with admin, do maintenance and offer fitness training. What a wonderful opportunity when through PfPs networking for national partnerships, Bruntville Primary was able to employ 15 local residents through Youth@Work in their fields of interest and gifting – IT, admin, foundation phase support and sports.

Chew on that 'boardroom head'. Is this not what Otto Scharmer's Theory U[40] asks of us? How can we activate our deeper levels of humanity in order to bridge the divides in our social, environmental and spiritual challenges? Many cynics remain on the periphery, this education system is way too broken, you will never fix it, they are not interested…watch this space. Next step in Bruntville primary is a call to action…

---

40 Scharmer's Theory U model shows how we can open our minds, emotions and will to moments of discovery and mutual understanding. See https://www.ottoscharmer.com/theoryu

neighbouring farmers, local employers, interested parties, national and international supporters, they will join. I invite you to walk through this portion of the Midlands and ask after Bruntville primary, a school in the heart of an often 'burning' township bordering the N3 highway, a hotspot for truck violence and other criminal activity. We keep you posted on this ripple, or more aptly the epicentre of a tidal wave of change emanating from this township school. Oh so much to measure and framework!

I have a confession, I have always fancied myself as a bit of a "closet conductor". At a basic level, conducting is supposedly very simple, it aims to keep an orchestra or a choir in time and together. The conductor serves as a messenger for the composer, it is his or her responsibility to understand the music and convey it through gesture so that the musicians in the orchestra can transmit a unified interpretation of the music to the audience. The musicians are of course all experts of their own instruments and the conductor creates the space of belonging where each musician can contribute to the overall excellence. How amazing then that I have the possibility of conducting a PfP circle in the KZN Midlands, allowing the Symphonia way and PfP methodologies (the composers) to stir and awaken. Music stirs emotion, it allows our mental wellbeing quartet of chemical messengers – dopamine, serotonin, oxytocin and endorphins to be "unleashed" and we vibrate differently. Being an LPF within PfP has welcomed the conductor part of myself back into the whole. I am not sure what the PfP song sounds like yet, but it has strong African rhythms anchored in experienced composers with lyrics that speak of struggles, gratitude, grace, belonging and possibility. The Midlands1 celebration event will be anchored in music…

For years this quote by Elizabeth Kubler Ross, Swiss-American psychiatrist has been above my desk:

> "People are like stained – glass windows. They sparkle and shine
> when the sun is out, but when the darkness sets in, their true
> beauty is only revealed if there is light from within."

What a gift it has been within the PfP context to experience this light from within, what we often refer to as 'shiny eyes'. Just yesterday I had Lions River business leader, Simon Francis share with us with a considerable glint in his eye, the awe of attending a parent meeting with Principal Slo Mhlongo. Shiny-eyed children performed with much expression a non-supportive and then a supportive household. In doing so, inviting parent conversations, whose contribution included an acknowledgement of personal struggles with curriculum, but leaving shiny-eyed, grateful for the opportunity to be included in making a difference and guided with how they can support.

I have a childhood memory of the Salvation Army moving through our suburb in Port Elizabeth, you heard them before you saw them and there was always a mad scramble for a coin to drop into the tin. Most important was to stop what you were doing and join in. It was such a sense of awe as the brass band would march past, cymbals crashing, tins shaking and barefoot children running onto the street, marching along and being swept up in the excitement. Experiences always arrive with music in my life and so this image of the music permeating a street, a suburb, a lifetime memory…this is PfP in me, my career and my community. It is who I am…when head, heart and feet align.

Like samp and beans, shisa and nyama, Partners and For Possibility!

Kubashnee (Kay) Moodley
Learning Process Facilitator and LPF Supervisor (Inland region)

I spent many years searching and working exceptionally hard, feeling that I always had more to prove than most of my colleagues because I am female and Indian. Perhaps a bit selfishly, I grasped the opportunities for learning that came my way and created a legacy of "I" with my work, achieving many successful projects, with amazing client reviews. The "I" was important to me for many reasons (a story for another day).

My concept of what "I" meant began to change when I started my PfP journey. The PfP programme was very different to any other leadership programmes I have facilitated, implemented or taught in the past. It was Servant Leadership at its best, something that I had unknowingly been searching for, and I couldn't believe my luck.

The universe was actually listening to me. The programme **released** my HEART, my compassion and care for school principals who I would have never ordinarily have engaged with nor been gifted to hear their stories. I was ignited with an overwhelming appreciation for humanity through the work that PfP did.

I was given the opportunity to stand on the balcony with soft eyes and watch humans connect, despite their differences of colour, gender or age. The most rewarding part was that I was able to leave the balcony and participate in the connections. I learnt the importance of "I" in others, and how "We" can show up for each other to achieve "Work" in communities for our children and our country.

This all happened through the guidance and structure of a well-administered programme, one that advocates equality and the possibility of "what if?" with a heart to serve. The concept of Ubuntu (I am because you are) was brought to life, with business leaders wearing their hearts on their sleeves and school principals starting to reflect on the possibility of being their own heroes.

I am proud, humbled, blessed and honoured to be part of the PfP Community.

Marichen Mortimer
Learning Process Facilitator in Tshwane

When I received the call in 2014 to join PfP, I was extremely curious to know what the organisation was about, what the journey between partners would look like and how I could possibly make a contribution to a cause that felt huge and challenging. How can I make a positive contribution to the educational landscape of South Africa?

As leadership development and education are both close to my heart, I embarked on the journey with goodwill and an open heart although I had no idea of where the journey would take me or my fellow journeymen and women.

My journey started with the Tshwane3 Leadership Circle. What an incredible experience; with 21 fellow South Africans, committed to making a difference, no matter the challenges we faced, personally and professionally. I have seen many examples of courageous and creative ways of tackling challenges in the schooling environment, personal hardship and how it was overcome, sharing across boundaries and tapping into the kaleidoscope of powerful and diverse perspectives.

I have learned the power of authentic leadership, showing up as your true self, caring and sharing and giving others the same gift. I have realised, once again, that we basically want similar things from life: love and acceptance and the opportunity to bring our unique gifts to the world.

Several years and seven leadership circle journeys on, I am amazed how I always learn. The socio-politico-economic environment is continuously changing, and the impact thereof is also altering the way in which we work with each other. I believe that through the PfP process we continue to learn and grow and become better versions of ourselves, which leads to better leaders, better society and better learners… our ultimate goal.

My PfP journey always reminds me of the Wild Fig Tree (Ficus Thonningii). The big, solid roots reflect the importance of the time we spend connecting with each other to build a solid foundation to our relationship. The trunk of the tree is the journey we walk together – never straight – sometimes we need to take a side road, only to come back. The branches are the training and learning we engage in and share along the way, and the leaves are the benefits that learners experience from our work. The delicious fruit from the Fig Tree is the gift of friendship we give each other. Precious and soul enhancing.

As a result of PfP, I have a wide network of friends from diverse backgrounds, languages, cultures, religious orientation and dreams. It is a colourful kaleidoscope of vibrant possibilities and I will treasure my time with each and every one for as long as I live.

Mel Tomlinson
Learning Process Facilitator in Nelspruit

How has PfP impacted my life? This is a huge question so I have categorised the elements that have touched me the most deeply:

The PfP community

I have always been a lone ranger, somewhat an outsider, not quite in with the mainstream but also not totally out. This was further entrenched by living in Nelspruit and starting my coaching business before there were other coaches in the town.

PfP has allowed me the wonderful opportunity to reconnect with the larger world out there, a world of coaches and one of knowledge and connection. I remember going to the retreat arranged for the PfP team in Ficksburg feeling so excited to be part of something not organised by me. The retreat, however, was difficult for me, highlighting how isolated I had become and how, despite feeling bold and brave, one uncomfortable experience sent me recoiling back to my comfort zone, afraid to step out. This has been invaluable for me in learning about myself, trusting my own wisdom and being willing to stay with the discomfort and show up again.

Connecting to the PfP community through regular Zoom calls has kept me in the loop. I still watch myself take the occasional "get out of jail free card", an old habit of disengaging when it suits me, but the awareness now forces me to actively engage at every opportunity, something that has contributed to my personal growth. I have learnt the importance of 'being in the room'.

Having only ever worked for myself, PfP has given me the amazing experience of working as part of a team, where I don't get to make the rules. This, too, has developed a side of me I longed to experiment with. I have learnt to listen, be more respectful and toe the line; something I have never had to do. The discipline to hand in journals, mark written work and attend my supervisory coaching sessions has at times stretched me, but I never saw it as optional, rather contractual and purposeful.

Being under the leadership of a remarkable team of committed and conscious people has given me a beautiful example of the many things I have read. Louise demonstrates vulnerability as a leader in a way I admire and aspire, to but am petrified of (Brene Brown would be proud). Robyn is the most amazing relationship-builder and has an insatiable capacity for people. I learn from her loving, patient and caring ways and always feel supported by her. Irma works so hard, stretches herself so far and has grown so much in the time I have known her. Jansie keeps everyone on the straight and narrow, at times frustrating me, but through that forcing me to voice my opinion regardless of protocol. Everyone has impacted me significantly.

The Partners for Possibility

This is probably my favourite part of PfP. I love my circles. I love each partner and partnership deeply. The biggest shift I made from my first circle to the second one has been relaxation; I guess similar to the difference between raising one's first and second child. I am more trusting of the process and more able to simply hold the space for the partners to grow at their own pace.

I have always seen myself as a bridge and thought my personal tag line should be "I straddle the divide". This could not be more apt in the role I play as LPF. I am most comfortable in the gap between two parties, being a bridge for them to meet on. I love gently nudging them along when they are slow or slowing them down when they are going too fast. I love watching the many creative ways in which each partnership approaches their particular set of challenges. I love watching the puzzle pieces change shape until they fall into their respective, perfect places. I love the perfect and beautiful combinations of people.

For me the circle is a place of coming home. In this time of being an LPF, my two best friends moved away. One to Johannesburg and one to New Zealand. All I can say is that what could have left a huge hole in my life simply allowed me to take more joy from my work and relationships, and I have had the opportunity to invest more in these new connections.

As an LPF I have had a platform to exercise and develop my own leadership skills with a variety of people at different stages of their lives. I feel accomplished and proud of the progress made in NEL2, my first circle, and excited about NEL4. I actively observe how my personal growth translates into benefit for the circle and see that where NEL2 ended NEL4 has begun. As I learn and grow, the partners learn and grow too.

PfP learning opportunities

I think the thing I am most grateful for is the many learning opportunities we are given in PfP. I try not to miss one masterclass or workshop offered to us. I have been on my own for so long, paying my way and creating my own opportunities that the generosity of PfP is something I always deeply appreciate. I feel that it is a brilliant example of abundance thinking.

Of all the workshops. I feel that Time to Think (TtT) has impacted me most deeply, with immediate benefits to my own coaching practice, my marital relationship and generally to my inner peace. Relieving myself of the need, and quite frankly bad habit, of having to personally come up with 10 solutions for every problem and instead trusting my clients to find their own wisdom was something I seemed to have missed in my initial coaching training and finally got, loud and clear, during TtT.

Increased efficiency

I am not sure I would have been confident to say yes to PfP had I known that I would downscale my business, losing my right hand, Manus, and Waheeda, my PA. I was already busy, but PfP helped me to see that I was simply busy being busy. Running my second circle with less support than before is still completely manageable and forces me to plan properly. In fact, I believe that my own business has been blessed with additional clients while I give of myself wholeheartedly to my PfP circle. I have always been a good delegator, and PfP has allowed me to exercise my faith in the fact that "everything is going to be alright". Every day is a new opportunity for a miracle!

Unexpected gifts

I often wondered why I was approached to be part of PfP. Although I never doubted that I had the ability to do the required work, I did doubt my understanding of the SA education system and its relevance to my life. To this day, I am still very challenged in this area.

School was something I did with relative ease and little push back. I achieved good marks and left with no need to ever return. I chose not to have children, so I escaped the school-mom-run, the sandwich-and-tuckshop club and the many other things that go with being a parent. I also missed the inside track on education as it is now, the changeover to Model C schools and had no language for anything school-related.

Joining PfP was a rapid learning curve, but nothing compared to the real learning I was exposed to when I was introduced to Jetro. Jetro appeared in a WhatsApp message one day when a principal posted a photograph on the NEL2 group of a child who had been through a particularly difficult time after losing his mom. It was instantly apparent to me that this message was for me; that I had been nominated and elected for this 'project'. I rallied around, put a post of Facebook requesting donations and began what initially appeared to be a reasonably easy-to-do, quick-fix. How difficult can it be to get a kid a school uniform, stationery and some clothes, top up their cupboards with food stuffs and throw some money at the problem?

That notion lasted about two minutes after I met Jetro. This sweet, well-behaved young man sprang into my heart instantly and my husband, Cobus, and I are now co-parenting (for lack of another word), Jetro with his great-granny, Maureen.

Jetro sparked my fury, my fear, my love and my compassion; all of the emotions I was saving myself from by not becoming a mom. Jetro made education my business because 'my kid' is directly impacted by it. Jetro rendered me useless; without tools and without strategy, crying on the shoulders of my NEL2 principals. When Jetro came home from school and sent me photos of how he was beaten with an electric pipe by his teacher for misunderstanding an instruction, I was mad. When I realised that this diligent student, now in Grade 8, did not grasp timetables, I was sad. When I saw his face light up during a week when he attended maths tuition, became a library member for the first time and went to gym with Cobus, my heart was glad. Oh my, what a flood of emotions!

This is the gift PfP has given me; not a gift I would have consciously chosen for myself, but one selected for me because I needed Jetro, I needed to really understand, connect and become committed, not just involved. I have no idea what Jetro will mean to PfP, but to me he means the world. He has also brought our NEL2 circle closer as everyone has a small stake in the life of Jetro and through him they can experience my love and compassion.

Yes, I am afraid of the wheel set in motion. I am very conscious of starting something and the importance of finishing what I have started. I am so out of my depth. I don't know when to speak up or shut up. I don't know who to speak to and what the repercussions will be. I am connected but still feel muted. I am brave but feel afraid to step out of line. I can make a difference, but is it the right thing to do for the right reasons?

All I know is that I am now part of an amazing organisation with support structures and processes that will gently hold me, guide me, try not to judge me and cheer me on in my endeavour to make South Africa a little better.

Merridy Edgson
Learning Process Facilitator, Western Cape

My amazing journey with PfP started in 2012. The programme was only two years old and I was starting my own new career as a coach and facilitator. After supporting four circles of partnerships in Cape Town I 'hung up my boots' while I packed up and moved to the countryside with the intention of starting a quiet life in the village of Darling. However, our move to Darling coincided with PfP growing into the rural areas and I was honoured when asked if I would assist in bringing this exceptional programme to schools in the Swartland and the West Coast.

At the time of writing, I am facilitating my sixth circle of partnerships and feel so privileged to have worked with more than 40 school principals and business leaders. The programme is now national and has touched over 1,000 schools and impacted almost 1 million learners. Wow! How wonderful to have been part of this.

This journey of self-awareness and leadership development has not only had an impact on our principals and their partners. It has also had a great impact on my personal development in the following ways:

- I have had the privilege of working with communities I hadn't ventured into before. I broadened my relationships and discovered friendships with people I may never have met in the past. Seeing things through different lenses has broadened my perspectives significantly.

- I am in awe of the principals and teachers in these schools whose commitment to their learners' well-being is exemplary. In spite of the apparent lack of resources in both school and community, it is heart-warming to see all the smiles and shining eyes.

- The programme attracts business leaders with open hearts and a commitment to change and I have so enjoyed my journey with each of them. I have witnessed the partnership relationships and noticed how each one unfolds differently. However, in almost all cases these relationships grow into firm friendships that last beyond the scope of the structured programme.

- As the partners and principals have reflected on their own journeys, I have been encouraged to reflect on mine. I notice how self-reflection is one of the most powerful motivations to change the way we show up in the world.

- I have been lucky enough to attend the PfP courses, Time to Think, Flawless Consulting and Community Building, at least six times each. Each facilitator and group brings a different dynamic and influence, and I learn something new every time.

- I have had the honour to work with the Symphonia for South Africa leaders, administrators and colleagues around the country. I have been inspired by the energy and opportunity for change that many of my LPF colleagues bring to this programme.

I am now 70 years old and I would like to thank PfP for making my belief in continuous development, personal growth and a life of purpose a reality.

Nicky Bush
Learning Process Facilitator in Cape Town and Time to Think facilitator

My passion is to work with people as they navigate different perspectives, celebrate diversity, learn and grow from one another. As an LPF, one of the roles I play in the partnership and group dynamic is to hold a safe space for very different people to come together to build a relationship and connect with the group. Diversity is the incredible gift that is offered in the partnership and among the group, allowing for different perspectives and an opportunity to generate and share ideas for new ways of doing things in a school environment, as well as support and solidarity for the common challenges faced.

When we come together as a Community of Practice, all the hierarchy from business and from the school environment is taken away and we meet as equals with a shared vision. One of the highlights for me is to see the 'lightbulb moments' when people take a deep breath and begin to move out of their comfort zones. To share an example of this; we hold the Community of Practise sessions at a different school every six weeks, so everyone in the group experiences all the different school environments in the leadership circle. At first, there are concerns, the principal at a school in Grassy Park is afraid of visiting a school in Khayelitsha as she has never been in the area before. The principal of the school in Khayelitsha is also afraid of visiting Grassy Park as he has never been in the area. Once they have taken the leap and visited areas they have never been in before, they are overwhelmed at how welcomed and embraced they are by the community. They experience such a wonderful example of nation building through small acts of courage and a willingness to move out of comfort zones.

In the past year I have facilitated a one day Time to Think workshop for many of the new partnerships that have been launched across South Africa. Time to Think is a platform from which all partnerships can start and be anchored in.

The Time to Think workshop focuses on building listening skills, experiencing generative attention and appreciation from each other as well as group equality and a collaborative, respectful and appreciative way of meeting and ensuring all voices are heard.

I would love to share some of the magical stories of transformation I have experienced in these workshops and a new way of being taken into the school environment. This time together offers opportunities to change single stories, celebrate diversity and come together as human beings with a vision for change.

The Stories...

Last year I worked with a group in the Northern Cape. For some of the partners, this was the first time they were meeting each other. For others, this was the first time they had been alongside people of different colour in a workshop. I had not anticipated the fear and resistance from some partners in the room. One of the women approached me quietly and asked if I could move the chairs slightly further apart from each other as she felt uncomfortable being so close together. She was struggling with sitting next to a person of a different colour, holding her own assumptions and untrue stories that needed be dismantled fast! It was a really difficult situation. I made sure everyone was as comfortable as possible and we started with a round to get all the voices in the room. We then moved into thinking pairs of three minutes each way. The question was "Who has shaped you to make you who you are today?" and the objective was to experience absolutely beautifully, uninterrupted attention as each person shared their story with another. When we came back into a circle to share as a round, the chairs were closer together. The partnership that had asked to move the chairs at the beginning had their arms around each other. When it came to their sharing they reflected back: *"We thought we were so different but actually we are sisters!"*

We all carry our own single stories that can define the relationships we have, the conversations we have, the way we view the world. What if we were willing to listen, give beautiful attention to a different story, a new perspective?

Sometimes the power of appreciation and being noticed can have a physical effect.

I was working with a group in De Aar (Northern Cape) where principals and business partners had come from afar. As a round we were sharing a time in our lives when we had felt really appreciated. It was a beautiful experience hearing all the stories of appreciation and realising the power and importance of appreciation in our lives. How do we bring it into everything we do? However there was one principal who had come into the room very quietly, she was very reserved and sat hunched up not wanting to share. When it came to her turn for sharing a story of appreciation, she quietly said "I don't think I have ever been appreciated in my life." Horrors! What to do? I was completely stumped. I decided to continue with a lump in my throat...

Then one of the principals stood up boldly and said he would like to appreciate her for her incredible commitment and courage to work and travel to her school every day, and the passion with which she does it. This was followed by another appreciation from another principal. The appreciations continued from every single person in the group and the effect was a physical change in this tired, sad principal who, appreciation by appreciation, slowly sat a little straighter, lifted her head a little higher and began to smile. By the end of the session she was sharing and laughing with the group. She felt acknowledged, seen and highly appreciated! Appreciation BUILDS, let's do it as often and as genuinely as possible!

From a Cape Town partnership, one of the principals shared a story of how experiencing Time to Think had changed the way he dealt with his learners at school. He said, "Before, when they were naughty, I would line them all up military style with their arms at their sides outside my office and they were not allowed to talk. After our Time to Think workshop, now, when a leaner is naughty, I ask them to join me in my office, I sit down with them, look them in the eyes and ask them to tell me their story, what is happening that you are behaving like this. One boy I discovered had lost his father and was acting out of pure devastation of the loss of his dad. He broke down when telling me the story and after our conversation was completely different in class. He felt noticed and cared for. He was more engaged in class and no longer acting out to get attention. I now always ask the learners to tell me their stories and I have found a whole new understanding of the bigger picture about what is truly going on."

A principal working in a poverty stricken area in Cape Town shared her story of the importance of bringing equality into her school, modelling behaviour and believing in her staff. She decided to move her little boy, who was in Grade 6 and who was attending a private, well-resourced school in a wealthy area, to her school in a poverty stricken area. She shared that he was nervous and made comments like "But these children are different to me, Mommy," but she entrusted her child into the care of the Grade 6 teacher and fully believed in the importance of integration. After one term, her child is thriving, making good friends and seeing many different sides to the story. We referred back to the danger of the single story. Before, her son had one story and that was that the children at mommy's school are poor. Now he has many stories… the children at mommy's school are poor and they are kind and they love to laugh and they are good at maths and sport.… After she modelled this to her staff, now many staff members are bringing their own children to the school. For me, this shows a whole new level of belief and confidence in the school and a sign of a very promising future.

This work seems to be unlocking stories and feelings, and creating safer spaces to share and support one another. Imagine an environment where principals and teachers can provide beautiful attention and appreciation to encourage amazing, independent thinking!

I believe that when we truly respect each other as human beings, we have the power to change our world, one conversation at a time.

Nomfuzo Ntolosi
Learning Process Facilitator, Johannesburg

"Mntanam, imfundo lilifa ongasoze walohluthwa mntu" – loosely translated: *"Education is your legacy; you have no future without education."* This random piece of advice would be offered by my grandfather when in a deep state of reflection about life, which was often the case. He would say this, in his very soft and ever gentle voice that appealed even to the 6 year-old in me to do nothing else but listen. For my grandfather, if nothing else, with these words he hoped to inspire me and my siblings to dream for a better life which, to him, seemed only possible when you have a certain level of formal education. I went on to hear these words, uttered by different people, in various contexts that contributed to shaping the adult I am.

I have taken so much from how this precious man who held his household of 15-20 family members at any given time, together through his leadership. Besides being an example of the change he wanted to see, his collaborative manner of engaging instilled in me the importance of the value that each person brings into any situation, no matter the age, level of education or life experience. He would not hesitate to call a gathering when he discerned that everyone's voice in the household would add value when particular family decisions needed to be made or levels of problem-solving were required – inviting every voice and affording it a chance to be heard. He led where he was, with who he was and what he had – quality of attention, ease, respect, and the list goes on – a true partner for possibility. There is a lot I did not understand about this approach at the time. At that young age I did not even know that these are behaviours that are written about and create a culture and practice of releasing brilliance in the individuals. The greatest learning from this experience is that we are the communities we are looking for.

Fast forward to 2016, I discover and become part of the many other concerned active citizens who are yearning to make a difference in the world – Partners for Possibility. Listening to the programme described and what it seeks to do, leadership development and principal support process, I had no hesitation in my mind, heart and spirit about where I needed to use my skills, experience and live my passion.

As an LPF, I have the honour and privilege of partnering with principals from under resourced schools and business leaders from the South African business community. These partnerships use the creative collective energy of humanity to co-create solutions for change in the schools.

The bounce in the step, the tall shoulders, the beaming smiles, heart prints, ever glowing flame of hope, is how I have experience this programme. Over the years I have witnessed with amazement the bounce in the step of our principals who are renewed and energised by the promise of the possibility of the school at the centre of the community. I marvel at the tall shoulders, as they begin to appreciate the gift of partnership involving all the possible stakeholders, including the ever magical and committed PfP staff, and that they don't have to carry all the problems of the school by themselves.

The eyes shine brighter with each experience of being seen and heard, through their thinking partnerships with the business leader, the triad conversations, training sessions designed to equip them for their leadership journeys, or the Community of Practice space where the different visions of what it means to be a school at the centre of the community are brought to life. As I journey with the principals I have a rare glimpse of what courage in practice looks like, as they, supported and encouraged by their business partners, (abundantly giving of their time, attention, presence, care, friendship, wisdom and passion), making the best of their circumstances, even in situations where inspiration remains a distant experience. Unconscious barriers that often keep individuals in comfort zones of possible complacency for change are challenged and broken. Deeply meaningful, caring and life enhancing partnerships are nurtured in this space and they go on to be partnerships for life. This is a lived experience of leadership as heart-work.

An affirmation with which I enter each new day, *shine where you are*, has taken on an expanded meaning through the Partners for Possibility experience. All the school entrances have the same vision inscribed in various ways – a vision of making a difference in the life of a learner. Here's to leading where we are, with what we have.

Paul Abrams
Learning Process Facilitator in Cape Town

I have spent much of my adult life trying to change the world. A noble goal that sounds good and has set me up for failure and disappointment.

The last few years have been rough. The world has been tough to save, downright unwilling if you ask me. Anger is growing. Poverty is getting worse. Our planet is being destroyed.

Then I learnt that I cannot and should not try to save the world. The idea is to start conversations with those around me. The conversations help us understand ourselves and each other and build relationships of trust. From that base we can start working together to change our immediate environment and heal, nurture and develop our communities. Then there is the possibility of transformation.

That is when PfP came into my life. A leadership programme focused on changing the world one conversation at a time. As an LPF I hold the space for the individuals, partnerships and the circle to conduct these crucial conversations. In the space that I hold there is diversity, life experience, incredible wisdom, a willingness to learn and, most importantly, delicious listening.

I no longer have to change the world. Being part of PfP gives me the opportunity to work with people who are passionate about their world, which will hopefully impact our children so that they can create their own future of possibility.

Paul Sturrock
Partner for Possibility and Learning Process Facilitator in Cape Town

Most school principals express feeling lonely and isolated: caught between the expectations of their employer, staff, parents and learners. Often, they experience very high stress levels which negatively impacts their health and relationships, at work and beyond.

Business leaders do not necessarily speak of loneliness, but other feelings linked to separation and feeling disconnected; amongst others, feeling disempowered in the corporate hierarchy; anxiety about their place in South Africa due to their ethnicity, class or gender, and the fear of travelling into areas they would normally avoid due to crime. In different ways, participants speak of the dehumanising impact of external forces in South Africa.

In this context, I have experienced and witnessed the following. Listening to my partner (principal), feeling her pain, being trusted, laughing and crying together and the energy of working together to make a difference. In the circles, principals appreciated the safe space to be vulnerable and to be able to talk about challenges without feeling judged. Business leaders experienced new respect for principals and gained insights into the complexities of our country. Participants moved beyond their comfort zones, took risks and discovered more of themselves. They experienced a connection with their partners and their circle that enabled them to be more fully human.

Rosie Chirongoma
Partner for Possibility, Learning Process Facilitator in Johannesburg and Time to Think Facilitator

I cannot tell my life story without talking about PfP and not in a cursory by-the-way manner. It's shaped the person I am, the relationships I have and want to be in, the work I do, the conversations I have, and the way I choose to move through the world. The threads from and to PfP run through so many parts of my life, it's incredible. Whenever I meet someone and we can't quite figure out how we know each other, it almost always comes back to PfP.

I've had the gift and absolute privilege to wear different hats at PfP; from business leader recruitment, to member of the leadership team, to partner to Johanna Ramodike at Siphethu Primary School, to becoming an LPF and, now, adding Time to Think facilitator to the list. I have grown!

I would never have applied for the business leader recruitment role. I don't think I was even clear what I was saying yes to in my conversation with Louise in Cape Town after I'd spent two days with her in meetings. When I'd first met her, she'd handed me the Community Building book and leaflets, so matter of fact, like I already belonged to this enterprise and just needed to familiarise myself with the information. It was simple and it felt right.

I've lived so far out of my comfort zone with PfP in every role I've had. The gift has been knowing I can live there and won't die. In fact, I'll grow, thrive and be stronger. I've learnt that I might just be good at things I never thought I was. I might just surprise myself. I carry that to this day. I'm bolder and braver. My heart has expanded and it keeps doing so. The knowledge I've been exposed to and absorbed completely has molded and shaped my thinking.

The greatest joy of my PfP journey has been having a front row seat to how something can grow from one person, Louise's dream for South Africa's children, into a movement. That's what PfP is. Louise's dedication, perseverance, unwavering conviction for the cause is like nothing I've ever encountered in my life and I don't know if I will ever again. It's held space for my own dedication, perseverance and conviction. Louise's light shines so bright, that I have no choice but to shine mine and I know that has a ripple effect.

When I shine my light, others shine theirs too. I'm part of a movement of shining lights in a world that can often be quite dark, and that is the most amazing thing about PfP; people from all walks of life, strangers whose paths would otherwise never have crossed are standing next to each other with love in their eyes. And I get to experience this all the time. My heart expands till it feels like it will burst. My assumptions, prejudices, stories all come tumbling down, and now I move through the world with curiosity, always looking for what might surprise me. What I might react to with Ben Zander's, "how fascinating!"

Savanthika Pillay
Learning Process Facilitator, Gauteng and Community Building Facilitator

We are living in disruptive and troubled times. The future of our children is looking bleak. We can sit on our hands or hold our heads, lamenting and complaining OR we can choose to make a contribution that creates the possibility of a better future. We can make a choice to work with hope rather than despair.

Václav Havel, one of the leaders of the Velvet Revolution in Czechoslovakia, describes hope as:

> *"Hope, in this deep and powerful sense, is not the same as joy that things are going well, or willingness to invest in enterprises that are obviously headed for early success, but rather an ability to work for something because it is good, not just because it stands a chance to succeed. The more unpromising the situation in which we demonstrate hope, the deeper that hope is. Hope is not the same thing as optimism. It is not the conviction that something will turn out well, but the certainty that something makes sense, regardless of how it turns out."*

PfP helped me find hope and it gave me a platform and a way to respond meaningfully to the education crisis that we are facing in our country. It gave me a role and allowed me to be of service in a way that was meaningful and respectful to the communities that I wanted to reach.

The idea of respect cannot be overstated. One of the criticisms levelled against 'do-gooders' or people who have inherited or acquired privilege, is that they assume they know what's good for others, what the solutions are and how they should be reached. They step in with an attitude of knowing and fixing and, in that way, they strip people of dignity and power.

PfP cannot be accused of making such an egregious mistake. The PfP programme calls on us to pause, to reflect on what was, to sense what is and to get to know what and who is in the system. Through this process we build relationships, give authentic and respectful attention and develop presence for deep thinking, together, so that the mind can break free to accept responsibility in a co-created relational space and build one's own personal and professional leadership.

This is the most essential work that happens on the programme and it is from this interior place that the partnerships start to think together about a project or a plan that would create a more hopeful future for the children in the school.

The children are the ultimate beneficiaries of this programme and they benefit because PfP takes care of the adults who are taking care of them.

There is an African Prayer that springs to mind:

> Let us take care of the children for they have a long way to go
> Let us take care of the elders, for they have come a long way
> Let us take care of those in between for they are doing the work

I will forever be deeply grateful to Louise van Rhyn who is the visionary and the soul force behind the PfP programme. She designed a brilliant and thoughtful programme. She provided hope and a way for ordinary people to make a contribution, to cross the bridge, to go over to the other side, to be one human being with another human being, to sit in community, to work together, to find belonging.

The impact of being part of PfP on members of our core team

I agree with Gary Hamel, visiting professor at the London Business School, that many organisations are no longer fit for human life. My commitment is to practice what we preach and co-create an organisation where people willingly share their gifts and creativity and feel that they can flourish.

It was heart-warming and humbling to hear how members of our team feel about being part of the organisation.

Dorcas Dube
Marketing and Communications Manager

"Wherever life plants you, bloom with grace." This quote by Isabella Martin summarises my PfP journey…

Life planted me in the PfP community in 2016 when I joined the team as Marketing and Communications Manager. As a 26-year-old, passionate about social change, I didn't realise that I wasn't given just a job, but the start to a fulfilling, worthwhile, life-changing learning journey.

On this PfP journey, I have learnt a lot and it would be impossible to list everything. Some of my key learnings over the years include:

- Relationship building is at the centre of success. The benefits of good relationships are far reaching and include the ability to focus on the possibilities and on unearthing gifts that can never materialise if relationships are not nurtured.

- I have always been a quiet voice, but I have realised that every voice matters. As a result, I have learnt to position my voice in spaces and make meaningful contributions. I have also encouraged my team to find their voices in each space. It's been a beautiful experience to watch the team blossom while finding their voices.

- One of the most important lessons on this journey has been the realisation that at the core of leadership is humanity. This has taught me to be a courageous leader who has a lot of compassion and care for people. Moreover, I learnt that self-leadership is the secret to servant leadership. This has kept me pressing on to the mission of changing lives and sending ripples of hope amidst the various challenges we experience.

- If I have a differing view, I have learnt to express it rather than "going with the flow". This has been a difficult but fulfilling lesson that has sometimes resulted in the need to have courageous conversations. Appreciation for differences is not always easy. However, as Stephen Covey points out: "Strength lies in differences, not in similarities." I can attest that my team has become stronger since I've grown in this respect.

- I learnt the importance of thinking time and silence. I have become a better listener and examine how I show up and how I converse. The former has prompted me to be conscious of my reflection through the gaze of others.

- One of the most fundamental aspects I have learnt is that I owe it to myself to become everything I ever dreamt of. Through PfP I have witnessed learners succeed against all odds. This has not only motivated me but made me believe in the power of dreams.

It's been a privilege to be part of the PfP community. To more learnings and sending ripples of hope!

Ernest Moore
Principal Liaison in the Western Cape & Former School Principal

When I first joined PfP, I had been a principal for just over 12 years and I was in a good space, having weathered those first few turbulent years which followed my secondment to 'steady the ship' at a school which was on the brink of either being closed or merged with a neighbouring school.

I had a great, committed and dedicated staff, supportive parents and receptive, well-disciplined learners. But I also had all the answers, or at least so I thought. When staff or parents came to see me with problems, I had the solution before they could even complete the question. I had only one challenge, or so I thought, and that was that my workload was too heavy. I was often criticised by my peers for the all the duties and responsibilities I had taken upon myself. There were however, two reasons for this, firstly, I felt that my staff was already overburdened and making so many personal sacrifices, that I could not add to their heavy workload. The second was, of course, my issues of trust, believing that the only way to get a job done, and done well, was to do it myself. I was ripe for Partners for Possibility!

My journey, as many others have undoubtedly testified, was amazing. Suffice to say that for me it was not only my own learnings that brought me joy, but witnessing how Grade Heads and SMT members slowly began applying the principles of Time to Think and Flawless Consulting in their own senior and grade meetings. This was not a request or requirement from my office, but, I believe, their own internalisation of its value.

If the first phase of my PfP experience could be likened to a journey aboard a Five Star super luxury coach along the picturesque Garden Route, then the second phase was an opportunity to be taken on a tour of the engine room and control centre of this magnificent carrier. Here I was given the opportunity to meet the behind-the-scenes people and the honour of working with the team who made this amazing journey possible. Here I got to experience first-hand the months of planning, the days of preparation and the hours of conversations that went into ensuring that the coach was absolutely ready before departure and that every passenger on board would enjoy optimal benefit from their journey. But I also got to see the maintenance crew at work, always on hand, not only ensuring that wheels did not come off, but ready to repair within an instant any misfortunes that might occur and to reassure passengers whenever the journey encountered unforeseen potholes or speedbumps in the road.

I've always agreed that if you cannot stand the sight of dirty dishes, stay out of the kitchen. But with Partners for Possibility, the opportunity of getting my hands wet has been one of the most rewarding experiences yet!

Gail McMillan
Member of the Monitoring and Evaluation team

After living for over 20 years in Europe and the Middle East, where I worked with homeless young people and other vulnerable groups, I returned to South Africa, and in 2014 I spent a few months working with a night-shelter organisation in Cape Town. During that period, I became increasingly aware of the devastating impact that an inadequate education continues to have on the lives and prospects of so many South Africans. I decided to look for an opportunity to contribute to improving basic education as a means of helping to prevent homelessness and other forms of suffering and indignity that so often afflict those who have not been equipped with sufficient education.

I starting looking into education-related NGOs that were operating in South Africa and PfP stood out for several reasons. Firstly, the organisation was focused on strengthening leadership, and my postgraduate studies in the UK had convinced me that competent and inspirational leadership, particularly at the 'coalface' level, is an absolutely critical factor in efforts to rescue ailing institutions, be they public, private or nongovernmental. At the time, I didn't know much about the impact of leadership in education specifically, but a bit of research revealed that the leadership practices and values of school principals are among the critical factors that explain variation in student outcomes between schools.

Beyond the clear rationale for strengthening school leadership, I was inspired by how the programme's partnership approach was helping to break down entrenched social barriers by bringing together South Africans with a common purpose but completely different backgrounds – and for long enough to develop a real understanding of each other's lives and realities.

Another feature of PfP that I found both interesting and encouraging was how the passion and commitment of its leadership and implementing team was matched by the skills needed to deliver their mandate. In almost every corner of the world there are non-profit organisations (NPOs) like PfP striving to tackle some of the most intractable and challenging problems that exist. Sadly many, if not most, struggle to fulfil their mission due to a lack of technical and organisational capacity (largely because of their competitive disadvantage against the private and public sectors in salary benchmarking). However, in PfP there seemed to be an unusually large number of exceptionally well-qualified professionals who were foregoing opportunities to make much more money elsewhere to be part of the movement started by founder Louise van Rhyn.

Fortunately for me, Louise welcomed me into the organisation as a volunteer, and I was subsequently offered a role in PfP's M&E team. Through that work, and especially through my contact with participating principals and business leaders, I soon realised that the programme's impact on them and its ripple effect through the schools and out into their communities was far more profound than I could ever have imagined. I have shed many a tear of joy while reading reflections from principals and business partners, and will always remember one principal saying 'I was on the verge of giving up, but PfP gave me back my life and my career.'

PfP was indeed fulfilling its mission; yet maintaining financial support for the programme was a persistent and exceptionally tough challenge. Among the reasons for this was the difficulty at an early stage in the programme's history in showing that it was positively impacting academic outcomes. Although others were involved in fundraising, Louise was clearly the driving force in ensuring that the programme kept going and, like others in the team, I worried about the toll this was taking on her.

I remember sitting beside Louise at a Global Leadership Summit event in 2015 and hearing Bill Hybels talk about the intangible qualities of great leadership. One of them is 'grit', which he described as passion and perseverance over the long haul and he likened it to Watty Piper's *Little Blue Engine* that refused to give up. Having worked with Louise for about a year by then, I had realised that grittiness was undoubtedly one of her characteristics. I know now, however, that I hadn't seen anything yet at that stage.

In the last few years there have been a couple of times when the survival of the PfP programme has been in serious doubt because of funding constraints, and the pressure on the leadership team has been immense. At those times and beyond, many people have worked hard and made sacrifices to ensure that our work could continue. However, in my mind, there is absolutely no doubt that without Louise's grit, PfP would not have survived and the programme impacts we have continued to see (including improvements in academic achievement) would simply not have happened.

I have never, *ever* known anybody personally who possesses more sheer, unrelenting tenacity to keep going against seemingly impossible odds in pursuit of a dream to make other peoples' lives better. I am grateful for the opportunity I've had to learn lessons in leadership from Louise and from the extraordinary group of active citizens that she has drawn into the PfP community. On several occasions, Louise's expression of faith in me has nudged me out of my comfort zone into a task I wouldn't have braved otherwise. That is real leadership, and I have gained new skills and grown in confidence each time. Above all, I value the chance I've had to contribute to turning our team's shared dream into a reality.

Jansie Rautenbach
Operations Lead and KZN Regional Manager

My journey with Symphonia for South Africa started in 2014 when I received a phone call from Louise van Rhyn to talk about my interest in working with PfP. At the time, I was building up a financial consultancy business after many years in the corporate world.

During this time, I had lengthy conversations with a good friend and ex-colleague about the state of our nation, poverty, inequality and the future of our children in this beautiful country. He introduced me to Symphonia for South Africa and the Partners for Possibility Programme as he thought I would fit perfectly into the team of people who runs PfP.

That is how I came to speak with Louise, and when she shared her vision with me I realised how well it resonates and that I share the dream. When I think back now, my first thought at the time was how Louise took a leap to accept me into the team, without hesitation, without rules, but with open arms and an open heart to bring what I can give, to walk together.

During the years that have followed, we have worked together on a daily basis. We have shared laughs and tears. There were times when I woke up in the morning and sat for some time in front of my laptop, trying to think what I was going to tell staff members and creditors as we could not pay them. We were totally understaffed and worked extremely hard. The hours were long, but we pushed on, never willing to let go of the dream. The vision we shared was that we have no choice; we have to bring South Africans together from all aspects of life and that we have to break down the barriers of apartheid, poverty, inequality and colonialism. Our plan has always been to do this by starting with the education system; but it is so much more than that. It requires each South African to take his neighbour's hand and walk together.

The learnings I have taken from PfP are endless. From Time to Think to Flawless Consulting to Community Building I have changed the way I work and the way I show up so drastically that my friends and family have seen a radical positive shift in me. I have the privilege of waking up every day and feeling joyful and happy. I never thought I would have a job that would become part of my being, where I could enjoy every moment and give children and adults "shining eyes".

PfP has many magic ingredients, but one of them that stands out for me is the make-up of the leadership team that runs the organisation. Every leadership team member has unique qualities that they bring and, in the end, we form a very strong, robust team that can conquer the world. We do not work alone, we walk together with trust and mutual respect and with care and compassion.

The essence of our work is the fact that we build the community to become one South Africa and that we break down the fences of apartheid and colonialism. It is breathtaking to see the shining eyes of a principal who has found his voice, who can stand up and say that he has a strong SMT and SGB, a school to be proud of with learners who have a future, and a community around the school which supports it.

Another magic ingredient of PfP is that we have a flat organisational structure and it is amazing to see how people are motivated and excited when their voices are heard. When they are given the opportunity to step up and lead, notwithstanding their rank or status in the organisation. This is what inspires people and what leads to inspirational and ground-breaking ideas and solutions.

Then, we also have an amazing team of Learning Process Facilitators, the backbone of our organisation. These are the men and women who bring the circles together and do the hard work on the ground. Each one has the passion for building the community they are in.

The organisation has grown rapidly over the past years and is now strong and stable, with very few of the cash flow challenges which Louise and I lost sleep over a few years ago. I remember how we expressed a wish during an event years ago where we said, "if only we had enough cash flow to have a good night's sleep". The goal has now shifted for me to how we can work alongside more school principals, business partners and organisations to build a stronger South Africa.

Since then, we have grown into a formidable organisation with a national footprint. I learned many lessons and had many moments of joy, but through this all I am mostly appreciative of the fact that PfP made me a better person who looks at the world with sympathetic eyes, with no judgement, with no expectations of what I want, but rather what I can do for my family, my neighbour, my community and my South Africa.

Now I am able to wake up and say "What can I do today to inspire someone to build South Africa, so that each child has the opportunity to get a proper education?"

Imagine if each business leader in South Africa took the hand of one school principal to build our country. One school at a time, one day at a time. Suddenly the vision becomes a reality.

The Symphonia team, and specifically Louise, has become my family and at the same time has given me the opportunity to become a true citizen. My wish is that we can look back in ten years and say, "We have brought our citizens together. We have given our children a future."

I will be forever grateful to Louise and the team for accepting me and allowing me to be part of PfP.

It has been a life-changing experience.

Justin Foxton
Stakeholder Engagement (KZN) and Community Building Facilitator

I clearly remember the day when I first heard about Partners for Possibility. I remember it because of the impact it had on me at a very deep and personal level, and I recall leaving my coffee meeting with Louise van Rhyn drunk with possibility.

Louise and I had never met before that meeting in Cape Town, but we had both recently returned from working stints in the UK, and, as it turned out, our hearts both burned with the same fire for change in South Africa; a fire ignited by the possibility of mobilising citizens in the co-creation of a new reality for our nation.

Our first meeting was probably a year or two before the actual start of my PfP journey, but as Louise shared her vision for partnering school principals of under-resourced schools with business leaders, in a profound co-learning leadership development journey, I realised that this was a prophetic voice speaking into our time; a post-rainbow nation, post-democratic voice that was leading us one person, one conversation at a time, into a new and utterly vital era of deep reparation, transformation and healing.

As an aside: Louise will tell you that the Dinokeng Scenarios*, in particular the scenario that encouraged us to "walk together", played a key catalysing role in the beginning of Partners for Possibility. I have never seen it quite that way. I believe that Louise's vision (shared and elucidated in different ways by others who, at the time, were also foretelling a new type of citizen leadership for our nation), played a key catalysing role for the scenario planners who developed the Dinokeng Scenarios. They may or may not have known it at the time, but Louise had already started to do the work and as such had already scattered the seeds of that particular scenario into the ether. The scenario planners were just breathing in those seeds.

I went straight back to my home in Kwa-Zulu Natal and began telling people about this extraordinary vision of cross-sectoral collaboration and development and how it could change South Africa – not just the education sector, but all sectors. Louise went on to build PfP, one leader, one school at a time. I went on to become an ardent PfP cheerleader.

On the day of that meeting, I remember that we both shared a deep nagging sense of unfinished business from the Truth and Reconciliation Commission; of a journey begun but ended too soon without fundamental shifts in our behaviour, or even a roadmap or some next steps. How could there be true reconciliation without some sort of action, redress or effort? It was a journey that was so incredibly powerful and profound of itself, but one that left so many unanswered questions. It couldn't take us into the new realm of healing and change that would be needed for us to succeed as one, unified nation.

But in the same breath, who were we to even try; to even talk of trying? Here at Melissa's Coffee Shop sat a Foxton and a Van Rhyn – dreaming about "making the country a better place". How dare we, after our complicity in screwing it up?

But I left with an even bigger question; the right question with a decade of time and thinking under my belt: How dare we not? By every definition, by absolute necessity, it needed to be people that looked and sounded like us. Such visions must be born from within the coddled cosiness of privilege for them to hold real, transformational, healing power. Because, of course, those most transformed by visions as big as Partners for Possibility would be us! – because the absolute power of Louise's vision that I sensed in our first conversation, but was only able to fully articulate a decade later, went way beyond education. Her vision was of a mechanism – a journey – that would take us as a people to a brand new level of consciousness; a profound depth of connectedness; a depth that we had not begun to think or even dream about as a people. And this would, like so many journeys of healing (and specifically racial healing), be a necessary process of breaking, re-breaking, resetting and recasting. Indeed, how could anyone like me – those of us who had never been materially impacted by the violence of apartheid – not require breaking and recasting? And what better place to do this work than in one of the 20,000 odd cast-iron cauldrons of discrimination and oppression and injustice (still to this day); an under-resourced school in post-apartheid South Africa?

On a personal level, this meeting came at a time when I was sensing my own deep complicity in the destruction caused by colonialism and apartheid. As an early middle-aged white fella who had grown up in the '70s, '80s and '90s, I had always parroted the old "it wasn't my fault" chestnut, closely followed by, "what can I do to make a difference?" I would add , just to complete my "redemption", that "even we" had had black kids at St. John's College, Houghton where I matriculated. But over the years, as I had allowed myself to begin to be properly broken by the vast and glaring inequalities of our nation and my sublime white, male privilege, I had grown nauseous of my own self-serving justifications and set myself on a course of rehabilitation: "Hello. My name is Justin. I am a privileged middle-aged white man and a recovering racist, and whilst I may not have been the architect of apartheid I certainly enjoyed (and still do) living in the building. I have done nothing significant to get out of the building, let alone break it down. So, if you will have me and I have anything of value to add: "thuma mina – send me".

At that time, I also realised properly (and shamefully), perhaps for the first time ever, that not all schools looked like my alma mater. Now, of course, I didn't expect every school to be hewed from the rock of Houghton Ridge and designed by Sir Herbert Baker. But I remember clearly wondering why "government" schools needed to be so austere; so bricky and barren (that nausea returns even as I write this). When I first went into a school that wasn't even bricky and barren, but inhumane, I remember feeling such a biting sense of shame. Not for what I had had. But for what I had chosen not to see.

And as I sipped my cappuccino and listened to Louise, I began to get excited beyond the definitions of "leadership development programme" and "principal support programme" and "improving education" (all of which PfP is in spades). I started to imagine that it would help people like me to see! That it would be the catalyst that caused scales to drop from our eyes. It would literally begin a process to call out our white-blindness and help us to see our way forward into a new and better way of being white in South Africa.** Although the term "woke"*** was not in common usage at that time, we as participants, practitioners and cheerleaders get more and more woke as we take our "long, loving (and I would add, painful) look at the real"**** through the lens of under-resourced schools and one another.

I didn't enter the PfP family as a partner on the programme. I transitioned from cheerleader to facilitator of the third and final workshop module of the year-long programme – Community Building. This took my understanding of PfP's "why" and my belief in the relevance of the programme to a new level. I then had the privilege of working together with the Learning Process Facilitators in my home province of Kwa-Zulu Natal and together we are currently building the KZN footprint.

As I have watched PfP from a distance and then at close range, I have been able to peel back the many layers and see the heart of a programme that is simple but radical and profound. I have heard the words of business leaders and principals – men and women; black and white – now friends for life – as they have spoken out about how this journey has changed them forever; their views of other races, their views of other genders, their views on inequality, privilege and patriarchy.

I have learned that the state of our education system is just a metaphor for our brokenness and that when we heal the deep rifts between us – hundreds of years in the making – education, and indeed all our other seemingly intractable issues, will be healed and transformed.

I have learned that when we show up with humility and kindness; when we drop our all-too-quick defensiveness and rightness and we really listen to each other – there is nothing we cannot do.

In finishing, I must say this: that coffee with Louise that day was a major signpost on the journey of my life; it challenged me deeply to work, to live a different life and it confirmed in me that the only people we can rely on to fix our mess is us.

And my deepest wish is that hundreds of thousands of South Africans will experience all of this and be able to join me in saying that the very biggest beneficiary of PfP is me!

*For more information visit www.dinokengscenarios.co.za

**I am referencing the transformative aspects of PfP to whiteness simply because I am white. The programme is, I believe, transformative in different ways for any race group.

However, I can only speak from my white perspective.

***Woke as a political term of African American origin refers to a perceived awareness of issues concerning social justice and racial justice. It is derived from the African American Vernacular English expression "stay woke", whose grammatical aspect refers to a continuing awareness of these issues.

**** Quote attributed to Friar Richard Rohr, Order of Friars Minor

Magali von Blottnitz
Monitoring and Evaluation Lead

I discovered PfP in 2016, after a zigzagging career path which traversed high-pressure work in the financial sector, through research, into teaching. In the early years of my professional life, I mostly enjoyed the stimulating environment of the corporate sector. There were always challenges to take on, and perhaps the most gratifying aspect of the job was that I could reap acknowledgement for the quality (and quantity!) of my work. I soon got caught in a spiral of increasing pressure though, which not only had the potential to create tension in my marriage, but also raised the disturbing question of the why? Why do I have to work so hard for my employer? For whose benefit? It became clear that I couldn't justify to myself the personal cost that such a career was going to have for me and my loved ones.

'Taking a break' from this career translated into getting involved in research, which was way too lonely for me, and then teaching. Oh, what a joy to interact with these teenagers, to help them make sense of the hours they had to spend in the classroom, to challenge them and be challenged by them, to see them discover their hidden talents for mathematics or their love of reading, after they had given up on themselves! Oh, what a fulfilment to accompany them on their own path of growth and see them craft their own journey into adulthood.

What I gained in purpose, I lost in acknowledgement though. No matter how much you give, how creative you are about your work, it's never enough: high school teachers are rarely recognised for their input into their learners' lives. Too much bureaucracy on the school management's side; too many frustrations for teenagers and their parents... So you learn to rejoice when you've been able to shift the needle away from this default position for a couple of kids, a couple of moms...

I also never quite learned to navigate the negativity in the staff room, the resistance to change and to collaboration, the rivalry and mobbing, the attacks against those who are trying to do things differently. There were a few of us, unconventional teachers, in the team – and I am probably the one who got myself most badly entangled in those toxic dynamics. I was deeply convinced that things were wrong but unable to find a way out.

Because the school where I was teaching was serving such a small and close-knit community, teachers' private connections with some of the families of our learners became an issue. We were given strict instructions to keep our personal relationships unconditionally out of the way of our teaching practice. Connecting with learners at a human level became suspicious. In the context of criticism and what was labelled as 'interference' by the parents, we were also requested to keep parents at bay and refrain from engaging with them.

So there I was, in 2016, objectively pretty successful as a teacher but bruised by the war of clans in the school and revolted, with every cell of my being, against a trend towards dehumanisation of teaching – unable to accept the divorce between my professional self and my human self – torn between the temptation to swim upstream, with a few other crazy ones, and the painful awareness that the creative, inspired, enthusiastic and optimistic part of myself, my joy to see the impact on learners of a teacher going beyond the call of duty, were perceived as a threat by my colleagues and would probably need to be turned off if I wanted to "fit in".

Looking back at this now, with all the lenses that PfP gave me to understand how those dynamics play out, I can see how I contributed to my woes. I can see how, in my desire to put the learner at the centre of my teaching work, I neglected to build the right quality of relationships with my colleagues. Having become a teacher out of passion rather than through the regular well-oiled and regulated pipeline, I neglected to be curious about how my colleagues saw their roles, what vision of education was driving them, and where the levers were that would have enabled us to work constructively together. I suppose that, deep inside, I just wanted them to be like me and, in my frustration about the gap, I probably came across as demanding and perhaps arrogant.

I can also see how things would have been very different if the leadership of the school had been equipped with skills to create a platform for the team to grow together and find common ground. I remember a conversation that a fellow unconventional teacher and I had with the principal, raising the possibility of the school organising a 'teambuilding exercise'. In his response, the principal made it clear that he knew nothing about teambuilding. He was leading the school to the best of his ability according to the guidelines of the education department. There were government circulars instructing subject teachers to collaborate to put together pedagogic projects. But there was no recipe in the circular to explain how to make this work in a context of a deeply divided staff. And since it wasn't in the circular, the teambuilding didn't happen.

So, I turned my eyes towards PfP. My first face-to-face meeting with some members of the PfP team took place in November 2016 during a day of strategic reflection facilitated according to Time to Think principles by Maryse Barak. The quality of interaction between members of the team was so different from anything that I had experienced in my professional life that a secret voice deep inside me told me that it could not be real – surely it had to be a well-rehearsed play put together to impress me! And yet there was so much authenticity and spontaneous imperfection in the day that even the conspiracy theory would not hold.

I can't think of any other experience, in my entire life, in which people made so much effort to understand different perspectives. Perhaps what scared me was the raw vulnerability in the room. It was as if your presence there was a naked one. There was no hiding, physically or emotionally. I was stirred. After that day of "initiation," I was half tempted to run away but my curiosity kept me there – I had to understand how all of this was possible.

And so began the most fascinating journey of discovery about a new universe. It is not by any means a paradise; but I very soon experienced it as a universe where I could be whole. Where, instead of feeling pushed to silence the humanity in me, I had to stretch it and grow it. Where every reading, every course, every interaction with members of the team, was giving me new keys to view myself differently within the various webs of relationships that I was living in. I became aware of my patterns, I paid attention to my relationships and how they were affecting my ability to reach my goals. I practiced new ways to grow these relationships, and the immersion in those practices helped to make them second nature for me. I need to qualify the sentence I've just written as there is still LOTS of room for improvement. And I remain hungry for more learning, more growth, more input.

It would be impossible to list all that has changed in me as a result of this journey but these are some of my new awareness and my practices:

- In the first place, the fundamental awareness that relationships are at the core of (almost) any work. I now have a better understanding of the specific time and effort required to achieve the right quality of relationship.
- Although listening was never a challenge for me, I used to neglect the quiet voices. I now realise the power of actively seeking out those voices and creating a space for them to speak into.
- That includes my voice too. Learning to position my voice in that space, as a contribution to the pool, is a muscle that I am still trying to build.
- In the interdependency between my work and that of other people, I need to collaborate, and that will happen more fruitfully if I follow some common-sense steps. This is not my comfortable place but I can call myself out when I

realise that I haven't been clear on expectations or that I haven't given people enough space to voice their concerns or if I haven't appreciated people enough for what they've done right.
- By definition, "courageous conversations" will always require courage. But I realise now that the courage is not about daring to pitch my voice higher than the rest (a very uncomfortable thing for me to do) but about showing up with honesty and appreciation for differences. The first time I experienced the power of plain authenticity in a situation of potential conflict, was a revelation for me. It is amazing how, in these stressful scenarios, the human psyche tends to create complicated scenarios of "playing a role", which are most likely to make matters worse. I am still a bit baffled by the simplicity and effectiveness of authentic humanity.

Nearly three years in, I have become quite comfortable in this universe of Symphonia, in this beautiful team of amazing personalities who all try their best to model radical respect, generative relationships and nurturing / appreciating the leader in every person. Of course, we are all on our personal growth path towards this aspirational vision but it has become a home for me, the place in which I can feel whole again.

I am back to a job where the risk of being sucked in by the work is very real, but the team's commitment to each other's wellbeing and shining eyes is there to help me figure out where to stop. And even if am sometimes acutely aware of how little my tiny cog means within the big broken machine that we are dealing with, there can be no doubt about the purpose of my contribution.

I dare to hope, too, that what my children have lost in contact time with me after I gave up my teaching job is partly made up by a more balanced and fulfilled mom, who is better able to hold a generative space for the family dynamics and to profoundly respect, love and honour them as they deserve.

Rama Naidu
Founding Board Member of Symphonia for South Africa and Facilitator of the Community Building and Flawless Consulting workshops

When Louise asked me if I wanted to relate my story of PfP I thought it would be an easy task and said 'yes' too quickly!

My reflections on this journey have made me realise that it has been life-changing in so many ways, both personal and professional.

Nothing prepared me for that first meeting with Peter Block and Louise in 2011. I expected nothing new, just something interesting. I was always looking for innovative ways to make my own work at the Democracy Development Programme more impactful, and perhaps this could give me some answers.

I went through the two days of the Community Building workshop completely mesmerized by everything Peter said about working in community and why the conventional approach simply exacerbated the problem of brokenness. In many ways, it was a crossroads for me and I became more and more uncomfortable with leading an organisation and wanting to do this work. Partners for Possibility gave 'hands and feet' to the work that I wanted to do in the world. Louise lived abundance and kept looking for ways for us to work together – it was the natural next step.

My whole approach to community work changed in an instant and from that moment on I knew this programme was revolutionary in its simplicity and its profound respect for relationships and the pursuit of a common humanity. I have been associated with PfP ever since that first meeting.

To cut a long story short, at the pinnacle of my career as CEO of a large NGO, I left the safety of my comfortable office and began to facilitate the Community Building workshops full time for PfP. I decided to follow my dream – and what an amazing journey it has been.

I have met the most amazing human beings all over the country, people who have stood up and actively sought to be a part of this nation-building project through signing up for PfP. Shifting their stories of despair and despondency into possibilities for a different co-created future always leaves me feeling humbled and privileged to be doing this work. I leave every workshop inspired by their stories and their willingness to truly engage each other in the pursuit of building this nation.

People often say to me, 'You must be tired of doing the same workshop all over the country,' and my answer is always the same: 'It is never the same workshop.'

PfP has opened hundreds of rooms for me, each with their own abundance, possibilities and amazing human beings. I feel privileged and humbled to be able to do this work. It has brought new meaning and purpose to my life.

Robyn Whittaker
Stakeholder Engagement Lead

In 2013 I was asked by the Governing Body Association of SA to read the National Development Plan draft policy on HIV and TB, and advise them on the implications it had for schools.

Reading the National Development Plan, and the response I had to it, remains a vivid and clear memory. As I read the document, I had a clear sense that I had found my work, and that my purpose fell within a place that I could assist in realising the vision held within the NDP. The small nagging voice within me saying "stop being so idealistic" had finally met up against a bigger, stronger, validated voice that spoke the same language as my heart and allowed me to dream – to dream BIG and to dream real about the impact that could be achieved if we collectively worked together as a nation.

The NDP sparked a vision in me for empowering schools to bring the diverse assets they needed from different sectors of society into their space, which was so strong and compelling that there was a sense of it having been birthed rather than thought. That evening I took a leap of faith and spoke to my older sister, explaining what had been sparked within me, and my commitment to find a way to support schools this way. Her affirmation, and the ability to vocalise my thoughts consolidated my internal commitment to work in this space.

I went to speak to a few organisations to ask them to support me and help me to realise this vision – and here I met the voice of dissent in a big way. The CEO of Aurum told me that doing this work would break my soul. Yet I left feeling more determined than ever to make it happen.

And then… a fellow SGB member introduced me to Symphonia SA and the Partners for Possibility programme….

When I looked at the vision of Symphonia for South Africa, and how it was being operationalised through the Partners for Possibility programme, and compared it to what I had written, it felt like a carbon copy. I attended the 2014 PfP celebration event and knew then that this was the work I was going to do, and that I had found the organisation I was going to do it in.

It took courage, coaching and a huge leap of faith to make the move but, in April of 2015, I left my medical practice to work for Symphonia SA and support the PfP programme. It was undoubtedly the best move of my life – I had a sense of being so true to myself, of stepping back into my 18 year old self and of my passion, my purpose and my work moving into alignment.

The sense of flow and of gratitude that I have in doing this work is constant – there is a deep, solid energy to the work. Undoubtedly, there have been some hard moments, but this feels to me like such human, necessary, *right* work that it seems bigger than our efforts or any frustrations we might face.

In many ways, Symphonia for South Africa has restored me to myself. It has validated, strengthened and equipped me, and spoken to the very deepest part of my belief system and my faith in humanity. It has surrounded me with people who are willing to dream big and then go out and make these dreams become reality. It has given me the space to envisage, create, think, explore, grow, dream, partner, laugh, touch lives and hearts and hopes with an incredible and committed group of people, right across our nation and, in fact, increasingly, the world.

This work – this programme – although so intellectually and academically robust, really does the one thing that counts most of all – it lets us be human with one another again. For those who participate as partners in the programme, as well as for the SSA team, it validates our dreams. It gives us courage to voice them and a space to go out and make them become real. It enables us to become pioneers, leaders and visionaries – able to create a new, better, joyful world out of what often feels so broken.

Being a part of this courageous, passionate, powerful and kind team has given me my voice back. It has allowed me to move from being an idealist to being a visionary. It has grown my confidence and let me show my heart and spirit with courage. I am forever grateful for this.

When I first joined Symphonia, I was inspired by the intent and the passion of the programme – by the way it created opportunities for people who had never previously known or been interested in knowing each other, to find one another. The ability to give agency to schools and school leaders, create exposure to different worlds and opportunities and connect people across the many boundaries dividing them was very appealing. The opening of new worlds to learners in communities that have never previously had this kind of exposure is wonderful. It seemed such a simple and yet miraculous process. The more I have been immersed in the programme, the more blown away I am by its practical, clear and yet intricate brilliance. There is no doubt in my mind that Louise has done something revolutionary in designing PfP in such a way that it is able to connect us as humans and unlock potential.

However, it is not only the care, intelligence and compassion with which she and our Symphonia for South Africa team have crafted, refined, delivered and nurtured the Partners for Possibility programme that makes me grateful. It is the tenacity, selflessness and perseverance that it takes to birth something as remarkable as this programme that remains near incomprehensible to me. Conceptualisation is one thing – a beautiful idea is always attractive. But to carry that beautiful idea into reality – and not just any reality but a vibrant, thriving, national reality – is something else altogether. This is because the CEO of Aurum was right – the road is paved with pain, naysayers and detractors, and it really does require sacrifice and commitment to stay the course.

My biggest learning from being at Symphonia, from working with Louise and this incredible team, is that courage, persistence and perseverance are worth a million brilliant ideas. This organisation epitomises the concept that "a journey of 1,000 miles begins with the first step". And it is human beings, not superheroes, who have to take those first steps and who have the blisters to show on their heels…

This work has shown me that it is the little things that count – everyday miracles performed by ordinary people who are courageous enough to listen to and follow their hearts and allow others to listen to and follow theirs. These are the things that change the world.

"Love, allowing the other to be a legitimate other, is the only emotion that is able to expand intelligence."[41]

When I think of Symphonia and PfP, these are the words that spring to mind:

- Courage
- Faith
- Tenacity
- Strong love
- Commitment
- Sacrifice
- Exposure
- Vulnerability
- Humanity
- Care
- Stepping in
- Self-belief
- Actualisation
- Connection
- Conviction
- Purpose
- Fulfilment
- Stretch

I am a changed person as a result of the privilege of working in this organisation. The exposure I have been granted to new worlds, new thinking and new contexts has shifted how I show up in the world. That exposure has been to both internal and external worlds and has offered me depths of insight into both myself and others that I value and treasure.

We still have work to do. The space that we find ourselves in now is different from the years of work spent in establishing and nurturing PfP. Our work now is to develop different muscles to ensure that we can continue to grow and can spread deep, wide roots to feed the tree PfP has become. This includes becoming better at self-care in the interests of long-term sustainability, attending with care to the internal team that delivers on this work, and building a strong, supportive network around Symphonia that can take our work deeper.

---

41   Maturana, R.H., & Verden-Zöller, G. (2008). *The Origin of Humanness in the Biology of Love*. Exeter, UK: Academic.

The community we belong to supersedes any individual one of us and yet it is also the place to which we can come home and can be enough, just as we are.

"If you want to bring about a fundamental change in people's belief and behaviour (...) you need to create a community around them, where new beliefs can be practiced, expressed and nurtured."[42]

I am forever grateful for having found such a community in Symphonia and am committed to doing all within my power to ensure the continued expansion of this work. I pray that a decade from now we will see the impact of our work stretching like a finely woven cloth right across our country, which will have transformed our social fabric in this, our homeland, our South Africa.

Selwyn Page
Western Cape Regional Manager

My earliest recollection of PfP is from a marquee on an overcast Saturday morning on Mandela Day at Kannemeyer Primary School in 2011. There, for the first time, I was asked, "What is your commitment to this community?" Reflecting on my time thus far I can see how my conversations have changed. In South Africa, with all the challenges we face, you can lose hope. Because of PfP, ordinary people are given the opportunity to discuss the very future of our nation in a space of mutual respect.

Now believe you me, as a "boytjie" coming from the Cape Flats, I was confronted with my own prejudice, stereotypes and assumptions. The saying "you don't know until you spend time with others" is true. The programme brings people from all spectrums of our rainbow nation together. Our numerous discussions about the challenges and the joys of working in the education sector has changed my behaviour. I am inspired by the many selfless volunteers who give up their time at personal cost.

Over the last three years I have attended countless celebration events and every time I wonder how we can get more people to hear the stories of personal transformation. At the core of what is actually happening is that my own character is being changed to be more tolerant of others, less bossy and certainly more appreciative of small victories. I identify myself as PfP/ Symphonia and have seen how this has impacted every aspect of my life.

As a member of the PfP team, I've always experienced the environment as a nurturing one in which I've been on a steep learning curve but have never felt overwhelmed. At the heart of my experience has been my own journey of transformation, because

---

42   Goodreads. (2000). Malcolm Gladwell Quotes. Retrieved from: https://www.goodreads.com/quotes/367442-if-you-want-to-bring-a-fundamental-change-in-people-s

I have realised that I can't be impactful until I have dealt with my own issues. On my PfP journey I have had to grapple with many complex matters and have often been surprised by what is possible when committed team members think together in a spirit of mutual respect.

I observe myself as happy within my skin, a work in progress, not the complete article but owning my story.

Reflections

It is deeply humbling to read my colleagues' reflections on their experience of being part of PfP. The last ten years have not been easy for any of us. I often refer to my skill in beating myself up for making mistakes and for not being the perfect leader at all times. However, reading these reflections reminded me that we need to practice what we preach and focus on what is strong rather than what is wrong. We have co-created a very special organisation and that we have much to celebrate and be proud about.

Leading Partners for Possibility for the last ten years has been the most phenomenal leadership development experience. I have learned more about leadership from being in this role and working with the amazing PfP community than I could ever have learned from going to a business school or doing a leadership course.

I feel privileged to have had the opportunity to be a member of the PfP Leadership Team and the PfP community. Few people ever get to build an organisation and a movement from an idea to a point where more than a million lives have been touched by our work. We trust that PfP will continue to have impact for many years to come and that we have done during the first 10 years will be a solid foundation for many years of impact in the future.

I feel deeply honoured and privileged to have had the opportunity to lead the PfP community.

Chapter 21

Concluding thoughts

I started this book-writing journey with doubts and reservations – not so much about the impact of our work – but definitely about our ability to tell our impact story in a way that would help us mobilise more funding for this work.

I did not realise it at the time, but I needed to hear from the 32 principals, 40 business leaders and many other adults whose stories are featured in this book. Visiting schools across the country and hearing stories of impact was a deeply healing experience for me.

I am reminded of Chimamanda Adichie's words: 'Many stories matter. Stories have been used to dispossess and to malign. But stories can also be used to empower, and to humanize. Stories can break the dignity of a people. But stories can also repair that broken dignity.'

In 2014 I had the opportunity to be one of the opening keynote speakers at an education conference in Spain. While we were waiting to speak, I had a conversation with one of the other speakers from a well-known philanthropic foundation. After we had spoken for a while I asked whether his organisation might be interested in funding the kind of work we did. He was quick to respond: 'No. We won't be interested. We only fund organisations that can show that they are moving the dial.'

This has been working me for many years. However, after writing this book I am finally able to lay this to rest. We may not be 'moving the dial' in ways that can easily be depicted in graphs or on a dial, but I am now more certain than ever that our work is having a profoundly positive impact on the lives of individuals and communities across South Africa.

Data that looks convincing and is simple to understand, while useful, sometimes tells us only a very small part of the story of positive change and can even mask the 'real' story altogether. A single-minded obsession with the matric pass rate, for example, tells us nothing about the massive proportion of students who drop out of school or the ongoing reduction in the number of students writing mathematics.

Evaluating the change processes that occur at multiple levels through PfP is a very challenging exercise. Our work happens in VUCA (volatile, uncertain, complex and ambiguous) environments where there are few simple causal links and change is not linear or easily predictable.

Most of the systems that are currently in use to measure impact originated in western liberal democracies, where the social and political environment is relatively stable and predictable. Popular monitoring and evaluation tools like logical frameworks, for instance, assume that social change is predictable, and they don't adequately account for external forces that can and will upset our change strategies. It is often assumed that only outside evaluators are sufficiently objective to produce convincing evidence of impact, but we have observed that external evaluators sometimes completely fail to see the significance of a shift that has occurred.

Many of the most significant impacts that occur through PfP, such as changing levels of empowerment in school principals or awareness among business leaders of the stark inequality that continues to characterise our education system, do not lend themselves to easy measurement. We may never be able to depict these kinds of impacts in ways that convince all stakeholders of the value of our work, but this doesn't mean that we aren't 'moving the dial' in ways that matter greatly for our country.

As the sociologist William Bruce Cameron wrote in 1963, 'Not everything that can be counted counts and not everything that counts can be counted.'

As the stories we have shared in this book attest, principals are being re-energised and enthusiastically leading change at their schools, learners are benefitting, and business leaders are getting a chance to contribute meaningfully to a better future for all our children.

For the purposes of this book, Theo and I have only been able to get to 3% of all the partnerships that have participated in PfP and to visit schools in only five of our nine provinces. This book, therefore, only scratches the surface in terms of all the beautiful stories that have emerged from partnerships for possibility across South Africa.

However, after hearing these stories, and reflecting on hundreds of others that I have heard during the last 10 years from principals, business partners, teachers, learners, education department officials and many other stakeholders, I know that we are moving the dial with regard to impact in schools.

I am personally even more excited about the extent that these stories testify to the nation-building aspects of our work. As Justin Foxton so eloquently pointed out, PfP is providing a platform from which citizens from different sides of our social divide are 'walking together' and truly engaging with each other in the pursuit of building this nation. In the process, men and women, black and white are being changed forever,

Chapter 21: Concluding thoughts

their views about other races and genders, inequality, privilege and patriarchy are transforming and, in many cases, they are becoming friends for life.

I recently attended a PfP celebration event in the Natal Midlands, held at Michaelhouse[43]. As we were listening to the stories of impact in eight schools in and around Nottingham Road, I marvelled at how PfP has impacted this community. There were 85 people in the room: principals and educators from under-resourced schools; business leaders; a nurse who has been partnered with a principal; an internationally-renowned singer who lives locally; the Chairman of the Michaelhouse Community Trust, who travelled from Johannesburg to be with us; business leaders and principals partners and many other citizens who were interested to know more about this process that seems to be building bridges across traditional divides.

We were all spellbound by the stories about what had happened in these eight schools. We were thrilled that every partnership ended their presentation by saying, 'We are not done. We still have lots of work to do and we are committed to do the work together.' I asked Karen McKenzie, our LPF in the Midlands, what had struck her about the evening. She said it was the composition of the people in the room and the fact that she has never been at a function in this community where there was so much diversity and such a strong sense of unity.

I remember feeling the same way when I recently attended the celebration event for the North Coast 3 Leadership Circle held at the Simbithi Eco-Estate. I was asked to say something in response to the stories we had heard. At the time, I was so moved by the experience of being in that room that, afterwards, I could not remember what I had said. Later, I read an article about the celebration that was published in the *North Coast Courier* and was reminded of my words: 'This is a case of citizens saying yes to a situation and making magic happen. I am so inspired by the power of human connection and when people meet with open hearts and open minds and an open will. I keep thinking that this is the work that Mandela dreamed about.'

Nelson Rolihlahla Mandela – a man who inspired us all with his example. I feel so privileged to have lived at a time when such a great statesman led our nation. In July 2007 he spoke at the last 46664 concert held in Hyde Park, London and he ended his speech by passing the torch to all those who care about the future of South Africa. He said, 'It is in **your hands**.' Although I was not at the concert, I remember seeing the footage and being deeply touched by those words. They have kept us going at times when the going was tough. I am absolutely convinced that he would have loved the work of Partners for Possibility.

---

43   A prestigious private school in Nottingham Road, KwaZulu-Natal

PfP is also an innovation in leadership development for leaders in all industries and sectors. We have shown how impactful the 70:20:10 framework can be at scale. I find it thrilling to listen to leaders talking about what they have learned and discovered through being part of PfP. When I think back on my years as a lecturer at a business school and a facilitator of 'piecemeal' leadership development modules and remember how frustrated I felt, I am so grateful to have had the opportunity to apply all my knowledge and experience in such a powerful process and to have been able to witness and experience its impact.

On the morning of 5 May 2009, I read the *Dinokeng Scenarios Report* and made a public commitment to dedicate the next ten years of my professional life to making the 'Walk Together' scenario a reality. To convey the essence of their message, the scenarios team quoted this African proverb: 'If you want to go fast, go alone. If you want to go far, go together.' I wanted to figure out a way to enable leaders to work together across boundaries to create a better future for all our children. It is humbling to know that our programme has achieved exactly that: enabled more than two thousand leaders to achieve results beyond what they could ever have envisaged. These leaders have discovered what it means to 'walk together' and the experience has changed their lives.

When South Africa's Vision 2030 was published in 2012 as the preamble to the National Development Plan (NDP), it was clear to all who read it that this was an audacious dream. We published the entire Vision 2030 text in the first PfP book because everyone in our team thinks it is one of the most beautiful vision statements they have ever seen, and we are absolutely committed to play our part to achieve this vision.

Trevor Manuel and his colleagues who authored the NDP knew that achieving it would require extraordinary effort, and they identified three indispensable enablers: leadership, active citizenship and a capable state. They also said that it would require cross-sectoral collaboration: business, government and civil society working together to address the significant issues facing our country. The stories in this book demonstrate that we have facilitated partnerships across sectors and show how business and education leaders have been working together to address the issues at under-resourced schools. In 2012, we committed ourselves to mobilise active citizenship and strengthen leadership in education, and the stories in this book illustrate how we have done that.

Not only have we positively impacted more than a thousand schools across the country, we have also started a movement of active citizenship in education. In 2010 Derek Sivers spoke at TED about how to start a movement. The video of his talk[44] has

---

44 Sivers, D. (2010). *How to start a movement*. Retrieved from: https://www.ted.com/talks/derek_sivers_how_to_start_a_movement

since been viewed more than 8 million times, and we have often referred to the video as a means of explaining how our movement has evolved. According to Derek, the first enabler for a movement is someone who is willing to stand up and be ridiculed. If what this person is doing is enticing enough, others will want to follow and join him or her. These followers transform the 'lone nut' into a leader. It is essential that the leader embraces these followers as equals and encourages them to urge their friends to join in. More people will be enticed to join because they want to follow their friends. We have seen exactly that: in towns and cities across the country people have joined our movement because their friends asked them to do so. And as a result of adults saying yes to these invitations, more than a million schoolchildren have benefitted.

At the end of 2019, we were welcomed as a member of the Million Lives Club[45]. This club acknowledges social enterprises that have reached more than a million lives through their work. It is a huge privilege to be recognised in this way, and it debunks a myth about scaling our kind of work. There are many people who feel strongly that this kind of work can't be scaled and that something special is lost when you attempt to do so.

We think the reason why we have been successful at impacting schools across the country, in tiny rural towns and big cities is because we have essentially been scaling intimacy. Being part of PfP in Modimolle, Limpopo is both a very different and fundamentally similar experience to being part of PfP in and around Simbithi on the KZN North Coast. In both cases, the role of the LPF is critical in facilitating a 'deep learning experience' for the leaders in these leadership circles.

I am specifically using the term 'deep learning' as acknowledgement to the work of Michael Fullan, Santiago Rincón-Gallardo and their colleagues who are committed to re-imagining education and (specifically) learning. In his most recent book *Liberating Learning: Educational Change as Social Movement,* Santiago defines deep learning as 'the result of the process and the result of making sense of questions that matter to us.' He defines pedagogy as 'the practice of supporting someone else's learning together with the guiding principles underlying such practice,' and then he refers to the 'dynamic relationship between an educator and a learner in the presence of knowledge, or the interactions that take place within the pedagogical core'.

For Santiago, 'the pedagogical core is not only the basic unit where learning happens,' but also 'a basic unit of social relationships of power and authority'.[46] He highlights the challenges with traditional hierarchical relationships where teachers know, and learners

---

45   Million Lives Club. (n.d.). *Celebrating Innovators Reaching New Horizons of Impact*. Retrieved from: https://millionlivesclub.org/
46   Rincón-Gallardo, S. (2019). *Liberating Learning: Educational Change as social movement.* New York: Routledge, p51-52.

should learn from the knowing teachers. We know these hierarchical relationships are no longer serving us in schools. I have seen how these relationships have no significant impact in business schools and leadership development programmes for adults. What makes PfP different is that the LPFs are committed to 'learn with' the PfPs in their leadership circle. The entire process is designed as a peer-to-peer learning experience where all participants are learning together. I am convinced that this contributes to the impact of the process.

When I started my doctoral studies, I was intrigued by the application of complexity science to organisational and leadership development. At the time, I was mostly interested in how to apply the idea of *organisations as complex responsive processes of relating* to my work with large corporates. I am convinced that one of the reasons for PfP's substantial impact is that the entire process is informed by complexity science (rather than scientific management or even systems change). We don't have preconceived ideas about the journey to be taken for every partnership because we recognise that every school and context is different. We therefore guide PfPs to start from where *they* are and then find their way to a better future (as defined by the partners rather than the programme). We encourage PfPs to take their own experience seriously and to use their experience in the school as their 'site of learning,' thereby validating their experience as valuable and important. We often hear from business leaders and principals that they value the fact that they were able to walk *their* journey and do what they deemed to be important rather than being told what they should do.

We have followed theorists who believe that the 'school is the unit of change in education' and have therefore focused our attention on schools. We believe that impact in thousands of schools will ultimately influence the entire education system. When we started in 2011 to argue for leadership development of principals as a key enabler for change in education, ours was a lonely voice. Today, nine years later, many people and organisations have joined forces and leadership development for principals is now firmly on the agenda.

When Ben and Roz Zander were in South Africa in 2008, we often talked about the idea that we can all lead from wherever we are. In their book *The Art of Possibility*[47] they call this practice 'Leading from Any Chair,' signifying that every musician in an orchestra has the power to influence the performance. Through PfP, we have given life to this idea. We have shown how every citizen can help to co-create a better future for our country – whether you are a farmer in Letsitele, a manager in a renewable energy firm in Pofadder, a midwife in the Natal Midlands, or a journalist in Nelspruit.

---

47 Zander, R.S. & Zander, B. (2000). *The Art of Possibility: Transforming Professional and Personal Life.* New York: Penguin.

Chapter 21: Concluding thoughts

A few years ago we pitched PfP to Carte Blanche, a popular TV programme that airs on Sunday evenings in South Africa. We thought our story about the power of active citizenship was worth sharing with the nation. The feedback from the producers was that it would have been interesting if there were more 'big names' involved. At the time, I felt quite deflated by their feedback but I am increasingly convinced that PfP is impactful *because* we have thousands of ordinary citizens involved rather than a few 'big names'.

During the last few months we have spent some time articulating our 'Why': **To be a contribution, reclaim humanity, cultivate community, ignite possibility and activate leadership** *so that* **people are inspired to let their light shine and work together to co-create a more just, equitable, caring and joyful future in South Africa**. We are grateful for every instance where this has happened. And we look forward to many more stories that illustrate the impact of our work in the future.

In 2013, Symphonia for South Africa received the Reconciliation Award from the Institute for Justice and Reconciliation in recognition of the impact of the Partners for Possibility programme in promoting education and, ultimately, reconciliation. When he handed us the award, Archbishop Emeritus Desmond Tutu said, 'When you read the newspapers, you want to cry. You really feel awful. And God cries. And then… God looks, and God sees the work of Symphonia… and then God starts smiling…crying, smiling, like the sun shining through the rain.'

As PfP is about to turn 10, I am smiling too. With a heart full of joy and gratitude.

Acknowledgements

Partners for Possibility: Stories of Impact is the result of the journey of discovery that Theo and I embarked on 10 years after the first PfP partnership was established. We set out to visit people who have been involved in PfP to find out how they had been impacted by their involvement in the programme.

PfP began with my own principal partner, Ridwan Samodien, agreeing to test a principal-business leader partnership with me in 2010. He is the co-founder of the programme and his saying yes to the idea opened the way for 1,198 principals to become part of the PfP community within 10 years.

For each of those principals there was a business partner, and we want to acknowledge and honour every single partnership for possibility who took the bold decision to join our pioneering programme. Without their commitment and active citizenship there would not have been any stories to tell.

By the time I asked Ridwan to be my partner, my thinking had been shaped by influential thought leaders in education and several other fields. They include Professors Jonathan Jansen, John Volmink and Brian O'Connell, Nancy Kline, Peter Block, Angeles Arrien, John McKnight and Benjamin and Roz Zander. They have been with me in thought and spirit every step of the way, and I am eternally grateful to them for their role in the original design of the PfP process and our subsequent refinements.

When we decided that this book would be a compilation of impact stories, we realised that we would have to restrict our visits to just a few places and would only be able to hear from a limited number of partnerships. Wherever we went, we were received with grace and enthusiasm. We experienced nothing but kindness and generosity from everyone we visited, and we would like to express our deep gratitude to all those who made themselves available for a conversation. This book would not have been possible without your stories.

We thoroughly enjoyed our visits to Letsitele, Simbithi and Nelspruit. It was a special treat to visit Burgert and Irma van Rooyen on their La Gratitude, Cobus and Mel Tomlinson in Abundance Lodge and Tony and Terry's beautiful home in Simbithi Eco Estate.

None of the work and impact described in this book would have been possible without the incredible passion and dedication of our enabling team members, workshop facilitators, leadership team and, especially, our Learning Process Facilitators. Without their commitment and support there would be no PfP, and I am profoundly grateful to each and every one of them.

Two of the long-serving members of the team, Sharon van Schalkwyk and Robyn Whittaker, are leaving the organisation this year and I would like to say a special thank you and pay tribute to both of them for their immense contribution to our work. Sharon joined PfP in 2013, first as a business partner, then LPF and finally as an LPF Supervisor. Robyn has been our Stakeholder Engagement Lead since 2016.

The impact that PfP has had over last 10 years simply would never have happened without generous financial support from a wide range organisations and individuals who have sponsored partnerships and funded specific endeavours such as independent evaluations of the programme. To date, we have received support from over 350 funders; too many to list here, but my heartfelt gratitude goes out to every single one.

Our special thanks also to the following organisations who contributed towards the production of this book by sponsoring case studies: Bestmed, Citadel, Inmarsat Global, Liberty, Multotec, Sphere Holdings and Woolworths Financial Services.

We feel extremely fortunate that, over the years, many prominent people have expressed their support and admiration for our programme. For this book, we received so many endorsements that we could not publish them all. However, we would like to sincerely thank every person who read the book and sent us an endorsement.

Thanks to Theo Garrun, my travelling companion, who did a great job of capturing the many stories we heard and to Gail McMillan who edited the manuscript and made grammatical and logical sense of it all. I am also grateful to Miranda Capellino, the talented design consultant who has been on this journey with us since the beginning and designed the evocative cover of this book.

Thanks to Knowledge Resources, Wilhelm Crous and Cia Joubert for believing in our concept and getting the book out under extremely difficult circumstances.

Finally, thank you to my amazing family, who have supported me every step of the way. None of this would have been possible without my wonderfully supportive husband Gerrit and my two gorgeous daughters Helen and Lize.

About the Authors

Dr Louise van Rhyn is a social entrepreneur. She believes the worlds' huge intractable problems can be solved through cross-sector collaboration and a solid understanding of complex social change. Her approach to change is shaped by more than 30 years of working as an Organisational Change and Leadership Development practitioner. She holds a Doctorate in Complex Social Change and has founded a few entrepreneurial organisations.

In 2008 she returned home to South Africa (after living in Europe) and started a social enterprise with a purpose to mobilise active citizenship around the significant social issues facing the country to contribute to a more just and equitable society.

In 2010 she launched Partners for Possibility (PfP), an innovative national building and leadership development process for business and school leaders. Business leaders develop their capacity to lead in a complex and unfamiliar environment by becoming a co-learning and co-action partner to a school principal. The focus of their partnership is to lead positive change in an under-resourced school, thereby reducing inequality in education. Through these partnerships previously under-resourced schools mobilise the gifts and contributions available from business and community members around the schools.

PfP brings leaders together in intimate learning partnership across traditional boundaries of race, ethnicity, gender, age, etc. Leaders are confronted with their biases and "-ism's" and get the opportunity to discover the richness and beauty of our diversity.

So far more than 2,200 leaders across South Africa have benefited from the programme and they've won many national and international awards for their innovative approach to enable business leaders to make a significant contribution in education while developing their leadership skills. Leaders report that they learn more about leadership from working with a school in an under-resourced community than attending a course at a business school. School leaders are equipped and empowered with the skills and agency to lead change at their schools.

Theo Garrun's education and early work experience were in teaching. He graduated with a BA (Geography and English) and teaching diploma from Wits University in 1978 and 10 years later he returned to Wits to do a BEd degree.

He taught at Highlands North Boys' High School for 16 years, and was deputy principal when he left, one year after spending two terms as acting principal. He taught for one more year, at St David's Marist Inanda, before leaving the profession to pursue his other passion – writing.

He worked for Independent Newspapers for the next 21 years, mostly as editor of The Star Workplace and, at the same time, as the Star's local and school sport correspondent. In the last five years he was there he created and edited the Saturday Star's School Sport supplement.

He took voluntary retrenchment in 2016, amid the turmoil resulting from the takeover of the organisation by new owners.

Since then he has been a freelance writer in various capacities. He has done quite a lot of corporate writing, and has continued to cover school sport, mostly for the online divisions of SA Cricket and SA Rugby magazines.

He is employed on a part time basis by Jeppe High School for Boys, in their communications department, creating content for their Website and social media channels and does a similar job for the TAG Foundation at King Edward VII School.

He is an active blogger – https://theogarrun.blogspot.com/ - commenting mainly on the role of sport in education at schools.

Index

6 conversations of community, 4
70:20:10, 4, 342

A

ABSA, 260, 263, 281
academic outcomes, 2, 39, 62, 166, 321
academic results, 2, 203, 211, 293
accountability, 46, 159, 164, 181, 212, 260
achievements, 43, 199, 202, 205, 211, 243, 249, 264
action learning, 9
activate leadership, 345
active citizenry, ii
active citizenship, 1, 5–6, 16, 19, 155, 283, 300, 342, 345
adopt, 8, 25
aftercare, 177, 179
Agnes Raboshakga, 229
Aleen Maharaj, 74
Alfonso Louw, 138
alive with possibility, 10–11, 14–15, 69
all the voices, 14, 98, 165, 273, 296, 311
Amahle Mngadi, 247
Andi Norton, 107
Andre Engel, 255
André Lamprecht, 117, 133, 161
Andrew Jackson, 27, 36–37
Andrew Thompson, 80
Andrew Windvogel, 216
Andries Breytenbach, 273
Andy Mahlangu, 252
Anita Moerman van Blankenberg, 295
Annemien Holtzhausen, 256, 278
Annual National Assessment (ANA), 57
apartheid, 41, 61–62, 67, 82, 117, 211, 283, 323, 326
appreciation, 61, 78, 147, 150, 246, 249, 264, 281, 283, 287, 290, 294, 303, 310–312, 319
Archbishop Emeritus Desmond Tutu, 345
Arnola Ross, 63
The Art of Possibility, 10–11, 13, 67, 273, 344
Arthur Collett, 274
Asset Based Community Development (ABCD), 95
Attie van Wyk Primary School, 198

authentic leadership, 294, 304
authenticity, 211, 260, 300, 330–331
autocratic, 33, 44, 47, 49, 163, 168, 170
Ayesha Ismail, 275
Ayn Brown, 17

B

Bantu education, 62
be a contribution, 72, 345
Belinda Petersen, 189
Benjamin Zander, 10–11, 163, 273
Bernice Kotze, 276
Bestmed, 234–238
Bizie Magwaza, 95, 204, 247
Bob Head, 25, 52–53
Bona Lesedi Secondary School, 225–226
Bongani Hlatshwayo, 172, 174
Book Banks, 151–152
books, 8, 57, 88–89, 91, 109, 129, 135, 137, 151, 169, 199, 202, 218, 248, 251
boundaries, 5–6, 9, 28, 59, 72–73, 75–76, 138, 209–210, 262, 271, 288, 304, 334, 342
Brainboosters, 29
Brand Pretorius, 20, 25
Brenda Scrooby, 296
Brian O'Connell, 7, 68
Brian Schreuder, 148
Bridgetown High School, 215–216
Bruntville Primary, 301
budgeting, 159, 192, 262
building capacity, ii
Burgert van Rooyen, 23, 27, 30, 39
Busi Vilakazi, 79
business as a force for good, 22, 133
business in society, 210
business-school partnership, 160
buy-in, 43, 71, 104, 172, 200–201

C

camaraderie, 293
Cami Maths, 34
capable state, 19, 342
Cape Wine Auction, 107

care, 56–57, 70, 73, 120, 180, 182, 288, 298, 301, 303, 312, 314, 318–319, 323, 335–336
career day, 261
career evening, 243–244
career guidance, 173, 183, 269
careers fair, 145
Carlin Symonds, 256
Cathalijne Bol, 78
celebrate, 35, 43, 68, 89, 123, 140, 310–311, 337
celebration, 28, 43, 47, 79–80, 121, 123, 195, 197–198, 220–221, 227, 245, 257, 333, 337, 341
Chantal Dawtrey, 191, 268
Character Transformation, 152, 154
cheerleader, 50, 110, 192, 325, 327
Chimamandla Adichie, 22
Chris Luyt, 234
Circuit Manager, 32–33, 35, 38, 70
Citadel, 225–228
classroom, 33, 37, 49, 56, 105, 107, 111, 173, 177, 201, 205, 207, 210, 241, 247
Click Foundation, 107, 181–182
Clive Naicker, 208
Cloetesville High School, 143, 146, 149
coaching, 4, 46, 75, 112, 180–181, 183, 204, 207, 273, 278, 289, 296, 299–300, 305, 307
co-action, 4, 26, 28, 64
Coba Röhm, 297
co-created future, 332
coexistence, 277
cohesion, 259, 266
co-learning, 4, 26, 64, 85, 325
collaboration, 3, 6, 19, 24, 59, 151, 153, 158, 175, 177, 186, 258, 260, 325, 328
collaborative, 1, 49, 78, 98, 148, 170, 288, 310, 313
comfort zone, 34, 77, 79, 84, 138, 164, 192, 207, 209–210, 213, 305, 316, 322
commitment, 23–24, 38, 40, 42, 55–56, 73–74, 76, 155, 178, 218–219, 265–266, 285–286, 309, 333, 335–336
communication skills, 84, 201, 253, 263
community, 4–10, 17–26, 41–46, 66–77, 80–86, 107–111, 113–118, 149–152, 170–174, 188–190, 198–203, 215–220, 230–233, 258–261, 280–286

Community Building training, 105, 146
Community Building workshop, 105, 115, 118, 168, 220, 266, 270, 332
community involvement, 76, 110, 113, 118, 270
Community Keepers, 113
Community of Practice (CoP), 29
Community: The Structure of Belonging, 4, 18
community-based solutions
compassion, 20, 39, 283, 298–299, 303, 308, 319, 323, 335
compassionate listening, 286
complex organisation, 26, 147
complexity, 39, 286, 344
conductor, 163, 273, 300, 302
confidence, 44–46, 49, 67, 69–70, 106, 110, 113, 165–166, 176–178, 189–190, 194, 199, 201, 269–270, 275–276
confident, 49–50, 59, 63, 103, 106, 165–166, 168, 170, 196, 199, 201, 203, 228, 252–253, 259–260
connectedness, 271, 326
connection, 11, 33, 71, 73, 116, 128, 139, 217, 226–227, 230, 285–286, 305, 315, 335, 341
consciousness-raising, 20, 207, 220, 241
contract, 20, 26, 47, 51, 56, 68, 201, 217, 265, 286, 293
contribute, 3, 5, 14–15, 18, 74, 76–77, 79, 83, 98–99, 137–138, 165, 222, 224, 320, 322
contribution, 69–70, 72, 136, 138, 147, 155–156, 163–164, 170, 224–225, 227, 234–239, 296–297, 304, 317–318, 330–331
contributors, 13, 163, 165, 170
conversation, 5, 8–13, 65, 68, 79, 104, 106, 126, 191, 193, 299, 301, 312, 315–316, 325–326
Corporate social investment (CSI), 73–74
courage, 169, 211, 277, 310–311, 314, 331, 333–335
courageous, 44, 106, 166, 203, 244, 304, 319, 331, 334–335
creative, 15, 24, 147, 185, 241, 304, 306, 313, 328–329
crossroads, 332
cross-sector collaboration, 3, 59
cultivate community, 345

culture, 50, 78, 150, 159, 165–166, 169, 173, 193, 202, 235, 274, 282, 285, 289, 313
curriculum, 18, 56, 61–62, 112, 152, 230, 257, 259, 302
Curriculum Assessment Policy Statement (CAPS)., 62

D

Dalton Ramaoma, 208
Daniel Navazo, 277
Darren Hele, 150, 155
Dave Morris, 238
Dave Wilson, 277
Davril Harmse, 64
DBSA, 297
Debbie Horne, 197
delicious listening, 168, 315
Dennis Coetzee, 256, 278
Dennis Wevell, 149
Deon Myburgh, 143
Department of Education (DBE), 33
Derek Sivers, 342
Desmond Zeelie, 26, 36
Dhiresh Ramdeen, 234, 236
Dina Cramer, 28, 186
Dinokeng scenarios
discipline, 13, 16, 51–52, 63–64, 152, 202, 212, 305
distributed leadership, 167, 170
diversity, 155, 238, 286, 310–311, 315, 341
Dominic Raphahlelo, 257, 286
Dorcas Dube, 318
dreams, 12, 25, 35, 42, 45, 65, 79, 153, 179–180, 216, 292, 305, 319, 334
Dysan Parasaraman, 77

E

early childhood development (ECD), 151
ecobrick, 84, 91
education system, 53, 61, 72, 77, 148, 256, 260, 290–291, 294, 301, 307, 323, 327, 340, 344
e-learning, 109–111
Elizabeth Masemola, 244–245
Elsie Chiloane, 103, 173
empathy, 31, 39, 78, 192, 211–212, 233, 271, 276
empowered, 24, 59, 88–89, 105, 169, 179, 188, 259–260, 265, 272, 292
energy, 15–16, 107, 110, 113–114, 117, 134, 136, 236, 270, 272, 279, 281, 313, 315, 333–334
engaged citizenry, ii
engagement, 70, 73–74, 104, 114, 170, 176, 192, 199, 227, 236, 258, 260, 297, 324, 332
entrepreneurial, 177, 184, 233
equality, 283, 286, 303, 310, 312
Eric Tiba, 27, 30–31
Erica Kempken, 175
Erika Human, 103
Ernest Moore, 319
Esikhisini Primary School, 234
Eugene Daniels, 5
evaluate, 211, 301
every voice, 163, 170, 297, 313, 319
evidence, 3, 19, 88, 166, 205, 272, 340
exposure, 46, 57, 77, 139, 172–173, 178, 195, 198, 201, 208, 233, 238, 277, 334–336

F

facilitated, 4, 17–18, 28–29, 36, 39–40, 47, 121, 123, 139–140, 144, 159–160, 177, 179, 227–229, 278–279
Famous Brands, 149–150, 155
Federated Employers Mutual Assurance Company, 150
Federated Employers Mutual Education Foundation (FEMEF), 150
Felicity Sasman, 202
Felix Hacker, 27, 38, 279
Fella's Army, 22, 115, 125–129, 249
financial management, 133, 191–192, 245
FirstRand, 208–209, 216–217
Flawless Consulting, 18, 44, 46, 51, 54, 68–70, 190, 200, 203, 259, 262–265, 276–278, 280–281, 295–296, 320
Florence van Rensburg, 279
FNB, 159, 215–217, 279
Frank Bradford, 81
Frank Terblanche, 191–192
Freddy Antwi, 211
Freek Mulder, 280
functionality, 2, 236
funders, 2, 61, 107, 112, 136, 148, 168
funding, 26, 40, 61, 108, 110, 124–126, 136–137, 149, 153, 176–177, 186–187, 217, 219, 233–234, 339

fundraising, 90, 105, 137, 152–153, 177, 264, 289, 321
Furqaan Jacobs, 253

G

Gail McMillan, 320
Garth Löest, 1
gated community, 74, 77, 81
Gauteng Department of Education (GDE), 20, 225
Gavin Alkana, 117, 119, 124–125, 133
generative attention, 310
generative conversation, 149, 299
generative relationship, 331
generosity, 7, 72, 115, 152, 289, 306
Geoff Lee, 281
George Khosa Secondary School, 191
Getrude Mafoko, 225
gifts and contributions, 4–5, 22, 95, 114, 135, 160
Gill Cox, 95, 100, 167, 247
Gill Leslie, 204
Gina Botha, 27
Glide and Ride, 96–98
GOBY, 169, 180–181
Gordon Institute of Business Studies (GIBS), 9
Graeme Morrison, 150
Graham Haird, 244–245
Grant Kelly, 211, 220
Grant Paulsen, 218
gratitude, 23, 28, 85, 174, 248–249, 251, 264, 286, 302, 333–334
Greg March, 281
Greg Vlotman, 7
Groep 91, 23, 25, 27–28, 30, 32, 36–40

H

Hasina Mahomed, 259
Head of Department (HOD), 32
healing, 4, 69, 90, 106, 296–297, 325–326, 339
heart, 22–23, 66, 69, 72–74, 122, 146–147, 220, 222, 292–293, 298, 300–304, 308–309, 313–314, 316, 333–334
heart of the community, 73–74
hearts, 2, 75–76, 86, 116, 165, 295, 297, 299, 303, 309, 324, 334–335, 341
Heidi Edson, 281

Henk van Rooyen, 27
Hillwood Primary, 115, 117–119, 121, 124–125, 127–129, 133, 136, 249
hold the space, 299, 306, 315
honoured, 31, 85, 165, 274–275, 303, 308, 338
hope, 12–14, 22–23, 69–70, 72, 91, 93, 107–108, 131, 133, 241, 246, 249, 280, 295, 317–319
HR, 17, 133, 192, 225, 294
humanising, 210
humanity, 116, 120, 277, 284, 296, 301, 303, 313, 319, 330–332, 334–335, 345
humble, 47, 49, 79, 192, 194, 233, 244, 253
humbling, 34, 72, 147–148, 154, 206, 210, 218, 279, 318, 337, 342
humility, 85, 211, 241, 284, 296, 327

I

Ian Macdonald, 22, 115–116, 124, 129–130, 136, 249–250
Ian Wilson, 96
ICT, 66, 109, 140, 143, 147–149, 151, 154, 191
identity, 3, 91, 209–210, 282
ignite possibility, 16, 345
immersion, 9, 330
impact, 2–3, 18–21, 23, 37, 45–46, 137–141, 179–180, 186–188, 196–198, 200, 220, 243–245, 295–296, 320–321, 339–345
improvements, 2, 30, 38, 48, 67, 98, 134, 144–146, 191, 202, 211, 224, 229, 233, 322
Imtiaz Adams, 259
inclusivity, 78, 212
indicators, 2, 39, 211
induction, 30, 32, 36, 82, 96
inequality, 3, 58–59, 176, 212, 286, 322–323, 327, 340–341
influence, 72, 77, 180, 186–187, 192, 198, 208, 210–213, 259–260, 266, 277, 279, 289, 291, 344
influencing skills, 9
Institute for Justice and Reconciliation, 2, 50, 345
Instructional Leadership Institute (ILI), 200
integrity, 78, 261, 283

interdependency, 330
invitation, 9, 12, 22, 36, 65
Irené Raubenheimer, 133, 139, 160, 245
Irma Jacobsz, 282
Irma van Rooyen, 23–25, 28, 31
Isaac Nkonwana, 27, 30
IT, 70–71, 113, 133, 140, 148, 175, 182, 301
Itumeleng Kgaboesele, 155

J

Jacinta Roest-Tshidzumba, 176
Jackie Warner, 264, 293, 298
Jaelyn Williams, 243
Jane Tsharane, 52, 55
Jan-Louis Pretorius, 23, 27
Jansie Rautenbach, 27, 322
Jessica Batts, 107, 110, 143
Jo Monson, 298
jobs, 68, 73, 91, 145, 159, 173, 175–177, 181, 186, 226
Johan Minnie, 229
John Matiso, 260
John Mdluli Primary School, 149
Jonathan Jansen, 118, 255
Joseph Kente, 221
Joseph Taylor, 79
journey, 17–18, 20–21, 33–36, 77–79, 255–260, 262–263, 267, 269–270, 274–287, 295–296, 300–301, 303–304, 318–320, 325–328, 330–332
joy, 9, 15–16, 107, 163, 170, 184–185, 273, 279–280, 297, 301, 306, 316–317, 320–321, 324, 328–329
joyful, 1, 185, 323, 334, 345
judgment, 15
Juliet Shilubana, 21, 27, 32

K

Kamentha Pillay, 282
Kannemeyer Primary School, 8, 61, 71, 90, 95, 154–155, 336
Karen McKenzie, 272, 300, 341
Karenne Jo Bloomgarden, 81
Kaross, 23–25, 28, 37, 40
Kate Baynes, 283
Katherine Persson, 129, 136
Kelly April, 253–254
Ken McKenzie, 284

Keran Coetzer, 97
Kevin Velensky, 260, 286
Khosi Ntuli, 155, 158
Khumbul'ekhaya, 215
Kim McNally, 301
kind, 2, 7, 59, 63, 113–114, 119–120, 122, 141–143, 153, 155–156, 160, 287–289, 334, 339, 343
kindness, 131, 194, 288, 294, 327
Klapmuts Primary School, 107
Klapmuts Sevens Tournament, 112
not knowing, 42, 299
Kobus van Wyk, 23, 27, 30
Komala Pillay, 284
Kubashnee (Kay) Moodley, 303
Kuruman, 276, 285, 289, 292, 297

L

Lavender Hill, 117–119, 121, 123–125, 127–128, 133–136, 138, 219, 250
Le Roux Conradie, 112
lead change, 43, 72, 78
leadership, 1–4, 8–11, 16–20, 51–59, 166–170, 195–200, 209–211, 256–260, 268–271, 285–287, 296–299, 303–306, 313–317, 321–323, 341–345
leadership capacity, 2–3, 27, 59, 64, 192, 197, 209, 243
leadership circle, 17–20, 23, 26–27, 29, 45, 48, 77, 103, 164, 250, 252, 264–265, 268, 270, 304
leadership development, 1–4, 9–10, 17–18, 20, 179, 196–197, 200, 206, 210, 233–234, 273, 275, 325–326, 342, 344
leadership style, 44, 47, 52, 105, 163, 166, 211, 296–297
leadership team, 72, 151, 186, 296–297, 316, 322–323, 337
learners with special educational needs (LSEN), 148
learnerships, 175–176
learning community, 168, 200, 207, 260
learning experience, 17, 31, 85, 157, 259, 286, 343–344
learning opportunities, 151, 211, 306
learning partnership, 4
Learning Process Facilitator (LPF), 17
Lebo Mokwele, 238–239
legitimacy, 220

Lephalale, 186
Lerato Lotlhare, 285
Letsitele, 20–21, 23, 25–29, 35, 37–41, 279, 344
Levana Primary, 117, 126, 133–137, 161
Liberty, 191–192, 229–234
Library, 7, 109, 135
Lidell Botha, 37
life-changing, 9, 18, 20, 55, 68, 80, 164, 228, 237, 244, 246, 255, 318, 324, 331
Limpopo Department of Education, 32
Linc Foundation, 81, 83, 88
Lindelani Singo, 41, 252
Lindiwe Ginya, 191
listen, 49–51, 54, 57–58, 102–104, 147, 168, 170, 189–190, 204–205, 220, 222, 260–261, 264–266, 279–280, 335
listen without judgement, 42
listening, 51, 54, 68–69, 72, 99, 102, 166, 168, 170, 259, 286–287, 296–297, 310, 313, 315
listening skills, 297, 310
literacy, 29, 88, 90, 123, 135, 159, 169, 181–182, 217, 238, 262, 285
Living Legends, 112
Liz Dewing, 286
Lizzie Seema, 47
Loretta Loggenberg, 197
Lorraine Hadfield, 110
Lorraine Mgobhozi, 194
Louise van Rhyn, 14, 67, 116, 264, 273, 293, 318, 321–322, 324
love, 46–47, 72, 85, 87, 99, 101, 129–131, 247–248, 283, 289, 292, 296, 306, 308, 335
Lowveld Media, 171–173
Lowvelder, 171–173
Lucille Meyer, 260, 286
Lukkie Matsabe, 164, 171
Lwazi (Jetro) Nkuna, 250

M

Madiba Day, 66
Magali von Blottnitz, 328
magnet for the gifts, 95, 114, 135, 202
Magri's Language Institute, 34
Magwaza Ngomana, 32
Mahatma Gandhi, 61, 178, 225

Makgatho Primary School, 52, 55
Makhanani Shilote, 27, 38
Malcolm Samuel, 73
Mamphela Ramphele, 7
management, 26, 30–31, 70, 139, 158, 166–167, 169, 191–194, 207–209, 211, 232, 240, 257–260, 271, 291
management style, 70, 147, 238
managerial skills, 263
Mandela Day, 48, 336
Mapula Trust, 127, 249
Marc McClure, 81–82
Marichen Mortimer, 263, 304
Marina Bidoli, 286
Marina Knox, 225
Mariza Lubbe, 110
Martin Tobias, 151, 164, 174
Mathipa Nelson Poopedi, 261
Matshedisho Pobe, 261
Matthys Ferreira, 171
Maud Langa, 234
Mavis Mpanza, 80
measure, 13, 136, 236, 300–302, 340
media, 32, 44, 66, 75, 87–88, 102, 112, 118, 142, 164, 171–173, 210, 291
Mediclinic, 143–149
Mel Tomlinson, 103, 106, 149, 164, 250, 305
Merridy Edgson, 308
Merryl Williamson, 81
Michael Bloomberg, 139, 143
Michael Byron, 127
Mike Stopforth, 287
Million Lives Club, 343
mission, 3, 50, 125, 209, 230, 246, 266–267, 300, 319, 321
Monitoring and Evaluation (M&E), 2
Montagu Drive Primary School, 202
morale, 124, 145, 148, 265, 284, 287
motivated, 66, 91, 96, 113, 128, 178–180, 186, 193, 256, 261, 264, 319, 323
movement, 79, 91, 179, 224, 277, 298, 316, 321, 337, 342–343
Mpumalanga News, 171–173
Mshwati Memorial Primary School, 87, 95, 204
Mthayiza Primary School, 103, 173
multi-faceted, 197, 207
multiplier effect, 136, 140
Multotec, 47–48
music, 50–51, 163, 167, 170, 238, 302–303

mutual growth, 276
mutual respect, 211, 279–280, 323, 336–337
mutuality, 8, 24, 207

N

Nadia Mason, 117
Nal'ibali, 169
Nancy Kline, 18–19, 288, 300
narrative, 5, 10, 171, 179
National Development Plan (NDP), 342
National Planning Commission (NPC), 19
National School Nutrition Programme, 58, 265
nation-building, 1, 3, 7, 27, 52, 91, 332, 340
Nedbank, 17–18, 103–104, 177, 179, 182, 184, 194, 211–212
negotiation skills, 205
Nelson Mandela, 1, 14, 41, 69, 210, 243, 245
Nelspruit, 22, 103, 106, 149–152, 154–155, 164–165, 171, 174, 250, 305, 344
network, 84, 86, 98, 121, 124, 137, 145, 147–148, 155, 217, 222, 227, 233, 255, 257
New Guelderland Combined School, 80
Nick Binedell, 9
Nicky Bush, 197, 310
Nimble, 138–140, 189
Nkateko (Eddie) Manzini, 244
Nolitha Fakude
Nomfuzo Ntolosi, 313
Nomsa Mhlongo, 27, 35
North Coast Agricultural College, 76, 81–83, 85–87, 91–92
nurture, 314
nutrition, 58, 153, 237, 265, 267–268

O

Obert Machimana, 27
Olievenhoutsbosch Secondary School, 229, 231, 233
open heart, 72, 304, 323
open-hearted, 13, 286
opportunity to speak, 244, 269, 275
Otto Scharmer, 52, 301
Outcome-Based Education (OBE), 62
ownership, 48, 71, 109, 157, 166, 169, 174, 259

P

parental involvement, 56, 146, 265
parents, 33, 43, 55–57, 64–67, 101–102, 104–105, 119, 136, 144–146, 173–175, 198, 201–203, 264–267, 283–284, 328–329
Parkgate Primary School, 167, 169
partnership, 29–31, 35–38, 41–43, 52–57, 117–118, 120–123, 137–140, 146–151, 155–160, 197, 224–229, 234–239, 256–259, 278–281, 309–312
pass rate, 1, 85, 146, 159, 191, 194, 227, 232, 265, 289, 339
passion, 12–13, 112, 116, 123, 129, 178–179, 223, 226, 235–237, 310–311, 313–314, 321–322, 324, 329, 333–334
passionate, 13, 59, 100, 121, 142, 186, 210, 218–219, 226, 236, 257, 283–284, 315, 318, 334
Paul Abrams, 203, 314
Paul Marketos, 252
Paul Sturrock, 315
Paulo Freire, 295
Pearl Nel, 215
Penreach, 151
people skills, 85, 201
perseverance, 205, 222–223, 287, 296, 316, 322, 335
persistence, 335
personal development, 185, 233, 256, 260, 270, 309
personal growth, 84, 140, 211, 234, 257, 279, 305–306, 309, 331
perspectives, 77–78, 142, 262, 287, 298, 304, 309–310, 330
Peter Block, 4–5, 10, 12, 18, 52, 64, 66, 69, 73, 115, 117, 171, 174, 268, 273
Peter Makgatho, 262
Peter Venn, 117, 126, 129, 134, 136
Petra Snyman, 288
PfP community, 1, 85, 99, 170, 196, 258, 261, 305, 318–319, 322, 337–338
Philip Mirvis, 207
Phinias Gololo, 288
pioneers, 9, 296, 334
Portfolio of Evidence (PoE), 205
positive impact, 2, 19, 79, 111, 177, 179–180, 296, 339

possibility, 7–8, 10–17, 24–26, 85–87, 122–125, 153–155, 268–271, 273–274, 285–286, 298–299, 302–303, 313–315, 324–326, 332–333, 344–345
power of partnerships, 260
powerful, 11, 13–15, 120, 123, 163, 165, 174, 201, 207, 211, 218, 287, 300, 304, 309
principal support, 313, 326
problem-solving, 177, 269, 283, 313
professional, 6, 10–11, 13, 220, 224, 227, 259–261, 264, 273, 277, 281, 292, 328–331, 342, 344
Prospect Farm School, 204
Protus Sokhela, 301
providing support, 133, 161
purpose, 1–2, 4, 68–69, 212, 218, 228, 235, 259, 278, 284, 288, 321, 328, 331–333, 335
purpose-driven business, 212

Q

qualitative, 2
quality education, 4, 61, 148, 202, 284, 290
quantitative, 2–3

R

radical respect, 331
Rama Naidu, 331
Ravi Perumal, 167
Raymond Ndlovu, 107
reading programme, 87–88, 133, 169, 175
reciprocity, 8, 24, 207
reclaim humanity, 345
reconciliation, 2, 50, 115, 325, 345
Reconciliation Award, 50, 345
refirement, 241
reflection, 27, 196, 277, 309, 313, 319, 330
reflective, 260, 264, 286
relationship, 15–16, 29–31, 36, 44, 48–51, 90, 110–111, 142–146, 148–149, 193–194, 197–198, 201–203, 220–222, 239–240, 304–305
Rembrandt Park Primary School, 47
Remco Bol, 78
Remgro, 107, 109–110, 112–113
report on what is working, 174
resilience, 35, 79, 123, 130, 206, 264, 288, 293

resources, 17, 89, 91, 96, 98, 101, 103, 119–121, 123, 133, 158, 176, 232–233, 237, 287
respect, 31, 45, 47, 85–86, 152, 199–200, 211, 213, 278–281, 283, 297–298, 301, 312–313, 331–332, 336–337
responsibility, 33, 62–63, 164, 166–167, 191–192, 216–217, 230–231, 233, 266, 270–271, 274, 276, 296–297, 300, 302
Richard Okhaa, 221
Richard Sonkwala, 1
Ridwan Samodien, 8, 62, 71, 154
Rina Vogler, 256, 278
Rob Broster, 121, 124, 126
Robyn Whittaker, 176, 192, 332
ROGZ, 133, 245–247
Ronel Baker, 262
Ronnie Frans, 107, 110, 154
Rosamund Zander
Rosie Chirongoma, 315
Rowan Gordon, 138

S

Sally Mampa, 263
Sam Jooste, 87
Samuel Skosana, 263
Sandile Mzoneli, 264, 292–293
Santiago Rincón-Gallardo, 343
Sarita Phillander, 289
Savanthika Pillay, 268, 317
scaling intimacy, 343
School at the Centre of Community (S@CC), 4, 5, 7, 10, 17, 64, 95, 114
school community, 17, 48, 55, 71, 140, 147, 173, 293–294, 298–299
School Governing Body (SGB), 31, 34, 36–37, 49, 56, 70, 89, 104, 145, 204, 220–222, 224, 258, 262, 264–267, 271, 287, 293, 301, 323, 333
school hall, 119, 217, 221, 267, 270
school improvement plan, 169, 205
School Leadership Forum, 262
School Management Team (SMT), 30–31, 33, 44, 47, 51, 56, 63, 71, 78, 83, 89, 146, 153, 160, 169, 190, 203–204, 209, 217, 224, 234, 257, 265–267, 275, 287, 301, 320, 323
school of choice, 35, 42, 44, 57, 66, 71, 80, 136, 199, 202

school pages project, 22, 171, 173–174
Sean Hendey, 194
security, 76–77, 91, 104, 120–121, 134, 144–145, 153, 168, 218, 236–237, 252, 294
self-awareness, 292, 309
self-confidence, 96, 199
self-discovery, 69, 283
self-esteem, 67, 69, 171, 227, 257, 262
self-leadership, 319
self-reflection, 309
Selwyn Page, 336
Senior Experten Service (SES), 83
Shapule Modjadji, 265
Sharna Fernandez, 218
shine, 13, 16, 87, 113, 123, 163, 171, 298, 300, 302, 314, 316, 345
Shine Literacy, 123
shiny eyes, 302
Sibongile Sibuyi, 149
Siddeeq Railoun, 220
Sihle Mdlalose, 204
Sikolo Setfu, 171–172, 174
Simbithi, 21, 73–86, 90–93, 96–97, 204, 341, 343
Simbulele Mgengo, 245
skills, 83–87, 136–137, 168–169, 177, 179–180, 182, 186, 188–191, 194–196, 198–199, 204–205, 256–259, 263–264, 268–271, 278–279
small group, 115, 264, 295
Snooky Msibi, 268
social constructivism, 10
social fabric, 115, 336
social justice, 2, 98, 328
soft eyes, 200, 303
sounding board, 46, 50, 54, 57, 110, 139, 141, 190, 227, 275
South Africa, 1–4, 6, 9–16, 78–79, 115–117, 215–216, 231–233, 273–274, 290–292, 308–310, 315–316, 320–327, 333–336, 339–342, 344–345
South Africa:
 Alive with Possibility, 10–11
 The Good News, 115
space, 35, 37, 68–70, 165–166, 198–199, 261–262, 283–285, 295, 297–299, 301–302, 314–317, 319, 330–331, 333–334, 336
Sphere Holdings, 155, 157
Sphokuhle Gxagxa, 249

sponsorship, 2, 45, 145, 150, 195, 199, 225, 230, 291
Square Hill Primary School, 218–219
St Agnes Primary School, 138
staff meetings, 165, 200, 261
stakeholder engagement skills, 199
stakeholder management, 194
stakeholders, 2, 5, 8, 49, 51–52, 148, 182, 185, 194, 258–259, 263–264, 266–267, 271, 278, 340
Stanley Charles, 153–154
Stephen Goddard, 289
Sthe Shabalala, 87, 91
stories, 2, 10–11, 20–22, 25, 28, 38–39, 58–59, 84, 114–115, 160, 170–172, 205–206, 241, 310–312, 339–342
strategic approach, 233
strategic leadership skills, 270
strengthen leadership capacity, 2, 59, 64, 192, 197, 243
strengthen the fabric of society
structured, 9, 99, 122, 258, 309
Stuart Gast, 110
success, 33, 35, 38–40, 66, 73, 75–77, 111, 113, 135, 146, 156, 271–272, 287, 290–291, 317–318
Sun International, 270, 281, 293
Sunjay Bodasing, 81
sustainable, 2, 7, 25–27, 29, 38, 76–77, 184, 188, 195, 230, 233, 237–238, 269, 279, 281
Suzie Allderman, 126
Suzzy Milazi, 27
Symphonia, 1, 10, 14, 273–274, 277–279, 282, 292, 295, 302, 309, 322, 324, 331, 333–337, 345
Symphonia for South Africa (SSA), 1, 72, 138, 148, 177, 228, 240, 292, 309, 322, 331, 333–345
symphonic leaders, 163
symphony, 10, 14, 16, 170, 273
systemic tests, 64, 67, 71, 136, 141, 201, 203

T

team building, 153, 209
teamwork, 33, 158, 166, 266
teenage pregnancy, 229, 231–232
tenacious, 147
tenacity, 322, 335
Terry Dearling, 73–74, 82, 95, 167, 204

Terry's Angels, 87, 204
Tersia Potgieter, 103
Thami Mkhize, 77
Thandi Jafta, 5
Thandi Puoane, 290
Theo Garrun, 21, 28
Theo van den Berg, 107
thinking council, 297
thinking environment, 288, 296
thinking partner, 19, 42, 46, 83, 125, 193, 227, 234, 239–240, 286
Thomas Hlongwane, 268
Thomas Holtz, 47
Thopodi Primary School, 238–239
thrive, 81, 280, 284, 316
Tim Maake, 27
Time to Think, 18, 72, 82–83, 88–89, 168, 190, 192, 198–199, 240, 259, 276–278, 296–297, 309–310, 312, 315–316
Tlhatlogang Secondary School, 155, 159
Tom Bassett, 93, 291
Tracy Rae, 269
training sessions, 31, 106, 257, 270, 273, 314
transformation, 15, 22, 114–115, 152, 154, 170, 190, 195, 198, 277, 286, 296, 310, 314, 337
Trevor Da Rocha, 253
Trevor Manuel, 19, 290, 342
triad conversations, 314
trust, 31, 33, 78–80, 108, 111, 127, 134–136, 143, 145–146, 149, 155, 249, 252, 260–261, 282
trusting relationship, 18
Twitter, 219

U

Ubuntu, 116, 257, 303
Unilever, 78–79
unit of change, 344
unit of transformation, 115
University of the Western Cape (UWC), 7, 205,
upliftment, 24–25, 83, 178, 222

V

Val de Vie Foundation, 107, 110, 112
values, 93, 148–149, 152, 154, 157, 193, 203, 235, 238, 249, 277, 283, 296, 301, 321

Vaughn Bishop, 180
vegetable garden, 32, 37, 46, 98, 105, 133, 153, 193, 237
Veronica Wantenaar, 68
Vincent Mabunda, 27
vision, 19, 42–43, 56–57, 84, 88, 109–114, 149–151, 153–154, 266–267, 301, 310–311, 314, 322–326, 333, 342
visionaries, 334
voice, 68–70, 120, 163, 170, 200, 205, 297, 306, 313, 319, 323, 325, 330–331, 333–334, 344
volunteer, 57, 89, 97, 145, 181, 202, 216, 218, 321
VUCA, 4, 8, 241, 339
Vulemehlo Primary School, 164–165, 171
vulnerability, 269, 305, 330, 335

W

Walk Together, 6–7, 53, 116, 342
walking together in education, 7
well-being, 90, 102, 167, 235, 309
Western Cape Education Department (WCED), 63, 108, 111, 141, 148, 149, 198, 243
Wimpie Mostert, 27
Windlab, 117, 122–123, 126, 129, 133–137, 249
work-readiness skills, 177
Workshop, 220
World Innovation Summit for Education (WISE), 2, 70

Y

Yeoville Boys' Primary School, 41, 252
Yolandi Strydom, 289, 292
Youth@worK, 22, 89, 96, 175, 177–179, 181–182, 184–187
Yvonne Johnstone, 264, 292

Z

Zamani Ngidi, 271
Zeenat Harper-Valentine, 270, 293
Zelda Schonken, 272
Zilungisele Primary, 87–88
Zuko Mlonyeni, 294

www.ingramcontent.com/pod-product-compliance
Lightning Source LLC
Chambersburg PA
CBHW080357170426
43193CB00016B/2742